CONVERTING HORIZONS

CONVERTING HORIZONS

Theological and Sociological

M. D. Litonjua

Copyright © 2019 by M.D Lintojua
ISBN 978-1-6455-0681-2

All rights reserved. No part of this book may be reproduced or transmitted in any form or by any means, electronic or mechanical, including photocopying, recording, or by any information storage and retrieval system, without permission in writing from the copyright owner.

The views expressed in this work are solely those of the author and do not necessarily reflect the views of the publisher, and the publisher hereby disclaims any responsibility for them.

Matchstick Literary
1-888-306-8885
www.matchliterary.com
orders@matchliterary.com

Preface

"No man is an island, entire of itself. Every man is a piece of the continent, a part of the main," John Donne wrote. "Any man's death diminishes me, because I am involved in mankind. And therefore never send to know for whom the bell tolls: It tolls for thee." John Donne's image of the human person is diametrically opposed to that of the deracinated individual of modern, especially American, culture, for whom his individualism is the highest value, his license to do whatever he wants is paramount, his desire to express whatever he feels or what pleases him is supreme.

The human person is a social being; he is enmeshed in a web of structured relationships, which social structures and social arrangements he and his fellows have created to enable them to live in community and society. He/she is a political animal; as a member of the *polis*, they have the capacity and ability, the power, to engage and participate in their own governance and that of their society. He/she is a cultural being; they share in the values and symbolic representations of a common culture, from which they derive the meaning for their existence, the common goal of their commonweal, and the destiny of their future.

Most of all, the human person is a historical being and should be a historically conscious human person. He/she bears the burden of the successes and failures of the past, encounters the vicissitudes of the present as they have been handed down to him, and makes of the future from the constraints and opportunities presented to him from history. Many times, however, the human person has not been conscious of the historical stream in which he is situated. Oftentimes, he makes the present immutable: things have always been the way they are today and will be tomorrow. This is especially true of religious matters: doctrines, moral teachings, liturgical practices, structures of governance, disciplinary actions are today what they were in the past; they never change, they will not change, they cannot change. The mantra becomes: tradition today, tradition tomorrow, tradition forever.

Historical consciousness is an epistemic breakthrough in religious studies. This is the singular achievement of Bernard Lonergan (1972: 315) who distinguished between theological knowledge that is classicist, and theological understanding that is historically conscious. For the former, reality is static, necessary, fixed, and universal. A religious truth couched in a doctrinal propositional form captures objective reality and is forever true and cannot be changed. For the latter, reality is dynamic, evolving, changing, and particular. It recognizes the historicity of human thought and action so that the articulations of one sociohistorical era are not necessarily those of another. "The world, both the world free of every human intervention and the human world fashioned by socially constructed meanings and values, is in a permanent state of change and evolution" (Lawler, Salzman, and Burke-Sullivan 2014: 113). It is essentially for this reason that anyone wishing to make a value judgment in the present cannot simply do it on the basis of its givenness in the past, argues a historically conscious theology against a classicist theology. This is Lonergan's contribution to philosophy and theology, a theory of knowledge that has been labeled "critical realism" (Fiorenza 2000: 214-21). In the foreword to David Tracy's (1970: xi) *The Achievement of Bernard Lonergan,* Lonergan allows himself a modest role in the process of renewal in Catholic theology: "It crystallized, burst into the open, and startled the world at Vatican II" – the process in which theologians "have gradually been adapting their thought to the shift from the classicist culture, dominant up to the French revolution, to the empirical and historical mindedness that constitutes its modern successor."

Closely connected to the historical consciousness of knowledge is Lonergan's key concept of horizon. If knowledge is historically situated, culturally conditioned, and positioned within a socio-political matrix, then there are different and varying horizons. Ordinarily horizon denotes the line at which the earth and the sky appear to meet, which constitutes the outer limit of one's physical vision. It determines my perspective, what I can see and cannot see. Beyond the horizon are the objects I cannot see; within the horizon are the objects I can see. But my physical horizon is not immovably fixed: it moves as I move, either receding in front of me or encroaching behind me. Personal physical horizon provides an analogy for personal horizon of knowledge. What lies within my personal horizon is an object of interest and knowledge: I can be attentive to it, try to understand it, make a judgment about its truth, and make a decision based on it.

Such personal horizons are socially constructed, the result of one's history, culture, social class, gender, race or ethnicity.

There are, therefore, many horizons and perspectives. What I know, appreciate, value, and love are from my perspective. Others have their own horizons and perspectives. This therefore negates or at the very least diminishes the old idea of knowledge as correspondence of mind to reality. The mind, via the senses, apprehends the totality of reality as it is, and what it apprehends is in complete correspondence to reality. The better understanding of knowledge is perspectivism: I apprehend reality from my perspective and understand reality only from that perspective. Others have different perspectives, based on their different histories and cultures, influenced by their varied social classes, genders, and races/ethnicities. One's knowledge is always related to one's perspective, is relative to one's interests and values, is therefore partial. This is what Karl Mannheim calls "relationism." This is not what Joseph Ratzinger excoriates as relativism, a cynical attitude that there is no truth, no objective reality, but anything goes. This is simply pluralism: a multiplicity of horizons, a diversity of perspectives. A tree is a poem to Joyce Kilmer, provides shade to a weary traveler, absorbs carbon dioxide and emits oxygen to an environmentalist, is lumber to a lumberjack.

Perspectivism leads to different conclusions derived from different perspectives, and results in conclusions that are true but are only partially true. It does not reject objective reality nor objective truth, but realizes that one's truth from one's perspective is only partially true. This is the basis for a legitimate pluralism in doctrinal beliefs and moral reflections, a profound methodological development in how the Catholic Church reflects on its relationship to the modern world, as propounded by *Gaudium et Spes*, Vatican II's Pastoral Constitution on the Church in the Modern World (Lawler, Salzman, and Burke-Sullivan 2014) . More importantly, because of the variety and diversity of horizons and their partiality of truths, perspectivism demands dialogue between different perspectives, interrelations between varying horizons, openness to partial truths of others. Feminist sociological theory is explicit about this. This is how Patricia Madoo Lengermann and Jill Niebrugge-Brantley (1988: 432) put it:

> People understand and act toward reality from the vantage point of their structurally patterned situations. Because this fact extends even to the sociologist, certainty about the truth becomes a suspect and elusive condition. That certainty can only be achieved if sociologists: (1) seek their facts at the point of intersection between the

understandings of the world held by differently situated and often oppositionally related groups; (2) stay focused not only on these different accounts but on the situated vantage points from which they arise; (3) remain sensitive to the situationality of their own professional efforts to know the world; (4) remain sensitive to the differences in perception that people may have about the requirements of their structural locations; (5) stay modest about their "certainty" and recognize its processual basis, its precarious state, and the permeability of all their concepts; and (6) stay constantly aware of and attempt to compensate for the ways that structural inequalities weight different groups' accounts of social reality.

For this to happen, however, another of Lonergan's key concepts, that of conversion, is essential. Conversion is the movement from one horizon to another, the ability to shift from one perspective to another, which involves openness to and acceptance of the "other" and "the different:" especially the stranger, the alien, the foreign, the subaltern, the poor, the exploited, the oppressed. Conversion is intellectual and moral. Intellectual conversion is the elimination of false ideas of reality, objectivity, and knowledge, namely that reality is simply what is out there, that objectivity is simply seeing what is out there and what is not, that knowledge is simply mentally looking and grasping objectively at what is real. "This myth confuses the physical world of sensation, the sum of what is experientially seen, heard, touched, tasted, smelled with the world mediated by meaning, which is a world known, not by sensation alone, but by the cognitive processes of sensation, understanding, and judgment. Knowing is not simply seeing, hearing, touching, tasting, smelling; it is seeing, understanding, and judging. Until knowers reach the judgment that their understanding is true or false, there is no knowledge" (Salzman and Lawler 2012: 224)

There is also moral conversion. After intellectual conversion comes moral conversion. Following judgment and the attainment of truth, there comes the decision about what to do with the truth, which involves the shift from one's decisions and choices to the satisfaction and attainment of values. "Moral conversion involves progressively understanding the present situation, exposing and eradicating both individual and social bias, constantly evaluating my scale of preferred values, paying attention to criticism and protest, and listening to others. Neither one instance of moral conversion nor one moral conversion leads to moral perfection, for after one conversion there remains the possibility of either conversion or relapse, and after one moral decision there is still required moral action. Conversion is not to be conceived as an on-off moment but an ongoing process" (Salzman and Lawler 2012: 224-25).

Finally, there is religious conversion, the final modality of self-transcendence involved in conversion, which Lonergan (1972: 239) himself describes: "Religious conversion is to a total being-in-love as the efficacious ground of all self-transcendence, whether in the pursuit of truth, or in the realization of human values, or in the orientation man adopts to the universe, its ground, and its goal." It is, Fiorenza (2000: 219-20) adds, "an affective self-transcendence of falling in love. . . . Religious conversion entails a love without conditions, reservations, or limitations. The knowledge of God is given in religious conversion and its unrestricted and conditional love. In linking love and knowledge, desire and self-transcendence, Lonergan places at the center of his method themes that were initiated at the beginning of the [20th] century by Rousselot and the *nouvelle theologie.*"

For me, this three-fold conversion of self-transcendence is especially demanded by the preferential option for the poor, the newest and most consequential development in Christian social teaching, which started with Latin American liberation theology and which has since been enshrined as an essential feature of contemporary Christian theology, ethics, and spirituality. In a continent wracked by poverty and oppression, in societies marked by deaths due to conflict and war and the desperate plight of migrants, in a world riven by a chasm of inequality where there is an epidemic of obesity and consumerism, on the one hand, and the destruction of want and starvation, on the other, a change of horizons, a shift of perspectives, intellectual, moral, and spiritual conversion are demanded (Litonjua 1998: 30-37).

First, we have to do away with romanticizing and idealizing poverty and the poor: "Blessed are you who are poor, for the kingdom of God is yours" (Mark 6:20). Nor should we spiritualize poverty: "Blessed are the poor in spirit, for theirs is the kingdom of heaven" (Matthew 5:3). Much less should we "eschatologize" poverty with the promise to the poor of "the pie in the sky, by and by." Otherwise, let us all be poor! Material poverty is a dehumanizing and a scandalous situation. It is hunger, sickness, pain, homelessness, misery, helplessness, and ultimately untimely death. The grinding poverty of many in the Two-Thirds World reduces them to the level of animals, degrades them, and deprives them of any choice in their lives and futures. That is why Gustavo Gutierrez (1973: 261), the father of Latin American liberation theology, requires that "the first form of poverty is to renounce the ideas we have of poverty." It is a renouncement of old perspectives, outdated horizons in theology, ethics, and spirituality.

This not to deny that poverty, even material poverty, can be an occasion and an opportunity that lead one to be more open to the transcendent on whom we all depend and to the poor neighbor – but certainly not as a cause. Spiritual poverty, taken voluntarily as a choice, can be a path towards growth in spirituality and holiness, understood not as an individualistic journey, but as a pilgrimage to God that includes the promotion of justice, love, community, and peace amongst the less fortunate of his people. This is what Gustavo Gutierrez (1973: 296) means by poverty as spiritual childhood, "the ability to welcome God, an openness to God, a willingness to be used by God, a humility before God."

Second, there must be a radical shift of horizon, a basic conversion, to the poor in their concrete situations as victims of injustice. This involves seeing the poor, no longer blaming them for their laziness, their vices, their lack of values and character, initiative and hard work that make then undeserving, but situating them in their long history of oppression, locating them within the social structures of injustice, placing them at the center of the institutionalized violence of society. This change in intellectual horizons requires an experiential aspect, a choice to share in a significant way with how the poor exist and survive, how they are mistreated, ignored, and rendered helpless. By entering the world of the poor, one begins to understand and experience their pain and struggles, as well as their hopes and aspirations. Experiencing the situation of the poor results in a new way of seeing reality, a new perspective, a new horizon, an intellectual, moral, and spiritual conversion, a new manner of being a Christian, a new way of being church.

Third, there must be solidarity with the poor, participation in their struggles against poverty, oppression, and institutionalized violence, working with, not for, the poor as they strive to liberate themselves to achieve their dignity, their aspirations and hopes. It demands a commitment to protest and work against what Pope Paul VI called "the international imperialism of money," the international structures of injustice, of domination and subordination. It is important to realize that poverty and exploitation are built into the social structures of power and privilege across and within nations. They are justified by ideas and beliefs in the inferiority and superiority of classes and peoples. The change in perspective, the shift in horizons, the necessary conversion required by solidarity with the poor are especially demanding in a global economy ruled by the ideology of neoliberalism, where, first, foremost, and last, the priority is economic growth, even to the detriment of the peoples of the world and the sustainability and survival of the planet.

***

The articles and review essays, published and unpublished, gathered here under the title *Converting Horizons*, share the motivation, orientation, and purpose of those found in my previous four collections, *Critical Intersections* (2006), *Creative Fractures* (2011), *Joint Ventures* (2012), and *Border Crossings* (2015).

1

EMPIRE AND THE INFANCY NARRATIVES OF MATTHEW AND LUKE

Christmas is the most popular of all feast days. Theologically, however, Easter is more important than Christmas, the Resurrection more significant than the Incarnation. For most Christians, however, Christmas is the most joyous, the most anticipated, and the most celebrated holy day and holiday. In fact, to a certain extent, Christmas has lost most, if not all, of its religious meaning. It is simply a period of buying and giving gifts, of coming together and having a good time, of enjoying good food and drink and merrymaking, a season especially of tremendous commercial success. The Christmas story of the child Jesus and his parents, especially Mary, of shepherds and angels and magi, narrated to the tune of Christmas carols has become an uplifting narrative, comparable perhaps to the other fables of childhood. Add to that is an environment festooned with Christmas trees, Christmas decorations, Christmas cards, and Christmas indeed is a wonderful season to be alive and well.

In many ways, this is a surprising situation in light of what Stephen Nissenbaum (1996) revealed regarding Christmasses past in the United States. "I discovered that Christmas had once occasioned a kind of behavior that would be shocking today: It was a time of heavy drinking when the rules that governed people's public behavior were momentarily abandoned in favor of an unrestrained 'carnival,' a kind of December Mardi Gras. And I found that in the early nineteenth century, with the growth of American cities, that kind of behavior had become even more threatening, combining carnival rowdiness with urban gang violence and Christmas-season riots" (Nissenbaum 1996: x-xi). In fact, the Puritans introduced the old colonial holiday of Thanksgiving as a more acceptable alternative to Christmas. "Thanksgiving was intended to offer New Englanders an opportunity for seasonal feasting after the conclusion of the harvest, an occasion that was not tainted by the pagan origin of Christmas, or its carnival associations" (Nissenbaum 1996: 313). On second thought, this should not come as a surprise if we remember that Christmas under Christian rule was precisely set to "baptize" Saturnalia, the ancient Roman festival in honor of the deity Saturn, celebrated with sacrifice, public banquet, and continual carousing and partying that overturned Roman social norms.

Victory in the battle for Christmas in America, in other words, the transformation of carnival Christmas into domestic Christmas, resulted from a convergence of interests of laborers and capitalists, producers and consumers, clients and patrons of an increasingly commercialized society, marked by the official recognition of Christmas as a legal holiday in the United States by mid-century. Nissenbaum's (1996: 318) parting words:

> [M]ost of the problems we face at Christmas today – the greedy materialism, the jaded consumerism, the deliberate manipulation not only of goods but also of private desires and personal relationships into purchasable commodities – are surprisingly old. They date, in fact, to the emergence of the domestic Christmas itself. And they were being publicly debated, and lamented, as early as the 1830s. . . .
>
> [T]here never was a time when Christmas existed as an unsullied domestic idyll, immune to the taint of commercialism. . . . [T]he domestic Christmas was the commercial Christmas – commercial from its earliest stages, commercial at its very core. Indeed, the domestic Christmas was itself a force in the spread of consumer capitalism.

The infancy narratives, as the Christmas story in the bible is called, are found only in the Gospels of Sts. Matthew and Luke; they constitute the first two chapters of each of the gospels. Matthew's narrative is significantly much shorter, taking only 31 verses, than Luke's which is 132 verses long. There are similarities, differences, and contradictions between the two infancy narratives. Most importantly, there are elements found in one and not in the other, and vice-versa, but in the popular reconstruction both narratives are amalgamated and harmonized to form one continuous and consecutive narrative. Most people are not aware that this is so.

For a start, therefore, let us see what is contained in Matthew (1-2):
1. The genealogy of Jesus stretching through the fourteen generations from Adam to David, the fourteen generations from David to the Babylonian exile, and the fourteen generations from the Babylonian exile to the Messiah.
2. An angel appears in a dream to Joseph to take Mary as his wife who is pregnant with Jesus.
3. Jesus is born in the family home in Bethlehem.
4. The visit of the magi from the east led by a prodigious star, who bring gifts of gold, frankincense, and myrrh (hence three magi? Matthew does not say so).
5. The family flees to Egypt to avoid the massacre by Herod of all boys two years old and under in Bethlehem and vicinity.
6. The family returns to Israel, departs for Galilee, where they settle in Nazareth.

Next, let us see what is contained in Luke (1-2):
1. The announcement of an angel to Zechariah of the birth of John.
2. The announcement of the angel Gabriel to Mary of the birth of Jesus.
3. Mary visits Elizabeth, and sings the Magnificat, also known as the Canticle of Mary.
4. John is born, and Zechariah prophesies (the Benedictus).
5. Caesar Augustus orders a census, when Quirinius was governor of Syria, for which reason Joseph and Mary journey to Bethlehem where Jesus is born in a manger, because there was no room for them in the inn.
6. An angel announces to shepherds in the field the birth of Jesus, and a multitude of heavenly hosts with the angel praise God: Glory to God in the highest and on earth peace to men of good will. Then the shepherds visit the child Jesus.
7. The circumcision and naming of Jesus.
8. The presentation of Jesus in the Temple where Simeon and Anna give praise to God (the Nunc Dimittis).
9. The family returns to Nazareth in Galilee.
10. The family journeys to Jerusalem for the Passover, and the boy Jesus is left in the temple.

11. Luke gives the genealogy of Jesus in 3:23-38, at the beginning of Jesus' public life and ministry after his baptism by John. Luke's genealogy is in reverse order of Matthew's, is longer, and differs substantially from Matthew's (see the parallel comparison in Vermes [2006: 37-40]).

On the other hand, as Raymond Brown (1993: 34-35) notes, it is important to indicate that the following eleven points are shared by the two infancy narratives:
    a. The parents to be are Mary and Joseph who are legally engaged or married, but have not yet come together or have sexual relations.
    b. Joseph is of Davidic descent.
    c. There is an angelic announcement of the forthcoming birth of the child.
    d. The conception of the child by Mary is not through intercourse with her husband.
    e. The conception is through the Holy Spirit.
    f. There is a directive from the angel that the child is to be named Jesus.
    g. An angel states that Jesus is to be Savior.
    h. The birth of Jesus takes place after the parents have come to live together.
    i. The birth takes place in Bethlehem.
    j. The birth is chronologically related to the reign (days) of Herod the Great.
    k. The child is reared at Nazareth.

The Issue of Historicity

The infancy narratives contain and describe events that could only be considered miraculous. While the historical and the miraculous are not necessarily and inherently a contradiction in terms, by the same token what is miraculous is not by that fact automatically not historical. It is the task of the historian, therefore, to inquire, before all else, into the historicity of the infancy narratives found in the Gospels of Mathew and Mark.

Citing the problems of corroborating witnesses and of conflicting details, Raymond Brown (1993: 36; see also Meier 1991: 208-30) in his magisterial work on the infancy narratives concludes that "close analysis of the infancy narratives makes it unlikely that either account is completely historical," which judgment he reaffirms in the updated edition of his book (Brown 1993: 576):

Because of disagreements between the two infancy narratives, because of the lack of confirmation of their material anywhere else in the NT, because of the failure of highly public events in the narratives to be confirmed extrabiblically, because of seeming irregularities (census affecting Galileans under Quirinius in Herod's time), because of total uncertainty about the evangelists' sources for what is narrated, I made a careful judgment (36 above), denying that both accounts can be "completely historical," and thinking it unlikely that either account is "completely historical.". . . Claims to certitude about historicity gained from unspecified tradition, from the experiences of later mystics, or from general piety are employing those tools to solve issues for which they have no relevance. If some find me too "rigorous" (or less kindly, skeptical and rationalist) when I admit that I do not know whether or some events are historical, they should be more rigorous in proving what they claim they know. But enough of what I regard as unpersuasive historicizing . . .

But even if the infancy narratives are not strictly historical, it does not mean that they can be dismissed, that they lack any meaning, that they are fictional, that they are false. Brown (1993: 29-32), for one, situates the infancy narratives within the Gospel tradition as testimonies of faith in the development of Christology. Belief in the resurrection was the chief moment associated with the proclamation of the divine identity of Jesus. Jesus did not claim to be divine during his lifetime, nor did the disciples who followed him proclaim him to be divine. With the resurrection, which cannot be proven as a historical fact, or, more properly, with the belief in the resurrection, which is a historical fact, the disciples of Jesus began to think of him as divine. There were a number of ways by which Jesus' divinity was understood and explained, but the Council of Nicaea, convoked by Emperor Constantine to resolve the issue, defined that Jesus Christ was one in being with the Father, was consubstantial with the Father (Fredriksen 1988; Ehrman 2014).

Mark retroactively pushes the self-identity of Jesus as divine to his baptism by John at the Jordan, when on coming out of the water, the heavens were torn open, the Spirit, in the form of a dove, descended upon him, and a voice came from the heavens, "You are my beloved Son; with you I am well pleased" (Mark 1:9-11). Matthew and Luke push the proclamation of Jesus' divinity further back to his virginal conception in the womb of Mary.

Matthew (1:20) writes that an angel of the Lord appeared to Joseph in a dream and told him: "Do not be afraid to take Mary your wife into your home. For it is through the holy Spirit that this child has been conceived in her." Luke (1:30) tells of the angel Gabriel saying to Mary: "Do not be afraid, Mary, for you have found favor with God. Behold, you will conceive in your womb and bear a son, and you shall name him Jesus." Finally, John (1:1) situates the Word in the beginning when the Word was with God, and the Word was God. "The Word became flesh and made his dwelling among us, and we saw his glory, the glory of the Father's only Son, full of grace and truth" (John 1:14).

Thus, Brown argues that the infancy narratives make sense as part of their respective Gospels in the backward process of Gospel formation and Christological development. "Matthew and Luke thought they were appropriate introductions to the career and significance of Jesus. To give them less value than other parts of the Gospels is to misread the mind of the evangelists for whom the infancy narratives were fitting vehicles of a message they wanted to convey. Indeed, from this point of view, the infancy narratives are not an embarrassment but a masterpiece" (Brown 1993: 38).

Geza Vermes (2006) attends to the historical oddities, difficulties, complexities, inconsistencies, and contradictions of the infancy narratives. Basically, he dismisses the infancy narratives as not the stuff out of which history is made. The legendary trappings of the infancy narratives enhance the essence of the joyful tiding announced by the nativity stories, the happy message that the Christian world identifies with Christmas, the sweet and simple story of Luke with angels, shepherds and jolly neighbours.

Joseph Ratzinger/Benedict XVI (2012) offers a spiritual reading of the narratives. For him, "what Matthew and Luke set out to do, each in his own way, was not to tell 'stories' but to write history, real history that had actually happened, admittedly interpreted and understood in context of the word of God." He simply ignores the inconsistencies and contradictions between the two narratives. The "facts" that defy explanation, foremost of which are the virgin birth and the resurrection, he calls miracles – "If God does not have power over matter, then he simply is not God." – a default position that resounds throughout history as not too far removed from *"Deus vult!"* of the Crusades and other ecclesiastical atrocities. He spiritualizes and allegorizes everything, including the ox and the ass that supposedly flanked the manger as "humanity made up of Jews and Gentiles – to acknowledge God." There is no mention of an ox and an ass in the manger in the infancy narratives of Mathew and Luke, but they do make an appearance in the apocryphal Gospel of the Pseudo-Matthew (Jenkins

2015: 14). My copy comes in large print, and it has the feel of a children's book, sans illustrations, addressed to adults.

Marcus Borg and John Dominic Crossan (2007: 25-32) also point out that even if the infancy narratives are not strictly historical and biographical in the modern sense of the words, they cannot simply be dismissed as false or fables, nor, for that matter can they be taken as factual, as religious fundamentalism and sentimentalism would like them to be. There is truth in the infancy narratives; there is meaning, personal and political, then and now, in them. Borg and Crossan (2007: 32-40) see them as parables, a form of story or narrative which is about meaning: "the meaning of a parable – its parabolic truth – does not depend on its factuality." Borg and Crossan (2007: 38-40) understand them as "parabolic overtures." An overture is a summary, synthesis, metaphor, or symbol of the whole. Matthew's and Luke's infancy narratives are overtures to their respective gospels, a miniature version of what will come, microcosms of their quite different gospels as macrocosms. That is why they are also quite different overtures.

The major theme of Matthew's overture is the basic parallel between Moses and Jesus, thus faith in Jesus is the fulfillment and consummation – not replacement and abandonment – of Israel. Moses was a law-giver whose law, the Torah, is contained in the Pentateuch, the first five books of the bible. Matthew structures his gospel so that Jesus gives five long addresses, the first of which is the Sermon on the Mount (Borg and Crossan 2007: 40-46). The core message of Matthew's gospel is the Kingdom of God, inaugurated by Christ. He emphasizes the kingly genealogy of Jesus, his birth in the Davidic city of Bethlehem, the visit of the magi from the east, and the disturbance in the mind of Herod of the news of Jesus' birth in his overture to the Good News of Jesus. He was a Jewish Christian, writing from a community of like Jewish Christians, and responding in opposition to other Jews who did not recognize Jesus as the Messiah and were antagonistic to communities of Jewish Christians.

Three important themes structure Luke's overture: his emphasis on women, the marginalized, and the Holy Spirit, themes which will animate his gospel-as-macrocosm (Borg and Crossan 2007: 46-52). Luke was a non-Palestinian writing to a non-Palestinian audience, made up mostly of Gentile Christians. In his infancy narrative overture, he announces many of the Christological themes of his Gospel: the fidelity of the Jewish Jesus to the Law and the Prophets, the importance of Jerusalem and the temple, the fulfillment of Old Testament prophecies, Jesus' concern for the poor, the marginalized and the lowly, the importance of women as ministers of the gospel, Christianity as a legitimate form of worship in the Roman world as Christianity spreads throughout the Roman Empire, guided by the Holy Spirit, the universality of salvation with the promise and advent of the Holy Spirit, Jesus as savior at a time of *pax Augusta*. Luke's is the Good News of Jesus to Gentiles.

Thus Borg and Crossan (2007: 52-53) conclude that

> the Christmas stories are primarily parabolic overtures, but based on biblical tradition rather than on historical fact. Each is its Gospel in miniature. When, therefore, Matthew 1-2 and Luke 1-2 are combined into a single Christmas story – for instance, in standard Christian imagination or the traditional Christmas crèche – that story is the entire Christian gospel in miniature. Get it, and you get everything; miss it and you miss all.

But the infancy narratives are not free-floating parables, like the story of Midas; they are "historical," not in the sense of factual, but in the demand that they be understood in their proper historical setting, in their first-century context. As such, the infancy narratives are subversive stories. They subvert the conventional ways of the world, of the way of seeing things as they are. They also subvert the conventional ways of seeing life and God, of how we should live in Christ. They subverted the dominant consciousness of the first-century world as they should of our own. They subverted the world in which Jesus and early Christianity lived as they should our world. "As stories told by his followers late in the first century, they are part of their testimony, their witness, to the significance that Jesus had to come to have for them. That significance had as its center a different vision of life, a vision they got from Jesus – from his teaching, his public activity, and his life, death, and vindication by God. That vision was embodied in Jesus, incarnate in Jesus" (Borg and Crossan 2007: 36-38).

The Historical and Social Context

The historical context of Jesus' birth, the society and world in which he was born, and of the events connected with and narrated about it are what I intend to focus on in understanding the meaning and significance of the infancy narratives of Matthew and Luke. And that fundamental historical and social context is of empire and colony, where the basic social distinction is between Roman citizen and non-Roman inhabitant, from which all other distinctions flow: materially advantaged and economically deprived, mighty with power and downtrodden because powerless, nobility and official retainers in their castles and exploited peasantry toiling in the fields, and finally flourishing with life or pinned to death. This is the same pathway that Richard Horsley (1989: xii-xiii) took, which became the signature characteristic of his work:

> The birth narratives and the crucifixion-resurrection narratives link Jesus explicitly with the history of Israel or even humankind, and more directly and immediately with the imperial Roman rulers and the Jewish rulers. Moreover, the latter are not simply the background or setting for the teachings and healings but are essential forces and actors in the overall history and historical significance of Jesus. This should also be clear as well that the Gospels do not simply take the political situation into account; rather, it is an integral part, the framing of the story as a whole.

With the assassination of Julius Caesar on March 15, the Ides of March, 44 BC, the suicides of the assassins Brutus and Cassius, the defeat of Anthony and Cleopatra at Actium, Octavian, Julius' adopted son, ascended to power and become the first Roman emperor, taking the name Augustus Caesar. He ruled from 27 BC to 14 AD. Directly ruling Palestine but dependent on Rome was Herod the Great who was ruling during the time of the birth of Jesus and who ordered the massacre of the innocents. Upon his death in 4 AD, his kingdom was divided among his three sons, with Herod Antipas becoming the tetrarch of Galilee and Peraea. He executed John the Baptist and was ruling at the time of Jesus' death. Pontius Pilate was the Roman procurator of Judaea, supposedly a ruthless governor, who was removed at the complaint of the Samaritans, among whom he engineered a massacre. He had Jesus crucified for claiming to be the King of the Jews, a political crime punishable by crucifixion for non-Romans. According to tradition, he committed suicide in Rome.

This constituted the immediate contours of the Roman Empire during the lifetime of Jesus, as it touched him, his family and society, his disciples and followers. It was empire in the form of the greatest and most powerful in history that constituted the historical and social context from which the Jesus movement emerged in Galilee and in which Christianity spread around the Mediterranean basin. Its reverse was the colonies of Palestine and of the Mediterranean world, where poverty and oppression ruled, where repression and domination were omnipresent, controlled as they were by the might of Rome. The Roman Empire was built on political intrigue and murder, on military might and terror, on territorial conquest and expansion. Its foundations rested on the exploitation of other peoples, its riches on plunder, its glory and grandeur on the exercise of force and violence. Romans themselves sought explanations of their ingrained traditions of violence in the mythical foundation of Rome, attributed to the killing by Romulus of his brother, who then supplied his followers with women kidnapped from the Sabines.

"Every empire bears the mark of the kind of society that creates it," writes Greg Woolf (2012: 82) in his chapter, titled "Slavery and Empire." Rome was a city-state run by its greatest families. It was also a slave-owning society, so that it depended for its management on the family and slavery, a very odd combination to modern ears. The families competed for political power and patronage, often resorting to political intrigue and political assassinations. The heads of these families lived a precarious life, often finding themselves seated on the thrones of power one day, and drowning in a pool of blood, by their own hand or by their opponents', the next. In the management of public and private proceeds of empire, family and slavery acquired more and more power as Roman power expanded. But at the heart of this enterprise was slave labor. Rome was an agricultural society, and its productivity could only be assured by slaves, recruited from the poor urban classes and from enslaved populations of conquered territories. Such were their numbers that when organized, e.g., by Spartacus, they could threaten the empire itself.

Roman prosperity was also attributed to the proper management of relations with the gods. Remember that the founder of Rome, Romulus, was considered to be the son of Aeneas' line and of the god Mars. Favor with the gods was the ideological legitimation of the fortunes of families and of the hegemony of the empire. Such was the desire to curry favor with gods that the Romans incorporated the gods of their conquered peoples into their own divine pantheon. The creation of emperor worship was a watershed in Roman religion such that the history of religion became a way of telling imperial history. The emperor was not god, *deus*, but was *divus*, deified or divinized or apotheosized human being. Julius Caesar was deified soon after his death. Caesar Augustus, credited with establishing a time of peace, *pax Augusta*, was revered as savior and god during his long reign. "The cult of the emperor became an integral dimension of Roman life for both the city and the *coloniae* of the empire.... Participation in the rites of the imperial cult provided a symbolic expression of Roman identity for peoples hundreds of miles from Italy" (Heyman 2007: 87, 225).

I argue that another way of understanding the infancy narratives of Matthew and Luke is to see them within the historical and social contexts of their times. One way of drawing out the meaning and implications of the infancy narratives is to understand them against the background of the might of the Roman Empire and the cult of its emperor. To see the warnings to Christianity that the infancy narratives provide is to study them against the future that Christianity sadly became: a version of what Christ fought against, a Christian empire. Jesus was against empire; Christianity itself became empire.

The infancy narratives announce the birth of a king of the Davidic line who with his coming inaugurates the Kingdom of God. This is the core message not only of the infancy narratives but of the entire Gospel tradition. But it is a king so unlike Caesar and a kingdom so different from Caesar's empire.

Caesar sat on his throne, figuratively atop a pile of corpses of political competitors, whom he had to eliminate through assassinations or in combat. His rule was one of fear and terror, crucifying non-Romans accused of threatening his claim, oppressing and exploiting conquered peoples for profit and gain and territory. The defiant speech that Tacitus put in the mouth of the Scottish chieftain Calgacus sums it all up: "To plunder, butchery, and rapine, they give the lying name of 'government'; they create a desolation and call it peace." Caesar lorded it over his empire, attended to by political sycophants and hangers-on, surrounded and guarded by military lackeys, and always on the look-out for ambitious usurpers. He was *divus* all right, descended from couplings of fictitious deity ancestors, and apotheosized for expanding the territorial limits of the empire and for his magnanimity to the statuary glory and grandeur of Rome.

Jesus was conceived by the Holy Spirit, born of peasant parents, and lived in rural Galilee, which was of absolutely no significance to empire. His birth was attended to by angelic hosts, by shepherds who attended their flock in the fields, and by wise men who travelled far from the east, all equally of no significance to empire. "Are you king of the Jews?" Pilate asked. "You say so!" he answered, "but my kingdom is not of this world." His kingdom is not one of military might, or of economic wealth, or of political power. His kingdom is one of justice and love, and of joy and peace. It is a kingdom in which the poor and the meek, those who hunger and thirst for righteousness, the pure of heart and peacemakers, those who are persecuted and reviled are welcomed and blessed. In Jesus, all are one; there is no longer Jew or Greek, slave or free, male or female. He is no deified human being but the Son of God, one in being with the Father.

The elements of the infancy narratives – genealogies, announcement by angels, virginal conception and birth, Bethlehem and Davidic descent, Herod and the slaughter of the innocents, angels and shepherds in the field, the magi from the East led by a star, the flight to Egypt, the return to Nazareth – have two purposes: to show that the prophecies of the

Old Covenant are fulfilled with the coming of Jesus, and to contrast Jesus and his kingdom with Caesar, his empire and his imperial theology. The infancy narratives contradict the tidings of *Pax Augusta;* they oppose Augustus as "savior" of the world.

Imperial Christianity

The "Our Father," the prayer Jesus taught us to pray, has two main parts. In the first part, we praise God: Hallowed be thy name. Thy kingdom come. Thy will be done. In the second part, we petition God: Give us this day our daily bread. Forgive us our trespasses. Lead us not into temptation. *Wait a minute.* We are asking God not to lead us into temptation? We are not saying: God, do not let Satan, or the devil, or the evil one lead us into temptation. We are saying: God, do not lead us into temptation. What is this temptation we asking God not to lead us into?

John Dominic Crossan (2010: 163-82) tells us first to look into the temptations Jesus experienced in the desert after his baptism, especially as narrated by Matthew (4:1-11). Right at the start, "Jesus," as Robin Griffith-Jones (2000: 35) put it, "is subjected to a threefold blandishment: to take a prophet's power over food in the desert; a priest's power over the temple; and a king's power over all the kingdoms of the earth." Jesus' answer to the first temptation was: "One does not live by bread alone, but by every word that comes forth from the mouth of God." His answer to the second temptation was: "You shall not put the Lord, your God, to the test." And to the third temptation, Jesus answered: "Away from me, Satan. The Lord, your God, shall you worship and him alone shall you serve."

Crossan (2010: 173-75) asks and points out:

> What, then, is the difference in precise content between worshipping God and worshipping Satan? *To obtain and possess the kingdoms of the world, with their power and glory, by violent injustice is to worship Satan. To obtain and posses the kingdom, the power, and the glory by nonviolent justice is to worship God.* They are, in other words, two ways of establishing our world and controlling our earth.
>
> The last and climactic temptation of Jesus is to use violence in establishing the kingdom of God on earth and thereby to receive it as the kingdom of Satan. *And so also for us....* The major temptation of God's Adversary is to lure us into the escalatory violence required to obtain the power and the glory of all the kingdoms of the earth. But what if we

did that "for God"? That is truly the last temptation. That is why Jesus did not say to God, "Do not let the devil lead us into temptation," but "Do not you yourself lead us into temptation." The last temptation concerns the violence, done for the name, kingdom, and will of God on earth. . . . Nonviolent justice or violent justice is the essential choice between God and Satan and their respective kingdoms.

The tragedy of it all is that it is precisely this temptation to deploy force, coercion, and violence in God's name that Christianity succumbed to. It is pointedly the warning and lesson of the Infancy Narratives that the Christian religion forgot as it became Christendom, the Christian empire.

It all began with Constantine. After defeating his brother-in-law Maxentius in battle at the Milvian bridge in 312 to become the sole emperor of the Roman Empire, a victory he attributed to the Christian religion, Constantine issued the Edict of Toleration in 313, which legalized Christianity. Constantine used the Christian religion to unify his empire through the unity of belief. He convoked what is now considered the First Ecumenical Council at Nicaea in 325 AD, which defined that Jesus was consubstantial with the Father. The Council also formulated a creed, expanded into the Nicene-Constantinopolitan Creed, which is recited today by Catholics at Mass. Thus, in turn, the Christian Church used the power of empire to impose orthodoxy on Christian belief, declaring in consequence heretical all other theological opinions that until then were freely discussed and debated. Empire utilized the cross to unify the empire, Church in turn used the sword to impose uniformity of belief, ridding the Church of all who would not toe the doctrinal line.

"Thus, began a new stage in the empire's persecution of Christians," Paula Fredriksen (2012: 62-63; see Ehrman 2003b) writes:

> By the end of the fourth century, the bishops' battle against Christian diversity had resulted in a practical victory for the "orthodox" church (that is, for the church now supported by the state.)
>
> Their victory affected not only the future but also the past. By banning the texts of "deviant" Christians, burning their books or impeding their being copied, the bishops got to remake the Christian past into their own image: the only documents to survive were the ones they approved. This ancient triage consigned countless gospels,

apocryphal acts, sermons, prayers, letters, commentaries, and theological treatises to the ash heap of history. The record of the Christian past, in short, was effaced by the church itself.

Theodosius in 381 declared Christianity to be the state religion of the empire, the beginning of the monotheistic state, "the first time in a thousand years of Greco-Roman civilization that free thought was unambiguously suppressed" (Freeman 2008). Christianity was now married to empire, church and state formed a union, and alliance between altar and throne established. This marriage of convenience and mutual support would end only with loss of the papal states in 1870, when Rome itself was absorbed as part of the Kingdom of Italy. Final resolution was reached in 1929 when the Vatican was recognized as a separate state. History has shown that the marriage of state power and monotheistic religion can have lethal consequences for minorities. In this particular case, religious minorities who dissented from official Christian orthodoxy – Manichaeans, Arians, Nestorians, Donatists, Marcionites, Montanists, Pelagians, Docetists, Adoptionists and a host of other dissenters – were put to the sword and completely disappeared from history (see Ehrman 2003a). "[M]ore Christians were persecuted by the Roman Empire after 312 than before" (Frederiksen 202: 27). Only the Jews escaped extermination, following the admonition of Augustine: Let them survive, but do not let them thrive! They were to be ongoing witnesses to the perfidy of a people and the fulfillment of Old Testament prophecies regarding the Christ. Jacob Neusner (1987: 146) admits that "Judaism endured in the West for two reasons. First, Christianity permitted it to endure, and, second, Israel, the Jewish people, wanted it to. The fate of paganism in the fourth century shows the importance of the first of the two factors."

This is perhaps the saddest and the most shameful aspect of imperial Christianity. As the early followers of the Jesus Movement weaned themselves from their Jewish roots to create their own identity, they engaged in political anti-Judaism against their former co-religionists. As Christianity spread around the Mediterranean basin and throughout the Roman Empire, a shift in perspective and tone began to intrude. Jews were now being blamed, not the Romans, for the death and crucifixion of Jesus. Even the Gospels evince this change. Mark (14:53) identifies the Jewish opponents of Jesus as "the high priest, and all the chief priests and the elders and the scribes," come together in the Sanhedrin. Also in Mark (15:6-15), "the crowd" presses Pilate to release Barabbas and to crucify Jesus, which, "wishing to satisfy the crowd," he did. Matthew (26:3-4) identifies the Jewish enemies of Jesus as "the chief priests and elders of the people," headed by high priest Caiaphas. He (Matt. 27:24-26) depicts Pilate as washing his hands, saying, "I am innocent of this man's blood. Look to it yourselves." And the whole people said in reply, "His blood be upon us and upon our children." Luke (23:1-25) presents Pilate as finding Jesus guilty of no capital crime three times, but was forced by the chief priests and the people to release Barabbas and condemn Jesus to be crucified. John (18:28-19:16) names the enemies of Jesus simply as "the Jews." It is as if Christianity, having forged its own identity, especially after the destruction of the Temple of Jerusalem in 70 AD, needed to curry favor with the power and might of the Roman Empire. "The result:" Paula Fredriksen (1988: 105) put it, "Rome and Christianity are both on the same side against the Jews."

Pontius Pilate is rehabilitated in the Gospels. Instead of the Procurator of Judaea, notorious for his cruelty for which he was recalled to Rome where he committed suicide, he is shown to be reluctant in finding Jesus guilty but was pressured by the chief priests and people to sentence Jesus to death. It was forgotten that crucifixion was a punishment instituted by the Romans for the political crime of sedition and rebellion. Pilate had the crime of Jesus nailed on the cross: INRI, Jesus of Nazareth claimed to be King of the Jews, a political crime if there is one. Yet, in the Gospels, Jesus' crime was blasphemy against the Temple from which he drove the sellers and thieves, but which crime is punishable by stoning. The Gospels, frankly speaking, are involved in revisionism. It is no wonder that when a famous celebrity or athlete becomes a born-again Christian and begins reading the Gospels, he also starts spewing anti-Semitic remarks.

The anti-Judaism of the Gospels will be transmogrified into racial anti-Semitism, which will run as a sinful strain in the bloodstream of the institutional Christian Church, infecting its doctrine and morals, its spirituality and liturgy, its canon law and ecclesiastical governance. The cross will be used as an ideological weapon to charge Jews of deicide and to confine them in ghettoes. Saints and sinners, Fathers and Doctors of the Church, popes and cardinals, bishops, priests and laity, all members of a sinful Church will be contaminated and corrupted. Christians will hate Jews – of all people. It will be forgotten that, first and foremost, Jesus was a faithful and devout Jew; his mother Mary and family and disciples were all Jews. By repudiating Jews, the Christian Church will in effect disown the Jewishness of Jesus and the Jesus Movement. The Jew-hatred of Christians will water and fertilize the anti-Semitic soil from which Hitler will rise to perpetuate the Holocaust. Thus, the urgent task of re-reading the New Testament and re-doing Christology after Auschwitz (see, e.g., Fredriksen and Renhartz 2002). It will only be at the Second Vatican Council (1962-65) that the sin of anti-Semitism will be repudiated and repented of.

John Wilkins (2014: 13), writing on the "Great Expectations" aroused by Pope Francis and his convocation of a synod on the family, notes the comment of the historian Eamon Duffy on the restoration of an absolute monarchy under John Paul II in the aftermath of the failed prescriptions of Vatican II about governance, that "centralized rule is by now a part of the Catholic Church's DNA." You have to beg to disagree. It has long been a part of the Catholic Church's DNA since the Christian Church became the successor to the Roman Empire.

In the centuries-long aftermath of the decline and dissolution of the Western Empire that started in the 5th century – Alaric and his Visigoths sacked Rome in 410 – Alan Ryan (2012: 188, 194) writes, Catholic Christianity became the one unifying force in Western Europe.

> It was the papacy, rather than the barbarian kingdoms that inherited the territory of the empire, that inherited the imperial conception of the state. This was not merely a matter of the papacy's mimicking the outward trappings of imperial office, although it did so. It was rather that the church was the means by which Roman notions of law-governed political community were transmitted to medieval Europe. . . [T]he papacy copied the thrones, tiaras, and robes of the Roman Empire, and in the course of time, the cardinals, who were originally the assistants of the popes in matters of liturgy and care of the poor, came to form a College of Cardinals that replicated the Roman Senate.

In greater elaboration, Peter Heather in *The Restoration of Rome* (2013), the sequel to his *The Fall of Rome* (2005), picks up from when the curtain fell on the Roman Empire in Western Europe, and tells the story of three great imperial pretenders who attempted to revive the Roman inheritance in Western Europe: Theoderic, Justinian, and Charlemagne. In the end the restoration of stable imperial power on a truly Roman scale proved possible only with the reinvention of the papacy in the eleventh century. Under the imperial rulers and pretenders from Constantine to Charlemagne, Heather (2013: 312) writes, "without any doubt, the emperor was the functioning head of the Christian Church. Others, including popes, played a part, but the imperial role in the formulation of correct doctrine, in defining and enforcing expected standards of practice, and in selecting personnel was paramount." Fast forward to November 11, 1215, Heather (2013: 350-51) continues:

> In the Fourth Lateran Council, we finally encounter a papacy which was recognizably functioning as the head of Western Christendom: calling councils of massed clergy, dictating the agenda, setting standards of belief and practice for clergy and laity alike, and attempting to have those standards enforced. . . . Not only did Innocent III claim total authority over the Western Church, and demonstrate the reality of that claim in the extraordinary gathering of churchmen who turned up in Rome for Lateran IV, but he based that claim on the assertion that his authority was of a higher order than any of the worldly rulers of Christendom.

Though that claim was rooted in the forged *Donation of Constantine*, the Pope became in effect the supreme monarch, *pontifex maximus*, of Christendom and the Catholic Church the restoration of the Roman Empire. In his review Michael Walsh (2014: 31) recalls Edward Gibbon's thought that the pope was the ghost of the Roman emperor seated on the throne of St. Peter, and adds that "perhaps he might have likened the current papal penchant for canonizing their predecessors to a revival of that imperial practice of deifying one's ancestors." In fact, Massimo Faggioli (2014: 7) points out, "the beatification and canonization of a pope by another pope is the ultimate phase in a long history of centralization of the politics of sainthood in Rome."

But earlier than that, and more than the external trappings of empire, Christianity had already imbibed and assimilated the rhetoric and ideology of empire. In the words of George Heyman (2007: 235):

> Steeped in the sacrificial milieu of the Greco-Roman world, Christianity not only fashioned its own sacrificial rhetoric to exalt Jesus as Lord, it also adopted the imperial model to organize *its* social structure. Just as sacrificial rituals brought identity and displayed imperial power, early Christianity used sacrificial rhetoric to achieve *its* social identity. If the adjective "success" applies to Christianity by the fourth century, it must be ascribed to the way it adapted Roman sacrificial discourse and imperial ideology. The "public transcript" of Roman

sacrificial discourse had been taken over and enhanced by the rhetoric of Jesus' death and later on by the witness of the Christian martyr. In place of the *pax deorum*, the Church envisioned the *pax Christi* (the peace of Christ). In place of the social control ritually portrayed in imperial sacrifices, uniting the center and periphery, Christianity ritualized Jesus' sacrificial death through Eucharist and baptism in the life of each believer. Just as the emperor and the imperial family were exalted along the "sliding scale of divinity," so too the Christian martyr shared (as much as theologically possible) in the exalted status of the risen Jesus. Just as Rome portrayed power and imperial benefits through ritual sacrifice, the martyrs' second baptism of blood infused them with power to do battle with the forces of Satan. However, unlike the Roman model, where only the emperor was apotheosized after his death, *all* Christians, especially those called by God to martyrdom, were guaranteed the reward of heaven.

Instrumentalized by empire and in turn instrumentalizing empire, Christianity was more than ready to become Christian empire. It culminates in the absolute monarchy of the papacy of Western Roman Christianity, wielding both temporal and spiritual power. Its apex were Gregory VII (1072-85), who claimed spiritual as well as temporal power over the whole Christian world, and Innocent III (1198-1216) who claimed authority not only over the whole church (Gregory VII already did that), but over the whole world as well. (Shades of the third temptation of Jesus in the desert! Did the pope finally get what Satan promised Jesus if he prostrates himself and worships him?) Much is made today of the violence of Islamists who would recreate a long-gone Islamic caliphate. Remember Benedict XVI's pointless reference to the violence of Islam in his speech at Regensburg? This is not to condone, much less dismiss, 9/11 and the barbarities of Al Qaeda and the Islamic State. But this is also not to forget the violence that marred the history of Christianity when it succumbed to the temptation Christians had always prayed God would not lead us into, when it became oblivious to the lesson of the infancy narratives that Jesus was not Caesar and that his Kingdom was not of this world. Suffice it for our purposes to mention three of the most egregious historical cases when the Christian religion married the lethal violence of the state to pursue its ends.

The Crusades, the Inquisition, and the collusion of Christianity with imperialism and colonialism are prime examples of the use of force, coercion, and violence in the name of God, to allegedly promote the cause of God. Pope Urban II issued the call to arms at the Council of Clermont in 1095 ostensibly to regain the holy places in Palestine from infidel hands. With that, the Crusades, a new era of papal-sanctioned brutality, were launched. *Deus vult!* – God wills it! –was the battle cry (Bartlett 1999). The Christian crusaders, martial heirs of the Roman legions, were mimicking the armies of imperial Rome. There were six major crusades. The first succeeded in the capture of Jerusalem from Muslim hands in 1099. It was brutal and barbarous, with blood running up to the knees in the streets of Jerusalem, according to some accounts. Jerusalem would be under the rule of the crusaders until its recapture by Saladin in 1187. The fall of Edessa prompted the second crusade in 1146, preached by St. Bernard of Clairvaux. The third crusade ended inconclusively with the truce between Richard the Lionheart and Saladin in 1192. The notorious fourth crusade in 1204 resulted in the murderous siege and sack of Constantinople, which was finally destroyed by the Ottoman Turks in 1453. The fifth crusade in 1228, marked by the conflict between Pope Gregory IX and Frederick II, the new Holy Roman Emperor, had become a political tool: the pope calling a crusade against the crusader who had recaptured the Holy Sepulcher in the name of Christendom. Angus Konstam (2002: 175) points out that "a once-noble movement had become corrupted, becoming a tool of an intolerant and domineering Church." The last crusade was led by the saintly Louis IX of France, but it was a tragic fiasco. With the fall of Acre in 1291, the crusader presence in the East ended, but its memory lingers to the present, polluting the relationship between Islam and the West, while being manipulated by radical Islamists for their own nefarious ends.

In the early thirteenth century, the violent crusading spirit was turned inwards into the very heart of Europe against the Cathars or Albigensians, a heresy that had taken hold in south-western France. In 1209, the Cistercian monk, Arnold Amaury, was sent by the pope to Languedoc to stamp out the heresy by any means necessary. His knights started their atrocities in the town of Beziers, through which they pillaged and slaughtered their way until they came to the Church of the Madeleine, which they burned with 7000 inhabitants locked inside. When the papal legate was informed that Catholics as well as heretics had taken refuge in the church, he replied: "Kill them all; God will recognize his own." Stephen O'Shea (2000: 6), in his chronicle of the Cathars, writes that "the sack of Beziers was the Guernica of the Middle Ages."

After the Cathars, the papacy was taking no chances, and in 1231 Pope Gregory IX established the Inquisition with the papal bull,

Excommunicamus. Dominicans and Franciscans were sent to Germany, France, and Italy to ferret out heresies. Accused heretics were given a month to recant without penalty, after which they were subjected to secret trials. Those found guilty were handed over to secular authorities for burning at the stake. The most infamous, because the most ruthless, of these heresy-hunters was the Spanish Inquisition, created by Ferdinand and Isabella, as an instrument against Jews and Muslims, in their *reconquista* of the Iberian peninsula. The Dominican friar, Tomas Torquemada, was the original "hammer of heretics," responsible for torturing and killing thousands, and thus for spreading a reign of terror across Iberia.

Not only do the offices of the Inquisition survive into the twenty-first century, Cullen Murphy (2012) points out, albeit under a less notorious name, but its spirit is more influential than ever in the modern world. The most important factor in the making of an Inquisition is the conviction that one is absolutely right against demonized evil. With an outlook of moral certainty, which is alive in some religious and secular circles, the unthinkable becomes permissible. Torture or, euphemistically, "enhanced interrogation techniques" become an integral part in the inquisitorial process as it has been justified in the so-called War on Terror. In the original Inquisition, Church officials would not sully their hands with blood, so they handed the condemned to secular authorities. This moral delicacy has its modern analogue in "extraordinary rendition," whereby a nation, to maintain its constitutional innocence and purity, hands over suspected terrorists to where they will be tortured. "Power corrupts," Lord Acton's dictum goes, "and absolutely power corrupts absolutely." The methods of absolute power may vary, but the impulse is the same.

The twin aims of Spain and Portugal were both to colonize and Christianize the Americas and the Philippines. Conquistador with sword and friar with cross sallied forth to conquer lands and souls for crown and church. As we used to say in the Philippines, the Spaniards arrived in the Philippines in the garbs of the conquistador who pointed with his sword to the land and claimed, "This is mine," and of the friar who pointed with his cross to the sky and promised the natives, "A pie in the sky, by and by." One result was the demise of peoples and cultures, oppression and exploitation, suffering and death. Not to be outdone, the Puritans aimed to convert the natives of America, but if they would not convert, the heathen – who were already condemned anyway – would be exterminated. Thus, they built their "city upon a hill," on the genocidal foundations of the original Americans, which will be compounded by the enslavement of another race.

How did we get from the fishermen of Galilee to bishops with gold-inlaid gloves riding horses into battle, or medieval authorities burning alive those whose consciences moved them to dissent, or missionaries killing peoples and destroying cultures to implant the faith? It was a journey travelled by the alliance of altar and throne, of monotheistic religion and state power, because Christianity neglected the lesson of the infancy narratives of Matthew and Luke that Jesus' kingdom was not like Caesar's kingdom, that Jesus' methods were not like those of Caesar, that God's way was not Rome's imperial theology. It was undertaken through political power and with military might, because Christianity ignored the all-important petition of the prayer taught by Jesus that God lead us not into temptation to use the weapons of the kingdoms of the earth promised by Satan to promote his cause, to spread his message, to establish his kingdom of justice, mercy, love, and peace, which is a contradiction of the highest order.

Even today, the Catholic Church, while it is shorn of temporal and political power, while it has accepted the separation of church and state, the freedom of conscience and religion, and the existence of human rights, continues to deploy its spiritual power to call on the state to enforce its teachings, when those teachings have lost their credibility and the faithful simply ignore them. Take the case of contraception and the Affordable Care Act. The Catholic Church in the United States has traditionally been known for three causes: labor, immigration, and healthcare. Even with the accommodations made by the Obama administration, and unlike Catholic nuns, the American hierarchy continues to oppose the ACA, because, according to them, it promotes contraception, a teaching with which the majority of moral theologians do not agree and which the majority of Catholics do not follow. They oppose it on the grounds of religious freedom, they say, *their* religious freedom, not the religious freedom of their non-Catholic employees and clients. Ultimately, however, it is against contraception that they are asking the state to enforce, because they have failed to persuade their members (Miller 2014).

Empire and its trappings are what confront Pope Francis. The temptation to use the coercive power of the state to advance the Church's program continues to bait bishops and priests. Marco Politi (2015: 54-55), a veteran journalist on Vatican issues, pinpoints the beating heart of the opposition to Pope Francis by some members of the worldwide episcopate by providing the basic context of his reform program which is:

> a coherent design to dismantle the imperial character of the papacy, its Caesarian absolutism, semidivine and fed by the aura of infallibility that has clung to the papal court. The formal title of the successors of Peter is itself pagan, for the

pontifex maximus was the chief priest of ancient Rome. . . . The "sacred" and grandiloquent character that has become attached to the bishopric of Rome does not derive from Christianity, much less from the Gospel, but from the later Roman Empire. "Everything having to do [with] the Emperor Diocletian was defined as 'sacred': his edicts, his bedchamber, his bodyguard, the papal chancellery," writes the historian Giovanni Filoramo, evoking the heightened rituality of the late imperial court. "Those granted an audience with the emperor were admitted to the 'adoration of the purple,' the hem of the imperial mantle."

This is the origin of the red shoes and red shoulder cape of the popes. It has nothing to do with the redness of blood or with any symbolic readiness for martyrdom. It is the red of absolute power. The custom of prostration before the pope and cardinals corresponds to the self-effacement of subjects in the presence of the Roman emperor and his great imperial counterpart and model, the Persian king of kings. The "Sacred Rota," the "Holy Inquisition," the "sacred palaces" of the Vatican, the "audience of kissing the hand," the "sacred congregations," the "kissing of the pope's slipper" – all are descended from the practices of the absolute oriental monarchies, where the sovereign's mere nod was the supreme law.

"Heads of the church have often been narcissists, flattered and thrilled by their courtiers. The court is the leprosy of the papacy," Francis confided to Eugenio Scalfari, founder of the newspaper *La Repubblicca*.

Borg and Crossan (2007: 166-67) are emphatic:

The Roman vision incarnated in the divine Augustus was peace through victory. The Christian vision incarnated in the divine Jesus was peace though justice. It is those alternatives that are at stake behind all the titles and countertitles, the claims and counterclaims. . . .

The terrible truth is that our world has never established peace through victory. Victory establishes not peace, but lull. Thereafter violence returns once again, and always worse than before. And it is that escalator violence that then endangers our world....

We face a similar choice each Christmas, and so each Advent is a time of repentance for the past and a change for the future. Do we think that peace on earth comes from Caesar or Christ? Do we think it comes through violent victory or non violent justice? Advent, like Lent, is about a choice how to live personally and individually, nationally and internationally.

Christmas is not about tinsel and mistletoe, or even ornaments and presents. But about what *means* we will use toward the *end* of a peace from heaven upon the earth. Or is "peace on earth" but a Christmas ornament taken each year from attic or basement and returned there as soon as possible?

Empire, Colony, and America

The Third World is the grouping of poor and underdeveloped countries of Latin America, Asia, and Africa. What is common to them is their shared histories of colonialism. To try to find out indigenous resources for their development, we often turn to their precolonial histories and cultures. This is not possible for Christianity. There is no history of Christianity before and without colonialism. Christianity is the product of empire. Even their Judaic roots grew under empire, four of whom are mentioned by Daniel (7:2-7, 17) – Babylonian, Medean, Persian, Macedonian – except when they themselves acted as empire in cleansing Canaan for their Promised Land and under the Maccabees.

But within three centuries, Christianity soon adopted the ways and ideology of empire, and itself became an empire. What started as an anti-imperial movement became established as the official religion of an empire. What is astonishing and disconcerting, to say the least, is that empire and colony do not figure much, if at all, in theological discourse and study. And yet it could be said that empire and colony are endemic to the history and development of Christianity, its doctrine and moral teaching, its governance and disciplinary structures; they continue to be challenges in the ways the Church conducts its business in society and the world. I suppose it behooves that the theologians who bring up the issue of empire and colony in the bible, in Christianity, in theology and ethics, and in the contemporary circumstances of the churches come from the margins of the dominant theological world. Some recent examples:

Richard Horsley has consistently argued against a depoliticized Jesus, a depoliticized Judea and Galilee, a depoliticized Roman Empire. "Trying to understand Jesus' speech and action without knowing how Roman imperialism determined the conditions of life in Galilee and Jerusalem would be like trying to understand Martin Luther King without knowing how slavery, reconstruction, and segregation determined the lives of African Americans in the United States" (Horsley 2003: 13). Accordingly, for him *Jesus and Empire* cannot be yanked from each other. Jesus and empire must be studied together; the meaning and implications of Jesus' life, teachings, and ministry – then and now – cannot come from a deracinated Jesus. A Jesus uprooted from his actual historical, social, economic, and political environment is an ethereal Jesus, worthy of being worshipped, perhaps, but not imitated and followed.

Complaining that so little attention has been devoted to the Roman imperial context of Paul's mission and his relations to it, Horsley (1997) edited a volume, *Paul and Empire*, whose selections represent a substantive or procedural shift from previous scholarly understandings. First, the emperor cult and the imperial patronage system offer the principal networks by which Roman imperial relations were established and, therefore, broaden our understanding of how power relations were constituted in political-religious and social-economic forms. Second, there is a significant shift in our understanding of the background and significance of many of the most basic Pauline terms and symbols, that is, over against Roman imperial religio-politics, not against "Judaism." Third, there occurs a serious broadening of Paul's basic agenda, i.e., that he was not simply catalyzing religious congregations of Gentiles, but was organizing an international anti-imperial alternative society based on local communities.

In *Christ and Empire*, Joerg Rieger (2007) advanced the proposition that our images of Christ have been shaped by empire at significant historical turning points, that the figure of Christ was inextricably bound to the bloody advance of empires in the past and even today is implicated in new and subtler empires. Historically, the spread of the Gospel was accompanied by cross and sword, by flag and cannon. We need to chip away at the violent colonial legacy of Christology to find the authentic Christ. Today, the most urgent theological issue is the ecological degradation and the survival of the planet under the conditions of globalization. But globalization also facilitates patriotic fundamentalism, prosperity preaching, and charismatic enthusiasm. The image of the cosmic Christ can initiate new kinds of relationships between peoples and the planet that resist the distortion of power under the conditions of empire. But it can be coopted, manipulated, and subverted, not by the direct exercise of political power, but by the more far-reaching influences of supposedly universal and neutral laws of the free market.

The Bible and the gun were literally conjoined when William Colenso, who worked as a printer in New Zealand, picked up a cartridge fashioned out of the pages of the Bible. The rolled-up paper came from 2 Samuel and bore the words: "How long have I to live?" This is how R.S. Sugirtharajah (2005a) starts his *The Bible and Empire*, in which he is concerned about what happens to colonial artefacts, most especially the Bible, when it is imposed forcefully on the natives or offered to them for their benefit. He demonstrates how the Bible has been used in a variety of ways by both the colonizer and the colonized, thus bringing to the fore personalities and issues seldom dealt with within the parameters of mainstream biblical scholarship. He is interested in "how different communities of interpreters, among both the colonized and the colonizers, appropriated, reappropriated and at times emasculated their favourite texts, and how, in the process, they themselves were shaped and moulded and their identity redefined. The colonial usage is testimony to the notion that every era produces the Bible in its own image and responds to it differently on the basis of shifting political and cultural needs and expectations" (Sugirtharajah 2005a: 2).

R.S. Sugirtharajah (2005b: 542) was the first to introduce postcolonial criticism to biblical studies. He takes seriously empire and colony in theological discourse. He refers to the empires that "were an outgrowth of industrial capitalism and were marked by distinct cultural domination and penetration which have created the myth of the West as the superior 'other', a myth which is continually evoked in international disputes, and in political, cultural and theological discourses" (Sugirtharajah 2005a: 2). "Postcolonialism is used here as an interventionist instrument which refuses to take the dominant reading as an uncomplicated representation of the past and introduces an alternative meaning. Postcolonialism allows silenced and often marginalized people to find their own voices when they are at loggerheads with the dominant reading" (Sugirtharajah 2005a: 3). Empire and postcolonialism are therefore in basic continuity with Jesus and empire.

In the aftermath of 9/11 as George Bush II launched his war on terror, a member of his administration expressed the conviction that "we are an empire now, and we mean to act like one." Empire used to be a derogatory term to denote the excesses and overreach, economic, political, and military, of the United States as a superpower. With the collapse of the Soviet empire, it now seemed honorable for the sole remaining superpower to wield the scepter of empire. In response to *The New Security Strategy of the United States of America*, issued by George W. Bush on September 17, 2002, which describes the New Empire with crystal clarity, Robert Bellah (2004: 26), in a volume of essays, edited by Wes Avram (2004), "Anxious about Empire," expressed great fear that "this latest American outburst of 'the arrogance of power' will mobilize most of the world against us."

John Judis (2004) dared to instruct what George W. Bush could learn from Theodore Roosevelt and Woodrow Wilson about the folly of empire. Theodore Roosevelt originally believed that the United States should compete with Europe in the struggle for colonies. But he became disillusioned with imperialist pretentions after the protracted colonial war in the Philippines. Woodrow Wilson, shocked by the brutality of World War I, saw imperialism not as an instrument of peace and democracy, but of war and tyranny. He advocated that the United States lead in eliminating colonialism, and in creating a "League of Nations," in which he failed. According to Judis (2004: 212), their lasting lesson is that "when America goes out alone in search of monsters to destroy – venturing on terrain upon which imperial powers have already trod – it can itself become a monster." It echoes Heather's (2005: 459) conclusion that "by virtue of its unbounded aggression, Roman imperialism was ultimately responsible for its own destruction."

All these led Cullen Murphy (2007) to wonder *Are We Rome?* Murphy sees a wide variety of similarities between Rome and America: the blinkered, insular culture of capital cities; the debilitating effect of venality in public life; the dysfunctionality of government because of the inability of parties to rise above narrow, partisan interests; the individualism of citizens that prevents them from cooperating for the common good; the distrust of central government and the misplaced belief in unfettered markets; the issue of borders and the bitter dispute over how to manage immigration. But Murphy argues that we resemble most the Roman Empire in the burgeoning corruption and paralysis of government and in our ignorant, arrogant condescension toward the world outside, two things that must be changed if we want to avoid Rome's fate.

If, indeed, America is not wholly Rome, there is no question that today America holds overwhelming power, economic, political, cultural, and military, which it has used for good and ill, which it can utilize for domination and oppression or for liberation and freedom, which it can deploy for narrow, vested interests or for the common good of the global community. There is no doubt that the United States is the main pillar that props the global capitalism that has wrought social deterioration in poor peoples' lives and their cultures, that has brought about ecological degradation and devastation, and that has resulted in a crisis of humanity (Robinson 2014). America also wields the greatest military firepower the world has ever known. America has a military budget that dwarfs the budgets of all other countries. America is "not an empire of colonies," Chalmers Johnson (2004: 23) points out, "but an empire of bases," dotting the entire world map, ever ready to protect and promote the imperial interests of the United States. In the view of officials in the Bush II administration, America is no longer bound by international law, the concern of allies, or any constraints on its use of military force.

What complicates the situation is that American imperial power has the support and the encouragement of both the political right and the religious right that have, for all practical purposes, captured the Republican Party. It is devoutly claimed that America is the exceptional country that can do no wrong, that it is mandated by divine providence to have dominion over the earth, a city upon a hill that is destined to bring freedom, democracy, and capitalism to benighted countries. America is No. 1! God bless America! Even conservative Catholic intellectuals have chimed in that American "democratic capitalism," a.k.a. unregulated markets, corresponds the most to the vision and demands of Catholic social teaching, and have wholeheartedly rallied to the immoral and disastrous invasion of Iraq and the questionable methods and techniques of the war on terror. God, if we are to believe these modern crusaders, has unleashed America as empire. It is no longer Jesus and Paul against the Roman empire, but Jesus and Paul with and for the American empire. It is now violent Christianity against violent Islam, a violent Book of Revelations against a violent Quran.

What then is expected of Christians who know that God's reign is the end of empires? (Gonzalez 2012). John Dominic Crossan (2007: 237) is constrained to ask: "How is it possible to be a faithful Christian in the American Empire? How is it possible to be a nonviolent Christian within a violent Christianity based on a violent Christian Bible? How is it possible to be a faithful Christian in an American Empire facilitated by a violent Christian Bible?" These are age-old questions raised and equally age-old answers given in the Infancy Narratives of Matthew and Luke. These are also immemorial temptations and perennial dilemmas posed by the prayer Jesus taught us to pray, that we ask God not to lead us into. At the minimum, Vincent Rougeau (2008: 22) proposes: "When the empire demands our services, Christians must determine whether what we are being asked to do is consistent with a Christian understanding of the common good, and ultimately we must be willing in certain instances to reject the worldly benefits that an unquestioning identification with the American empire might offer."

2

EVOLUTION AND THE BODILY RESURRECTION OF JESUS

The Resurrection of Jesus is the central mystery of the Christian faith. Easter, therefore, is the main Christian feast day. The Paschal Mystery – the Passion, Crucifixion, and Resurrection of Jesus – is what we commemorate during Holy Week. It is the core of Christian evangelization; it is the Good News of the gospels. The Resurrection of Jesus formed, and forms, the foundation of the new community called Christian and a new understanding of God.

Jesus' resurrection is the ultimate vindication of his life and ministry, of his message of redemption and of his promise of salvation; his exaltation as Lord. Jesus' resurrection is the fulfillment of the prophecies of the Old Testament, that he indeed is the Messiah, the Christ, so that Jesus Christ became his name and surname. Jesus' resurrection is also the main presupposition of the emergence of the Christian group as a new community. The Christian community's claim is that God's salvation has been revealed in the cross and resurrection of Jesus. Thus, as Pheme Perkins (1984: 18) put it, "it is the condition for the emergence of Christian speech itself." Finally, Jesus' resurrection anticipates the eschatological victory over death. Jesus' resurrection is the foretaste of our own resurrection, the harbinger of our own redemption and salvation. The Risen Christ foreshadows our life of union with God. Paul in 1 Corinthians 15:13-19 sums it all up:

If there is no resurrection of the dead, then Christ has not been raised; and if Christ has not been raised, then our proclamation has been in vain and your faith has been in vain. We are even found to be misrepresenting God, because we have testified of God that he raised Jesus – whom he did not raise if it is true that the dead are not raised. For if the dead are not raised, then Christ has not been raised. If Christ has not been raised, your faith is futile and you are still in your sins. Then those also who have died in Christ have perished. If for this life only we have hoped in Christ, we are of all people the most to be pitied.

Resurrection and Divinity

The centrality and significance of Jesus' resurrection for Christian faith and life are perhaps better understood and appreciated if we take a look at what historical criticism tells us about the resurrection and divinity of Jesus Christ. The task of historical criticism is to try to retrieve what really happened behind the testimonies of faith that are the gospels (Litonjua 2011). Joseph Fitzmyer (2008: 66) points out:

In regard to the historical criticism of the Synoptic Gospels, we have learned through this method to distinguish three stages of the gospel tradition: (I) what Jesus of Nazareth did and said (corresponding roughly to A.D. 1-33); (II) what apostles of Jesus preached about him, his words, and his deeds (corresponding roughly to A.D. 33-65); and (III) what evangelists wrote about him, having culled, synthesized, and explicated the tradition that preceded them, each in his own way (corresponding to A.D. 65-95). The relationship of Stage III to Stages I and II is the problem for modern readers of these Gospels, and therein lies the crucial need of the historical-critical method of Gospel interpretation.

Firstly, there is a general consensus among biblical scholars that Jesus during his lifetime did not claim and proclaim himself as God, as divine. Neither did his disciples consider him as divine, as God. This is what historical criticism tells us about the divinity of Jesus in stage I of the gospel tradition.

Secondly, between stage I and stages II and III there intervenes the resurrection of Jesus from the dead or, more precisely, there occurs a change in the consciousness of Jesus' disciples, they begin believing that he rose from the dead. This belief in the resurrection of Jesus by his disciples is indisputably verified by historical criticism.

Now comes stage II of the gospel tradition. Jesus' disciples begin preaching that Jesus rose from the dead. They proclaim that because of his resurrection, Jesus is exalted as Lord, Jesus is the long-awaited Messiah, Jesus is divine. Through Jesus' passion, death, and resurrection, we are redeemed and saved from sin. Communities of his followers are formed in which the Risen Jesus is proclaimed, the Divine Christ is worshipped, his message is preached, and new followers are baptized in his name.

There were different ways by which the divinity of Jesus as derived from the belief in his resurrection was explained. There were debates and conflicts about how Jesus could be in some way divine, as we will see later.

In state III of the gospel tradition, we now have documentary evidence of the faith of the early communities of the followers of Jesus. It must be remembered that the letters of Paul, the synoptic gospels of Mark, Matthew, the gospel and acts of Luke, and that of John are not strictly historical and biographical documents in the modern senses of the words, although they contain historical facts and biographical elements. They are primarily testaments of the faith of the communities of the followers of Jesus, to whom were preached and proclaimed and who, in turn preached and proclaimed, the message and life of Jesus. St. Paul's Letters were written in the 50s. Mark's Gospel is considered the earliest of the four, written in the 60s, with Matthews's and Luke's written in the 70s, and John's the latest, written in the 90s.

These documents are retrospective documents. They look back at the events of Jesus' life and ministry, his words and actions, i.e. in stage I, through the eyes of faith, interpreting them and communicating them in the light of their belief in his resurrection. They look at the events and happenings in state I of the gospel tradition through the prism of the passion, death, and resurrection of Jesus. They retroactively apply what they have come to believe of Jesus, the Risen Lord and Savior, to what he said and did when he walked the plains and hills of Galilee, ministering to the poor and the lowly. They retroject the post-resurrection Christ back to the pre-resurrection Jesus.

A simple example may help clarify. Jesus says: "Let us go to Jerusalem for the Passover." The disciples object and resist: "Why go to Jerusalem? You have antagonized the high priests who accuse you of blasphemy. You have also antagonized the Romans for claiming to be the King of the Jews.

If you go to Jerusalem, you are putting yourself in peril." Jesus replies: "Let us go anyway." And they go to Jerusalem where Jesus is captured, bound for trial, and crucified.

As now found in the Synoptic Gospels, through the lens of the Resurrection, the time of the Passover in Mark 14:1 ("The Passover and the Feast of the Unleavened Bread were to take place in two days' time.") is turned in Matthew 26:2 into Jesus' final prediction of his death ("You know that in two days' time it will be Passover, and the Son of Man will be handed over to be crucified."). In Luke 13:33 Jesus declares his final destination where his work will be accomplished ("Yet I must continue on my way today, tomorrow, and the following day, for it is impossible that a prophet should die outside of Jerusalem.").

In other words, the events that took place in Jerusalem during the Feast of the Passover are retroactively recounted as having been predicted by Jesus in his lifetime, as having been foretold by the pre-resurrection Jesus. It was as if the evangelists writing in stage III of the events in stage I realized: "That is why he insisted on going to Jerusalem for the Passover. He knew that he would be captured, tried, and crucified. That was the only way in which he could bring about our redemption from sin." This the disciples realized after he rose from the dead.

(Raymond Brown [1994: 1468-91] somewhat tediously and torturously discusses Jesus' predictions of his passion and death – [the three famous detailed predictions are Mark 8:31; 9:31; and 10:33-34] – but the most he can conclude is that "subtlety does more to the likelihoods than a negative vote [by the Jesus Seminar] that Jesus did not make (and perhaps could not have made) any of the predictions attributed to him." But, the conclusion of the Jesus Seminar on this matter, is it not more consonant with Brown's own backward process of Christological development?)

The belief in the resurrection led to the belief in his divinity; it was a journey from Jesus to Christ (Fredriksen 1988). Bart Ehrman (2014) addresses how Jesus became God, while Richard Rubenstein (1999) narrates when Jesus became God. Paul did not know Jesus of Nazareth, nor did he evince much interest in him. Paul knew only the Risen Christ, from whose resurrection he reasons backward to his divine Sonship and forward to his imminent Parousia. Salvation comes in and through the great eschatological fact of Christ's resurrection. The believer can have a foretaste of this salvation, through the grace of the Spirit received in baptism, which would be realized fully at the Parousia.

What Raymond Brown (1993: 32) calls "the backwards process of Gospel formation and christological development" applies to the four evangelists. Mark retroactively pushes the self-identity of Jesus as divine to his baptism by John at the Jordan, when on coming out of the water, the heavens were torn open, the Spirit, in the form of a dove, descended upon him, and a voice came from the heavens, "You are my beloved Son; with you I am well pleased" (Mark 1:9-11). Matthew and Luke push the proclamation of Jesus' divinity further back to his virginal conception in the womb of Mary. Matthew (1:20) writes that an angel of the Lord appeared to Joseph in a dream and told him: "Do not be afraid to take Mary your wife into your home. For it is through the holy Spirit that this child has been conceived in her." Luke (1:30) tells of the angel Gabriel saying to Mary: "Do not be afraid, Mary, for you have found favor with God. Behold, you will conceive in you womb and bear a son, and you shall name him Jesus." Finally, John (1:1) situates the Word in the beginning when the Word was with God, and the Word was God. "The Word became flesh and made his dwelling among us, and we saw his glory, the glory of the Father's only Son, full of grace and truth" (John 1:14). Thus, Christ was not only divine because and when he rose from the dead, nor only at the beginnings of the Jesus Movement, nor only at the first instant of his humanity, but at the eternal origins of cosmic time.

The importance of this development is captured most recently by James Carroll (2014a: 48):

> If Jesus were not regarded as God almost from the start of his movement, he would be of no interest to us. We would have never heard of him. Nothing but his divinity accounts for his place in Western culture (or in my heart): not his ethic, which was admirable, but hardly uncommon; not his preaching, which was firmly in line with Jewish proclamation; not his heroic suffering, which was typical of many anti-Roman Jewish resisters; not his wonder-working, which was attributed to all kinds of charismatic figures in the ancient world.

This is not to contradict James Carroll, but only to point out that, like everything else in human life, there can be a downside. To share in the Kingdom of God which he came to inaugurate, Jesus lays down the beatitudes, nine of them in Matthew (5:3-11) and four in Luke (6:20-22). What are we to do with them? Jesus ends his Parable of the Good Samaritan (Luke 10:29-37) with these words: "Go and do likewise." It was all about imitating and following Jesus. But with the Christological controversies of the 4th and the 5th centuries, it became who Jesus Christ was, not what he did and taught; it became worshipping Christ, not imitating and following him. How do you imitate and do likewise a divine being? All the questions about Jesus are preempted by his divinity. Did he walk on water? Of course, he was divine. Did he know the future? Of course, he was God. Did he work miracles, and so and so forth. The Council of Nicaea in 325 came up with a creed, later to be expanded by the Council of Constantinople in 381, which Nicene-Constantinopolitan Creed is recited today by Catholics at Mass. It was a set of propositional truths to be believed, to be intellectually adhered to; not one word about the beatitudes, about the preconditions for participating in God's reign.

Moreover, as Carroll (2014b: 13-15) expostulates at length, the divinity of Jesus Christ trumps his humanity, including his Jewishness. "[W]hile 'Jesus' can be routinely understood as a Jew, 'Christ' is taken to be the claim that cuts him off from his Jewishness.... His being 'Christ' worked against his being 'Jesus,' because his elevation up the pyramid of what scholars call 'high Christology' . . . had the practical effect of obliterating the single most cogent note of his identity as a man." Two points, therefore. Is Jesus that the Gospels claim to have been rejected by the Jews the human Jesus of history, or the divine Christ of faith that the evangelists projected back in their Gospels? If Christian memory did not obliterate Jesus the Jew, would the polemical anti-Judaism of the Gospels not have transmogrified into the racial anti-Semitism of Christian history, which in turn fertilized the soil from which the evils of Hitler and the Holocaust sprouted? That is why, James Carroll (2014b) insists, that after Auschwitz, we must retrieve and reclaim the Jewishness not only of the human Jesus, but also of the divine Christ for Jesus Christ actually to become the Son of God for the secular age.

Christianity and Judaism

The divinity of Christ as a result of his resurrection was not the only thing that was retroactively applied in the founding documents of Christianity. As the Jesus Movement moved out of Palestine and spread around the Mediterranean as Christianity, the situation in Palestine under the Romans had changed. As a consequence of the Jewish revolt in 66 AD, the temple of Jerusalem was burned down by Titus in 70 AD. By mid-second century Jerusalem itself disappeared after the insurrection led by Bar Kochba. In its place was erected the pagan city Aelia Capitolina, and in its temple area, a shrine to the God Zeus and the emperor Hadrian. "The destruction of Jerusalem and of the Second Temple," wrote Paula Fredriksen (1988: 81), "was a major blow both to the political aspirations and to the religious institutions of Judaism. The Supreme Jewish Court, the Sanhedrin, ceased to exist; the sacrifices required by the Torah and restricted to the Temple could no longer be performed."

The Christian communities spread around the Mediterranean basin. "Once the movement that formed around the memory of Jesus spread from rural Palestine to the cities of the Roman Empire," Fredriksen (1988: 17) noted, "it did not leave Judaism behind. On the contrary, it followed the lead of the Hellenistic synagogue both sociologically and theologically. Early Christian communities adopted the Jewish practice of meeting regularly once a week for group worship. They too established philanthropies for the needy, offered group support in time of persecution, and took responsibility for the burial of the dead. Such social structures sustained and gave expression to the strong sense of community and solidarity that distinguished these groups within their pagan environment."

The Christian communities in the Mediterranean world were soon faced with three incontrovertible facts: the continuing resistance by, if not conflict with, Jews; the attraction and therefore the influx of Gentiles to Christianity; and the prolonged delay of the End which Jesus himself thought and taught was imminent. These had an impact in the way the gospels were written, in the way events and happenings were retrospectively narrated. I wish to limit myself to two examples which will have lasting and disastrous historical effects.

The first concerns the relationship of Christianity to Judaism. For Paul, salvation only comes in and through the great eschatological fact of Christ's resurrection. But trying to understand Paul's views on Christ and the Law, Fredriksen (1988: 160), points out, is to "enter into the deepest exegetical quagmire of New Testament scholarship." As traditionally understood, by Augustine and Luther, for example, although Fredriksen (1988: 161-65) discussed also two other more positive views, Paul rejected Judaism as a religion of works-righteousness. "The Torah only entangled man in self-righteousness, inducing him to think that he could earn salvation through the accumulation of good works ("legalism")" (Fredriksen 1988: 60).

To explain Jewish resistance to Christianity, Mark insists that Israel had always rejected the Gospel, from the earliest days of Jesus' mission to the last, while the Gentiles have always been receptive. Mark (3:31-35) even has Jesus reject his (Jewish) mother and brothers, "for whoever does the will of God is my brother and sister and mother." And why did the Jews reject Jesus? Because, Mark answers, Jesus had already rejected them together with their religion. This mutual hostility and rejection were retrojected into Jesus' times and words. But Fredriksen (1988: 181) raises "an awkward problem" created by Mark: "Was the Gospel rejected by Jesus' Jewish contemporaries the same as the Gospel rejected by Mark's?

Did Jesus before his death and resurrection, in other words, proclaim as Mark's community did the post-resurrection Jesus?"

Matthew was a Jewish Christian, whose community at Antioch was riven with shifting relationships between Jewish and Christian Gentiles, living as they did in the shadow of a larger Jewish community. Matthew (23:1-26) shows the sharpest hostility to Jews, decrying the title "Rabbi" for their teachers, calling Pharisees hypocrites, blind guides, blind fools, whitewashed tombs, full of the bones of the dead and of all kinds of filth, and puts them in the mouth of Jesus, such that the word "pharisee" has become synonymous with "hypocrite" and the reputation of Pharisees has forever been denigrated. Raymond Brown (1997: 215, 79) states that "the Matthean rejection of the title 'Rabbi' (23:7-8) is unique," and adds that Matthew's "picture is hostilely exaggerated, reflecting later polemics between Christians and Jews." But the damage has been done. Mark Allan Powell (2009: 121-22) notes that "Matthew's Gospel often has been accused of fostering anti-Semitism . . . and anti-Semitic people throughout history have used it . . . to justify hatred and abuse of Jews, characterizing them as 'Christ-killers' and as people accursed by God."

Luke's Gospel and Acts differ from Mark's and Matthew's portrayal of intractable and inevitable hostility between Christians and Jews in the past. He emphasizes the continuity and historicity of salvation revealed in scripture. For Luke, the object of God's redemptive acts and the partner in his covenant is the Jewish nation, Israel. Luke's Jesus is a traditionally pious Jew. Who, then, is Jesus' Jewish opposition? "The Jews of the Diaspora are the true villains of Luke's piece. The Sanhedrin and the people of Jerusalem had acted against Jesus in ignorance; but the Jews of the Diaspora act from malice and jealousy against his church" (Fredriksen 1988: 193-94). Thus, "Luke leaves Paul in Rome on [a] dual note of pessimism and confidence: pessimism about the Jews' ability to receive the Gospel, confidence in the Gentiles' positive response" (Fredriksen, 1988: 195).

John's Jesus is the preexistent, supremely divine Son. "As he travels repeatedly between Jerusalem and the Galilee," Fredriksen (1998: 199, 200, 210) wrote, "this Jesus encounters, not fellow Jews, but sons of darkness, denizens of the lower cosmos, who can never receive the word of God. . . . Through his Christology, John rotates the axis of Christian tradition ninety degrees, away from the historical, horizontal poles of Past/Future to the spiritualizing, vertical poles of Below/Above." Thus, we find in John "not only a developed and retrojected Christology but also an equally developed and retrojected polemic against the competition." John explains that "the root cause why Jews do not accept Jesus is that they *cannot*. They are not 'of God,' they do not 'know God,' and therefore they cannot recognize his Son. . . . Jesus never called them, since he knew that they were not his sheep. In this sense, then, Israel did not reject the Gospel: the Gospel was not really offered to them. And though the Jews' 'failure' was divinely predestined, they are accountable nevertheless" (Fredriksen 1988: 2001).

The second issue relates to the gospel depictions of the trial of Jesus. Mark (14:53) identifies the Jewish opponents of Jesus as "the high priest, and all the chief priests and the elders and the scribes," come together in the Sanhedrin. Also in Mark (15:6-15), "the crowd" presses Pilate to release Barabbas and to crucify Jesus, which, "wishing to satisfy the crowd," he did. Matthew (26:3-4) identifies the Jewish enemies of Jesus as "the chief priests and elders of the people," headed by high priest Caiaphas. He (Matt. 27:24-26) depicts Pilate as washing his hands, saying, "I am innocent of this man's blood. Look to it yourselves." And the whole people said in reply, "His blood be upon us and upon our children." Luke (23:1-25) presents Pilate as finding Jesus guilty of no capital crime three times, but was forced by the chief priests and the people to release Barabbas and condemn Jesus to be crucified. John (18:28-19:16) names the enemies of Jesus simply as "the Jews." It is as if Christianity, having forged its own identity against Judaism, especially after the destruction of the Temple of Jerusalem in 70 AD and the disappearance of Jerusalem by mid-second century, needed to blame Jews for the death and crucifixion of Jesus to curry favor with the Roman Empire. "The result:" Paula Fredriksen (1988: 105) put it, "Rome and Christianity are both on the same side against the Jews." Christianity's cross and Constantine's sword were the weapons of destruction of the Jews.

I have often wondered why when a famous athlete or a celebrity becomes a born-again Christian and begins reading the New Testament, s/he also starts spouting anti-Semitic slurs. Because they do not realize – who could on their own? – that the anti-Judaism of the Gospels is the polemics of an intersectarian dispute. But it is also true that the polemical anti-Judaism of the Gospels was transmogrified into racial anti-Semitism that had wreaked havoc on world and church and had resulted in the deaths of millions. The cross became an ideological tool to charge Jews with deicide and to confine them into ghettoes. Anti-Semitism ran like an infectious disease in the life and structures of the Christian churches, soiling their doctrine, morals, worship, and governance, contaminating head and members, saints and sinners alike. Even today, traditionalist Christians, including adherents of the schismatic Pius X Society, continue their anti-Semitic tirades and malicious practices. Christian anti-Semitism was the fertile soil from which sprung the horrors of Hitler and the Holocaust. That is why, after writing a massive and masterful volume on the Church and the Jews, James Carroll (2001, 2014), as does John Meier (2001), insists that "recovering the permanent Jewishness – not just of 'Jesus,' but also of 'Christ' – defines the essential work that Christians must do after Auschwitz."

Resurrection in the Gospels

Edward Schillebeeckx (1979: 380) asked: "What brought the disciples who had left Jesus in the lurch at the time of his arrest and crucifixion together again – and together now in the name of Jesus, acknowledged as the Christ, Son of God, the Lord?" He points out first: "The primary and immediate reply to this cannot be: the reality of the resurrection itself. The resurrection in its eschatological 'eventuality' is after all nowhere recounted in the New Testament; nor of course could it be, because it no longer forms part of our mundane, human history; it is *qua* reality, meta-empirical and meta-historical: 'eschatological.'" Schillebeeckx's (1979: 381) reply: "What actually took place between the two historical events – Jesus' death and the apostles' preaching – we are bound to say at once: the conversion of the disciples, who 'notwithstanding' Jesus' scandalizing death came together again – and did so in the name of this same Jesus, through a recognition of the paucity of their faith. It is a process of conversion between the two historically accessible elements."

This conversion process, which Schillebeeckx designates as the Easter experience, involved a relationship to the Jesus of Nazareth whom the disciples let down, and a relationship to Jesus as the Christ to whom they return. It is the experience of grace as forgiveness and as empowerment. It was an act of sheer grace on God's part that enabled the disciples who had first taken offense at Jesus to subsequently proclaim him as the only bringer of salvation. It was an experience of a renewed offer of salvation from God, which meant that after Jesus' death, salvation through the heavenly Jesus meant that the disciples' return to Jesus became a return to the living, crucified One. Thus it is that the disciples' experience of Jesus' resurrection stands at the heart of the Christian movement.

But where and how did this experience of and belief in the Risen Christ originate? Popularly it is taken to be the empty tomb, whose emptiness is often understood also as the ultimate proof of the fact of Jesus' resurrection. For one thing, Pheme Perkins (1984: 91-95) argued, "there was no unified tradition about the empty tomb in early Christianity. . . . At almost every point, the [four gospel] accounts go in separate directions. It is impossible to harmonize them in such a way as to produce a single, simpler tradition that has then been redacted by the narrators." Resurrection does not automatically imply an empty tomb. Finding the tomb empty was not the source of early Christian belief that Jesus had been raised. In fact, "the introduction of the appearances into the tomb traditions was an 'apologetic' for the tomb stories. By themselves the stories of the empty tomb do not prove anything. Consequently, they must be combined with kerygmatic traditions and appearance stories in order to be a significant part of the Christian kerygma" (Perkins 1984: 91).

The earliest example of resurrection proclamation is the formula in 1 Cor. 15:3-5: "Christ died for our sins in accordance with the scriptures; he was buried; he was raised on the third day in accordance with the scriptures; he appeared to Cephas, then to the twelve." The formula is pre-Pauline. Then follows a list of witnesses to the resurrection in vv. 6-7, which is an addition to the formula: "After that he appeared to more than five hundred brothers at once, most of whom are still living, though some have fallen asleep. After that he appeared to James, then to all the apostles." From v. 8, Paul is speaking of his own case: "Last of all, as to one born abnormally, he appeared to me. For I am the least of the apostles, not fit to be called an apostle, because I persecuted the Church. But by the grace of God I am what I am, and his grace to me has not been ineffective. Indeed, I have toiled harder than all of them; not I, however, but the grace of God that is with me. Therefore, whether it be I or they, so we preach and so you believed." The tradition therefore focuses on the experience of seeing the Lord. The conviction that Jesus has been raised was founded on the vision of the Lord. We cannot presume to reach the direct experience of those who became convinced that Jesus had been raised, if that could be described at all. But from Paul we may presume that it was a spiritual experience that carried with it the conviction of a revelatory encounter with God, one that was overpowering and empowering.

Hans Kung (1976: 346-48) pointed out four difficulties as well as their reverse advantages of the Gospel depictions of Jesus' resurrection, two of which are notable for our purposes.

> *Third difficulty.* There is *no direct evidence* of a resurrection. There is no one in the whole New Testament who claims to have been a witness of the resurrection. The resurrection is nowhere described. . . .
>
> The reverse side. The very reserve of the New Testament Gospels and letters in regard to the resurrection creates trust. The resurrection is neither depicted nor described. The interest in exaggeration and the craving for demonstration, which are characteristic of the apocrypha,

make the latter incredible. The New Testament Easter documents are not meant to be testimonies for the resurrection but testimonies to the raised and risen Jesus.

Fourth difficulty. A close analysis of the Easter accounts reveals insuperable *discrepancies and inconsistencies.* Attempts have indeed been made constantly to combine and harmonize them into a uniform tradition. But – to sum it up briefly – it is impossible to establish agreement about 1. The people involved: Peter, Mary Magdalene, the other Mary, the disciples, the apostles, the twelve, the Emmaus disciples, five hundred brethren, James, Paul; 2. The locality of the events: Galilee, a mountain there or the lake of Tiberias; Jerusalem, at Jesus' grave or a meeting place; 3. The whole sequence of appearances: morning and evening of Easter Sunday, eight days and forty days later. At every point harmonization proves to be impossible, unless we are prepared to accept textual changes and to minimize the differences.

The reverse side. Obviously, no one at the time needed or wanted a unified scheme or a smooth harmony, still less any sort of biography of the risen Jesus. The New Testament authors are not interested in any kind of completeness nor in a definite sequence and least of all in a critical historical investigation of the different pieces of information. From here it is clear that there is something more important to be stressed in the individual narratives: for Paul and Mark the calling and mission of the disciples; for Luke and John it is more the real identity of the risen with the pre-paschal Jesus (perception of the identity and ultimately proof of identity by the demonstration of his corporality and his sharing food, with a constantly greater emphasis on conquering the doubts of the disciples). At the same time it becomes clear that any how, when or where of the narratives is secondary in importance by the comparison with the fact – of which there is no doubt in the different sources – of the resurrection which in every context is clearly not identical with death and burial. What is required is a concentration on the true content of the message and this in turn will make possible a renewed investigation into the historical discrepancies.

Kung (1976: 348-61) then makes several additional clarifications that are helpful in understanding the resurrection of Jesus that his disciples believed in, from which I extract passages pertinent to our discussion.

> *Resurrection or raising?* In the New Testament "resurrection" is rightly understood a "raising by God." It is essentially a work of God on Jesus, the one crucified, dead and buried. "Raising" places God's whole action on Jesus at the center. It is only by God's life-creating action that Jesus' deadly passivity becomes new, vital activity. It is only as the one raised (by God) that he is the one who (himself) has risen.
>
> *Raising up as a historical event?* Since according to the New Testament faith the raising is an act of God within God's dimensions, it can *not* be a *historical* event in the strict sense: it is not an event which can be verified by historical science with the aid of historical methods. For the raising of Jesus is not a miracle violating the laws of nature, verifiable within the present world, not a supernatural intervention which can be located and dated in space and time. There is nothing to photograph and record. What can be historically verified are the death of Jesus and after this the Easter faith and the Easter message of the disciples. But neither the raising nor the person raised can be apprehended, objectified, by historical methods.
>
> But just because it is God's action according to the New Testament faith which is involved in the resurrection, this cannot be a merely fictitious or imaginary but in the most profound sense a *real* event. What happened is not nothing. But what happened bursts through and goes beyond the bounds of history. It is a transcendental happening out of human death into the all-embracing dimension of God. Resurrection involves a completely new mode of existence in God's wholly different mode of existence, conveyed visually and in need of interpretation.

Corporeal resurrection? No, if "body" simply means the physiologically identical body. Yes, if "body" means in the sense of the New Testament *soma* the identical personal reality, the *same self* with its whole history. In other words, no continuity of the body: questions of natural science, like that of the persistence of the molecules, do not arise. But an identity of the person: the question does arise of the lasting significance of the person's whole life and fate. In any case therefore not a diminished but a finished being.

The question persists: How about the body of the risen Christ? How about the bodily Jesus seen in the appearances? The question is important, because if it was a *bodily* resurrection, it was something that *did* happen to Jesus, and not just to the consciousness of his disciples. "We have to avoid two extremes: one which denies all bodily reality to the resurrection and make it something that happened to the disciples alone; and the other that exaggerates the bodily character of the resurrection and makes it an event that was equally available to the disinterested observer and the person of faith" (Mc Brien, 1994: 436-37). My own conclusion is that the risen Jesus did have a body. Not a resuscitated body. Not a purely spiritualized body. Not, therefore, an ethereal body. But a body transformed into a new mode of existence that could be touched, seen, and listened to, but also a body transformed into a different manner of being that could pass through walls, that walked on water, that could be with the Father. It is a transformed body that could only be apprehended in faith. It is this kind of marvelous transformation that awaits us all, that awaits the whole of creation itself, because God had raised Jesus from the dead, because Christ had risen and has been exalted at the right hand of God.

I leave the last word to Kung:

The ultimate reality. The message with all its difficulties, its time-bound concrete expressions and amplifications, situational expansions, elaborations and shifts of emphasis is basically concerned with something simple. And – despite all discrepancies and inconsistencies of the different traditions in regard to place and time, persons and the sequence of events – the different primitive Christian witnesses, Peter, Paul and James, the letters, the Gospels and Acts, are agreed that the *Crucified Jesus lives forever with God, as obligation and hope for us.* The men of the New Testament are sustained, even fascinated, by the certainty that the one who was killed did not remain dead but is alive and that the person who clings to him will likewise live. The new, eternal life of the one is a challenge and real hope for all.

The resurrection faith is not an appendage to faith in God, but a radicalizing of faith in God. It is a faith in God which does not stop halfway, but follows the road consistently to the end. It is a faith in which man, without strictly rational proof but certainly with completely reasonable trust, relies on the fact that the God of the beginning is also the God of the end, that as he is the Creator of the world and man so too he is their finisher.

The resurrection then does not only have apologetic value, the strongest possible corroboration of Jesus' messianic claims. Jesus' resurrection means that Jesus lives in a new and more powerful way than before. The resurrection is the principle of our new being. Jesus is the resurrection and the life. This is the resurrection of Jesus, which the disciples believed, which propelled them to preach the Good News, which changed the world. That is why the resurrection is the central mystery of the Christian faith, the foundation on which the Christian religion is built, the longing which animates all Christians and the entire creation.

What Kind of Divinity?

Because the followers of Jesus believed that he rose from the dead, they were led also to believe that he was in some way divine. It was because of the early Christians' faith in the resurrection that they came to acknowledge the divinity of Jesus. Belief in the resurrection was the chief moment associated with the proclamation of the divine identity of Jesus. Jesus did not claim to be divine during his lifetime, nor did the disciples who followed him proclaim him to be divine. With the resurrection or, more properly, with the belief in the resurrection, the disciples of Jesus began to believe also that he was divine. The divinity of Jesus would be pushed backed by the evangelists and retroactively applied in their gospels.

To repeat, Mark pushes the self-identity of Jesus as divine to his baptism by John at the Jordan, when on coming out of the water, the heavens were torn open, the Spirit, in the form of a dove, descended upon him, and a voice came from the heavens, "You are my beloved Son; with you I am well pleased" (Mark 1:9-11). Matthew and Luke retroactively push the proclamation of Jesus' divinity further back to his virginal conception in the womb of Mary. Matthew (1:20) writes that an angel of the Lord appeared to Joseph in a dream and told him: "Do not be afraid to take Mary your wife into your home. For it is through the holy Spirit that this child has been conceived in her." Luke (1:30) tells of the angel Gabriel saying to Mary: "Do not be afraid, Mary, for you have found favor with God. Behold, you will conceive in your womb and bear a son, and you shall name him Jesus." Finally, John (1:1) situates the Word in the beginning when the Word was with God, and the Word was God. "The Word became flesh and made his dwelling among us, and we saw his glory, the glory of the Father's only Son, full of grace and truth" (John 1:14).

But how did they understand his divinity? There were a number of ways by which Jesus' divinity was understood and explained. The variety and diversity of opinions regarding Jesus' divinity would constitute the great Christological debates of the 4th and 5th centuries. There were two extremes. On the one hand there were those that denied the humanity of Jesus for the sake of his divinity, that is, that Jesus was not truly human, but only took the appearance of being human. They were later labeled Docetists and Gnostics. On the other hand, there were those who denied the divinity of Jesus for the sake of his humanity, namely, that Jesus was human but was adopted by the Father or that he was divine – a creature created in time by God for the creation of the world – but inferior to the Father. The former were the Adoptionists and the latter was taught by Arius. Especially against the Arian view, the Council of Nicaea (325) proclaimed the oneness in being or consubstantiality of the Son with the Father. The Son was of the same substance (*homoousios*), not only of similar substance (*homoiousios*), with the Father. He is, as Christians recite in the Nicene Creed, "God from God, Light from Light, true God from true God, begotten, not made, one in being with the Father. . . For us and for our salvation, He came down and became flesh, was made man, suffered, and rose again in the third day."

Another Christological controversy centered on the unity of the divine and the human in Christ. The Antiochene school, with Nestorius as its most extreme example, regarded the unity of the divine and human in Christ loosely to defend his full humanity: There were two natures in Christ, human and divine; Mary was the mother of Christ, *Christotokos*, but not the mother of God, *Theotokos*. The Alexandrian school, with Monophysitism as its extreme expression, exaggerated the unity of the divine and human in Christ to defend his divinity: There was one divine nature in Christ. The Council of Ephesus (431) confessed that "a union of two natures has taken place; hence we confess one Christ, one Son, one Lord. In accordance with this union without confusion, we profess the holy virgin to be Mother of God, for God the Word became flesh and was made human and from the moment of conception united to himself the temple he had taken from her." Thus, Nestorian diophysitism and monophysitism were both condemned.

The Council of Chalcedon (451) offered a synthesis of these Christological controversies with this definition:

> Following, therefore, the holy fathers, we confess one and the same Son, who is our Lord Jesus Christ, and we all agree in teaching that this very same Son is complete in his deity and complete – the very same – in his humanity, truly God and truly a human being, the very same one being composed of a rational soul and a body, coessential with the Father as to his deity and coessential – the very same one – as to his humanity, being like us in every respect apart from sin. As to his deity, he was born of all ages from the Father before all ages, but as to his humanity, the very same one was born in the last days from the Virgin Mary, the Mother of God, for our sake and the sake of our salvation: one and the same Christ, Son, Lord, Only Begotten, acknowledged to be unconfusedly, unalterably, undividedly, inseparably in two natures, since the difference of the natures is not destroyed because of the union, but on the contrary, the character of each nature is preserved and comes together in one person and one hypostasis, not divided or torn into two persons but one and the same Son and only begotten God, Logos, Lord Jesus Christ – just as in the earlier times the prophets and also the Lord Jesus Christ himself taught us about him, and the symbol of our Fathers transmitted to us.

There is a sense that Chalcedon synthesized and settled the great Christological struggles and controversies of the first five centuries of Christianity. To the extent that Christological dogma was touched upon in subsequent councils of the Church, it was simply a matter of reiterating the teachings of the earlier councils, in particular of Nicaea, Ephesus, and Chalcedon. Docetists, Gnostics, Adoptionists, Arians, Subordinationists, Nestorians, Monophysites have all been condemned.

These Christological controversies were not only intellectual debates between theologians and theological schools. They involved emperors and empresses and their courts, as well as, the masses who often took their fight to the streets. Theological differences became political conflicts in which hate, murder, violence, ethnic cleansing, and even warfare figured. The violent debates divided the empire, making religious life fraught with contradiction and conflict. These religious conflicts illuminate the nature and destructiveness of those dark places in human history in which religious convictions turn hateful and vicious, bloody and violent. Philip Jenkins (2010) called them *Jesus Wars: How Four Patriarchs, Three Queens, and Two Emperors Decided What Christians Would Believe for the Next 1,500 Years.*

Richard Rubenstein (1999: 224-25) writes of the end of these Christological controversies:

> One year after he banned Arianism, Theodosius officially declared [in 382] Christianity the religion of the Roman Empire, thus bringing the movement begun by Constantine the Great full circle. The formerly persecuted sect became a state church with the power (and, according to some, the duty) to suppress or control its rivals. A religious community once harboring diverse strains of belief became an orthodoxy committed to doctrinal unity and the extinction of heresy. And the loose, decentralized organization of the earlier Church gave way to a more hierarchical structure, with power concentrating in the hands of a few great bishops. With the elevation of Jesus to God, orthodox Christianity broke the intellectual links that bound it to both Judaism and Greco-Roman paganism. Increasingly autonomous both as a faith and as an organization, the Roman Church was now positioned to survive even the collapse of the Roman Empire. [Which it did, effectively becoming its successor, the restoration of Rome (Heather 2013).]

Recently, it has been pointed out by Diarmaid MacCulloch (2009: 227-28) that "the label 'Monophysite' has widely been replaced by 'Miaphysite'. That derives from a phrase for 'one nature' (*mia physis*) which Bishop Cyril [of Alexandria] habitually and undeniably used, in writings which retained a wide esteem in both Greek East and Latin West. . . . [T]o use the 'Miaphysite' label is to point to the fact that Cyril was not crudely talking about 'one nature' in Christ; he would have said that Christ's nature might be single, but it was also composite."

It is also to point out that Chalcedon did not settle everything. Miaphysite Christianity had extraordinary histories of mission, endurance, and suffering in Asia and Africa. Western Christians know very little about these centuries of struggle, scholarship, sanctity, and heroism. Jenkins (2008) also wrote of *The Lost History of Christianity: The Thousand-Year Golden Age of the Church in the Middle East, Africa, and Asia – and How It Died.*

"Western Christians," MacCulloch (2009: 284) adds, "have forgotten that before the coming of Islam utterly transformed the situation in the Eastern Mediterranean and Asia, there was a good chance that the centre of gravity of Christian faith might have moved east to Iraq rather then West to Rome."

In 1951, on the occasion of the fifteen hundredth anniversary of the Council of Chalcedon, Karl Rahner wrote an article, originally titled "Chalcedon: End or Beginning?" but which now appears as "Current Problems in Christology" in the first volume of his *Theological Investigations.* As Elizabeth Johnson (1990: 11-12) puts it, "surveying the Catholic scene, Rahner judged that Christology was in a sorry and stagnant state. . . . Christology was just repeating the old neo-scholastic understanding about two natures in one person without genuine contemporary understanding. . . . [C]hristology by and large ignored the genuine humanity of Jesus Christ, a matter of scriptural and dogmatic truth." The lure of Docetism was stronger than the temptation of Arianism. In other words, Christian teaching and preaching were all about a divine Christ. In the main and for the majority of ordinary Christians, this remains to be true (Litonjua 2011).

Insights from Evolution

The truths of the Christian faith must be understandable to be credible. In trying to make them understandable and not contrary to reason, theologians turn to scientific knowledge and utilize its concepts and explanations. To give but one example, Thomas Aquinas, in order to explain and make credible the real presence of Christ in the Eucharist, utilized the Aristotelian theory of substance and accidents, and came up with the theory of transubstantiation. Today, that explanation is encountering difficulty because we no longer talk in terms of substance and accidents, but we think and speak of molecules, cells, atoms, genes, etc. One of the tasks of theologians, therefore, is to reformulate the traditional formulations of the faith taking into account the current state of scientific knowledge and rendering them into explanations that are more understandable and credible to contemporary men and women. Pope John XXIII in his opening address at Vatican II pointed out that "the Christian, Catholic, and apostolic spirit of the entire world expects a step forward toward a doctrinal penetration and a formation of consciousness in faithful and perfect conformity to the authentic doctrine, which, however, should be studied and expounded through the methods of research and through the literary forms of modern thought. The substance of the ancient doctrine of the deposit of faith is one thing, and the way in which it is presented is another" (Abbott 1966: 215).

In addition to this instrumental use of modern scientific research and thought in reformulating the doctrines of the faith, a greater and a more important task is engaging modern science, asking how it can clarify truths of the faith, what insights it can give for their deeper understanding, what implications for the life of faith does it offer, what conclusions can be derived to make the truths and the life of faith more meaningful in the lives and relationships of contemporary men and women. To achieve these worthy ends, it will be necessary for theology and theologians, not necessarily individually but corporately, to have a working knowledge of the scientific enterprise, to know and absorb the most important scientific findings, to be able to be conversant with scientists, and above all to respect the integrity and autonomy of science itself.

But for theology to be able to do so, it must have the appropriate attitude toward nature and the world which are the subject of empirical science. David Tracy (1981: 408) has posited that a major aspect of theology's task is "to develop a language that is both faithful to the tensive character of the religious language employed for the originating religious event and faithful to the demands of critical reflection . . . Two major conceptual languages have served as the principal candidates for this task of theology: analogical and dialectical languages." The analogical imagination sees a basic continuity between God and the world so that, in the words of Gerard Manley Hopkins, "the world is charged with the grandeur of God." Starting with the foundational sacramentality of Jesus Christ, the church, the entire creation, and the ordinary can be, and are, sacramental. They reveal and disclose God's power, grace, and love. The dialectical imagination perceives a basic discontinuity between God and the world. There is a basic rupture between God's revelation of salvation and the human condition. Over against the "sacrament" in the analogical imagination, the "word" in the dialectical imagination calls for judgment against idolatry, power, and pride.

Bernard Lonergan (1972: 315) distinguished between theological knowledge that is classicist and static, and theological understanding that is historically conscious. For the former, reality is static, necessary, fixed, and universal. A religious truth couched in a doctrinal propositional form captures objective reality and is forever true and cannot be changed. For the latter, reality is dynamic, evolving, changing, and particular. It recognizes the historicity of human thought and action so that the articulations of one sociohistorical era are not necessarily those of another. "The world, both the world free of every human intervention and the human world fashioned by socially constructed meanings and values, is in a permanent state of change and evolution" (Lawler, Salzman, and Burke-Sullivan 2014: 113). It is essentially for this reason that anyone wishing to make a value judgment in the present cannot simply do it on the basis of its givenness in the past, argues a historically conscious theology against a classicist theology.

In the debate on *Gaudium et Spes,* Vatican II's Pastoral Constitution on the Church in the Modern World, Joseph Komochak (1994: 87) identified two differing theological orientations among the members of the progressive majority: Augustinian and Thomist.

> The typically Augustinian approach works with a sharp and unmediated distinction between sin and grace, natural reason and faith. The natural world appears to have no solidity or substance except as a sign pointing beyond itself to the spiritual and supernatural. The dramatic contest between sin and grace monopolizes attention, distracting it away from the natural, or rather subsuming it under religious categories so that, on the one hand, we are "*natura filii irae*" and, on the other, our "true" nature is only recognized in the supernatural. [It was this selfsame Augustinian theological bent that made Joseph Ratzinger, as Cardinal-Prefect of the Congregation for the Doctrine of the Faith, condemn Latin American liberation theology and German political theology. But his theological vision imploded when the City of Man, in the form of the secular press and the legal profession, laid bare the pedophilia scandal in the City of God on earth, the institutional Catholic Church.]

> The typically Thomist approach, in contrast, effects a theoretical differentiation of the natural, not in order to deny that the drama of sin and grace is the only real drama of human history but in order to promote a more accurate understanding of it. "Nature," if you will, theoretically mediates the practical drama. It has its own solidity or substance, its own laws, its created autonomy. Sin is what falls short of or contradicts nature, and grace is what heals and transcendently fulfills nature. This permits

one at once to differentiate the genuine limitations of nature without having to label them as sinful and to affirm the power of grace as the fulfillment and not the destruction of nature. This is why St. Thomas could embrace the new world opened to Christian culture by Aristotle's philosophy and by Arabian science without believing, as many Augustinians did at the time, that this was a profanation of the sacred because it implied that an understanding of nature was possible in other than religious terms.

A theological orientation that is analogical, historically conscious, and Thomist, which respects the integrity and autonomy of nature and the world, is better able to engage the insights of evolutionary science (Litonjua 2015a). Robert Bellah has pointed out that "the meta-narrative that is really the only one intelligible to all well-educated people everywhere in the world is the meta-narrative of evolution, which is in turn embedded in a narrative of cosmological development since 13.7 billion years ago in the Big Bang" (Horn 2011). Evolution – cosmic, biological, and human – has become today's main scientific paradigm. Evolutionary science has impacted the natural sciences of physics, chemistry, and biology, the behavioral sciences of psychology, sociology, and cultural anthropology, as well as, the practical sciences of agriculture, medicine, and aging. Evolutionary science has done the most to upend popular understandings of the cosmos, of nature, of human origins and behavior which turned out to be misconceptions. "Darwin's spectre," Michael Rose (1998) writes, hovers over the modern world.

Holmes Ralston (2010: xi) has proposed that there had been three Big Bangs. Big Bang is the figurative term given to the explosive event of energy that started the universe. The first Big Bang is the primordial explosion some 13.7 billion years ago that generated an expanding magnitude of matter-energy and initiated a process that produced stars, galaxies, and everything else in the cosmos, and that continues up to today. The second Big Bang, some 10 billion years ago, generated life and began an evolutionary process that now covers the earth with complex creatures interacting in life-sustaining eco-systems. The third Big Bang, more than three billion years ago, marked the emergence of human beings, mammals with minds and wills who think symbolically and act with deliberate, free intent. Humans belong on a spectrum with others in a community of life. Having themselves continued to evolve, humans have populated the globe with a restless inventiveness that creates, accumulates, and transmits ideas and technologies across generations so that evolution now proceeds by way of culture as well as biology.

Robert Bellah (2011; Litonjua 2015b) locates the emergence of religion in cultural evolution which became conterminous with biological evolution. As hominids evolved into humans, they developed consciousness, intelligence, and self-awareness, engaged in play, dance, and ritual, acquired the capacity to symbolize and the ability for language. Symbolic capacity contributes to the evolution of religion by the development of piety, awe, equanimity, self-transcendence, and spiritual renewal. Language, symbols, and the cultural developments derived from them contribute to religious ability to find meaning in existence. Interacting with other humans, they formed groups to solve their common problems in their specific environments. In the process, they created social institutions and cultural systems. Together with marriage and the family, education, the economy, and political system, humans constructed religion, a system of symbols that relates them to the grounds of their ultimate existence and that bestows meaning on the world and renders therefore life meaningful, especially at "three points," in the famous formulation of Clifford Geertz (1973: 100), "where chaos – a tumult of events which lack not just interpretations but *interpretability* – threatens to break in upon man: at the limits of his analytic capacities, at the limits of his powers of endurance, and at the limits of his moral insights."

There are two core elements of modern evolutionary theory which theology has to contend with: the emergence of new life forms and the continuity of the evolutionary process. "While the former bears relevance for our understanding of how life and anthropologically important phenomena such as 'mind' and 'consciousness' came to be, the latter plays a crucial role in how we view our existence within the earth's fluid and changing biosphere" (Putz 2002: 85). Prospectively, the former also raises the question of how human life will likely become or will further evolve into, and the latter opens the possible future and final destiny of nature and the world which continue to evolve.

As species evolved, they achieved higher and higher levels of complexity, a process which science calls "emergence." The concept of emergence connotes that something is coming out of hiding, coming into view and appears, coming to exist and be. Evolutionary scientists use it to describe the spontaneous appearance of new biological forms as a result of nature's various elements interacting with each other. As interactions multiply over long periods of time, new forms appear and they are more and more complex. These new forms are not something that are added externally, but grow within and out of the same fundamental matter although having different properties and functions. Organized with more complexity, the new forms develop new powers and enter into more diverse networks of relations. As a result, new levels of reality appear over time that require new concepts and language to describe them accurately.

Elizabeth Johnson (2014: 175-75; see also Rahner 1978: 178-202; Putz 2002: 85-105) points out that Karl Rahner confronted this phenomenon with his theologically relevant idea of the self-transcendence of matter:

> Pondering this reality, Karl Rahner proposes that we embrace a fundamental idea: matter has the capacity to transcend itself. Matter can do this because it has been endowed by its Creator with an inner tendency, a quiet, powerfully pulsing drive, to become something more. The foil against which Rahner places this dynamic assessment of matter is the philosophical dualism which radically separates matter and spirit, considering matter passive and devoid of movement. . . . A human person is a dynamic unity of matter and spirit, an embodied spirit in the world. . . . [A]s physical beings, persons are able to go beyond themselves toward infinite mystery in every intellectual question, every act of love. . . . "Matter develops out of its own inner being in the direction of spirit" (Rahner).

Analogously, the social sciences, specifically sociology, study how people construct socially emergent phenomena. To start with a simple example: Ten boys want to play basketball. To be able to do so, the boys divide themselves into two teams; each team assigns who will play center, forwards, and guards. There are rules to follow, and there are sanctions for the violation of those rules. What they have done is construct the social structure of basketball: a goal, a division of labor, a hierarchy of authority, specific roles, rules, and sanctions. After their game, the social structure vanishes. Some social structures have lasted a long time and are called social institutions, long-lasting solutions to group problems. Five of them are basic institutions, found in all societies, because they are social arrangements that enable people to live and work together as groups. These are marriage and the family, education, the economy, political system, and religion. But they assume different forms depending on the culture of the group involved.

These social structures are emergent phenomena; they arise, they emerge, they are constructed by people as they interact with each other in solving their problems. They are constructed by the processes of externalization and objectivation, and become internalized through socialization (Berger and Luckmann 1967). Famously, they were called by Emile Durkheim, a founding father of sociology, "social facts." Social facts are not physical facts, but they should be treated as physical facts. Similar to physical facts, they facilitate behavior and enable people, but they also constrain and coerce. They confront us as facticities, social forces often beyond the control of the individual. When considerations of class, race, gender, disability, sexual orientation, and, most importantly, power are built into them, they can become discriminatory, oppressive, and lethal to the poor and the powerless. Thus, social structures can become structures of injustice and violence. They then constitute social sin (Litonjua 2007: 19-33). The emergent phenomena of social structures can throw analogous light on the concept of "emergence" that science uses in explaining the development of complex new forms in evolution, or the concept of "self-transcendence" that Karl Rahner utilizes in explicating the direction toward spirit of matter from it own inner being.

The second core idea of evolutionary science is the continuity of the evolutionary process. Put most simply, evolution is the story of change over time, minute and enormous changes over long stretches of time. It is the story of the robust and variegated tree of life, branching out in all directions but being pruned time and time again. It is the story of who lives and dies, therefore, who is found adaptable to its environment, who has the opportunity to pass on traits to the next generation, and to the next, and to the next. It is the story of a simple mechanism, natural selection, discovered by Charles Darwin and made more complete by the genetic theory of heredity of the Austrian Augustinian monk Gregor Johann Mendel to form the modern neo-Darwinian synthesis. It is the story that has altered our view of nature and the world around us, as well as, how we view ourselves. It is the story of the cosmos, of all life on earth, and of human life, and how we are inextricably bound to one another.

Evolution does not create from nothing, nor does it evolve into the most perfect forms. Evolution develops from pre-existing forms, selects their most adaptive traits, mutates them, and passes them on from generation to generation, becoming more and more complex along the long evolutionary path until they emerge into new life forms. And the process continues. The continuity of the evolutionary process is evidenced from the fact that "all organisms carry useless remnants of formerly functional structures that make no sense except as holdovers from different ancestral states – the tiny vestiges of leg bones, invisibly embedded in the skin of certain whales, or the nonfunctional nubs of pelvic bones in some snakes, surviving as vestiges of ancestors with legs" (Gould 2001: xi).

This is equally true of the human species. Most recently we have evolved from chimpanzees, our closest living relatives, to hominids, to humans. But our upright position is a recent evolutionary development. Evolution has taken a spinal column well adapted for horizontal, four-footed locomotion and pressed it into vertical bipedal service. It works well, but overtime stresses and strains bear on the human backbone to make bad backs symptomatic of hard work and old age. Our appendix seems only to make us sick; our feet are poorly constructed to bear the brunt of walking and running; our eyes are prone to optical errors and lose their ability for close focus as we age. Plague, pestilence, and parasite, as well as, typhoons, hurricanes, and tornadoes are all indications of the imperfections of the evolutionary process. Evolution is a continuing process but there are limitations inherent in an evolutionary universe.

Theologically, Karl Rahner sees creation as the expression of God. Creation is not simply the making of an external object, and the world is not only a product that was made. Creation is God's self-communication. Created reality therefore, including the spirited body or embodied spirit that is the human person, is endowed with an inner dynamism in an ongoing process of active self-transcendence. In the Incarnation God became *flesh*, became matter. "[C]reation and Incarnation [are] not two disparate and juxtaposed acts of God 'outwards' which have their origins in two separate initiatives of God. Rather in the world as it actually is we can understand creation and Incarnation as two moments and two phases of the *one* process of God's self giving and self-expression, although it is an intrinsically differentiated process" (Rahner 1978: 197). "Jesus, then," Rahner (1978: 280) adds, "is the historical presence of th[e] final and unsurpassable word of God's self-disclosure: this is his claim and he is vindicated in this claim by the resurrection. He is of eternal validity and he is experienced in this validity. In this sense in any case he is the 'absolute savior.'" The risen Christ is the ultimate promise of the final fulfillment of God's self-communication to his creation.

Oliver Putz (2002: 94) clarifies that "Rahner is not interested in a scientific analysis of evolution as such; his is solely a theological attempt to actualize Catholic theology in the light of the questions presented by modern evolutionary theory." In particular, Rahner theologically addresses evolution's concept of "emergence" of new life forms in the continuity of the evolutionary process with the concept of active self-transcendence in the continuation of cosmic, biological, and human evolution. For Rahner, it is in the risen Jesus that the irreversible self- communication of God to his entire creation on the one hand and the free and definitive response and acceptance on the part of humanity are unified.

Faith in the resurrection is not only about a past event, but about the Risen Christ ever bringing about something new for humanity and the world. It is hope in the gratuity, universal scope, and effectiveness of his saving grace where all creation and all fruits of human efforts will find their place in "a new heaven and the new earth." Thus, the fact of the bodily resurrection of Jesus from death has implications for how we might imagine our Christian life today and tomorrow, and how we might conceive of our final destiny. The truth that God raised Jesus from the dead and exalted him also has consequences for how we should relate to creation and how we can imagine creation's crowning glory. This is in keeping with what Paul says in Romans 8:19-23: "Creation awaits with eager longing for the revelation of the children of God . . . Creation itself will be set free from bondage to decay and share in the glorious freedom of the children of God . . . All creation is groaning in labor pains until now, and not only creation, but we ourselves, who have the first fruits of the Spirit, we also groan within ourselves as we wait for adoption, the redemption of our bodies."

The theological and spiritual task of imagination and hope in explicating the implications of the bodily resurrection of Jesus in the light of cosmic, biological, and human evolution is twofold: its implications for the human person, composed of body, mind and spirit, and its consequences on the whole of creation in its eschatological fulfillment.

We, human beings as spirited bodies and embodied spirits, continue to evolve. "We human beings are involved in our own evolution," Robert Bellah (2012: 448) writes, referencing Jurgen Habermas (1975), "and cannot escape making judgments that are evaluative as well as cognitive." Evolution today, as far as human beings are concerned, is coeval with cultural evolution. In fact, it is generally the received wisdom that human biological evolution stopped when humans appeared, marking the advent of cultural evolution. Culture then freed humans from the pressures of natural selection. This argument that behavioral modernity somehow froze human evolution is dependent on the notion of a static environment, which is obviously not the case. Culture itself has increasingly become an important part of the human environment.

Accordingly, Gregory Cochran and Henry Harpending (2009: 1) "intend to make the case that human evolution has accelerated in the past 10,000 years, rather than slowing or stopping, and is now happening about 100 times faster than its long-term average over the 6 million years of our existence. The pace has been so rapid that humans have changed significantly in body and mind over recorded history." They point out: "Our approach leans heavily on genetics – and with genetic information accumulating at an incredible rate, due to the ongoing revolution in molecular biology, it is an approach that we believe has been very fruitful. ... Genetic history addresses changes in underlying hardware, changes in body and brain, which also matter" (Cochran and Harpending 2009: ix-x). They further argue that the evolution of new complex adaptations takes long, "but it underestimates the importance of simple adaptations, those that involve changes in one or a few genes. ... [D]ramatic consequences of small genetic changes are possible because DNA is a bit like a recipe or a computer program: A change in a single letter can sometimes have a huge effect. .. This is a new picture of recent human evolution. It implies that humans have changed not just culturally, but genetically, over the course of recorded history, and that we must allow for such changes when we try to understand historical events. The implications of this contention are vast: If correct, it means that peoples in different parts of the world have changed in varying ways, since they adopted different forms of agriculture at different times – or in some cases not at all" (Cochran and Harpending 2009: 10, 17, 66-67).

So human biological evolution continues, together with cultural evolution. Cultural change is important and has been dramatic. New ideas, new techniques, new forms of social organization have been powerful influences on the historical process, and we all look forward, and maybe even contribute, to further cultural evolution, including ethical, moral, religious, and spiritual evolution. But there is no reason to demand that biological human evolution no longer happens, that we humans have reached the apex of evolution. There is an element of arrogance in such a contention. "If researchers in the human sciences continue to ignore the fact of ongoing natural selection," Cochran and Harpending (2009: 227) assert, "they will have thrown away the key to many important problems, turning puzzles into mysteries. ... In doing so, they're ignoring tremendous opportunities: not just in decoding the past, but in shaping the future as well."

Theologically, I believe we can also say that the resurrection points to the continuing unfolding of the unlimited potential of all created matter, most especially of the embodied spirit that is the human person. The risen Christ beckons to the future of evolution brought to self-reflective awareness, a conscious evolution. This is, of course, the basic idea of Teilhard de Chardin who expressed the conviction that we are the crest of an ongoing evolution of the universe, co-creators of an unfinished evolutionary process toward more being. It is an overall process of life toward convergence, complexity, and consciousness. John Haught (2010: 138) vividly depicts Teilhard's vision of the future:

Teilhard thinks about the God of evolution not as "up above" so much as "up ahead." God comes into the world from out of the future. Only by shifting to a futurist, hope-filled perspective can Christian thought connect the promises of God to Darwin's new picture of life. The universe, as evolution implies, is still coming into being. It is a work in progress, and for now it remains unfinished. It continues to be drawn toward an unpredictable and open future by the attractive power of God who creates the world by offering it new possibilities for becoming *more* – opportunities for more intense and valuable modes of being. . . .

The God of evolution continually creates a new world not *a retro*, by pushing things forward from the past, but *ab ante*, by drawing the world toward a new future from up ahead. The future is the primary dwelling place of God. Even though God is also present now and in the past, God is most powerfully effective *now* by opening the totality of things to an endlessly resourceful future. God is intimately involved in each present moment precisely by opening this moment to a new future. The world rests on this future, Teilhard says, as its "sole support." Whatever stability the universe has, in other words, lies not in the dispersed elements of its material past, but in the fidelity of the force that draws it toward the future. "The grandeur of the river is revealed not at its source but at its estuary."

Michael Crosby (2014) situates evolutionary consciousness within the context of the crisis of Western Catholicism which "is not so much a crisis of relativism as much as the inadequacy of an organizational model of church that too often reflects a culturally received, historical patriarchal model still based on a 'flat earth' cosmology." He continues:

[T]he Word's enfleshment in creation, the Incarnation and the Resurrection must now find its continued embodiment in all the members of the Body of Christ. This demands that we continually evolve into ever deeper consciousness of our need to incarnate a new cosmic order (2 Corinthians 5:17). Consciousness of this reality invites us to evolve in our relationships and institutions from the "old order" of sexism, ethnocentrism or classism (Galatians 3:27) to ever greater forms of equality reflecting the Trinity.

Matter continues to evolve in complexity and consciousness. Creation continues to groan for redemption and rebirth. The resurrection prefigures our bodily and human transformation. The risen Christ will also eschatologically redeem and transform God's creation. Eschatology refers to the last things, usually understood as death, judgment, heaven, and hell. The popular image is that of an analogous spiritual Big Bang, in which the world will come to an end, all will be raised in a general resurrection, Jesus will descend in his second coming as Judge, and judgment will result in the just being welcomed to heaven and in the condemned being relegated to the fires of hell.

This popularized description of eschatology, of life after death, of salvation and resurrection, of heaven and eternity contradicts modern biblical scholarship, does not lead to responsibility toward society, the world, and the planet, and does not even comport well with the best findings of evolutionary science. Salvation is not saving souls for a disembodied eternity, but transforming persons for participation in the new heaven and the new earth of the promised resurrection. The world is not evil, but the entire creation will undergo renewal, redemption, and rebirth. "The search for a timeless eternity outside of nature," John Haught (2003: 52) points out, "has made the physical universe seem to be only a staging area for the human religious passage."

But Bishop N.T. Wright (2008: 211-12) is emphatic:

> To put it bluntly, creation is to be redeemed; that is, space is to be redeemed, time is to be redeemed, and matter is to be redeemed. God said "very good" over his space-time-matter creation, and through the redeeming of this world from its present corruption and decay will mean transformations we cannot imagine, the one thing we can be sure of is that this redeeming of creation will not mean that God will say, of space, time, and matter, "Oh, well, nice try, good while it lasted but obviously gone bad, so let's drop it and go for a nonspatiotemporal, nonmaterial world instead." But if God really does intend to *redeem* rather than reject his created world of space, time, and matter, we are faced with the question: what might it look like to celebrate that redemption, that healing and

transformation, in the present, and thereby appropriately to anticipate God's final intention?

Since the promise and the hope for the future is not only for individuals, but for the world and the entire creation, "one should neither need nor want a ticket out of the created order into an eternal realm," Jon Meacham (2012) concludes in a recent Easter issue of *Time*. "One instead should be hard at work making the world godly and just."

> To hope for a better future in this world – for the poor, the sick, the lonely and depressed, for the slaves, refugees, the hungry and homeless, for the abused, the paranoid, the downtrodden and despairing, and in fact for the whole wide, wonderful, and wounded world – is not something *else*, something extra, something tacked on to the gospel as an afterthought. And to work for that intermediate hope, the surprising hope that comes forward from God's ultimate future into God's urgent present, is not a *distraction from* the task of mission and evangelism in the present. It is a central, essential, vital, and life-giving part of it (Wright 2008: 191-92).

The eschatological future diffuses new being from Jesus' risen bodiliness to the whole transfigured cosmos. It entails a unity between Creator and cosmos that does not obscure divine transcendence but implies immanence. It does not collapse physical cosmos into divinity. God will be all in all, but Jesus' risen bodiliness remains God's body in a decisive, unique, and causal way through the hypostatic union of human and divine in Christ. I cannot think or imagine a deeper theological, spiritual, and mystical reading of and reflection on the universe in the light of the bodily resurrection of Jesus, by utilizing what evolutionary science tells us about what started with the big bang, began evolving from inorganic to organic matter, from single cell to multi-cellular organisms, from vegetative to animal life, and continued to evolve from mammals to primates to hominids to humans – made in the image and likeness of God – and will evolve until its reaches its transformation, fulfillment, and consummation in resurrected glory.

3

OUR SISTER, MOTHER EARTH, OUR COMMON HOME: COLOGY, RELIGION, AND POPE FRANCIS

The most famous or notorious – depending on one's predilection – article on the ecological crisis was Lynn White, Jr.'s (1967) "The Historical Roots of Our Ecological Crisis," published in the journal *Science*. In it, it has repeated been mentioned, White declared that "Christianity is the most anthropocentric religion the world has seen," and pointed out that "by destroying pagan animism, Christianity made it possible to exploit nature in a mood of indifference to the feelings of natural objects." In this connection, although White did not specifically made reference to it, Yahweh's "command" to the man he created in his image, male and female he created them, is usually trotted out: "Be fertile and multiply; fill the earth and subdue it. Have dominion over the fish of the sea, the birds of the air, and all the living things that move on the earth" (Gen. 1:28). But White did write that "Christianity bears a huge burden of guilt."

But what is usually not mentioned is the conviction that White expressed at the end of his article (see also Erickson 2015):

> More science and technology are not going to get us out of the present ecological crisis until we find a new religion, or rethink our old one. . . . Possibly we should ponder the greatest radical in Christian history since Christ: Saint

> Francis of Assisi.... The key to an understanding of Francis is his belief in the virtue of humility – not merely for the individual but for man as a species. Francis tried to depose man from his monarchy over creation and set up a democracy of all God's creatures. With him the ant is no longer simply a homily for the lazy, flames a sign of the thrust of the soul toward union with God; now they are Brother Ant and Sister Fire, praising the Creator in their own ways as Brother Man does in his.... His view of nature and of man rested on a unique sort of panpsychism of all things animate and inanimate, designed for the glorification of their transcendent Creator, who, in the ultimate gesture of cosmic humility, assumed flesh, lay helpless in a manger, and hung dying on a scaffold.

Now, another Francis is on the world stage. The first pope who is a Jesuit, the first who hails from a Third World country, Argentina, and the first to take on the name of Francis, has become, in so short a time, the most open, expansive, and inclusive Bishop of Rome, a designation he prefers to the exalted and preeminent title of Supreme Pontiff of the Catholic Church, since Good Pope John XXIII, the convener of the Second Vatican Council. After the imperial rule of John Paul II and the dour pessimism of Benedict XVI, with Pope Francis have come fresh winds of pastoral change, high hopes and fervent aspirations of a more lively and joyful faith, and expectations of a more fruitful engagement with society and the world, and of great acceptance from people of all walks of life. He has issued an encyclical, "On Care for Our Common Home," whose Italian title, *Laudato Si'*, is taken from St. Francis of Assisi's *Canticle of the Creatures:* "Praise be to you, my Lord, through our Sister, Mother Earth, who sustains and governs us, and who produces various fruit with colored flowers and herbs."

Science, Technology, and Industrialization

It is estimated that modern humans – *homo sapiens sapiens* – emerged fairly recently from the evolutionary process that started with the Big Bang some 13.5 billion years ago. "Only about 50,000 years ago did they sweep out of Africa, and in a matter of a few thousand years they replaced all other species of humans across the Old World. These new Africans did not just look like us; now they acted like us. They invented tools far more sophisticated than those of their ancestors – hafted spears and spear-throwers, needles for making clothes, awls and nets – which they made from new materials like ivory, shells, and bones. They built themselves houses and adorned themselves with jewelry and carved sculptures and painted caves and cliff walls" (Zimmer 2001: 295). An overview of the evolution of human societies is instructive.

The earliest type of societies that humans constructed were hunting and gathering societies. They mark "a critical juncture in our evolution as a species. For, at this point, *cultural evolution replaced biological evolution as the primary means of adaptation and change in human societies*" (Nolan and Lenski 2004: 81). They were relatively small in size, their size being constrained by the scarcity of their resources. They were nomadic, moving for place to place, in search of the resources for maintaining subsistence and survival, which took the form of hunting animals and gathering plant foods. They are the most egalitarian of societies, especially between sexes, equality being determined by the contribution to economic subsistence. The men go hunting for animals and they do not always come home after the hunt with prey, but women, more often than not, come home with their baskets filled with fruits, berries, and other foraged foods. They had a division of labor, with men charged with hunting while women were assigned the gathering of plant foods. For most of human history or until around 8000 BCE, humans lived in hunting and gathering societies.

The shift to horticultural societies was due to three things: environmental change, population growth, and increases in cultural change and technology. The emergence of horticultural societies is considered today to constitute the first great social revolution in human history. The practice of horticulture is referred to as swidden or slash-and-burn cultivation, which meant clearing new gardens by cutting and burning existing vegetation to be able to plant new crops and trees, made possible by the invention of the hoe or digging stick. Horticulturalists also domesticated small animals. The dog has the distinction of being the first animal to be so domesticated. With the cultivation of plants and trees, and the discovery that manure could be used as fertilizer, horticultural societies enjoyed a stable source of surplus, a growth in population, permanent settlements, as well as, increase in societal complexity and social differentiation. Horticultural societies appeared some ten thousand years ago or around 8000 BCE.

Agrarian societies, the second great social revolution in human history, emerged during the period which was the most fertile in fruitful discoveries and inventions in human history prior to the sixteenth century. The innovations included the wheel and it application to wagons, the plow and its harnessing to animals to till the land, pottery, wind power for sailboats, writing and numerical notation, and the calendar. Collectively, they transformed the conditions of life in society. The plow had the greatest potential for social and cultural change, and led to the replacement of horticulture (*horti cultura*, the cultivation of a garden) by agriculture (*agri cultura*, the cultivation of a field). The plow and the harnessing of the energy of domesticated large animals led to greatly increased productivity. Urban communities increased in size and complexity and became recognizable as "cities." Empire-building occurred on a greatly expanded scale, with Egypt unified as an entire country under a single ruler for the first time in history. This is the period historians refer to as "the dawn of civilization."

In the early agrarian societies, religion was a powerful ideological force that united the society, motivated its people, and directed their efforts towards a goal. Eqypt was such a theocracy. Thus, Nolan and Lenski (2004: 145) lay down the principle: *"Technological advance created the possibility of a surplus, but to transform that possibility into a reality required an ideology that motivated farmers to produce more than they needed to stay alive and productive, and persuaded them to turn that surplus over to someone else."* The agrarian surplus also made possible the appearance of fulltime service workers, who did not need to till the soil, but could offer their services for pay. They would grow into bureaucracies in religion, government, and military. Codes of law were formalized, the most famous of which is the Code of Hammurabi, and monetary systems established that facilitated the movement, the exchange, and ultimately the production of goods and services. The increasing size and complexity of agrarian societies also meant increasing inequality. Three cleavages were especially serious: between a small governing class and the large mass of people who had no voice in political decision but who produced for the governing class; between the urban minority and the far more numerous rural population; and between a small literate minority and the illiterate masses. Agrarian societies appeared some five thousand years ago or around 3000 BCE.

The discovery that iron could be carburized and could be turned to steel marks the transition to agriculturally advanced societies. Other innovations included the catapult, the crossbow, gunpowder, horseshoes, stirrups, the clock, printing, all of which made for economic, political, and military power, with mid-nineteenth China being the largest advanced agrarian society. Cities became larger but were notoriously unhealthy, especially for the common people. Thus, one characteristic of advanced agrarian societies was the disasters that occasionally overtook them and caused sharp increases in the death rate, the most devastating of which was the Black Plague. Government was the basic integrating force, run for the benefit of a tiny elite. The proprietary theory of the state defines the state as a piece of property that its owners may use for their personal advantage.

This they did by owning a grossly disproportionate share of the land and appropriating not less than half of the total national income, even though they were only two percent of the population. Peasants, free and enslaved, bore the entire brunt of producing for the entire society. They were listed as part of the livestock and slaves, like livestock, were to be disposed of when no longer productive.

In the religious sphere the most important development was the emergence and spread of three new religions, Buddhism, Christianity, and Islam, each of which proclaimed a universal faith and succeeded in creating a community of believers that transcended societal boundaries. The advanced agrarian world, seen from its underside, was often unattractive, but one attractive accomplishment of advanced agrarian societies was in the arts. In sculpture, painting, and architecture, these societies left monuments of lasting beauty. Cathedrals, churches, mosques, pagodas, temples, palaces testify to an impressive development of the arts. Achievements in literature may appear less impressive because of our inability to appreciate them in their native languages and contexts. Toward the end of the era, the invention of new musical instruments and the genius of composers like Bach, Handel, Mozart, and Beethoven combined to produce an outpouring of magnificent music that since then has transcended musical tastes in space and time.

Industrial societies, the third great social revolution in human history, arrived some two hundred years ago or around 1800 CE. Industrialization refers to the use of nonhuman and nonanimal resources of energy, such as steam and mechanical power, and later electricity and oil, more than the utilization of human and animal sources of energy in the previous types of societies. England was the first truly industrial society, the first society to derive more than half of its income from productive activities involving machines powered by inanimate sources of energy. Nolan and Lenski (2004: 195-200) mention three main causes of industrialization: the accumulation of technological information throughout the agrarian era, such as discoveries and inventions in agriculture and mining, metallurgy and transportation, engineering and construction, most especially improvements in ships and navigation, exemplified by the compass; the conquest of the New World that brought in vast quantities of gold and silver, that produced inflation, and that in turn stimulated feverish enterprise; and the Protestant Reformation and the printing press that undermined traditional beliefs and values, changed attitudes toward work and innovation, which resulted in the pursuit of economic development. The Industrial Revolution itself was comprised of three critical innovations:

new energy, new machines, and new materials. Collectively, innovations in these three areas have transformed the world.

The impact of these technological innovations were first registered and felt in the economy, which saw tremendous increases in production and consumption, and consequently in the rising standard of living. Due to the use of machines, there was a shift from labor-intensive to capital-intensive industries, growth in the size of work organizations, increase in organizational specialization, and increased employment of men and women outside of the home. Industrial societies also saw the rise of market economies and the evolution of the modern corporation. But the initial effects of industrialization were harsh: migration to urban areas which were unable to cope with the sudden influx; the abrupt disruption of traditional relationships which provided meaning and support; a multitude of social ills inflicted on an uprooted and vulnerable mass of the population – misery, poverty, alcoholism, crime, vice, physical and mental illnesses; the inhuman conditions of employment in the "dark, satanic mills" of the factory system. The transition from agrarianism to industrialism was traumatic for the vast majority of peoples in all societies making such a transition.

Industrialization brought about an expansion of the bounds of human consciousness and knowledge that led people to raise questions about themselves, about society, about how they were governed. The first thing to go was monarchy and the divine right to rule, which in turn shook the thought forms of the theistic religions, exemplified by the Catholic Church's longstanding opposition to and struggle with religious liberty, separation of church and state, human rights, and democracy. Historical success favored the ideas of popular sovereignty and democratic governance. People preferred to be citizens rather than subjects. But not before the political scourges of Italian Fascism and German Nazism were defeated in the Second World War and before the Cold War with Communism ended with the collapse of the Soviet Union. The new threat is the terrorism of religious fundamentalisms. Industrialization also gave states of whatever political ideology tremendous military capacity to wage war, including weapons of mass destruction like nuclear bombs, that has made the twentieth century a most violent century.

In the economic realm, the competition was between capitalism and socialism. Capitalism itself was coterminous with industrialization so that it eventually held sway over industrial economies. But the Great Depression soon showed that the volatility of laissez-faire capitalism had to be tempered with government intervention. In the 1970s, laissez-faire capitalism reappeared under the guise of neoliberalism and soon brought us the Great Recession. State and market have to balance each other to prevent further economic catastrophes and to bring about prosperity for all. This is especially important because the increased productivity brought about by industrialization has also expanded the range of inequalities that includes race and ethnic, age and gender, educational and occupational stratification. The Great Recession exposed the yawning gap in income and wealth between the one percent of the richest and the rest of the population. There is a symbiotic relationship between economic and political power, with one feeding the other, that constitutes a vicious cycle. Growing economic and political inequality is not only economically unsustainable but politically perilous for democratic stability.

The impact of industrialization on population and family life has been no less dramatic. Improvements in nutrition contributed to better health and longer life spans; lower birth rates followed lower death rates; modern science and medicine, as well as, modern hygiene and sanitation raised the standards of living. The young no longer work, but spend time in the new stages of childhood and adolescence. The traditional functions of kinship and family have been altered. Romantic love became the basis for marriage and the nuclear family, shrunk in the number of children, spread. They were now a matter of choice than of necessity. The family remained an economic unit, no longer of production but of consumption. Nowhere are the effects of industrialization on society's norms, values, and sanctions seen more clearly than in the changing roles of women. They obtained the right to vote, they became educated, and they increased their participation in the labor force. Today, women outnumber men in academic degrees earned; their labor force participation is no longer complementary but necessary in maintaining the family's standard of living; many have been elected to and occupy high political offices, although, as of this writing, there has not yet been a woman president of the United States nor a female chief justice of the U.S. Supreme Court.

Most importantly, *"industrial societies are the first in human history in which the greatest threats posed by the biophysical environment are products of prior human activity"* (Nolan and Lenski 2004: 293). Put differently, more damage and destruction have been done to planet earth in the last two hundred years of industrialization than in all the previous kinds of human societies combined – and humans are the predators! The basic reason for this ecological flaw is the worldview promoted by industrialization. Industrial humans see the planet mainly as a source of resources and a sink for wastes. They see planet earth as a machine. What do you do with a machine? You use it, misuse it, abuse it, run it down, and replace it. But there is only one planet earth. Sustainable ecological consciousness has to start with a new, but really old, fundamental image of the earth, that of a human organism. We need to rediscover Native Americans' view of Mother Earth. What do you do with the living organism of Mother Earth? You protect it, you nourish it, you cherish it. There is only one planet earth, a spaceship earth traveling through the immensity of space and time of the cosmos, and we live or die with it.

Thus, White (1967) was correct in seeing science and technology as lying at the historical roots of our ecological crisis. "Natural science conceived as the effort to understand the nature of things, had flourished in several eras and among several peoples. Similarly there has been an age-old accumulation of technological skills, sometimes growing rapidly, sometimes slowly. But it was not until about four generations ago that Western Europe and North America arranged a marriage between science and technology, a union of the theoretical and the empirical approaches to our natural environment. The emergence in widespread practice of the Baconian creed that scientific knowledge means technological power over nature can scarcely be dated before about 1850, save in the chemical industries, where it is anticipated in the 18th century. Its acceptance as a normal pattern of action may mark the greatest event in human history since the invention of agriculture, and perhaps in nonhuman terrestrial history as well. Almost at once the new situation forced the crystallization of the novel concept of ecology; indeed the word ecology first appeared in the English language is 1973. Today, less than a century later, the impact of our race upon the environment has so increased in force that it has changed in essence."

White added the important idea that "what people do about their ecology depends on what they think about themselves in relation to things around them. Human ecology is deeply conditioned by beliefs about our nature and destiny – that is, by religion. . . . The victory of Christianity over paganism was the greatest psychic revolution in the history of our culture." Christianity inherited from Judaism a concept of time as non-repetitive and linear, but also a striking story of creation in which the human is the pinnacle. God was the wholly other, thus Christianity established the dualism between man and nature, as well as the understanding that man exploit nature for his proper ends. Nature was perceived primarily as a symbolic system through which God speaks to men. But with science and technology, it was less the case of decoding the physical symbols of God's communication, but the effort to understand God's mind by discovering how his creation operates. Thus, White asserted that "modern Western science was cast in a matrix of Christian theology. The dynamism of religious devotion shaped by the Judeo-Christian dogma of creation, gave it impetus."

It was earlier pointed out that in early agrarian society, such as that of Egypt, religion was an ideological force that united the society, motivated its people to produce more than what they needed for subsistence, and persuaded them to turn over the economic surplus to make of Egypt a powerful theocracy. It is not surprising, therefore, to say the least, that the Christian religion also performed the same underlying role in providing the rationale, the motivation, the assumptions, and the drive that resulted in the extraordinary achievements of Western science and technology. But as industrialization proceeded, deepened, and spread, the religious ideology became an industrial mind-set that saw nature simply as a source of resources to be plundered and as a sink of wastes that needed to be discarded. The ideology became a secular industrial hubris – overweening pride, overreaching arrogance – that saw and treated the earth as a machine to be used, misused, and abused. "The earth, our home," Pope Francis (2015a: 21) will say, "is beginning to look more and more like an immense pile of filth." In this we are all implicated, including the religion that provided its original underpinnings.

Religion, Ethics, and Ecology

Nature and culture were distinguished one from the other in that nature is that part of the created world that is untouched by human hands, that is not the product of human ingenuity, that has not been manipulated and exploited by human technology, while culture is human-made, the product of humans as they began to live in groups, as they tried to solve their group problems and to make sense of their communal existence. Nature is the mountains, the wilderness, the rivers, the forests, rain, and snow, as well as, earthquakes, the regularity of seasons, tornadoes, hurricanes, and typhoons. Nature happens, culture is made to happen. Nature takes forever, it moves with infinite slowness and spontaneity, it changes imperceptibly through the many periods of its history. Changes in culture are more dramatic, often brought about visibly and palpably by advances in science and technology. Cities and high-rise buildings, transportation on land, sea, and air, means of expression and communication, as well as, built-in, planned obsolescence, decay and destruction by human hands, human waste, pollution, plunder, and spoliation. The thing is that culture advances at the expense of nature, nature is not left unblemished as culture seeks to make it a source of resources and a sink of wastes.

Bill McKibben (1989: 8) has pronounced that we humans have crossed and stepped over the critical threshold: we are at the end of nature.

> By the end of nature I do not mean the end of the world. The rain will still fall and the sun shine, though differently than before. When I say "nature," I mean a certain set of human ideas about the world and our place in it. But the death of those ideas begins with concrete changes in the reality around us – changes that scientists can measure and enumerate. More and more frequently, these changes will clash with our perceptions, until, finally, our sense of nature as eternal and separate is washed away, and we will see all too clearly what we have done.

When humans began to exploit – in its original, nonjudgmental meaning of "to use," "to utilize" – nature, a new word came to existence: *environment*. Nature was transformed into environment, "a nonhuman world whose life and death, current shape and future prospects, are in large measure determined by human beings." One important consequence is that "in a sense modern industry, development, land use, and technology means that if ever a clear-cut distinction between nature and people was ever possible, it is no longer. Human beings and the environment now form a dialectical unity, each side affecting, and being affected by, the other. If we still depend on nature for food and water, air and minerals, every wild ecosystem depends on some political arrangement for protection, and every living thing is affected by human-made climate change, importation of exotic species, habitat loss, and pollution" (Gottlieb 2006: 5).

It all began in the distant past when humans and their archaic ancestors invented tools to help them find food, shelter, and clothing. As societies evolved to become more complex and advanced, human utilization of natural resources increased. But until about two hundred years ago, such utilization of natural resources or economic development, as it later came to be called, was sustainable, meaning that it did not lead to environmental degradation such that, in the words of the Brundtland Report, "it meets the needs of the present without compromising the ability of future generations to meet their own needs" (Martens and Schilder 2001: 813-815). Sustainability was underpinned by the belief that dependence on the earth requires responsibility, not destruction (Cobb 1992). With the Industrial Revolution which meant the substitution of non-human and non-animal sources of energy for human and animal sources, a dramatic change in economic development occurred and the exploitation of the environment increased exponentially. Attitudes toward the earth also changed: it simply became a means for human satisfaction. Today the poverty of the many and the excessive consumption of the few are driving forces of environmental degradation and economic development is no longer sustainable.

Environmental problems have reached a critical point; they have become a global crisis. Roger Gottlieb (2006: 5-6) explains it well:

> [T]he scope of the crisis makes for a totally new life situation.... Our plight today is *global*: there simply is no escape from it on this planet.... It has decisively changed people as well, inscribing itself in our bloodstreams, our breasts and prostates, our very mother's milk, all of which carry an unhealthy amount of toxins. It also taints our sense of what is to come, as we realize, perhaps only subliminally, that the future is likely to be worse than the past. The environmental crisis includes not only devastating particular events (Chernobyl, Bhopal, [Fukushima], a thousand-square-mile dead zone in the Gulf of Mexico) but a way of life which appears as a slow, seemingly unstoppable, deterioration in the quality of air, food, water, land, and life. At the worst, the crisis provokes a deep fear that the earth will cease to be a healthy setting for human life.

Gottlieb (2006: 4-5) lists at least eight major dimensions of the environmental crisis, "each of which by itself would be a critical problem, but all of which together make for perhaps the most significant challenge human beings have ever faced."

1. Climate change
2. Staggering accumulations of chemical, heavy metal, biological, and nuclear wastes
3. Loss of topsoil from overuse of chemical agriculture and the destruction of forests
4. Crisis of biodiversity
5. Loss of wilderness
6. Devastation of indigenous peoples
7. Unsustainable patterns and quantities of consumption
8. Genetic engineering

The environmental crisis has led to the importance of ecology. Ecology is the study of the relationships of organisms to their physical environment and to one another. Within the biosphere – the total expanse of water, land, and atmosphere able to sustain life – the basic ecological unit is the ecosystem. Each ecosystem consists of a community of plants and animals in an environment that supplies them with raw materials for life. The ecosystem is delimited by the climate, altitude, water, soil characteristics, and other physical conditions of the environment. An ecosystem may be small as a tidal pool or a rotting log, or as large as an ocean or a continent-spanning forest (Lagasse 2000: 861). In fact, James Lovelock (1979) formulated the Gaia hypothesis, which holds that the earth is a single living organism; it must be studied therefore as a single ecosystem. The most important characteristic of an ecosystem is interdependence and delicate balance between and within its constituent parts. The earth is a community of life in which humans are interdependent with all the other elements of the earth; we must live in delicate balance with all them, not in excess nor in deficiency. Social systems of all kinds depend on the "health" of the natural system. In Barbara Ward's graphic image, we are traveling in spaceship earth, we live or die with it.

With the awareness of the degradation of the environment and human complicity in it – the anthropogenic concept (Weart 2011) – with the consciousness that humans are bound up with the fate of the earth and that therefore we as humans have the responsibility to clean up our mess and remake God's creation in his own image and likeness, factors like these have forced reevaluation of religious traditions and sacred texts, of traditional religious concepts and ideas, reappraisal in theology and ethics (McDonagh 1990), such that we now have environmental theology (Hart 2004), environmental ethics (Smith 1997), and religious environmental activism (Gottlieb et al. 2006). But first religion and ethics must make an honest disclosure. For one thing, as Gottlieb (2006: 6) points out, "the first critical questions about humanity's modern relation to nature, wilderness, and industry were not raised by prominent theologians or religious leaders, but by freelance spiritual types, anticommunist Western Marxists, secular philosophers, or nature lovers." Former Vice-President Al Gore (1992) must be mentioned in this regard.

Christianity today strongly resists "dominion theology" that would subdue the earth and make humans have dominion over the entire creation to serve their purposes. But if truth be told, and honesty requires that it be told, it must be admitted that this ideology, derived from its Judeo-Christian heritage, has ruled Western industrial countries, inspired, and motivated their accomplishments in science, technology, industry, and urbanism. In fact, from the time Christianity allied itself with Roman imperial power, Christianity had sought to destroy what it considered the "other:" other religions with their shrines and symbols, other versions of

Christianity with their scriptures and writings, other peoples, other lands, other cultures.

Spain and Portugal flew the banners of Christianization and colonization to subdue and dominate the indigenous peoples and cultures of Latin America and the Philippines, to exploit their lands for plunder and profit, and in the process destroy and make the peoples and their cultures disappear from the face of the earth. The Puritans for their part landed on the shores of North America, intent to build a city upon a hill on what they considered to be their New Jerusalem. The result was the genocide of Native Americans and the enslavement of blacks, which did not fit into their supremacist Christian mindsets, and their expulsion from their original lands and the latter's despoliation. The scramble for Africa and its dismemberment into colonies for the exploitation of their populations and natural resources was perpetrated by the nations of Europe, the home and center of Western Christianity. There is much that the Christian religion is guilty of, that it needs to acknowledge in brutal honesty, that it needs to repent of.

There is also much that religion can offer. In fact, religion must confront the ecological crisis. Gottlieb (2006: 11-14) also addresses this issue: "This crisis is, among other things, a spiritual problem, affecting both the passion and the intimacy of religious life." Part of the essential role of religion is to remind people of human life's "ultimate concerns," a phrase from Paul Tillich, to pursue not power, pleasure, and wealth, but the most lasting and authentic values of love of God and his creation, of the neighbor, especially the poorest of them. Religion also uses the language of sin not to apply only to what is wasteful, inefficient, or troublesome, but to matters of the highest importance, essential to the health not only of our rivers and lungs, but of our souls as well. "Thus, religion attuned to the environmental crisis can help us, in Joanna Macy's phrase, 'sustain the gaze,' that is, to focus on what is actually happening long enough to see what we are doing to ourselves, our planet, and our future. In helping us to maintain this focus, religion can thus enable us to take at least the first step [and other further steps] toward collective change."

Religion also offers practical and political help in arriving at solutions. Gottlieb (2006: 10-12) writes: "Ethics requires politics. . . . [R]eligious people must engage in political life if they are to fulfill the minimum ethical requirements of their faiths – if, that is, the consequences of the way they live are not to make a mockery of what they claim are their values. (People do often make much of how hard this is, ignoring the fact that a committed religious life is always difficult: loving our enemies or giving up attachment to desire is, after all, no day at the beach.) . . . If the environmental crisis means that religion has to change, it is also the case that over centuries religions have developed powerful resources to help us understand and respond to critical forms of suffering and justice. ... [F]or hundreds of millions of people religion remains the arbiter and repository of life's deepest moral values. In this context religions provide a rich resource to mobilize people for political action." This mobilization and participation can, in turn, also revitalize the meaning of politics in its original Aristotelian sense as the citizen's duty in and to the *polis* from the partisan, ideologically polarized, and ultimately dysfunctional politics of today that we all decry (Kearns 2011).

The reappraisal in theology started with a new appreciation of creation. In the past, it is not an exaggeration to say that creation was simply the starting point for theological reflection that was soon bypassed to move on to salvific truths of the faith that were primarily centered on Christ's redemption and resurrection. A new appreciation of creation was started by such theologians as Thomas Berry (1992), Wendell Berry (1978), and Matthew Fox (1986), the latter to be driven from his Dominican Order and ultimately from the Catholic Church. Creation spirituality made us realize that creation has a value and autonomy of its own, that our human lives and our destiny as humans are tied up with the fate of the world, and that therefore we must be concerned with what was happening not only in, but also to the world, to nature, to the environment. The reappraisal in turn led to rethinking and reevaluating God, humanity, and the world, and even the meanings of redemption, salvation, and resurrection not only of humans, but of the world as a whole, of the entire creation. Thus, ecological theology, ecological ethics, ecological aesthetics, ecological justice are studied for their implications and applications in all aspects of Christian life (Haring 1981, Ryan 1994).

Ethics most especially enters the picture. Of all the ecological problems humanity faces today, the most serious and most dangerous, because of its catastrophic potential, is climate change. But it is also the most contentious, whose cast of characters includes leading scientists, professional skeptics and denialists, radical activists, powerful lobbyists of fossil-energy industries, loud-mouthed media gurus, and ideological pundits, all playacting their roles before a confused, anxious, and passive public (Pooley 2010). In a landmark study, Stephen Gardiner (2013: 3; also Gardiner 2011) declares that climate change is a prime example of a global environmental tragedy, given that the relevant facts are known, and yet effective action is so difficult, and indeed has so far eluded us. This is the real global environmental tragedy. "In my view, the global environmental tragedy is most centrally an ethical failure, and one that implicates our institutions, our moral and political theories, and ultimately ourselves, considered as moral agents."

Gardiner explains how the tragedy comes about through the metaphor of the perfect storm, borrowed from Sebastian Junger's true story – and movie – of the *Andrea Gail*, a fishing vessel caught at sea during the rare convergence of three particularly bad storms and ultimately destroyed as a result. Like the *Andre Gail*, we are beset by three forces that are likely to throw us off the course, and may even sink us to oblivion. "The first storm is global. Its key feature is that the world's most affluent nations, and especially the rich within those nations, have considerable power to shape what is done, and to do so in ways which favor their own concerns, especially over those of the world's poorer nations, and the poor people within those nations" (Gardiner 2013: 7).

The second storm is intergenerational. Its key feature is that the current generation has more power to affect the prospects of future generations, but not vice versa. For Gardiner (2013: 7), "the intergenerational storm is the most prominent of the three. Here the possibilities for taking advantage are deep." The third storm is theoretical. In dealing with the first two storms, we do not have robust theories to guide us, particularly in the relevant areas of intergenerational ethics, international justice, scientific uncertainty, and the human relationship to animal and the rest of nature. "This not only complicates the task of behaving well, but also renders us more vulnerable to the first two storms. Each of the three storms hampers the course of ethical action, and threatens to blow it seriously off course. But taken together they are mutually reinforcing, and the challenge becomes profound" (Gardiner 2013: 7).

Most importantly, Gardiner (2013: 45-48, 301-38) warns that "when the global, intergenerational and theoretical storms meet, they encourage a distinct problem for ethical action on climate change, the problem of moral corruption." Moral corruption involves the use of distraction, complacency, selective attention, unreasonable doubt, delusion, pandering, and hypocrisy to confuse, pervert, subvert our understanding of the complexity and enormity of the perfect storm of climate change to prevent, forestall, delay action. "Since climate change involves a complex convergence of problems, it is easy to engage in *manipulative* or *self-deceptive* behavior by applying one's attention to only some of the considerations that make the situation difficult." As Gardiner (2013: 47-48) puts it more forcefully:

> In conclusion, the threat of moral corruption reveals another sense in which climate change may be a "perfect" moral storm. Its complexity may turn out to be *perfectly*

convenient for us, the current generation, and indeed for each successor generation as it comes to occupy our position. For one thing, it provides each generation with a cover under which it can seem to be taking the issue seriously – by negotiating weak and largely substanceless global accords, for example, and then heralding them as great achievements – when simply it is simply exploiting its temporal position. For another, all this can occur without the exploiting generation actually having to acknowledge that this is what it is doing. If it can avoid the appearance of overly selfish (or self-absorbed) behavior, an earlier generation can take advantage of the future without the unpleasantness of admitting it – either to others, or, perhaps more importantly, to itself.

In the end, therefore, the perfect moral storm that is the ethical tragedy of climate change – as with all ethical problems and all ecological dilemmas – can only be solved by the answers to the questions about who we are and what we want to be as moral agents in a moral universe. The danger is that we become, if we are not yet already, victims of moral manipulation and self-deception.

Pope Francis' Ecological Vision

Pope Francis' encyclical *Laudato Si'* (2015) on care for the earth may well be as significant and momentous as Leo XIII's *Rerum Novarum* (1891) on the condition and rights of labor and John XXIII's *Pacem in Terris* (1963) on nuclear war and peace. It is one of the longest, if not the longest, of the encyclicals in the Catholic Church's history for its comprehensiveness. Following John XXIII who addressed his *Pacem in Terris* "to all men and women of good will," Pope Francis in *Laudato Si'* wishes "to address every living person on the planet," "to enter into dialogue with all people about our common home." Accordingly, since women hold up half of the sky, as a Chinese proverb puts it, and in spite of the adamant resistance of previous papacies and episcopacies, Francis does not hesitate to use inclusive language.

It certainly is a milestone in Catholic Social Teaching, to "which is now added" *Laudato Si'*, the Pope himself asserts. At the outset, Francis refers and recalls the ecological concerns of his immediate predecessors, Paul VI, John Paul II, and Benedict XVI to affirm his traditional focus and continuity. At the same time, Francis' encyclical also stretches beyond them. "This is what makes *Laudato Si'* the most significant addition to the corpus of social teaching since *Rerum novarum*. In essence, the new encyclical suggests that our responsibilities extend across time as well as space, and that they include the entirety of creation. *Laudato si'* thus develops a broader notion of solidarity – solidarity not only within generations but also between generations, and solidarity not only with our fellow human beings but with the whole earth and all its creatures" (Annett 2015).

Another feature distinguishing *Laudato Si'* lies in the footnotes (Ahern 2015). Vatican II defined the doctrine of collegiality, which means that the pope and the bishops of the Catholic Church constitute a college, and while the pope can exercise his authority by himself, the college of bishops with the pope can also – if not better or best – exercise collegial authority. The young Joseph Ratzinger (1964: 64) then wrote an article proposing that "the bishops' conferences are one of the possible forms of collegiality." But as chief enforcer of belief at the Vatican and in the face of the assertive and well-managed national episcopal conferences, he became the chief opponent of collegiality, emasculating their competence and authority. In 1998, John Paul issued *Apostolicos Suos* which degraded the theological status of national conferences of bishops. Similarly, the Synod of Bishops created by Paul VI in the wake of Vatican II had only advisory status.

It is such a pleasant surprise, therefore, to see twenty citations from eighteen national and regional bishops' conferences in *Laudato Si'*, most of whom speak from the Third World, where two-thirds of the world's Catholics live, which regions became Catholic through colonial expansion, and which have been marginalized in church governance. The tradition in citations in papal encyclicals, Kevin Ahern (2015) points out, "reflects a specific theology of the papacy that understands the pope to be the primary teacher of Catholic doctrine with a strict division of roles between teacher and student. As such, the pope would never need to learn from sources 'below' him." *Laudato Si'* departs from this tradition. As do the references to St. Francis of Assisi and Patriarch Bartholomew, to the theologians Romano Guardini and Teilhard de Chardin, and, most surprisingly, to a Sufi Muslim mystic. "From a theological point of view, the inclusion of specifically religious texts from outside the Catholic tradition raises interesting questions about the development of doctrine. What does it mean for an official statement of social doctrine to draw from a Muslim mystic? What does this say about the role of the Holy Spirit beyond the church" (Ahern (2015)?

The citations make the point that the issues raised by Pope Francis are more than his personally but are collectively the bishops' all over the world, as well as, the world's. More importantly, this is in line with Francis's

(2013a, no. 32) call in *Evangelii Gaudium* "for a juridical status of episcopal conferences" with "genuine doctrinal authority," because "excessive centralization, rather than proving helpful, complicates the Church's life and her missionary outreach." Conservative Catholic critics often claim that the teachings on racism, war and peace, and economic justice of national bishops' conferences lack authoritative competency because of their national origins. They cannot make this excuse for *Laudato Si'*. Pope Francis who prefers the title "Bishop of Rome" to that of "Supreme Pontiff" aims to revive the doctrines of collegiality and synodality, the importance and dignity of local churches therefore for church governance, which had been downgraded by previous imperial papacies (O'Malley 2015b).

Underlying Pope Francis' ecological vision is that of the earth: "our common home is like a sister with whom we share our life and a beautiful mother who opens her arms to embrace us," which is taken from St. Francis of Assisi's *Canticle of the Creatures*. "This sister now cries out to us because of the harm we have inflicted on her by our irresponsible use and abuse of the goods with which God has endowed her" (no.1). In Chapter 1, therefore, Pope Francis draws a picture of how the earth is maltreated and abused, how our common home is groaning in pain and suffering. It is devoted to a fresh analysis of our present situation, of what is happening to our common home. Pollution and climate change, the issue of water, the loss of biodiversity, the decline in the quality of human life and the breakdown of society, global inequality, as well as, weak responses to them are addressed.

For Francis, these problems have the result that "the earth, our home is beginning to look more and more like an immense pile of filth" (no. 21). He argues that "these problems are closely linked to a throwaway culture which affects the excluded just as it quickly reduces things to rubbish" (no. 22). He recognizes anthropogenic causes: "[A] sober look at our world shows that the degree of human intervention, often in the service of business interests and consumerism, is actually making our earth less rich and beautiful, ever more limited and grey, even as technological advances and consumer goods continue to abound limitlessly" (no. 34). He emphasizes that "the deterioration of the environment and of society affects the most vulnerable people on the planet . . . Today, we have to realize that a true ecological approach *always* becomes a social approach; it must integrate questions of justice in debates on the environment, so as to hear *both the cry of the earth and the cry of the poor*" (nos. 48-49; original italics).

In the section on weak responses, Pope Francis mentions that we lack the culture needed to confront the crisis, we lack leadership, we lack the establishment of a legal framework such that power structures based on the techno-economic paradigm overwhelm politics, freedom, and justice. Our politics are subject to technology and finance. The current global economic system is defenceless before the interests of a deified market. Meanwhile, we see the rise of a false and superficial ecology that bolsters complacency and a cheerful recklessness.

Addressing the most serious and dangerous of ecological problems, that of climate change, the Pope makes the claim that "a very solid scientific consensus indicates that we are presently witnessing a disturbing warming of the climactic system. . . . [A] number of scientific studies indicate that most global warming in recent decades is due to the concentration of greenhouse gases (carbon dioxide, methane, nitrogen oxides and others) released mainly as a result of human activity" (no. 23). Thus, Pope Francis puts his authority behind the solid scientific consensus on anthropogenic climate change.

This is significant in light of what Stephen Gardiner called "moral corruption" behind the ethical tragedy of climate change, i.e., the efforts to deny, subvert, distort, pervert, confuse, and manipulate understandings of anthropogenic climate change so as to promote inaction. Even before the encyclical was issued, conservative Catholic commentators were already criticizing the pope: that he did not have the scientific expertise to expound on scientific issues, that his papal authority did not extend to non-religious claims, that he is asserting as certain what has not been proven scientifically, that he is being duped by people who should know better. Francis recognizes "such evasiveness [that] serves as a licence to carrying on with our present lifestyles and models of production and consumption. This is the way human beings contrive to feed their self-destructive vices: trying not to see them, trying not to acknowledge them, delaying the important decisions and pretending that nothing will happen" (no. 59).

One last preliminary point. Pope Francis is also accused of dismissing the role of population in environmental problems. In fact, he counters the reasons usually proposed for population control (no. 50). But listen to Stephen Gardiner (2013: 443-56) who addresses in an appendix population and its environmental impact, especially on climate change.

> [T]he important issue about population is not really how many people there are. In itself, this tells us nothing and threatens little. The issue is the environmental impact that people have, in particular, on the so-called carrying capacity of the planet. Thus, the population element of global environmental problems concerns how the number of people in the world interacts with the environmental

> impact per person to produce the total environmental impact of humanity. On this issue, however, there is reason to believe that for some problems [like climate change] the most important variable is the environmental impact per person, not the total human population. . . .
>
> It is affluent people in general, and especially in the rich countries, who currently contribute most to our main global environmental problem [i.e., climate change], so it is essential that they take the lead in action, and quickly. This should be the political priority, especially since it is also a politically necessary prerequisite for preventing the developing countries from following a Western path.

The rest of the encyclical, especially Chapters 2 to 4 and 6, elucidates Pope Francis's theological, spiritual, and pastoral vision of ecology, from which I will gather key elements that constitute what, I think, is distinctively his ecological vision that might well be subtitled "Integral Ecology: Everything Is Interconnected." (A metaphysical reflection on Thomas Aquinas and relational ecology is given by Rothrock [2015]).

The Gospel of Creation. Pope Francis starts with the biblical accounts of creation, which "contain, in their own symbolic narrative language, profound teachings about human existence and its historical reality." The first is that "human life is grounded in three fundamental and closely intertwined relationships: with God, with our neighbor and with the earth itself" (no. 66). "These ancient stories, full of symbolism, bear witness to a conviction that we today share, that everything is interconnected, and that genuine care for our lives and our relationships with nature is inseparable from fraternity, justice and faithfulness to others" (no. 70). We are not God, called to dominate and subjugate the earth. "The Bible has no place for a tyrannical anthropocentrism unconcerned with other creatures" (no. 68). The earth, as with the entire universe, was here before us and it has been given to us to cultivate but also to care and protect. We admire the grandeur and immensity of creation, open to God's transcendence. But it is also a fragile world we live in, entrusted by God to human care. "The ultimate destiny of the universe is in the fullness of God, which has already been attained by the risen Christ, the measure of the maturity of all things" (no. 83).

Pope Francis' vision of the fullness of creation reminds me of Karl Rahner, about whom I (Litonjua 2012) had earlier written:

Karl Rahner sees creation as the expression of God. Creation is not simply the making of an external object, and the world is not only a product that was made, but it entails the self-communication of God. Creation is God's very self-communication. As such, God is present in the world, and this universal presence of God is at once the divine offer of grace. God is present in every corner of the world and of the universe; his grace is available in every nook and cranny of human life, but is most palpable in the innermost recesses of the human spirit. Creation is not God himself; that would be pantheism. But creation is permeated with God's presence and grace; that is panentheism. "The world is charged with the grandeur of God," the Jesuit poet Gerard Manley Hopkins echoes Rahner, for which "Glory be to God for dappled things."

Second, "we are called to recognize that other living beings have a value of their own in God's eyes: 'by their mere existence they bless him and give him glory,' and indeed, 'the Lord rejoices in all his works' (Ps 104:31)" (no. 68). The rest of creation is not simply subordinated to the good of human beings, neither simply as a means for their happiness nor as resources for profit and gain. This is a distorted anthropocentrism. Pope Francis quotes the German bishops who taught that, where other creatures are concerned, "we can speak of the priority of *being* over that of *being useful*" (no. 69).

Pope Francis gives an almost lyrical paean to human dignity and uniqueness in no. 81, after which he writes in equally poetic terms: "The entire material universe speaks of God's love, his boundless affection for us. Soil, water, mountains: everything is, as it were, a caress of God. The history of our friendship with God is always linked to particular places which take an intensely personal meaning; we all remember places and revisiting those memories does us much good. Anyone who has grown up in the hills or used to sit by the spring to drink, or played outdoors in the neighborhood square; going back to these places is a chance to recover something of their true selves" (no. 84).

This leads Erickson (2015) to note that:

> Beauty carries a lot of ethical weight in this encyclical. Despite the vast ecological devastations, the letter evokes the beauty of our ecological contexts in its descriptions and logic argues seeing that beauty urges respect of other

creatures. Learning to see beauty in the everyday is an intrinsic part of an ecological conversion to the earth. (Think of it this way: By my account the word "ecology" occurs thirty-three times in the encyclical. The word "beauty" occurs twenty-seven times.)

Third, "the earth is essentially a shared inheritance, whose fruits are meant to benefit everyone. . . . Hence every ecological approach needs to incorporate a social perspective which takes into account the fundamental rights of the poor and the underprivileged. The principle of the subordination of private property to the universal destination of goods, and thus the right of everyone to their use, is a golden rule of social conduct and the first principle of the whole ethical and moral order" (no. 93). Earlier, Pope Francis pointed out that "the deterioration of the environment and of society affects the most vulnerable people on the plant: 'Both everyday experience and scientific research show that the gravest effects of all attacks on the environment are suffered by the poorest'" (no. 48). He added and we repeat: "Today, we have to realize that a true ecological approach *always* becomes a social approach; it must integrate questions of justice in debates on the environment, so as to hear *both the cry of the earth and the cry of the poor*" (no. 49).

Parenthetically, according to *The Tablet* (2015), Leonardo Boff was one of key influences whose campaigning, knowledge, and writing influenced the Pope's thinking on the environment. Pope Francis, who previously welcomed Gustavo Gutierrez, the father of Latin American liberation theology, invited Boff to submit material for inclusion in the encyclical. Boff, a Franciscan friar and Brazilian theologian, left the priesthood after continued clashes with Cardinal Joseph Ratzinger who silenced him over his views on the church and on liberation theology. It was part of Ratzinger's larger campaign against theologies emanating from the margins and championing the cause of liberating the poor and the laity (Cox 1988). Boff (1995, 1997) wrote *Ecology and Liberation* and *Cry of the Earth, Cry of the Poor*, an ecotheology of liberation. He said: "Along with the poor, you have to add the Earth as the 'great pauper' that is oppressed and devastated. It's the ecotheology of liberation. It is not as if we went from red theology to green theology. It is the same liberating impulse."

Pope Francis draws an important implication that "a sense of deep communion with nature cannot be real if our hearts lack tenderness, compassion and concern for our fellow human beings, [especially the poor and the helpless]. It is clearly inconsistent to combat trafficking in endangered species while remaining completely indifferent to human trafficking, unconcerned about the poor or undertake to destroy another human being deemed unwanted. . . . Everything is connected. Concern for the environment thus needs to be joined to a sincere love for our fellow human beings and unwavering commitment to resolving the problems of society" (no. 91). St. Francis who recognized the sun and moon, earth and air, fire and water, his own body, all animals and plants, and death itself as brothers and sisters, also entered into a mystical union with Lady Poverty.

Conversely, "it follows that our indifference and cruelty towards fellow creatures of this world sooner or later affects the treatment we mete out to other human beings. We have only one heart, and the same wretchedness which leads us to mistreat an animal will not be long in showing itself in our relationships with other people. Every act of cruelty towards any creature is 'contrary to human dignity.' We can hardly consider ourselves to be fully loving if we disregard any aspect of reality . . . Everything is related, and we human beings are united as brothers and sisters on a wonderful pilgrimage, woven together by the love God has for each of his creatures and which also unites us in fond affection with brother sun, sister moon, brother river and mother earth" (no. 92).

Pope Francis ends his Gospel of Creation with a gaze on and of Jesus, the sacrament of God, who in his sacramentality has also made the earth, nature, and creation as a whole a sacrament of God's presence and grace (Himes and Himes 1990). "In the Christian understanding of the world, the destiny of creation is bound up with the mystery of Christ, present from the beginning: 'All things have been created through him and for him' (Col 1:16)" (no. 99). According to St. Paul (Romans 8:19), we all groan inwardly as we await, and the entire creation groans in labor pains and in anticipation, for the redemption and coming of the Risen Christ in glory.

One last point. David Cloutier (2015) comments on the image of creation oriented to the praise of God in chapter 1 of Pope Francis' encyclical as perhaps "one of the most spiritually revelatory for many readers; while it pours out of the psalmody, it isn't always a functioning part of the Catholic spiritual repertoire." He goes on to add that "certainly the chapter is a jarring contrast with any kind of social Darwinist picture of nature as 'red in tooth and claw,' and its robust conviction that creatures bear inherent purposes is a challenge to ideologies of science that see nature as blind."

But ignore "social Darwinist" and "ideologies of science," and listen to a contrarian viewpoint. Lisa Sideris (2006) argues that to ignore Darwinian evolutionary processes that are central to biological and ecological science, to fail to incorporate evolutionary science into religious descriptions of, and ethical prescriptions for, nature creates a number of problems.

First, "an inaccurate understanding of the natural world may generate ethical imperatives toward nature that are inappropriate for, and even disruptive of, natural processes. . . . The ethics proposed (or implied) for remedying suffering are oriented toward the establishment or perhaps *re-creation* of a world that is, as far as we know, biologically impossible. Put differently, . . . Christian environmental ethics still remains too otherworldly, too preoccupied with a prefall ideal of the natural world." Secondly, "neglecting Darwinism means that religious environmentalists cut themselves off from a vital source of information about nature but also from a vital source of environmental and animal ethics. . . . Darwin's theory is arguably the most important development in the history of science in clarifying the place of humans in nature and our relationships, past and present, to all other forms of life. Ecotheologians wishing to steer Christianity away from an overtly anthropocentric worldview should find a valuable reference point in Darwinism." Third, "some ecotheological accounts of nature so little resemble an evolutionary account that they could virtually pass for creationism or other arguments from design" (Sideris 2006: 448).

I cannot elaborate on these ideas in this paper. Suffice to note Sideris' (2006: 461-62) concluding remarks while quoting James Gustafson:

> I would argue that a failure to value nature as it really is – in its *given* ordering rather than its prefall or eschatologically anticipated perfection – constitutes a lack of piety, a failure to show respect and gratitude for the deity who created and sustains this ordering. Theologian James Gustafson argues that the desire to alter or perfect this basic, natural ordering implies a denial of God as God, a refusal to "consent" to the patterns and processes that manifest the deity in the realm of nature. An ecocentric ethic, by which I mean a general presumption in favor of respecting natural processes and intervening cautiously and with regard to the broader ecological context, can also be a theocentric ethic. . . . Humans as finite beings are participants in natural processes that we did not create and cannot fully control. Processes such as natural selection, and the natural ordering more generally, have value that is independent of humans and relative to God, even while humans may find this ordering disconcerting or even, at times, wasteful and improvident. Interdependence in nature is inseparable from conflict, and both are born of

the same natural processes. A truly ecological, evolutionary ethic must take all of the available facts of nature into account, not merely those that point to the sort of world we wish to live in.

Technological Anthropocentrism. After depicting the fullness of creation, Pope Francis undertakes an examination of the human roots of the ecological crisis. He identifies two such roots: the technocratic paradigm and modern anthropocentrism.

First, technology has brought humankind tremendous advances and benefits in improving the quality of human life. "Never has humanity had such power itself, yet nothing ensures that it will used wisely, particularly when we consider how it is currently being used" (no. 104). Technological hubris in the hands of totalitarianism has killed millions. Even today, the mushroom cloud of nuclear technology threatens the entire planet. "The basic problem goes even deeper: it is the way that humanity has taken up technology and its development *according to an undifferentiated and one-dimensional paradigm.* . . . [M]any problems of today's world stem from the tendency, at times unconscious, to make the method and aims of science and technology an epistemological paradigm which shapes the lives of individuals and the workings of society. The effects of imposing this model on reality as a whole, human and social, are seen in the deterioration of the environment, but this is just one sign of a reductionism which affects every aspect of human and social life. . . . The technological paradigm has become so dominant that it would be difficult to do without its resources and even more difficult to utilize them without being dominated by their internal logic" (no. 106-08).

The dominant technocratic paradigm has gone global with the globalization of the unfettered market such that finance, the most technical field in economics, now overwhelms the global economy. Technological specialization makes it difficult to see the larger picture; the fragmentation of knowledge leads to partial solutions to the urgent problems of the environment. "To seek only a technical remedy to each environmental problem which comes up is to separate what is in reality interconnected and to mask the true and deepest problems of the global system. . . . There is also the fact that people no longer seem to believe in a happy future; they no longer have blind trust in a better tomorrow based on the present state of the world and our technical abilities. There is a growing awareness that scientific and technological progress cannot be equated with the progress of humanity and history, a growing sense that the way to a better future lies elsewhere" (no. 111-13). All of this shows, Pope Francis asserts, the urgent need for us to move in a bold cultural revolution.

Second, "modern anthropocentrism has paradoxically ended up prizing technical thought over reality . . . Modernity has been marked by an excessive anthropocentrism . . . a Promethean vision of mastery over the world. Instead, our 'dominion' over the universe should be understood more properly in the sense of responsible stewardship" (no. 115-16). Pope Francis emphasizes that "there can be no renewal of our relationship with nature without a renewal of humanity itself. There can be no ecology without an adequate anthropology" (no. 118). Furthermore, "if we fail to acknowledge as part of reality the worth of a poor person, a human embryo, a person with disabilities – to offer just a few examples – it becomes difficult to hear the cry of nature itself; everything is connected" (no. 117). Here are encapsulated the three emphases of the Pope: a correct anthropology, a passion for nature, and an option for the poor.

Part of the misguided anthropocentrism that the Pope decries is practical relativism – more dangerous than doctrinal relativism – which leads to a misguided lifestyle. "When human beings place themselves at the centre, they give absolute priority to immediate convenience and all else becomes relative. Hence we should nor be surprised to find, in conjunction with the omnipresent technocratic paradigm and the cult of unlimited human power, the rise of relativism which sees everything as irrelevant unless it serves one's own immediate interests" (no. 122). The Pope adds: "It is also the mindset of those who say: Let us allow the invisible forces of the market to regulate the economy, and consider their impact on society and nature as collateral damage. In the absence of objective truths or sound principles other than the satisfaction of our own desires and immediate needs, what limits can be placed on human trafficking, organized crime, the drug trade, commerce in blood diamonds and the fur of endangered species? Is it not the same relativistic logic which justifies buying the organs of the poor for resale or use in experimentation, or eliminating children because they are not what their parents wanted" (no. 123)?

It might be surprising to many to find Pope Francis devoting several paragraphs to the need to take account of the value of labor in an encyclical on the environment. But correct anthropology demands a correct understanding of labor, a proper relationship between human beings and the world around us, between human beings and things requires asking the question of the meaning and purpose of all human activity. Francis asserts that "we were created with a vocation to work. . . . Work is a necessity, part of the meaning of life on this earth, a path to growth, human development and personal fulfillment. Helping the poor financially must always be a provisional solution in the face of pressing needs. The broader objective should always be to allow them a dignified life through work.... In order to continue providing employment, it is imperative to promote an economy which favours productive diversity and business creativity" no. 128-29). Again, everything is connected: nature, working men and women, the economy, and the poor.

Thus, it is not surprising that Pope Francis also touches on new biological technologies and gives guidance on human intervention on plants and animals which includes genetic manipulation by biotechnology, genetic modification, whether vegetable or animal, medical or agricultural. "Certainly, these issues require constant attention and a concern for their ethical implications. A broad, responsible scientific and social debate needs to take place, one capable of considering all the available information and of calling things by their name" (no. 135). "But when technology disregards the great ethical principles, it ends up considering any practice whatsoever as licit. . . . [A] technology severed from ethics will not easily be able to limit its own power" (no. 136).

Integral Ecology. This lies at the conceptual heart of Pope Francis' ecological vision. But as John Conley (2015) points out, although the term is widely used in contemporary environmental circles, it needs conceptual clarification to indicate the distinctive version of integral ecology that the Pope is defending and promoting. Some environmentalists conceive of integral ecology as a multidisciplinary study of environmental entities, from geological, biological, and economic perspectives, for example. Some economists use integral ecology to insist that environmental issues cannot be divorced from questions of production, distribution, and consumption. Some naturalists defend integral ecology as a form of naturalism in which human activity is wholly inscribed within, and therefore only understood and explained by, material nature and terms.

The term "integral" has distinctive Catholic echoes. Pope Paul VI in his 1967 encyclical *Populorum Progressio*, On the Development of Peoples, called for "integral development," the development of the whole man and of all men, a development therefore within the broader framework of the religious and moral maturation of the human person. In a book originally published in French in 1936, Jacques Maritain expounded on the theory of "integral humanism," a type of Christian politics that would and could join the secularist humanist in promoting civic democracy, but would insist on the religious source and ultimate destiny of the human person. With the exception of the naturalistic conception, Pope Francis' integral ecology draws from these various understandings and is most compatible with those who insist on the inseparability of the different and various aspects of ecological problems. Pope Francis's integral ecology respects and serves the "integrity" of all creation: it includes environmental, biological, social, economic, human, and personal dimensions, because everything is interconnected.

Economic and Social Ecology. The encyclical starts Chapter 4 with a consideration of ecology as the study of the relationship between living organisms and the environment in which they develop. Everything is interconnected. Even "time and space are not independent of one another, and not even atoms and subatomic particles can be considered in isolation" (no. 138). Determining the environmental impact of a concrete undertaking often needs studying how they relate in the context of the larger units of ecosystems. "Nature cannot be regarded as something separate from ourselves or as a mere setting in which we live. We are part of nature, included in it and thus in constant interaction with it. Recognizing the reasons why a given area is polluted requires a study of the workings of society, its economy, its behaviour patters, and the way it grasps social reality. . . . We are faced not with two separate crises, one environmental and the other social, but rather with one complex crisis which is both social and environmental. Strategies for a solution demand an integrated approach to combating poverty, restoring dignity to the excluded, and at the same time protecting nature" (no. 139).

Economics cannot only be about continued increases in growth, in the production, distribution, and consumption of goods and services. "[T]here is a need for an 'economic ecology' capable of appealing to a broader vision of society. The protection of the environment is in fact 'an integral part of the development process and cannot be considered in isolation from it.'. . . Today, the analysis of environmental problems cannot be separated from the analysis of human, family, work-related and urban contexts, nor from how individuals relate to themselves, which leads in turn to how they relate to others and to the environment" (no. 141).

There is also a need for a social ecology. "[T]he health of society's institutions has consequences for the environment and the quality of life. 'Every violation of solidarity and civic friendship harms the environment.' In this sense, social ecology is necessarily institutional, and gradually extends to the whole of society, from the primary social group, the family, to the wider local, national and international communities. Within each social stratum, and between them, institutions develop to regulate human relationships. Anything which weakens those institutions has negative consequences, such as injustice, violence and loss of freedom" (no. 142). The big problem is that some countries are institutionally weak, which results in people inequitably profiting from them, in the lack of respect for law, in well-framed laws yet remain a dead letter, in problems, like drug use, taking place in one area but having a direct or indirect effect on other areas. The overall result: "behavior is corrupted, lives are destroyed, and the environment continues to deteriorate" (no. 142).

Cultural Ecology. "Together with the patrimony of nature, there is also an historic, artistic and cultural patrimony which is likewise under threat. This patrimony is part of the shared identity of each place and a foundation upon which to build a habitable city. . . . Culture is more than what we have inherited from the past; it is also, and above all, a living, dynamic and participatory present reality, which cannot be excluded as we rethink the relationship between human beings and the environment" (no. 143). Pope Francis sees the main threat in consumerism. "A consumerist vision of human beings, encouraged by the mechanisms of today's globalized economy, has a leveling effect on cultures, diminishing the immense variety which is the heritage of all humanity. . . . There is a need to respect the rights of peoples and cultures, and to appreciate that the development of a social group presupposes an historical process which takes place within a cultural context and demands the constant and active involvement of local people *from within their proper culture.* Nor can the notion of quality of life be imposed from without, for quality of life must be pursued within the world of symbols and customs proper to each human group" (no. 144).

Pope Francis especially decries the exploitation and degradation of cultures. "The disappearance of a culture can be just as serious or even more serious, than the disappearance of a species of plant or animal. . . . [I]t is essential to show special care for indigenous communities and their cultural traditions. They are not merely one minority among others, but should be the principal dialogue partners, especially when large projects affecting their land are proposed. For them, land is not a commodity but rather a gift from God and from their ancestors who rest there, a sacred space with which to interact if they are to maintain their identity and values" (no. 145-46). In an age when neoliberal globalization is steamrolling societies and cultures, commercializing and commodifying everything, Pope Francis' call for "a bold cultural revolution" (no. 114) is urgent.

Ecology of Daily Life. "Authentic development includes efforts to bring about an integral development in the quality of life, and this entails considering the setting in which people live their lives" (no. 147). In other words, the integral development of Paul VI, the development of the whole man and of every man, must include consideration of the environment, which "influence[s] the way we think, feel and act. In our rooms, our homes, our workplace and neighborhoods, we use our environment as a way of expressing our identity" (no. 147). When our environment is disorderly, chaotic, or noisy, we are not integrated and happy.

The encyclical mentions the renovation and beautification of inner cities, the protection of public areas where the poor congregate from criminal activity, the environmentally-friendly design of buildings, neighborhoods, and public spaces, lack of housing which is a major issue for human ecology, unsanitary slums or dangerous tenements, ecologically-safe systems of public transport available to those who cannot afford the means of private transport as part and parcel of the ecology of daily life. Another profound reality necessary for a more dignified environment is based on what Benedict XVI called an "ecology of man," the recognition that "our body itself establishes us in a direct relationship with the environment and with other living things. The acceptance of our bodies as God's gift is vital for welcoming and accepting the entire world as a gift from the Father and our common home . . . Learning to accept our body, to care for it and to respect its fullest meaning, is an essential element of any genuine human ecology" (no. 155).

The Common Good. A central and unifying principle of social ethics is the common good, "the sum of those conditions of social life which allow social groups and their individual members relatively thorough and ready access to their fulfillment." At a time when there is not much mention of the common good in philosophical and public discourse, it is imperative to be reminded that human ecology is inseparable from the common good: the good of each and every person is ultimately the common good, and vice versa. "Underlying the principle of the common good is respect for the human person as such, endowed with basic and inalienable rights ordered to his and her integral development. . . . In the present condition of global society, where injustices abound and growing numbers of people are deprived of basic human rights and considered expendable, the principle of the common good immediately becomes, logically and inevitably, a summons to solidarity and a preferential option for the poorest of our brothers and sisters. . . . [T]his option is in fact an ethical imperative essential for effectively attaining the common good" (no. 157-58).

Intergenerational Justice. "The notion of the common good extends to future generations. . . . Intergenerational solidarity is not optional, but rather a basic question of justice, since the world we have received also belongs to those who will follow us. . . . 'The environment is part of the logic of receptivity. It is on loan to each generation, which must then hand it on to the next.' An integral ecology is marked by this broader vision" (no. 159). "What kind of a world do we want to leave to those who come after us, to children who are now growing up? . . . We need to see that what is at stake is our own dignity. Leaving an inhabitable planet to future generations is, first and foremost, up to us. The issue is one which dramatically affects us, for it has to do with the ultimate meaning of our earthly sojourn" (no. 160-62). We need a renewed sense of intragenerational solidarity and justice, in which an option for the poor is a priority, and an urgent moral need for intergenerational solidarity and justice.

Thus, Pope Francis' "integral" ecology respects the integrity of creation, calls for an integrated approach in the analysis of environmental problems and for the search of integrated solutions to ecological degradation and devastation across generations.

***

Chapter 5 of *Laudato Si'*, subtitled "Lines of Approach and Action," outlines the paths of dialogue which can help us escape the spiral of self-destruction which currently engulfs us. It begins by pointing out that "interdependence obliges us to think of *one world with a common plan*. . . . A global consensus is essential for confronting the deeper problems, which cannot be resolved by unilateral actions on the part of individual countries" (no. 164). Among the worldwide problems mentioned are: highly polluting fossil fuels, the protection of biodiversity and desertification, climate change, the elimination of extreme poverty, the scandalous level of consumption. The encyclical calls for dialogue on the environment in the international community, dialogue for new national and local policies, dialogue and transparency in decision-making, politics, and economy in dialogue for human fulfillment, and religions in dialogue with science.

Laudato Si' is notable for statements like these: "Politics must not be subject to the economy, not should the economy be subject to the dictates of an efficiency-driven paradigm of technocracy" (no. 189); "[E]nvironmental protection cannot be assured solely on the basis of financial calculations of costs and benefits. The environment is one of those goods that cannot be adequately safeguarded or promoted by market forces. Once more, we need to reject a magical conception of the market" (no. 190); "[G]iven the insatiable and irresponsible growth produced over many decades, we need also to think of containing growth by setting some reasonale limits or even retracing our steps before it is too late" (no. 193); "The principle of the maximization of profits, frequently isolated from other considerations, reflects a misunderstanding of the very concept of the economy" (no. 195); "[E]conomics without politics cannot be justified, since this would make it impossible to favour other ways of handling the various aspects of the present crisis. The mindset which leaves no room for sincere concern for the environment is the same mindset which lacks concern for the inclusion of the most vulnerable members of society" (no. 196).

The sections ends: "Any technical solution which science claims to offer will be powerless to solve the serious problems of our world if humanity loses its compass, if we lose sight of the motivations which make it possible for us to live in harmony, to make sacrifices and to treat others well" (no. 200); "The gravity of the ecological crisis demands that we all look to the common good, embarking on a path of dialogue, which demands patience, self-discipline and generosity, always keeping in mind that 'realities are greater than ideas'" (no. 201).

***

The last chapter is devoted to "Ecological Education and Spirituality," whose premise is that "it is we human beings above all who need to change. We lack an awareness of our common origin, of our mutual belonging, and of a future to be shared with everyone" (no. 202).

A New Lifestyle. "Compulsive consumerism is one example of how the techno-economic paradigm affects individuals. Romano Guardini had already seen this: 'The gadgets and technics forced upon him by the patterns of machine production and of abstract planning mass man accepts quite simply; they are the forms of life itself'" (no. 203). "Obsession with a consumerist lifestyle, above all when few people are capable of maintaining it, can only lead to violence and mutual destruction" (no. 204). "Yet all is not lost. Human beings, while capable of the worst, are also capable of rising above themselves, choosing again what is good, and making a new start, despite their mental and social conditioning. We are able to take an honest look at ourselves, to acknowledge our deep dissatisfaction, and to embark on new paths to authentic freedom" (no. 205).

A New Covenant. Environmental education should broaden its goals beyond being centered on scientific information, consciousness-raising, and the prevention of environmental risks. It should aim at developing an ethics of ecology and of creating an ecological citizenship. The encyclical stresses the importance of the family in developing educational sensibility and a generous spirit. "In the face of the so-called culture of death, the family is the heart of the culture of life" (no. 213). Political and religious institutions have also an important role to play in ecological education. Lastly, "the relationship between a good aesthetic education and the maintenance of a healthy environment cannot be overlooked.' By learning to see and appreciate beauty, we learn to reject self-interested pragmatism. . . . Our efforts at education will be inadequate and ineffectual unless we strive to promote a new way of thinking about human beings, life, society and our relationship with nature" (no. 215).

Ecological Conversion. For Christians, "the ecological crisis is also a summons to a profound interior conversion.... [W]hat they all need is an 'ecological conversion,' whereby the effects of their encounter with Jesus Christ become evident in their relationship with the world around them. Living our vocation to be protectors of God's handiwork is essential to a life of virtue; it is not an optional or secondary aspect of our Christian experience." (no. 217). This conversion entails gratitude that the world is God's loving gift, a loving awareness that we are not disconnected with other creatures, but joined in splendid universal communion, and generous care for all of God's creation.

Ecological conversion resides in "Christian spirituality [which] proposes an alternative understanding of the quality of life, and encourages a prophetic and contemplative lifestyle, one capable of deep enjoyment free of the obsession with consumption.... Christian spirituality proposes a growth marked by moderation and the capacity to be happy with little. It is a return to that simplicity which allows us to stop and appreciate the small things, to be grateful for the opportunities which life affords us, to be spiritually detached from what we possess, and not to succumb to sadness for what we lack" (no. 222). Therein lie joy and peace which we all long for already on earth.

"Care for nature is part of a lifestyle which includes the capacity for living together and communion.... Love, overflowing with small gestures of mutual care, is also civic and political, and makes itself felt in every action that seeks to build a better world. Love for society and commitment to the common good are outstanding expressions of a charity which affects not only relasionhips but also 'macro-relationships, social, economic and political ones'" (no. 228, 231). Thus, ecological conversion leads us to the conviction that love of God and of neighbor must also find expression in civic and political love, love for the least of God's creatures, animal and human, for the earth, and for society.

Trinitarian Sacramentality. Sacramentality is a uniquely Catholic idea, the privileged way in which God took human form in Jesus and takes up all the elements of his creation, inorganic and organic, life in animal and human forms, and makes of them effective signs of his presence and grace. Sacramentality culminates in "the Eucharist [which] joins heaven and earth; it embraces and penetrates all creation. The world which came forth from God's hands returns to him in blessed and undivided adoration: in the bread of the Eucharist, 'creation is projected towards divinization, towards the holy wedding feast, towards unification with the Creator himself.'

Thus, the Eucharist is also a source of light and motivation for our concerns for the environment, directing us to be stewards of all creation" (no. 236).

"The world was created by the three Persons [of the Blessed Trinity] acting as a single divine principle, but each one of them performed this common work in accordance with his own personal property. Consequently, 'when we contemplate with wonder the universe in all its grandeur and beauty, we must praise the whole Trinity.'. . . The divine Persons are subsistent relations, and the world created according to the divine model, is a web of relationships. Creatures tend towards God, and in turn it is proper to every living being to tend towards other things, so that throughout the universe we can find any number of constant and secretly interwoven relationships. This leads us not only to marvel at the manifold connections existing among creatures, but also to discover a key to our own fulfillment. The human person grows more, matures more and is sanctified more to the extent that he or she enters into relationships, going out from themselves to live in communion with God, with others and with all creatures. In this way, they make their own Trinitarian dynamism which is imprinted in them when they were created. Everything is interconnected, and this invites us to develop a spirituality of that global solidarity which flows from the mystery of the Trinity" (no. 240).

"Mary, the Mother who cared for Jesus, now cares with maternal affection and pain for this wounded world. Just as her pierced heart mourned for the death of Jesus, so now she grieves for the sufferings of the crucified poor and for the creatures of this world laid waste by human power. . . . At her side in the Holy Family of Nazareth, stands the figure of Saint Joseph. Through his work and generous presence, he cared for and defended Mary and Jesus from the violence of the unjust . . . He too can teach us how to care; he can inspire us to work with generosity and tenderness in protecting this world which God has entrusted to us" (no. 241-42).

"We are journeying towards the Sabbath of eternity, the new Jerusalem, towards our common home in heaven" (no. 243), the encyclical ends with a prayer for our earth and a Christian prayer in union with creation.

Laudato Si' is at once an act of faith in humanity, an act of hope in the future, and an act of love for all of God's creation.

Conclusion

I leave the last word to Lynn White, Jr. (1967):

> Both our present science and our present technology are so tinctured with the orthodox Christian arrogance

toward nature that no solution for our ecologic crisis can be expected from them alone. Since the roots of our trouble are so largely religious, the remedy must also be essentially religious, whether we call it that or not. We must rethink and refeel our nature and destiny. The profoundly religious, but heretical, sense of the primitive Franciscans for the spiritual autonomy of all parts of nature may point a direction. I propose Francis as a patron saint for ecologists.

4

THEOLOGICAL PARADIGM SHIFTS AT VATICAN II

2015 marks the fiftieth anniversary of the closing of the Second Vatican Ecumenical Council (1962-65). Vatican II, as it is more commonly referred to, is the most significant event in the history of Catholicism and of Christianity, for that matter, in the twentieth century, if not since Martin Luther's Reformation in the sixteenth century. What exactly happened at Vatican II? The battle for the meaning of Vatican II continues unabated between conservatives and liberal Catholics (Faggioli 2012). Some argue for the continuity of Vatican II with previous periods of the Catholic Church, which ultimately means that nothing significant happened at the Council. Some even repudiate the teachings of the Council as a betrayal of traditional Catholicism; at Vatican II, they hold, the Catholic Church succumbed to the spirit of the modern age.

Dramatic changes happened at Vatican II. These changes can even be considered seismic shifts in the Catholic Church's doctrinal and moral teachings, its life and liturgy, its discipline and governance, and its relationship to other Christian churches, other religions, and the world. In a nutshell at the Second Vatican Ecumenical Council the Catholic Church made a *rapprochement* with the modern world, which since its emergence in the long nineteenth century, the Church had adamantly opposed. To understand therefore what the Catholic Church achieved at Vatican II, it is necessary to take a look at the historical reality of modernity, its values and orientations, its demands and conditions, which unfolded in the nineteenth century. To grasp the meaning and implications of the *aggiornamento* or updating that John XXIII laid down as the overarching program of Vatican II, it is urgent to comprehend the Roman Catholicism that was constructed in the nineteenth century in opposition to the modern world.

In the best one-volume account of Vatican II, John O'Malley (2008) identifies three issues-under-the-issues, underlying issues of which various issues were surface manifestations: 1) the problem of change in the Church, subsumed under the heading of the development of doctrine; 2) the relationship of center to periphery, that is, how authority is properly distributed between the papacy and the rest of the Church; and 3) the style or model according to which authority should be exercised. But before all else, O'Malley (2008: 53-92) in his second chapter discusses "the long nineteenth century" which constitutes the background of the deliberations and debates at the Council, specifically the Italian *Risorgimento*, modernity, liberalism, and the negative stance that various papacies took in opposition to them.

Similarly, the most important volume of essays (Schultenover 2015), originally published in *Theological Studies*, commemorating the 50the anniversary of Vatican II, starts off with a long 39-page preface by Stephen Schloesser (2015: xi-l) on the historical preconditions of a paradigm shift in the reform of Vatican II. He spends roughly 70 percent of it on the long 19th century (from the Enlightenment to the beginning of World War I) and 25 percent from World War I to the present. It is a shift from reproach to *rapprochement* which continues to collide. "The paradigm shift in the reform of Vatican II," according to Scholesser (2015: l), "may not always (or even often) have informed magisterial documents during the half century following it (1965-2015). Yet it remains waiting in the wings, ever ready for the wise scribe – in words used by Paul VI when paying homage to Leo XIII – who 'knows how to bring both new and old things out' of the Church's treasure-house."

Earlier, on the 25th anniversary of Vatican II, Giacomo Martina (1988) gave a much narrower historical context of the Council. The period from 1945 to 1959 was marked by significant changes in the world: the end of colonialism and the rise of the Third World, rapid and intense industrialization transforming agricultural societies into industrial ones, dramatic changes in the mentality and consumerist lifestyles of people brought about by the spread of television. "The Church of October 1958," Martina (1988: 13) averred, was "a church on the defensive, immobile, in the face of a rapidly changing world." Still obsessed in extirpating the amorphous evil of modernism, the church hierarchy was also beset by calls for a more open attitude towards democracy after the defeat of Fascism and

Nazism and in the face of Communism, by new theological and pastoral orientations, exemplified in questions raised by church-state relations and concordats a la Franco's Spain and debates on worker-priests and artificial birth control. Martina recalled the intransigence shown by the Papacy and the Roman Curia to the disciplined theologians who will play a large role at Vatican II. He sketched "the preconciliar ecclesiastical atmosphere in Rome," concretized in the courses he took at the Gregorian University, which had to be cleared by opening the windows at Vatican II.

I take a slightly different approach. First, I explain and utilize Thomas Kuhn's theory of scientific revolutions, which coincidentally appeared in the very year, 1962, that Vatican II opened but which has undergone revision. Second, following Eric Hobsbawm's trilogy on the long nineteenth century – *The Age of Revolution* (1962), *The Age of Capital* (1975), and *The Age of Empire* (1987) – I discuss three theological paradigm shifts involved at Vatican II, which more or less encompass the significant conflicts and changes at the Council. These are: "the Age of Reason" is about the shift from faith to reason, characterized by the Enlightenment; "the Age of Liberty" involves the shift from absolutism to liberty, typified by the French Revolution, and "the Age of Equality" concerns the shift from hierarchy to equality, evidenced by the spread of democracy, all three of which are aspirations and orientations of the modern age against which the Catholic Church fought. This paper therefore is an exercise in the historical sociology of religion, specifically that of theological or religious knowledge.

Thomas Kuhn and Paradigm Shifts

It was a perennial question. How does scientific knowledge grow? What accounts for the increase in scientific knowledge? How do scientists acquire and further develop scientific knowledge? The usual answer is: slowly and progressively by additional research and studies, by replication and continued experimentation, by further hypothesis-testing and theory-building. But how do great advances in science happen? What accounts for scientific breakthroughs? What occurs when giant strides in science are achieved? There is Isaac Newton's aphorism, "if I have seen farther, it is by standing on the shoulders of giants," which Robert Merton (1985) spun into a whimsical tale of intuitive leaps, false starts, mistakes, loose ends, and happy accidents that actually clutter up the subterranean of scientific inquiry. On the more serious level, Merton (1973) in his sociology of science made a sharp distinction between science as a cognitive system and science as a social system. As a sociologist, he proffered competency only over the latter.

In contrast to the common image of scientific development and progress as a linear, albeit with numerous digressions, pitfalls, and false byways, process of cumulative knowledge, Thomas Kuhn (1970) argued such a process cannot explain scientific breakthroughs, such as the revolutionary leaps in scientific achievement from Ptolemy's geocentric to Copernicus' heliocentric theory of the earth revolving around the sun in astronomy, from Priestley's phlogiston to Lavoisier's oxygen theory of combustion in chemistry, and from Newton's laws of gravitation and motion to Einstein's relativity theory of space and time in physics. Such scientific revolutions which are non-developmental episodes play a greater role in scientific advancement. They are not mere accretions to accumulated bodies of knowledge, but each constituted a revolutionary "transformation of the scientific imagination" which resulted in a new conceptual framework through which scientists viewed reality and the world.

Such scientific revolutions, new ways of seeing and thinking, were made possible by changes in scientific paradigms. Thus, paradigm change constituted the structure of scientific revolutions. Paradigms, as defined by Kuhn (1970: viii), were "universally recognized scientific achievements that for a time provide model problems and solutions to a community of practitioners." Margaret Masterman (1970) identifies three categories: metaphysical, sociological, and construct paradigms. At the broadest level of generality, paradigm refers to unquestioned presuppositions, metatheoretical assumptions regarding the object of study, which are not usually made explicit, but which underlie and guide research and study. More restricted is the meaning of paradigm as a disciplinary matrix which represents the shared commitments of a disciplinary community, including symbolic generalizations, beliefs, and values. And the most restricted use is paradigms as exemplars, referring to the concrete accomplishments of a scientific community which serve as shared examples, "a time-tested and group-licensed way of seeing" (Kuhn 1970: 189) in concrete problem-solving. In a postscript to the second edition of his book, Kuhn (1970: 187) states that "the paradigm as shared example is the central element of what I take to be the most novel and least understood aspect of this book."

Two aspects are central to the theory of paradigm change: the cognitive nature of the paradigm, and the community structure of its practitioners. A paradigm provides the framework of assumptions, disciplinary matrix, and exemplars, with which a community of scholars pursues its work. It defines the types of questions that may legitimately be asked, the types of explanations that must be sought, the types of solutions that are considered acceptable, as well as, the methods of inquiry suitable for studying them.

But what is equally, if not more, important is the structure of the group which collectively holds a paradigm. A community of scientists provides the possibility of consensus with regard to assumptions, symbolic generalizations, beliefs, values, and, most of all, exemplars which constitute a paradigm. A shared paradigm creates a scientific community: a professional grouping with common assumptions, interests, journals, and channels of communication. Thus, a paradigm both presupposes and demands an integrated community of practitioners. The communal nature of a paradigm is of the essence of the concept, and constitutes the sociological base of Kuhn's theory of paradigm change in scientific revolutions. In fact, Kuhn (1970: 176) in his aforementioned postscript writes that "if this book were being rewritten, I would therefore open with a discussion of the community structure of science."

The period of scientific development by accumulation, of scientific progress through accretion is called by Kuhn as the period of normal science. It is a period characterized by the stability of a paradigm. The scientific community does its work within the parameters of a given dominant paradigm. Normal scientific activity primarily consists in "puzzle-solving" within the confines of the dominant paradigm. The members of the scientific community undertake their work, pursue their efforts within the boundaries of the accepted paradigm; they do not question but accept, explicitly or implicitly, the assumptions, the disciplinary matrix, and the exemplars of the given paradigm. They are locked in, as it were, within the worldview of the established framework which guides the direction of normal research. Anomalies are set to one side, or accommodated by *ad hoc* modifications. Normal scientific activity is essentially one of building on previous research based on the accepted paradigm, of finding answers to still outstanding questions with the use and within the purview of the same paradigm. This is the common image of scientific knowledge as proceeding from replication and accumulation from previous study and research.

When problems accumulate and "puzzles" mount that remain impervious to solution despite repeated attempts to solve them within the framework of the given paradigm, the state of "normal science" gives way to a period of crisis. Crisis leads the scientific community to examine its assumptions and to search for alternatives. Doubts and questions are raised about the paradigm itself, about its symbols, beliefs, values, and exemplars. The period of crisis is a period in which questions of basic theoretical and methodological significance are examined. The hitherto coherent scientific tradition with its networks of conceptual, theoretical, instrumental, and methodological commitments is subjected to ferment and turmoil. Out of the crisis, a new paradigm emerges – or several new ones or parts of new ones appear – which challenges the worldview of the old dominant paradigm.

When the new paradigm shows itself supreme over the old paradigm in its capacity to solve problems and puzzles left unsolved, it gains ascendancy and acceptance, initially by a small group of practitioners. When the new paradigm earns general acceptance by the scientific community at large, the old paradigm is displaced and declared bankrupt, and the new paradigm becomes the dominant exemplar in scientific research. Scientific activity returns once more to the state of normal science.

A major change of paradigms has far-reaching consequences that it amounts to a scientific revolution. Scientists usually resist such upheavals which subvert assumptions and commitments that have permeated their thinking. Adoption of a new paradigm demands a gestalt switch which produces a consequent shift in views, a new way of raising questions and seeking solutions worthy of scientific inquiry. It involves a veritable "conversion" of the scientific imagination which results in the transformation not only of the world in which scientific work is pursued but also of the world which is the very object of scientific work.

From this it becomes apparent that Kuhn has moved beyond the traditional concerns of the sociology of science. Thomas Kuhn has replaced Robert Merton in the basic constellation of problems that the sociology of science has to tackle. His theory both applies to the content and methodology of science and accounts for the sociological underpinning of scientific ideas and methods. To formulate it differently: unlike Merton's approach, Kuhn does not separate the cognitive system and the social system of science. Paradigm stability and change, normal science and scientific revolutions involve both the cognitive and social systems of science. Changes in the cognitive and social systems of science account for paradigm change and scientific revolutions.

Thomas Kuhn's *The Structure of Scientific Revolutions* has deservedly become the most influential and debated book in the history, philosophy, and sociology of science since it was published in 1962. Its impact has been felt in diverse fields of inquiry, leading students of various disciplines to assess the utility and relevance of his theory of scientific revolutions to their own concerns (Gutting 1980).

A main difficulty, however, needs to be pointed out. Thomas Kuhn applied his theory to revolutions in the so-called hard sciences. A scientific revolution in the hard sciences happens when one paradigm is displaced by another. Paradigms in the hard sciences are incommensurable. One completely replaces another. Two or more paradigms cannot co-exist. Thus, to take an example, the Copernican revolution in astronomy completely negated the Ptolemaic conception of the universe. With the triumph of the Copernican worldview, nothing of the Ptolemaic view remained. The question therefore is: can the Kuhnian theory of paradigm change be applied to the so-called soft sciences, to the humanities, the behavioral sciences, to theology and religious studies?

George Ritzer (1983: 430-42), for example, applied Kuhn's ideas to present a schema for analyzing sociological theory. True to the sense of Kuhn's key concept, he understands paradigm in three usages. It serves to differentiate one scientific community from another, for example, physics from chemistry, sociology from psychology. It can be used to differentiate between different historical stages in the development of a science, the paradigm that dominated nineteenth century physics, for example, from that of the twentieth century. Paradigms can also be utilized to differentiate among subcommunities *within* the same science. Thus, contemporary psychoanalysis, for example, is differentiated in Freudian, Jungian, and Horneyian paradigms. Attending to the third usage, Ritzer (1975; 1983: 434-35) argued that sociology is also a multiple-paradigm science, which he labels as the social facts paradigm, the social definition paradigm, and the social behavior paradigm.

In three masterworks, Hans Kung (1992, 1995, 2007) utilized the concepts of paradigm and paradigm change to chart the historical and theological developments in the three monotheistic religions of Judaism, Christianity, and Islam as a succession of paradigm changes. He first identified the abiding substance of the faith in Judaism, Christianity, and Islam. This remains constant throughout the historical changes each religion experiences and undergoes, throughout the controversies and debates each religion is subjected to. But this abiding substance of the faith takes on different historical forms. Theology is a dialectic between challenge and response. Different understandings of the truth of the faith and different emphases in the practice of the faith appear in history depending on the challenges faith faces, the problems it has to solve, the threats to its integrity, and the dangers in its beliefs and practices. It is these historical forms that Kung differentiated and categorized under the heading of paradigm changes. Thus, Kung was able to clarify the basic continuity and the historical discontinuities in the history of each religion, to highlight what is new and what is opposed, resisted, and debated in each paradigmatic period.

Hans Kung's panoramic survey of the theological histories of the Judaism, Christianity, and Islam in terms of the paradigm changes each has undergone is no mere chronological periodization of their histories.

While the abiding substance of the faith in each religion is constant, Kung identified the dramatic changes each has taken in its historical forms, categorizing them under the headings of distinctive paradigms. Each paradigm, therefore, constitutes an epoch-making basic model in historical form, characterized by a constellation of distinctive presuppositions, orientations, values, and beliefs. With the use of paradigms to delineate historical forms, Kung made better and clearer sense of historical development; he indicated new thematic and methodological insights a la the *longue duree* of the new historiography; he showed systemic changes in history of the decisive variables of religion against the background of its fundamental constants.

More importantly, the paradigm shifts each religion has taken in its theological history allowed Hans Kung to do several things. First, it allowed him to point out that some historical changes are in historical fidelity to what is abiding and constant, while some historical changes are in radical discontinuity with and even perhaps perversions of the original message, the decisive revelation event, and the distinguishing feature of the faith. Paradigm change always involves gains and losses. Kung evaluated what is gained and what is lost against the constant center and abiding substance of the religious faith. Second, it enabled him to show that some historical forms of the faith have become absolutized, rendered immutable because declared to be of the abiding substance when in reality they are only historically contingent. He emphasized the relativity of historical developments and therefore the need to contextualize developments alleged to have been ordained with divine sanction. Third, it permitted him to raise questions about the possibility of changes in historical forms to meet new challenges, to answer different questions, to inculturate in indigenous cultures, to continue to be relevant in postmodern times. At strategic stages in his paradigmatic narrative of the theological histories of the three religions, he offered critical and self-critical questions and reflections based on the paradigmatic change in historical form he had just discussed (Litonjua 2011).

I myself have utilized Kunh's paradigm theory to make sense of the breakthrough wrought by Latin American liberation theology, which Joseph Gremillion (1976: 136) believed was "the first school of theological thought to arise outside of Western Europe since that of the Cappadocians and Eastern Church colleagues of 400-600 A.D." While the perennial theological task is *fides quaerens intellectum*, faith seeking understanding, the task undergoes different modalities, emphases, and directions due to the broader social and ecclesial contexts theology finds itself in, to the different challenges it has to confront and respond to. The broader social context was that of the underdevelopment and dependency of the Third World, while the wider ecclesial context was the reforms of Vatican II and Medellin. In response, Latin American theology focused on the theological task as critical reflection on praxis, on theology as addressed to the non-person, and as a theology of and for liberation (Litonjua 1998). I contented that these were aspects or characteristics of the paradigm shift that Latin American liberation theology enacted in theology.

Utilizing once more Thomas Kuhn's theory of paradigm change, I try to make sense and clarify the significant changes wrought by the Second Vatican Council (1962-65) in Catholicism through three shifts in paradigm: from faith to reason, from absolutism to liberty, and from hierarchy to equality. These shifts undertaken by Vatican II amount to the Catholic Church's *rapprochement* or armistice with modernity and the modern world. The presentation therefore for each of the paradigm changes takes place in three steps: a brief understanding of the paradigms of faith, absolutism, and hierarchy in pre-modern times which also governed Catholicism, the shifts in paradigm to reason, liberty, and equality introduced by the Enlightenment, the French Revolution, and the Democratic Revolution respectively, which the Catholic Church reproached, opposed, and condemned – but whose condemnations I will not dwell upon – and the changes at and of Vatican II that indicate and represent them as paradigm changes of *rapprochement* with and acceptance of the modern world.

Faith and the Age of Reason

Charles Taylor (2007: 25-26) encapsulates the main concern of his *magnum opus, A Secular Age*, in this question: "why was it virtually impossible not to believe in God in, say, 1500 in our Western society, while in 2000 many of us find this not only easy, but even inescapable?" His initial answer is that "many features of their world told in favor of belief, made the presence of god seemingly undeniable," of which he highlights three:

> (1)The natural world they lived in, which had its place in the cosmos they imagined, testified to divine purpose and action, and not just in the obvious way which we can still understand and (at least many of us) appreciate today, that its order and design bespeaks creation; but also the great events in this natural order, storms, droughts, floods, plagues, as well as years of exceptional fertility

and flourishing, were seen as acts of God, as now the dead metaphor of our legal language still bears witness.

(2) God was also implicated in the very existence of society (but not described as such – this is a modern term – rather as polis, kingdom, church, or whatever). A kingdom could only be conceived as grounded in something higher as mere human action in secular time. And beyond that, the life of various associations which make up society, parishes, boroughs, guilds, and so on, were interwoven with ritual and worship . . . One could not but encounter God everywhere.

(3) People lived in an "enchanted" world. This is perhaps not the best expression; it seems to evoke light and fairies. But I am invoking here its negation, Weber's expression "disenchantment" as a description of our modern condition. This term has achieved such wide currency in our discussion of these matters, that I'm going to use its antonym to describe a crucial feature of the pre-modern condition. The enchanted world in this sense is the world of spirits, demons, and moral forces which our ancestors lived in.

It was, in other words, an Age of Faith. The palpable sense of the divine shone through and penetrated the "porous self" of pre-modern "man," as sunlight passes through a multi-colored stained glass, not as it does through a dark tinted glass, dimly, of the "buffered self" of the modern individual, as Taylor describes them. "There has been a titanic change in our western civilization. We have changed not just from a condition where most people lived most 'naively' in a construal (part Christian, part related to 'spirits' of pagan origin) as simple reality; to one in which almost no one is capable of this, but all see their option as one of many. We all learn to navigate between two standpoints: an 'engaged' one in which we live as best as we can the reality our standpoint opens us to; and a 'disengaged one in which we are able to see ourselves as occupying one standpoint among a range of possible ones, with which we have in various ways to coexist" (Taylor 2007: 12).

The rupture began with the Enlightenment, an intellectual movement that began in England in the 17th century, developed in France and spread to Germany in the 18th century, and eventually affected all of Europe and every sphere of human life and thought. It was a philosophical outlook that was critical of religious knowledge claims and of the social and political authoritarian claims of the state. It considered human reason, and human reason alone, as solely adequate to comprehend the world and to deal with human problems. The Age of Enlightenment was the Age of Reason. Kant, the greatest of the Enlightenment thinkers, described enlightenment as the emergence of man from his self-imposed infancy. It is infancy because it is the inability to use one's reason without the guidance of another. It is self-imposed because it does not arise from the deficiency of reason itself, but from the lack of courage to use it without external guidance. Thus, the watchword of the Enlightenment: *Sapere aude!* Have the courage to use your reason!

It was not as if there was no concern with and appreciation for human reason before the Enlightenment. Christian theologians, for one, taught that whereas there are truths inaccessible to human reason and known only by faith, there are also truths that human reason can discover about God. Above all, they sought to show the compatibility of the revealed truths of faith with human reason, their credibility. It was the theological task, in the formulation of St Anselm, of *fides quaerens intellectum*, faith seeking understanding. "For Aquinas, the human intellect has a natural light that suffices to attain certain truths; therefore, man does not need any special illumination to reach true knowledge, as Augustine held. According to Aquinas [via Aristotle], true knowledge comes from experience, which we acquire through our senses rather than from 'above'; sensory cognition, in turn, is subject to the process of abstraction, and it is by means of this process that we attain intellectual knowledge of reality" (Fidora 2012: 46).

But the general mental atmosphere and cultural ethos of premodern times was one of faith, not of reason. Thus, the Enlightenment was contrasted with the supposed darkness of irrationality and superstition of medieval times. The leading beliefs shared by Enlightenment thinkers were: the central capacity of reason enables man to think and to act correctly; all men and women are equal in respect of their rationality; humanity as individuals and as a whole can progress to perfection; tolerance is to be extended to other creeds and ways of life; beliefs are to be accepted on the basis of reason, not on the authority of priests, sacred texts, or tradition. "Thus, Enlightenment thinkers tended to atheism, or at most to a purely natural and rational deism, shorn of supernatural and miraculous elements and designed primarily to support an enlightened moral code and, in some cases, to account for the fact that the universe is a rational system, wholly accessible to human reason. The Enlightenment devalues local 'prejudices' and customs which owe their development to historical peculiarities rather than to the exercise of reason. What matters . . . is that one is an individual man, united in brotherhood with all other men by the rationality one shares with them. In general, the Enlightenment plays down the non-rational aspects of human nature" (Inwood 1995: 236).

Anthony Pagden (2013: ix) waxes eloquent on why the Enlightenment still matters:

> The "Enlightenment" – that period of European history between, roughly, the last decade of the seventeenth century and the first of the nineteenth – has had a far greater and more lasting impact on the formation of the modern world than any of the intellectual convulsions that preceded it. The Renaissance and the Reformation, although they too transformed the cultures of Europe, and subsequently the whole of Christianity, in irreversible ways, are for most people today simply periods in history. Not so the Enlightenment. If we regard ourselves as modern, if we are forward-looking, if we are tolerant and generally open-minded, if stem-cell research does not frighten us but fundamentalist religious beliefs do, then we tend to think of ourselves as "enlightened." And thinking this, we are in effect declaring ourselves to be the heirs, however distant, of a particular intellectual and cultural movement [called the Enlightenment].

There has been much criticism today of Enlightenment values, such that we are told we are now living in postmodern times. I will address three issues that have validity. First, the Enlightenment is accused for its sole reliance on reason, which supremacy of reason led to the excesses of the French Revolution that enthroned a prostitute as goddess of reason on the high altar of Notre Dame. There is no excusing the Reign of Terror. But the emphasis on reason must be understood in context, as is everything historical must be. To cite but one example: John Locke's *A Letter Concerning Toleration* appeared three years before Cotton Mather's witch chronicle, *Wonders of the Invisible World*. As pointed out by Adam Goodheart (2015) in his review of Stacy Schiff's *The Witches: Salem, 1692*: "The whole scholarly infrastructure of the 17th century – books, universities, learned societies – helped disseminate accounts of witchcraft and its dangers to the far ends of the Christian world." Salem of 1692 in which the accusations by children of the witchcraft of their elders, leading to their executions and hangings, is only the most salient example of the irrationality and insanity that prevailed in the premodern world.

Today, we indeed are living in postmodern times. After the pendulum had swung to its opposite extreme, it is now resting more in balance. The limits of reason are recognized, the importance of nonrational, not irrational, elements of life – faith, love, emotions, intuition, experience – are accepted, without giving up on reason and rationality. The best compliment to the Enlightenment, however, is that we know the limits of reason by the use of reason itself.

Second, the Enlightenment is criticized for positing universals that apply primarily to males, ignoring "difference," "the other," what was considered "alien." True enough in that the Enlightenment did not give importance to what we not consider significant: gender, race, ethnicity, sexual orientation and identity, for example. But the Enlightenment's drive towards universals derived from the heroic attempt to be "free from prejudice, the burden of accumulated customs, and the slavish devotion to false beliefs" (Pagden 2013: 149), to accord each "man," if you will, his innate dignity, rights, and destiny, to produce, as David Hume proposed, a secular ethics based on the science of man. In fact, the Enlightenment could be said to have secularized Christianity's basic idea that all of Eve's progeny belonged to a single community, which basic unity required that no distinction be made on the basis of origin, nation, or any other physical property. In fact, some of them, most notably Rousseau, went to the other extreme and considered savages as "noble," and among them no people had such a sublime character of mind as the savages of North America. "By the second half of the eighteenth century, however, any idealized image of the Amerindian as heroic or noble (or even 'good') savage had largely evaporated, to be replaced by the vision of a corrupted, despondent victim of European oppression" (Pagden 2013: 213).

Today, in post-Enlightenment times there is much emphasis on the differences between people, biologically derived or socially constructed, special rights and therefore privileged constituencies. At the same time, there continue to be violations of the rights of groups, based on ascribed and acquired statuses, outright physical violations of women, children, migrants, and the dispossessed, forgetting that we all share in something universally innate, our humanity.

Third, the Enlightenment is faulted for being "unhistorical," a battle cry of the Romantic Movement. "What the Romantics understood by 'unhistorical' was the Enlightenment rejection of the past as the source of tradition and of the allegiance to kin, hearth, king, and religion. In this respect, at least, they were very largely right" (Pagden 2013: 177).

There were many histories written during the period, Pagden (2013: 177) writes, "the more important ones were comparative studies of human actions and behavior. Their strategy was to employ the history of one particular people, or of one specific moment, to illustrate something about the history of the species as a whole." Moreover, "all of these histories . . . were attempts to construct a 'history of mankind,' a history . . . called 'philosophical historicism' – an account not of the simple facts of the past but of the *possibilities* that existed for human beings in time" (Pagden 2013: 179). No better testimony is given to the historical consciousness of the Enlightenment than that of Jurgen Habermas: "Thinkers from Vico to Condorcet . . . shifted the teleology of nature into the dimension of history," to which Pagden (2013: 180) adds, "And what that history would reveal was that the final destiny of the species must be the creation of a universal, cosmopolitan civilization."

The Enlightenment was the birth of modernity and the modern world, especially with its emphasis on reason, on the universal attributes of humans, and on the historicity of events and happenings. Historical consciousness will be very important in that it will tear away the absolutisms of church and state, the unchangeability of dogma and morals, and will reveal possibilities for the present and the future.

My first main point is that Vatican II initiated a paradigm shift from faith to reason, as the first step in its rapprochement with modernity, a shift that did not do away with faith but a shift that respected the necessity and autonomy of reason even in the understanding and practice of the Catholic religion, a shift therefore not along the lines of the hard sciences but of the soft sciences. Such a paradigm shift involved a change in the unquestioned presuppositions regarding faith and revelation, in the disciplinary matrix in which the community of faith lived and worked, and in the shared examples in ways of seeing and solving problems connected with religion. To put it succinctly, there must be *credibilitas* before there can be *credentitas*, teachings and practices must be reasonable and credible before they can be accepted and acted upon. They simply cannot be imposed from above, even with anathemas.

A few examples will suffice. In announcing the convocation of the Council on January 25, 1959, Pope John XXIII framed the purpose and program of the Council as one of *aggiornamento*, updating. Updating of what to what? What needed to be updated to what forms of updating? It could not be nostalgia, looking back to older, outdated ways of belief. It could not be restoration, as John Paul II and his cardinal-point man, Joseph Ratzinger, did, bringing back what has just been recently rejected. It could only be bringing up to date the doctrines, moral teachings, disciplinary rules, and social structures of the ecclesiastical institution to formulations and forms that meet the needs and aspirations of contemporary men and women. "It is a question of bringing the modern world into contact with the vivifying and perennial energies of the gospel," Pope John (Abbott 1966: 703) wrote in his Apostolic Constitution, *Humanae Salutis*, of December 25, 1961, officially convoking the Second Vatican Council. To achieve this, there had to be a cultural paradigm shift to more rational approaches to understanding the modern world, a world that is no longer of unitary faith, but one of dizzying pluralism of all sorts: of faiths and no faith, of philosophies, of ideologies, of ways of life, and of lifestyles.

In his opening address to the Council, *Gaudet Mater Ecclesia*, Pope John (Abbott 1966: 712-16) made three specific points: 1. He took note of the prophets of doom, who "in these modern times see nothing but prevarication and ruin." Instead, the Pope saw that "in the present order of things, Divine Providence is leading us to a new order of human relations which, by men's own efforts and even beyond their expectations are directed toward the fulfillment of God's superior and inscrutable designs. And everything, even human differences, leads to the greater good of the Church." 2. He pointed out that "the salient point of the council is not the discussion of one article or another of the fundamental doctrine of the Church." Instead, he called for presentations and formulations "studied and expounded through the methods of research and through the literary forms of modern thought. The substance of the ancient doctrine of the deposit of faith is one thing, and the way it is presented is another." 3. In opposing errors, he indicated that "nowadays the Spouse of Christ prefers to make us of the medicine of mercy rather than of severity. She considers that she meets the needs of the present day by demonstrating the validity of her teaching rather than by condemnations." With these points, Pope John distanced the Church from the policies of retrenchment and hostility to the modern world and the reign of intellectual terror toward Catholic thought and theology of the Piuses. He created an atmosphere of openness and freedom and an air of optimism and hope that will bear fruit aplenty in the Council.

As a result of the Council, the Mass was no longer an ancient rite in an alien tongue to which the people were mere spectators, but is a communal celebration of the Eucharist in which all the faithful are led to a full, conscious, and active participation, which is their right and duty by reason of their baptism. Revelation is not now narrowly understood as the truths revealed by God for human salvation, where the main concern is *intellectus fidei*, the intellectual adherence to the deposit of faith as authoritatively taught by the Church. Revelation is first and foremost God revealing himself and his love, which understanding enjoins Christians to discern the signs of the times in the aspirations of men and women, in the events and happenings in the world, and to respond to them in faith, justice, and love. The Church of Christ is not a *societas perfecta*, wholly sufficient unto itself, but is the people of God on pilgrimage, a sign and an instrument of the Kingdom of God to the world, to all peoples, nations, and times. Mission is not merely the conversion of pagans and the implantation of churches in foreign lands, often as in the past with the help and arms of colonialism, but is spreading and making present the Good News of Jesus Christ, the task of manifesting the love of God for all peoples and cultures, his design to give unity to all of humanity and to history its fulfillment. Understood this way, the term "missions" is unbiblical and meaningless. The whole Church is missionary.

But the most eloquent and heart-felt sign of this paradigm shift towards rapprochement with modernity is the opening paragraph of *Gaudium et Spes*, The Pastoral Constitution on the Church in the Modern World. "First," John O'Malley (2015a: 15) points out, "the title of the document is 'The Church *in* the Modern World,' not the Church for the modern world, nor the Church against the modern world. In other words, the Council recognizes as a fact of life that each and every one of us, even Church members, constitute the modern world. We cannot in any way step out of that reality, even if we want to. Therefore, neither can the Church step out of it." The opening paragraph in inclusive language reads:

> The joys and the hopes, the griefs and the anxieties of the people of this age, especially those who are poor or in any way afflicted, these too are the joys and hopes, the griefs and anxieties of the followers of Christ. Indeed, nothing genuinely human fails to raise an echo in their hearts. For theirs is a community of people united in Christ and led by the Holy Spirit in their journey to the kingdom of their Father; they have welcomed the news of their salvation which is meant for all of humanity. That is why this community realizes that it is truly and intimately linked with humanity and its history.

John O'Malley (20015c: 112; 2015d: 132) also emphasizes, and repeats in several of his publications, that one distinguishing characteristic of Vatican II is the "style" in which it formulated its enactments, a style which comports more with the sensibilities of contemporary men and women.

It most characteristically employed a vocabulary new for councils, a vocabulary filled with words implying collegiality, reciprocity, tolerance, friendship, and the search for common good. Instead of ignoring this distinctive feature, explanation and analysis of the documents' literary form seem to be indispensable for understanding the council....

The message of [Vatican II] speaks to our world today – a world wracked with discord, retaliations, hatred, bombs, preemptive attacks, wars, threats of wars, as if never to end. The message of the council is profoundly countercultural while at the same time responding to the deepest yearnings of the human heart: Peace on earth. Goodwill to men.

Absolutism and the Age of Liberty

Eamon Duffy (2011: 82) opens his vignette of Pope Paul III (1534-1549), one of his ten popes who shook the world, with these words:

By the beginning of the sixteenth century, the papacy was Europe's most important institution, the court of final appeal in tens of thousands of lawsuits, a centre of patronage and raw power. Imagine the EU headquarters, the United Nations and the International Court of Human Rights all rolled into one, and you begin to get the idea. And then add the World Bank, because in many ways the Pope and cardinals had become more like the chief executives of a global business corporation than priests of the Christian Gospel. Some of them, of course, were pious and conscientious; more were grizzled and experienced diplomats and power brokers. Wealth and power often made them forget their vocation – you did not have to be a priest to be a cardinal, and many had mistresses, and families turning into dynasties. They were also important patrons of art, science and learning: the world's best writers, painters and philosophers flocked to Rome to mop up some of the wealth swilling through the courts of the Pope and his cardinals.

It was a time of absolutes, underlined by a precise theory of power. All power is ultimately from God. But he has delegated power to the Pope in sacred things and to the Emperor in secular matters. Both Pope and Emperor ruled by divine right. But in the fifteenth century both Pope and Emperor lost their preeminence. The Great Schism of 1378-1417 showed that the pope had become merely one of the Italian princes, engaged in the incredibly complicated and unscrupulous game of Italian power politics. The new national monarchies in France, Spain, and England had their own territories in which Pope and Emperor could not interfere, having acquired, largely owing to gunpowder, power over and allegiance from their subjects. With the fall of Constantinople to the Turks in 1453, however, and the disappearance of the Eastern Empire, therefore, the Western Empire regained importance and began to flourish again, with the Papacy becoming the most important institution in Europe by the beginning of the sixteenth century. Hence, Eamon Duffy on Paul III.

But greater problems loomed on the horizon. Martin Luther in 1517 launched the Reformation which would leave all of Christendom divided against itself. But what destroyed the power and credibility of the Catholic Church, indeed of any church and religion itself, was the terrible Wars of Religion between the 1550s and 1650s, which left vast tracts of Europe in smoldering ruins, with millions, calculated at 5.75 million, dead in the carnage. The "Peace of Westphalia" in 1648 succeeded in creating lasting peace, with the formula *cuius regio eius religio,* the religion of the ruler is the religion of the region, the first treaty among sovereign nations, with the papacy the only party to the conflict to refuse to endorse the treaty. Westphalia transformed the disordered, divided monarchies of Europe into modern nation-states which they are today. The remarkable historical process that began with the Reformation in the sixteenth century, in the most widely repeated genealogy of the modern world, prepared the ground for the Enlightenment, which was followed by the Scientific Revolution and, in politics, the Democratic Revolution. But the seismic event, allowing for the interregnum of Napoleon, that really destroyed the absolutisms of church and state, of throne and altar, of pope and king was the French Revolution of 1789.

The French Revolution was a political upheaval of global importance. The fixed order of the *ancien regime* was already undermined by Enlightenment thinkers, but France was still governed by privileged groups – the nobility and the clergy – while the emergent productive forces, the bourgeoisie, were taxed heavily and the lower classes of peasants and farmers were subjected to forced labor and feudal dues. Put differently, France's economic and intellectual development was not matched by social and political changes. The direct and immediate cause of the upheaval was the chaotic state of government finance and the consequent loss of confidence in the state, which hid the powerful contradictory forces simmering under the surface. The usual focus of the narratives on the French Revolution is the heads rolling from under the guillotine, the fate of Louis XVI and Marie Antoinette, the conflict to the death between Jacobins and Girondists, and the reign of terror that ultimately consumed the revolution. But the French Revolution, which appeared to be nullified by the dictatorship of Napoleon, had far reaching consequences. It ended feudalism, it dissolved the absolutism of altar and throne, it cast into oblivion the divine right of kings. It threw open the floodgates of Enlightenment ideas: the freedom of the individual, the equality of citizens, tolerance of others, universality of human rights, a social contract between ruler and ruled, the separation of church and state, sovereignty of nations, national honor and pride. The French Revolution had an extraordinary effect in the making of the modern world.

Specifically, Anthony Pagden (2013: 389) observes:

> The liberals of the post-Revolutionary era, Alexis de Tocqueville, Benjamin Constant, and John Stuart Mill, saw the Revolution – for all its admitted excesses, for all that it had finally collapsed into the brief but bloody reign of Napoleon – as a necessary evil that ultimately cleared the way for the liberal-democratic order that ultimately came to replace the *ancient regime* throughout Europe. It had, as Tocqueville said of it in 1858, "regulated, coordinated, and legalized the effects of a great cause." That "great cause" was the cause of what today we might call loosely "liberal democracy," which, for all the suffering the West has undergone in the succeeding centuries (not to mention what the rest of the world has suffered at the hands of the West), is very much the political system under which most of us now live.

But it is precisely this liberal democracy that the Catholic Church had most difficulty with. Liberalism gives priority to the individual, while conservatism to tradition and social hierarchy over individual rights. Today, liberalism is usually equated with democracy, given its emphasis on individual political rights. But until the mid-twentieth century, most liberals were not democrats, since they believed that not everybody, such as women, the poor, and ethnic minorities, deserved such rights as the right to vote. Liberalism grew out of the conviction that toleration was the only alternative to the Wars of Religion. Both sides in the conflicts came to the conclusion that the state could not impose or assume a shared devotion to a single faith, and that the only stable basis for a political regime was to separate church and state. Liberalism has extended this principle from the sphere of religion to other areas of social life where citizens have conflicting beliefs. The term "liberal" has been stigmatized in the United States, forgetting that the Founding Fathers were liberals and that the Declaration of Independence and the Constitution are liberal documents. Liberalism is the only humane response to the inevitable pluralism and diversity of modern societies.

The Syllabus of Errors, a document containing eighty condemned theses, attached to Pius IX's encyclical *Quanta Cura* of December 8, 1864, anathematized political liberalism and the separation of church and state. With his loss of absolute temporal power over the Papal States, Pius IX grew more intransigent and had his absolute power over spiritual matters defined at Vatican I (1869-70). It is worth noting that Lord Acton uttered his famous aphorism – "Power tends to corrupt, and absolute power corrupts absolutely." – in connection with definition of papal infallibility at Vatican II to which he was opposed. At the same Council, the Catholic position on the relationship between church and state found expression in the thesis/hypothesis formula. The ideal or thesis was the union of church and state, and the model was Generalissimo Francisco Franco's Spain. In situations where it cannot be obtained, the hypothesis was toleration, until such time that it could be changed. The autocratic absolutism of the Papacy, the centralization of power and control in the Roman Curia, and the enfeeblement of the worldwide Episcopacy were meant to be bulwarks against the modern spirit and the values of the Enlightenment and the French Revolution.

It is no wonder then that the question of religious liberty was the most controversial topic debated at Vatican II. There was even what was called the "black week" during the third session of Vatican II (November 14-21, 1964), a series of events that caused disturbance among large members of the conciliar assembly, among which was the postponement of the vote on the much-awaited text on religious liberty (Tagle 2002: 387-452). The Catholic Church claimed religious liberty for itself, but is there also religious liberty for other churches, and can the state allow for that? John Courtney Murray had devoted his lifework to the proposition that the First Amendment of the U.S. Constitution – "Congress shall make no law respecting an establishment of religion, or prohibiting the free exercise thereof." – was not only compatible with Church teaching, but was the correct doctrinal and moral position on the separation of church and state. The Declaration on Religious Freedom, *Dignitatis Humanae,* was passed on December 7, 1965. It was a momentous paradigm shift from absolutism to liberty: it broke the relationship that was established by Constantine way back in 313. "A long standing ambiguity has finally been cleared up," Murray (1966: 673)) exulted. "The Church does not deal with the secular order in terms of a double standard: freedom for the Church when Catholics are a minority, privilege for the Church and intolerance for others when Catholics are a majority."

The Declaration states that the human person has a right to religious freedom, and that such a right has its foundation in the very dignity of the human person. The right entails two things, similar to the First Amendment of the U.S. Constitution: immunity from coercion, and immunity from restraint. The Declaration would clear up and open pathways to relationships with other Christian churches, to dialogue with Jews and other religions, to the promotion and defense of human rights for all people, and would bring new clarity to the relationship between church and state, between church and society, between church and world. But Murray left an unfinished agenda, and it remains unfinished fifty years since the end of Vatican II. A second argument needed to be set afoot, Murray (1966: 674) envisioned, "the theological meaning of Christian freedom. The children of God, who receive this freedom as a gift from their Father though Christ in the Holy Spirit, assert it within the Church as well as within the world, always for the sake of the world and the Church." The Catholic Church claims freedom for itself and other religions in the secular sphere. But it denies it to its members within the Church. Papa Wojtyla bestrode the world stage as a colossus for human rights, but he paternalistically treated Catholics as immature dependents. Ditto for Ratzinger as Cardinal-Prefect and Papa, although less flamboyantly.

A certain perversion, moreover, has crept into claims for religious liberty. Marilynne Robinson (2015) observes that "movements that present themselves as religiously motivated have now begun to regard the state as aggressively secular, and as enforcing secularism, precisely in maintaining institutional distance that was meant in the first place to protect religious freedom: they have begun to regard the state with a hectic moral aversion, and at the same time to meddle in or stymie public life by asserting a presence in governments national and local. The defense against these movements has often taken the form of secularism that is contemptuous of religion – religion for these purposes identical with the unbeautiful phenomenon that now so loudly claims the title for itself." She accuses this religious resurgence of having brought "a harshness, a bitterness, a crudeness, and high-mindedness into the public square . . . Its self-righteousness fuels the damnedest things – I used the word advisedly – notably the acquisition of homicidal weapons. I wonder what these supposed Biblicists find in the Gospels or the Epistles that could begin to excuse any of it." She alleges that "if the word [sin] is spoken now it is likely to be in one of those lately bold and robust big churches obsessed with sins Jesus never mentioned." She raises questions to those who have turned the figurative into the literal, of affection for the traditions of Christianity into hostility toward those who are known or assumed not to share them, and have therefore made religion the opposite of itself: "Does the word 'stranger,' the word 'alien,' ever have a negative connotation in Scripture. No. Are the poor ever the object of anything less than God's loving solicitude? No. Do the politics of those who claim a special fealty to the Bible align themselves with its teachings in these matters? No, they do not, not in contemporary America, certainly." No wonder, then, Robinson sadly notes, that "Christianity is stigmatized among the young as a redoubt of ignorance, an obstacle to the humane aspirations of the civilization. The very generosity and idealism of young people is turning them away."

It seems that religious liberty for which Catholics fought so hard and which was ultimately granted at and by Vatican II is now utilized, subtly to be sure, to establish, to enshrine the teachings of religion as laws of the land, applicable to all without exception, especially when those same teachings are spurned by their followers. Religious liberty, touted by its proponents but criticized as counterfeit by its opponents, is used, without acknowledgement of course, as a cover for prejudice and discrimination once more against the "other," the "different," the "alien," the "heretic." In the not too distant past, religion was the justification for slavery and segregation, and the rationale against women's rights and racial minorities. The more salient issues today are well-known by now: contraception, abortion, homosexuality, gay marriage. The shift from absolutism to liberty in this case has taken a dangerous and vicious turn.

Religious liberty was supposed to be a, if not *the*, means for religious tolerance. It now sometimes appears that it is becoming an instrument for religious intolerance. In the aftermath of the 2015 U.S. Supreme Court decision in *Obergefell v. Hodges*, legalizing same-sex marriage, a number of voices opposed the decision and demanded exceptions on the basis of the free exercise of religion. A county clerk refused to grant marriage licenses to gay couples. A pediatrician refused to treat the children of gay couples. A florist refused to provide flowers and a baker refused to bake cakes for the weddings of gay couples. A fast food restaurant refused to serve fried chicken to gay couples. All of them allege that homosexuality and gay marriage are against their religion. Their refusal constitutes, they say, an exercise of religion which is constitutionally protected. This so-called "exercise of religion," how different is it from: "We do not serve blacks," "We do not hire women," "No Chinese and dogs allowed," from the recent past. They were at one time or another also justified with biblical quotations and moral affirmations.

In contrast to groups of nuns supporting the Affordable Care Act, sometimes derisively referred to as Obamacare by its opponents, e.g. Network, whose executive director is Sister Simone Campbell, and the National Coalition of American Nuns, the U.S. Catholic Bishops opposed the universal health care insurance program, their longtime goal – with the defense and promotion of labor and immigrant rights – as a national conference because of its mandate to cover contraception for those who would want it. The Obama administration granted accommodation to Catholic institutions, which by the way include non-Catholic employees and clients, if they submit a written request, so that the coverage is given directly by the insurance company and does not go through the institution. But the Catholic bishops consider that an undue burden on their exercise of religion.

The Catholic Church in the Philippines mobilized the entire Catholic population to oppose the bill – which passed anyway – proposed by President Benigno Aquino III to provide contraceptives to low-income women, knowing fully well that women of means, including perhaps the female relatives of bishops and priests, can easily avail themselves of them. Is it really about religious liberty or about a religious teaching, in this specific case, about contraception that the majority of Catholic moral theologians dissent from and that the majority of Catholics do not accept? Has religious absolutism taken the guise of the "exercise of religion"? Has this "exercise of religion" become the scapegoat for prejudice and discrimination? If so, how is this different from the religious absolutism of the Taliban who would impose "sharia" on the entire population? Religious absolutism, how many crimes in the past have been committed in your name! Religious liberty, how many crimes are now being committed in your disguise?

Hierarchy and the Age of Equality

Peter Heather (2006, 2013) followed his *The Fall of the Roman Empire* with its sequel, *The Restoration of Rome*, captivating narratives of the death of an old empire and the birth of a new one in the Catholic Church. In 476 AD, the curtain fell on the Roman Empire in Western Europe, but the conquering barbarians, responding to Rome's continuing psychological dominance and the practical value of many of its institutions sought to reignite the imperial flame and restore the power and the glory that were Rome's. The three greatest contenders for the task, Theoderic, Justinian, and Charlemagne, restored enough of the Roman West to stake a claim to the Western imperial title, but none of their empires long outlived their founders' deaths. Not until the reinvention of the papacy in the eleventh century would Europe's barbarians find the means to restore a new kind of Roman Empire, the Catholic Church.

Heather (2013: 414) concludes his study:

> [O]nce the papacy had been reinvented to serve their [the Christian leaders and intellectuals in the post-Carolingian period] wishes, it operated like a one-party state in demanding compliance with its vision of proper Christian piety. Limited as it certainly was in political and military terms, therefore, the papacy certainly created an empire nevertheless, and in some important ways a much more powerful and oppressive one than the first Romans had ever managed. The projection of their imperial values never got past the landowning elites, where their papal successors targeted the entirety of the population. And where the spread of Roman law in the first empire allowed consent to overturn constraint among the provinces of the empire, in the new Rome, consent to its legal authority was in fact the path to constraint, a constraint that was being exercised over the entirety of the constituent population. That, of course, may be one reason why the new Roman Empire has so far lasted approximately twice as long as its predecessor.

Peter Damian (Heather 2013: 388) put it most succinctly:

> Now the Roman Church, the see of the apostles, should imitate the ancient court of the Romans. Just as of old the earthly Senate strove to subdue the whole multitude of the peoples to the Roman Empire, so now the ministers of the apostolic see, the spiritual senators of the Church Universal, should make it their sole business by their laws to subdue the human race to God, the true emperor.

For most of their existence, humans lived as hunters-gatherers. Theirs were small nomadic tribes, egalitarian in their relationships, all adults contributing as they did to their subsistence economy. As human groups grew in size and surplus, they also became more complex in their social, economic, and political organization. Hierarchy set in as stratification developed based both on achieved status, like skills, talent, and wealth, and on ascribed status, such as gender, birth, and race. Chiefdoms came to existence, followed by fiefdoms and kingdoms and monarchies, to culminate in empires, the greatest of which in the ancient world was the Roman Empire. This was true not only in the political field of governance and dominance, but also in religious realm of gods and goddesses, in the spiritual life of piety and sacrifice. If in the political field there was a pyramidal structure on which on the top sat the emperor with all the power and might, in the spiritual realm there was also a pyramid on which the top point of the pyramid was occupied by a supreme being and below whom were great gods, local gods, household gods, demi-gods, and daimonia.

The Catholic Church is the restoration of Rome. More than the architecture, the statuary, the legal code, and the fashion, the Catholic Church inherited and replicated in its institutional life the Roman imperial model of overarching bureaucratic authority. At the top of the ecclesiastical pyramid of the Catholic Church is the pope, the supreme pontiff, infallible in doctrine and morals, holding *plenitudo ordinis and iurisdictionis,* the plenitude of order and jurisdiction, with his Curia, whose power emanates and is derivative from its proximity to the papacy. Below the pope is a myriad of offices: three different kinds of cardinals, archbishops of various kinds, bishops, monsignori of different types, and priests. Except for the major orders of bishop, priest, and deacon, these titles do not have much historical, therefore biblical, warrant; they have been created to spread and gather benefices. Bishops are supposed to be the heads of local churches, but for all practical purposes, even after Vatican II, are treated as executives of local branches of the universal church. The diaconate was reinstated by Vatican II, but for all practical purposes deacons are a little better than altar boys. Priests hold the awesome power to change the bread and wine into the body and blood of Christ at Mass, a view derived from an individually constricted theology of the Eucharist. All of these office-holders are male, with women explicitly and doctrinally excluded from these offices. At the bottom is the laity, whose three roles, as traditionally enunciated, are to pray, to pay, and to obey.

The modern world has done away with absolute monarchies. It considers dictatorships illegitimate. It abhors tyrants. Together with reason and liberty, modernity extols equality. This is mainly the result of the democratic revolution that has swept the modern world. Democracy – government of the people, by the people, and for the people, in Lincoln's famous formulation – is today considered the best and the right form of governance. "We, the people" starts the preamble of the U.S. Constitution. "We are the people" is the rallying-cry of protests against authoritarianism, and everybody understands what it means. Democracy rests as foundation and requirement on the political equality of all citizens, which in turn rests on the recognition and acknowledgement of the human dignity of all people. Thus, democracy evolved not only as the rights of propertied men were recognized, but also of women, of the poor, of racial minorities. Today, it is argued that extreme economic inequality also threatens democracy: the very rich can buy their way, while the very poor live inhuman lives. Democracy is messy: it demands knowledge, deliberation, and participation of concerned citizens; it involves dialogue, argumentation, and debate in the public square. It does not primarily lie in the existence of political parties, in political campaigns, slogans, and elections. In Winston Churchill's quip, democracy is the worst form of government, except for all the other forms that have been tried and have failed.

The prominence, if not the primacy, given to the hierarchical and patriarchal nature of the Catholic Church, its pyramidal structure of authority and governance with the consequent enfeeblement of the episcopacy and the deadening passivity of the laity are also challenged by modernity, specifically by the democratic revolution. This paradigm of hierarchy and autocracy has not fully shifted to one of equality and inclusivity, but it was not for want of trying at Vatican II.

In the Dogmatic Constitution on the Church, *Lumen Gentium*, the chapter, The People of God, comes before the chapter, The Hierarchical Structure of the Church. The mere placing of the chapter indicates a most important point: before there is hierarchy of office, power, and honor, there is first and foremost the basic unity and equality of all members of the Church, in virtue of their common baptism. In fact, office, power, and honor are not for the self-aggrandizement of individuals, they are for service to the entire People of God. Instead therefore of a pyramidal structure, it is better to depict the structures of the Church as circles upon concentric circles. Joseph Ratzinger would later dismiss the image of the People of God as sociological, as if what is sociological is inherently opposed to what is theological, as if theology did not need sociologically concrete realities for it not to become ethereal musings.

In the same Dogmatic Constitution, it is declared that the universal call to holiness applies to the entire People of God, not just to celibate clerics. Thus, the dichotomy usually made in the recent past that virginity is a more perfect state than marriage is rendered null and void. In virtue of the selfsame baptism, all the faithful have the right and the duty to participate consciously, fully, and actively in the liturgy, as demanded by the very nature of the liturgy. Vatican II also declared, as indicated earlier, that the whole People of God is missionary, thus the duty to spread the Good News of Jesus, to make his love and justice present in all cultures is incumbent on the entire Church, not only on so-called missionaries.

In the path-breaking decrees on ecumenism, *Unitatis Redintegratio*, and on interreligious dialogue, *Nostra Aetate*, Vatican II extended respect and welcome to other Christians and other religions, and invited them to share in dialogue the riches of their traditions for the sake of the unity of Christianity and of solidarity with the world, especially the poor and disadvantaged. Joseph Ratzinger would pour cold water on these initiatives, by issuing *Dominus Jesus*, to arrogantly extol once more the uniqueness of Jesus Christ and the necessity of the Catholic Church for salvation, to judge offensively the followers of other religions to be in a "gravely deficient position" and their institutions as not truly churches but merely "ecclesial communities."

But over and above these advances in rapprochement with the modern principles of the dignity and equality of all, the Catholic Church remains adamant and intransigent regarding the question of the priestly ordination of women. Even Pope Francis has stated that the case is closed: no priestly ordination of women in the Catholic Church. What is one to do, then, asks Francis Sullivan (2014), if one does not find the reasons given for such denial credible? And the non-credibility and non-acceptance of the Church's position is widespread. Again, the issue of *credibilitas* for *credentitas*. Shockingly, Sullivan finds the answer in an early article of Ratzinger that criticisms of papal pronouncements are possible and even necessary to the degree that they lack support in the faith of the whole Church. I suppose this holds true also for homosexuality and gay marriage, which the Catholic Church continues to oppose but which are finding more and more acceptance, even among Catholics?

Vatican II also tried also to introduce changes into the pyramidal structure of authority and governance of the Church. It revived the ancient tradition of episcopal collegiality, which asserts that the worldwide episcopate constitutes a college, which with and under the pope, has supreme authority and bears pastoral responsibility not only for their individual local churches but for the Church as a whole. Collegiality is an expression of the communion that exists in the Church and is closely related to the catholicity of the Church. The debate over it became the most contested in the Council, arguably even more than that on religious liberty. It was one of the four issues that led to the "black week" of Vatican II (Tagle 2003), after Paul VI had a note of interpretation attached to the already voted upon text. The note emphasized that collegiality did not do away with papal primacy, which note collapsed the conservative opposition to collegiality. It presaged also its death in the actual and continued hierarchical and autocratic governance of the Church. Paul the VI constituted the Synod of Bishops, but only with consultative powers. John Paul II and his Cardinal-enforcer of belief defanged the national conferences of bishops, even though Ratzinger as peritus at the Council touted it as an organ of collegiality. Cardinal Ratziner reduced the International Theological Commission to a personal channel of his conservative theological opinions, notably on Latin American liberation theology and on ecumenism and interreligious dialogue. The Catholic Church therefore remains one of the last absolute monarchies on earth.

Pope Francis has given indications that his will be a more collegial Church. In one of the general congregations preceding the conclave that elected him, he insisted that the Church had to move from its self-referential mode and more resolutely undertake its mission of bringing the joy of the Gospel to the world (Vallely 2015: 151-52). *"Papa Bergoglio,"* John O'Malley (2015b: 70) reminds us, "the first pope in fifty years not to have participated in the council, is also the first pope to have grown up in the postcouncil church and thus to have accepted the council as a fact of life. His immediate predecessors often seemed incapable of forgetting the battles of the council in which they had been engaged, but Pope Francis has no such memories." He uses Vatican II's term, People of God, for the Church, a "field hospital," he adds, where the immediate task is to tend to the wounds and show mercy, a place of refuge and solace for those bloodied in their daily struggles. He has expressed his unstinted fidelity to Vatican II. "According to a reliable report," O'Malley (2015b: 71) writes, "had Cardinal Bergoglio been elected in the conclave in 2005, he would have chosen to be called John XXIV because of the deep inspiration he derived from the "good pope," *il papa buono*. Pope Francis projects the image of a person not unlike Pope John to whom he is often compared." One of Pope John's intention for the Council was to make cooperation and participation the mode the Church operates both internally and externally.

After his election, Pope Francis presented himself to the people that were gathered to await him as the Bishop of Rome, thus highlighting his membership in the College of Bishops. He formed a Commission of Cardinals, originally eight but now nine, to oversee the reform of the Curia and the governance of the Church, in the first place, with regard to its finances. He called a Synod of Bishops to consider pastoral approaches to the problems of modern married and family members. It was unlike all the other previous synods. It took place in two stages with a year separating them and before each of which he had a questionnaire distributed to be answered by the Church at all levels, although not a few bishops refused to do so. He opened the Synod to frank and open discussions by everybody present, which they did. As of this writing, the Synod has ended, and we do not know what Pope Francis will do with the conclusions voted upon in the Synod and submitted to him. But the Synod was collegiality in full display with differences in debate, conflict, and contestation in open and frank view.

Pope Francis has also spoken of his desire to implement synodality in the Church. Council and synod are synonymous; synod is simply the Greek word for the Latin, *concilium*. But whereas former synods in the history of the Church were decision-making bodies, ever since Paul VI created the Synod of Bishops, a new definition of synod is that it is strictly consultative, points out John O'Malley (Salai 2015). The Synods of Bishops convoked by Francis' predecessors were not even consultative, but pro-forma synods of already-arrived-at conclusions. The Synod of Bishops convoked by Francis is more accurately an expression of collegiality, and hopefully will also become an expression of subsidiarity – of decentralization, in secular political parlance – in the Church, as it was in the earlier years of the Church. Subsidiarity is the institutional response to a particular task which is best handled by those most proximate to it. Subsidiarity is grounded in the principle that large institutions should not usurp the responsibility of smaller institutions in the solution of problems that the latter are better able to handle; the role of the large institution is to support the smaller institution, not to replace it. Synodality recognizes that there are different contexts, different problems in different situations, that affect different groups. Synods on the national, regional, or diocesan levels may be better able to discern the peculiarities of their contexts, their problems and situations, and to come up with solutions better suited to those problems.

Paul VI in *Octogesima Adveniens* (1971, no. 4) located responsibility for the analysis and solution of social problems in local communities and churches: "It is up to the Christian communities to analyze with objectivity the situation which is proper to their own country, to shed on it the light of the Gospel's unalterable words and to draw principles of reflection, norms of judgment and directions for action from the social teaching of the Church." Mary Elsbernd (1995: 39, 60) noted, however, that this "central expression of a historically conscious methodology in magisterial teaching" underwent intentional distortion and reversal under John Paul II. She ended by saying that "the credibility and integrity of Catholic social teaching requires that it retrieve the fundamental insights sketched in *Gaudium et Spes* and elaborated in *Octogesima Adveniens*.

If this is true of social problems in the application of the social teachings of the Church, this is also true of pastoral approaches to doctrinal and moral issues necessitated by the different contexts of the People of God in different areas of the globe. It is a vision of the Church in which not everything comes down from the top of the pyramid, but coresponsibility is spread out throughout the Church in its tasks of evangelization, manifesting the mercy of Jesus and the joy of the Gospel to the peripheries: the marginalized, the neglected, the disaffected, and the disaffiliated.

Conclusion

At Vatican II, the Catholic Church met the twentieth century, and finally found itself *in mundo huius temporis*, in the world of this time, as the Latin title of *Gaudium et Spes* reads. It was a meeting impressed upon it by Pope John XXIII – "certainly trembling a little with emotion, but with humble resolve nevertheless," he said when he announced the Council on January 25, 1959 – without the tools of condemnation nor of definition, but with an openness to and dialogue with "the signs of the times" in the modern world and in the wider Christian and religious communities. The meeting entails a journey, long, arduous, and winding, with not a few bumps, potholes, and detours along the way. Even now, as Cardinal Carlo Martini of Milan asserted in his final interview (Allen 2012), "the church is 200 years behind the times." But – as a Chinese proverb puts it, a journey of a hundred miles always starts with a first step – the first steps have already been taken. The entire People of God, with their prophetic voices, transforming deeds, and liberating lives, has to complete the journey in courage and hope.

5

1898 AND AMERICA'S EMPIRE IN THE PHILIPPINES: RACE, RELIGION, IMPERIALISM, AND COLONIALISM

1898 was a significant milestone, an important turning point in American history. It had been more than thirty years since the Civil War ended in 1865 and, although the South was segregated, a new generation of Americans had come of age, children of those who fought in the War between the States, as it was known in the South. Industry was expanding, moving the country from being an agricultural society to one where factories and machines dominated the economy. Henry Ford and his Model T were paradigmatic of this period of industrial inventiveness. At the same time, the period which coincided with the Gilded Age was also characterized by the emergence of the Progressive Movement whose aim was to tame a runaway capitalist economy, to bust engorged business trusts, and to legalize the rights of workers. If Henry Ford stood for business interests, Theodore Roosevelt became the champion of government for the people.

But most of all, 1898 saw America's first venture into imperialism, the beginning of American expansionism therefore, the arrival in full force of the modern age in the Western Hemisphere, the birth of the American Century. The outbreak of the Spanish-American War in 1898 in Spanish-held Cuba led, in succession, to the possession of Puerto Rico, Hawaii, Guam, and ultimately to the American defeat of the Spanish in the Philippines in the South China Sea. The Philippines, thus, became

America's first empire, after a tumultuous debate between pro- and anti-imperialists, represented by President William McKinley and Mark Twain respectively. 1898, according to David Traxel (1998), was "a year without rival in United States history for its extravagant adventure and far-reaching significance."

"[E]mpire is not an epithet. It is a form of government in which a dominant power exercises control over the destiny of others through direct territorial rule (e.g., colonies) or indirect influence (e.g., military, economic, or cultural heritage)" (McCoy, Scarano, and Johnson 2009: 4). Ian Tyrrell (2009: 544) adds: "The United States is manifestly an empire because it has exerted power over other people; it has occupied other countries, changed their political regimes, and fought wars over the control of the territory of others. It has sought to influence other peoples indirectly as well." After counting seventy empires in world history, Niall Ferguson (2004: 14-15) notes wryly, "To those who would still insist on American 'exceptionalism,' the historian of empires can only retort: as exceptional as all the other sixty-nine empires."

What role did race and religion play in America's first adventure in imperialism? How did race and religion impact the way colonization was conducted? How did race and religion, imperial expansion, and colonial subjugation interact with each other? What were the consequences of these interactions? These questions mark the terrain that I wish to explore. I distinguish between two periods: the period of imperial expansion, when the debate centered on what to do with the Philippines, the different options that were open to the United States; and the period of colonial subjugation, when having decided to hold on to the Philippines, how the United States dealt with the Philippines, its first imperial outpost.

Historical Context

What was the world like in 1898? To get our historical bearings right, it is necessary to make a few observations regarding the United States, Spain, and the world as a whole.

First, the last decades of the nineteenth century for the United States, especially the 1890s, were tumultuous. To mention simply the economic and political aspects, the country was experiencing rapid industrialization and urbanization. Americans had reconstructed the South, settled the Far West, built a network of railroads, and expanded their great industrial system. With the depression that began in 1893, some businessmen became convinced that industry had become too efficient that it was producing more goods than customers at home could buy and consume, and yet it had to continue producing. The bitter protests of the time that resulted from the inequalities of the new industrial society, exemplified by bloody labor disputes, led many to believe that the nation was threatened with internal collapse. Some politicians advocated a more aggressive foreign policy to provide an outlet for frustration, specifically more markets for the goods that industry was overproducing, that would otherwise destabilize domestic life. Senator Albert J. Beveridge of Indiana perfectly captured the sentiment when in 1899 he cried: "Today, we are raising more than we consume. Today, we are making more than we can use. Therefore, we must find new markets for our produce, new occupation for our capital, new work for our labor."

The problem was that Frederick Jackson Turner had announced the "closing" of the American frontier, from which Americans believed they had acquired their most distinctive characteristics: their rugged individualism, their egalitarianism, and their democratic ideals. "Manifest Destiny" had reached its continental limits. At the same time, Alfred Thayer Mahan became convinced that all the world's empires, beginning with Rome, had relied on their power to control the sea. In his influential book, published in 1890, *The Influence of Sea Power upon History, 1660-1783,* Mahan laid out a program to transform the United States into a great world power, by constructing a first-class navy. By 1898 the U.S. Navy ranked fifth in the world, and by 1890 it ranked third. The consequential presidential election of 1896 which was "the first lavishly financed presidential campaign" (Traxel 1998: 19) was won by William McKinley – he was reelected in 1990 – who with his assistant Secretary of the Navy Theodore Roosevelt would almost make Mahan's vision a reality in the quest for empire. When McKinley succeeded Grover Cleveland in 1897, the acquisition of Hawaii moved rapidly forward, Queen Liliuokalani having been deposed by a coup led by Sanford B. Dole, a prominent pineapple planter. Hawaii was proclaimed an American territory in 1898, and sixty one years later, joined the union as the fiftieth state. It was time for "the Eagle to spread its wings and scream" (Traxel 1998: 11).

Second, Spain, for its part, had been in decline ever since the defeat of the Spanish armada in 1588. Most of Latin America had gained their independence in the 17th century. By the 1890s what remained of the vast Spanish empire of Philipp II were the islands of Cuba and Puerto Rico in the Americas and the Philippines in Asia. A revolt of the Cubans in 1868 had taken years for the Spanish to subdue. In 1895 the Cubans staged another revolt, destroying large parts of the islands. The Spanish army, led by General Valerian Weyler, responded in kind, forcing large numbers of Cubans in concentration camps. Denied adequate food, shelter, and sanitation, an estimated 200,000 Cubans, one-eighth of the population, died of starvation and disease. American opinion was inflamed by such tactics ascribed to "Butcher" Weyler, as he was known in the U.S. press. Many Americans sympathized with the Cubans, who reminded them of the anticolonial war they themselves waged over a hundred years before. The sensationalism of the yellow press and its jingoistic accounts, especially those of William Randolph Hearst and Joseph Pulitzer, however, were not enough to bring about American intervention.

The flashpoint came with the explosion of the battleship *Maine* at Havana harbor in February 1898, which killed 262 sailors. The battleship was sent to Cuba by McKinley in late 1897 to protect U.S. citizens and their $50 million worth of property after riots broke out in Havana. Although subsequent investigations revealed that the most probable cause of the explosion was a malfunctioning boiler, Americans were certain that it was the work of Spanish agents. The U.S. and Spain exchanged formal declarations of war in April, and the Spanish-American War commenced. Assistant Secretary of the Navy Theodore Roosevelt cabled Commodore George Dewey, whose selection to command the U.S. Navy's Asiatic Squadron was recently engineered by Roosevelt, to proceed immediately from Hongkong to Manila to destroy the Spanish fleet at Manila Bay lest they come to succor the Spanish in Cuba. Dewey arrived at Manila Bay on May 1, 1898, and easily destroyed the decrepit Spanish fleet. [1]

Ferdinand Magellan, generally considered the first circumnavigator of the world, arrived in the Philippines in 1521, but before he could return to Spain was killed by Lapu-lapu, a local chieftain. The expedition of Miguel Lopez de Legazpi and the Augustinian friar Andres de Urdaneta in1565 started in earnest the pursuit of the twin aims of the Spanish crown: the colonization of the islands and the Christianization of its inhabitants. The Philippine revolution against Spain erupted in 1896, with eight provinces rallying to its cause, but was crushed by the Spaniards, its leaders exiled to Hongkong. With the outbreak of the Spanish-American War, the Americans brought back the leader of the Filipino revolutionaries, Emilio Aguinaldo, from Hongkong to the Philippines to re-start the war against Spain. In less than a month Emilio Aguinaldo had secured practically the whole of Luzon, with the exception of the port of Cavite and Manila, and thereby declared the independence of the Philippines from Spain on June 12, 1898. But the First Philippine Republic was short-lived. A congress was convened to promulgate a constitution and the Philippine Republic was inaugurated on January 23, 1899, but before the government could function, hostilities broke out between Filipino and American troops on February 4. The Philippine Revolution gave way to the Philippine-American War. It was a brutal three-year war which ended in 1902. By then the United States had annexed the Philippines.

Third, the world in 1900 was imperialism at high tide. The scramble for Africa in the 19th century resulted in the continent being carved out by competing European colonial powers. The Far East was also being contested by British, French, Belgian, and German powers, always with an eye to the vast markets of the feeble Chinese Empire. Americans could not insulate themselves from the imperialist fever raging throughout Europe. The experience of subjugating Indian tribes and of enslaving Africans had established precedent for exerting control and domination over subject peoples. Besides, the continental frontier had closed, the economy was overproducing, and there was not an infinite number of territories still to be conquered and colonized. There was also the philosophic justification for expansionism and colonialism in the distorted interpretation of Darwin's evolutionary theory in the form of Social Darwinism, that nations and races struggled constantly for existence and only the fittest could survive: it was the law of nature that the strong dominate the weak. This was the background against which American debates on imperialism and anti-imperialism were conducted. "The annexation of the Philippines is the culminating event in the historical literature on race and imperialism in the late nineteenth century" (Love 2004: 164).

Race and Imperialism

A popular textbook on American history (Brinkley, Freidel, Current, and Williams 1991: 593) states: "The American republic had been an expansionist nation since the earliest days of his existence. Throughout the first half of the nineteenth century, as the population of the United States grew and pressed westward, the government continually acquired new territory for its citizens to occupy: the trans-Appalachian West, the Louisiana Territory, Florida, Texas, Oregon, California, New Mexico, Alaska, and more. It was the nation's 'Manifest Destiny,' many Americans believed, to expand into new realms."

It continues: "But the expansionism of the 1890s, the new Manifest Destiny, involved acquiring possessions separate from the continental United States: land territories, many of which were already thickly populated, most of which were not suitable for massive settlement from America, few of which were expected ever to become states of the Union. The United States was acquiring colonies. It was joining England, France, Germany, and other expanding nations in the great imperial drive that was, by the end of the century, to bring much of the underdeveloped world under the control of the industrial powers of the West."

Race and racism saturated the cultural and political landscape of the United States at this time. They are a vital part of the story and history of American imperialism. Eric Love (2004: xii) writes: "No one can doubt that the United States was originally conceived as a white nation or deny that the deliberate and systematic exclusion of nonwhites was a vital part of American nation-building throughout the nineteenth century." Americans held to a racial ideology, the belief that the white race was superior to nonwhite races, that nonwhite races were inferior and, therefore, were meant to be subjugated to serve the white race. Racial prejudice meant that nonwhites show attitudes of respect and deference to white people, while nonwhites were looked down upon, treated as mere extensions of property, and considered as means for the aggrandizement of whites. White supremacy decreed that institutions establish and maintain a racial social order, in which power and privilege are reserved to whites, while nonwhites are discriminated against, exploited, and oppressed. "The impenetrable and largely (though never completely) unquestioned conviction that the United States was a white nation and that every advance, domestic and foreign, should be pursued for the exclusive benefit of white citizens insinuated itself and shaped every important expansionist project of the nineteenth century, and all constituted formations of a racial – and racist – social order" (Love 2004: xiii).

What then was the relationship of racism to expansionism, specifically to the expansionist project of annexing the Philippines? The traditional narrative [2] has it that racism – the superiority of the white man, the inferiority of the nonwhite – was the inspiration and motivating force for expanding the territory of the United States. It was the destiny of the white race, specifically of the United States, to subdue and have dominion, as Genesis puts is, over the peoples considered biologically and culturally inferior, alien, and unassimilable. It was "the white man's burden" to advance empire. The racial ideologies of Anglo-Saxonism, Social Darwinism, benevolent assimilation, civilizing and Christianizing missions, all rooted in white supremacy, justified the annexations that followed the war with Spain in 1898, and that brought millions of people of color under the jurisdiction of the United States and that made the country a world power. There might be economic reasons for doing so, territorial justifications, political contestations, and global power considerations, but underlying all these reasons were racist ideology and white supremacy. The latter facilitated, rationalized, impelled, and removed the constraints for the United States to achieve empire. Daniel Schirmer (1972: 83, 88) pithily expressed the sentiment: "The imperialist posture, in attitude and ideology as well as in practice, stimulated white racism.... If imperialism abroad bolstered white supremacy at home, . . . white supremacy at home was an aid to imperial expansion abroad."

Eric Love (2004) disagrees with the traditional narrative of race over empire. He does not disagree with the prevalence of race and racism in the expansionist history of the United States, nor does he deny considerations of white supremacy in the imperialist designs of the United States. He emphasizes the elements of racial exclusion in racism and white homogeneity in white supremacy, which acted as constraints in the expansionism and imperialism of the United States towards peoples who were considered biologically and culturally inferior, who were alien and unassimilable. Instead of expanding into their lands, instead of trying to integrate them into American society, racial exclusion and racial homogeneity wanted to exclude them from the white man's land lest they contaminate the purity of the white race and mongrelize it.

In his preface, Love (2004: xi-xii) explains at length the thesis of his book:

> [R]acism had nearly the opposite effect: that the relationship between imperialists of the late nineteenth century and the racist structures and convictions of their time was antagonistic, not harmonious (and no class understood this more acutely than the foreign policy establishment itself); that imperialists, contained by the expectations and demands of the racial social order, neither spoke nor acted in the manner usually presented in the historical literature; that they did not overwhelm the racist invective of the anti-imperialists with more potent racial rhetoric (fighting fire with fire); that, instead, they reacted with silences, disinguous evasions, and denials that race had anything to do with their expansionist projects. In short, imperialist knew . . . that in an era marked by as much racial fear, hatred, reaction, and violence as the last decades of the nineteenth century – by the collapse of Reconstruction; the reversal of civil rights and equal protections, condoned by the U.S. Supreme Court; by the final suppression of native Americans; by the defeat of the Federal Elections Bill of 1890 (called the "Force Bill" by its enemies); by segregation, disenfranchisement, and the lynching of thousands of African Americans; by immigration restriction and other reactions against the so-called new immigrant groups, such as the founding of

the American Protective Association and the Immigration Restriction League; by Chinese exclusion and gentlemen's agreements – no pragmatic politician or party would fix nonwhites at the center of its imperial policies. Yet that is precisely what the rhetoric of "benevolent assimilation" and the "white man's burden" would have done and what the dominant narrative insists the student of history believe. . . . In short, the principal goal of the late-nineteenth-century racial social order was the exclusion of those racial and ethnic groups cast as "nonwhite" from equal access to and participation in America's economic, political, social, and cultural mainstream.

Love's (2004) study is organized around four attempts by American policymakers, made between 1865 and 1900, to annex territories away from the continent that were occupied by significant numbers of nonwhite people. They are: President Ulysses Grant's effort in 1870 to annex Santo Domingo, now the Dominican Republic; the U.S. attempt to annex Hawaii in 1893, which failed because it was blocked by the pillars of the racial order, both old and newly raised; the successful annexation of Hawaii in 1897 and 1898, whose justification was that, in fact, Hawaii was a *white* nation, a justification that privileged white racial brotherhood, not white supremacy or benevolent assimilation; and the successful annexation of the Philippines, achieved not by exploiting race as the dominant narrative portrays but because imperialists were able to cover it over with distracting appeals to war fervor, jingo patriotism, and politics.

The history of the United States attests to this policy of nonwhite exclusion for white homogeneity. It had done away with the native population of Americans, reducing what remained of them to reservations; it had enslaved blacks, then segregated them without due civil and political rights; it had excluded the Chinese, the first time in 1882, who with their coolie labor helped built the railroads. Even certain groups of European immigrants felt the sting of inferiority and exclusion. As European immigration swelled, it also changed its origin from countries of northern and western Europe to those of the south and east. These "new immigrants" – Jewish, Slavic, and Mediterranean – diverged in their social norms, culture, and religion, which elicited nativist fears, antagonism, and even violence. The Naturalization Act of 1790, the first definition of citizenship established by Congress, granted that status to whites only.

The possibility of expanding beyond the continental borders of the nation ignited a debate between imperialists and anti-imperialists. Some anti-imperialists, heeding the warning of George Washington against foreign entanglements, argued that what differentiated the United States from European countries was that the country had no imperial ambitions and inclinations, was not in search of colonies and enemies abroad. Other anti-imperialists contended that expanding into foreign territories would mean assimilating other peoples and cultures, extending to them the rights of citizenship, and allowing them to participate in the life of the nation, which would adulterate the purity and homogeneity of the superior white race. Some imperialists were gung-ho about showing off the superiority of the white race, dominating inferior races, and subjugating them for the benefit of the white race. The U.S. was already late in the race and game for empire. Other imperialists downplayed the issue of race, and propounded the need for new markets for the products that the American economy was overproducing, the political importance of naval power and the necessity for foreign bases, and the geopolitical competition for territories against Germany, England, and France. Both imperialists and anti-imperialists were tainted with the prevailing racism and white supremacy, whether they meant the inferiority of nonwhites and the right of whites to subjugate them or whether they intended the exclusion of nonwhites to preserve the purity of the white race.

After Commodore Dewey defeated the Spanish fleet at Manila Bay on May 1, 1898, his squadron laid anchor at the bay, waiting for American troops to arrive from San Francisco in three months time. Meanwhile, in spite of trench works bristling with the guns of fifteen thousand Filipino soldiers ringing the city of Manila, the Philippine revolutionary republic having consolidated its gains throughout the entire archipelago, save for Manila, the Spanish in typical Iberian haughtiness cut a deal with the Americans, and, after a mock battle, surrendered the Philippines to the Americans. On December 10, 1898, the Treaty of Paris, in which Spain relinquished Cuba, Puerto Rico, the Philippines, and the Marianas in exchange for $20 milllion, was signed. The Treaty was submitted to the U.S. Congress on January 4, 1899. By now the awaited American troops had arrived, and hostilities between American and Filipino soldiers erupted to start the Philippine-American War on February 4, 1899. The Treaty of Paris, opposition to which collapsed with the outbreak of war, was ratified on February 6, 1899, by a vote of fifty-seven to twenty-seven, one more than the necessary two-thirds. The McEnery Resolution was also passed which was indefinite as to the potential duration of the colonial enterprise, but specific in denying American citizenship to Filipinos.

Thus, the treatment of the Philippines was in marked contrast to the beneficence granted to Cuba, Hawaii, and Puerto Rico. The U.S. allowed

Cuba its independence, but burdened it with the Platt Amendment, which provided that Cuba cede territory to the United States for use as military bases – Guantanamo, principally – and the right to intervene to preserve life, property, and liberty, whenever Washington deemed it necessary. As for Hawaii, as mentioned earlier by Eric Love (2004: xvii), its proposed annexation failed in 1893, but succeeded in 1898. What intervened between the two dates was the coup against Queen Liliuokalani led by Sanford Dole which changed the justification against the assimilation of degenerate races and indolent natives to a rationale in favor of annexation of what had become a *white* nation, with a claim to privileged white brotherhood in the union of states. In contrast, "the U.S. Congress translated [a] pseudo-science [of race] into a national eugenics policy by means of laws that put the Filipinos, deemed unalterably Asian, on the path to eventual independence in the Jones Act of 1916. When Congress enacted another version of the Jones Act for Puerto Rico just a year later, it deemed Puerto Rico sufficiently 'white' and imposed U.S. citizenship on the island's entire population" (McCoy, Scarano, and Johnson 2009: 20). Filipinos were not deemed racially worthy of citizenship, much less of joining the Unites States as a state.

Eric Love (2004: 196-200) also points to the disillusionment of Theodore Roosevelt, the arch-imperialist who led his ragtag troops to charge up a hill during the Spanish-American War, with the imperial project. He dismissed the Philippines as a "white elephant," a conspicuous point of weakness in the nation's security, a dangerous burden to the nation. When Roosevelt took over the Canal Zone, not all of Panama was taken, despite the support for doing so. The Americans took only territory, on either side of the canal to build it and to suit its defense. It was a new policy without annexation, without race.

It is also worth mentioning Mark Twain (Shaw and Francia 2002: 57-68), the most famous of the anti-imperialists, whose biting satire, "To the Person Sitting in Darkness," originally published in *The Sun* of New York in February 1901 is enshrined in the annals of anti-imperialist writings. Eric Love (2004: 86) mentions that in his Sandwich Island lecture (published in a collection of his speeches in 1910), Twain talked of Hawaiians' decline with dark and gruesome levity. Their numbers have fallen from 400,000 to 55,000, at the time of Twain's lecture, with the arrival of the first white men and their motley and deadly companions: "various complicated diseases, and education, and civilization, and all sorts of calamities." Their extinction was inevitable, Twain said, a sad eventuality but not without its benefits. "When they pick up and leave we will take possession as their lawful heirs." Twain might have been an anti-imperialist, but his was certainly a racist-exclusionary sentiment.

A final word from Love (2004: xix) in his preface:

> [I]n the long history of the United States, racism has always been destructive toward innovation and progressive change. . . . Racism is not only a burden borne by its most obvious victims: it was a problem of power as well. The dominant narrative's insistence that racism effectively loosened the restraints on policymakers, allowing them to advance outward and extend their domination over territories and peoples at will, strikes me as disturbing, and not simply because this presumption – if my argument is correct – is for the most part historically inaccurate. Convictions of American exceptionalism, in those instances where it has been corrupted by white supremacy, deformed the nation's capacity to engage with much of the world on a just, moral, equal, and democratic basis consistent with its creed. Certainly, without the restraint of racism, our interactions with peoples of color around the world over more than two centuries might have been more constructive, materially and morally, than they have been.

Religion and Imperialism

The discussion of the role of religion in American imperialism, specifically in the decision to annex the Philippines, usually starts with the account President William McKinley himself gave to a delegation of Methodist dignitaries who came to see him in 1903.

> When next I realized that the Philippines had dropped into our lap I confess I did not know what to do with them. I sought counsel from all sides – Democrats as well as Republicans – but got little help. I thought first that we would take only Manila; then Luzon; then other islands, perhaps, also. I walked the floor of the White House night after night until midnight; and I am not ashamed to tell you, gentlemen, that I went down on my knees and prayed Almighty God for light and guidance more than one night. And one night late it came to me this way – I do not know how it came: (1) that we could

not give them back to Spain – that would be cowardly and dishonorable; (2) that we could not turn them over to France or Germany – our commercial rivals in the Orient – that would be bad business and discreditable; (3) that we could not leave them to themselves – they were unfit for self-government, and they would soon have anarchy and misrule over there worse than Spain's was; and (4) there was nothing left for us to do but to take them all, and to educate the Filipinos, and uplift and civilize and Christianize them, and by God's grace do the very best that we could for them, as our fellowmen for whom Christ also died. And then I went to bed, and went to sleep, and slept soundly, and the next morning I sent for the Chief Engineer of the War Department (our map maker) and told him to put the Philippines on the map of the United States (pointing to a large map on the wall of his office), and there they are, and there they will stay, while I am President (de la Costa 1965: 250).

Note the signal words that McKinley used: *educate, uplift, civilize,* and *Christianize.* Not only was the account to a group of Methodist clergyman, then the largest Protestant denomination in the nation, self-serving, not only did it completely ignore the Christianization of the Philippines by Catholic Spain for over three and a half centuries – the population of the Philippines today continues to be more than eighty percent Catholic – but those words were action words that revealed how Redeemer America considered itself and how it looked down on a benighted people like the Filipinos. America had to educate them because they were illiterate. America had to uplift them because they were downtrodden. America had to civilize them because they were barbarians. America had to Christianize them because they were pagans. America was not only a knight on horseback and in shining armor riding to rescue a woman in distress, but a missionary clad in religious raiment and upholding a cross come to bring the light of truth and goodness to a people mired in intellectual and moral darkness. It was a picture that was no different from the Spanish colonizer and his missionary sidekick.

In fact, George Anderson (1969: 279-80) pointed out, quoting Edward McCall Burns, that "one of the principal clues to knowledge of America is the sense of mission which has run like a golden thread through most of her history. To a greater extent than most other peoples, Americans have conceived of their nation as ordained in some extraordinary way to accomplish great things in the world.' . . . But the gospel of Manifest Destiny had its roots in the concepts of Anglo-Saxon racial superiority, of America as the center of civilization in the westward course of empires, the primacy of American political institutions, the purity of American Protestant Christianity, and the desirability of English to be the language of mankind." American national identity at the close of the nineteenth century was intertwined with race and religion. In truth, "race is so tightly associated with religion that the two labels often function as a single idea" (Harris 2011: 25). McKinley, in other words, was preaching to a rapt choir.

Part and parcel of this gospel of Manifest Destiny was anti-Catholic sentiment. "There was a predominant feeling that Anglo-Saxon, Protestant, republican America was God's measure and means for the establishment of His Kingdom on earth, and Protestants then generally viewed Roman Catholicism as a sub-Christian, if not anti-Christian, force" (Anderson 1969: 297). Americans were warned of the dangers of immigrants and their un-American ideas, especially of the Catholic Church, guilty of "rum and Romanism." In fact, the war itself was God's instrument for striking another blow "at that system of iniquity, the papacy." In spite of this, Renato Constantino (1975: 285-86) avers that "the Catholic Church in the United States also used its influence to encourage the American government to occupy the country. Cardinal James Gibbons and Archbishop John Ireland, both of whom had close connections with the Republican Party and with McKinley himself, were advocates of annexation. They saw American conquest as the only way to salvage the vast economic interests of the Church in the islands. Spanish rule had collapsed; if the Americans did not take over, the Philippine Revolutionary government would retain power."

The issues of racial inferiority and white domination, of racial exclusion and white homogeneity that rived both imperialists and anti-imperialists also bedeviled Protestant annexationists and religious anti-annexationists. The debate was further complicated by two facts in American religious history and identity. American religious history was rooted in the ideological struggles of the Reformation. "Students were taught that the Roman Church was a thoroughly corrupt, authoritarian institution that prevented its followers from achieving the level of independent thought and critical consciousness necessary for American citizenship. Successive ways of immigration only fortified anti-Catholic sentiment. . . . The upshot of the history of Catholic-Protestant rancor in the United States was that by the nineteenth century, for many Americans the word *Christian* was not synonymous with the word *Catholic*. Rather, the use of 'Christian' during this period carries an implicit opposition to the Church of Rome. Hence McKinley's words lay out a plan of action that sees 'civilization' as

'Protestant' and 'education as inculcation into a national culture based in Protestant ideas" (Harris 2011: 15).

The second complicating factor was the appropriation of Enlightenment ideals for religious ends. "Nineteenth-century Americans saw themselves within a fusion of Protestant Christian and Enlightenment identities . . . . In the popular understanding of American identity, the United States was a means to a divine end, a country established by God to fulfill God's plan. But America's identity could be accomplished only if her citizens continuously enacted the [Enlightenment] values on which their unique civilization had been founded. In practice this meant that any proposal for a radical change in national trajectory had to be carefully scrutinized to make sure it conformed to American ideals" (Harris 2011: 18). Both of these complicating factors played themselves out as underlying issues of race and religion in the debate on imperialism vs. anti-imperialism, annexation vs. anti-annexation. Christian imperialists argued that it was a Christian duty to "convert" Filipinos into a civilized people. Christian anti-imperialists retorted that the exceptional nature of American civilization should not be compromised by racial amalgamation. The core belief on which they agreed was that "the United States was a nation of white Protestants under a special mandate from God to represent freedom and fair-dealing to the rest of the world" (Harris 2011: 13).

In an interesting and enlightening volume, Susan Harris (2011) uses Mark Twain as a measure of nineteenth-century American understanding of who they were and how the government that represented them should be conducting itself on the global level. In the process, she clarifies the issues of race and religion underlying the debate on the annexation of the Philippines, as well as, Twain's contradictions and changes of mind regarding race, religion, national identity, imperialism and anti-imperialism. Harris (2011: 20) writes:

> Twain clearly perceived the problem with which his compatriots were blindly struggling: in the end, the American story of freedom and civil liberties was a narrative generated by and applicable to only one religious and ethnic identity – an origins myth for white Protestants. Hence the struggle: the decision about what to do with the Philippines exposed the contradictions under which most white Americans lived. On the one hand they ardently espoused the exemplary narrative of American freedom, and on the other, they fervently believed that those freedoms were generated from the Reformation,

formulated by the Puritans, and could be fully enacted only by white Protestants.

Race and Colonialism

President Theodore Roosevelt declared the Philippine-American War over on July 4, 1902, but the last Filipino revolutionary general, Macario Sakay, surrendered only on September 13, 1907. The savage conflict left at least 20,000 Filipino combatants and at least 250,000 – but possibly as many as a million – noncombatants dead from war or war-related causes. By the war's end, more than 4,000 U.S. soldiers had been killed, and 3,000 wounded. A total of approximately 200,000 U.S. troops had served in this, the first war fought by the U.S. on Asian soil. It "was a shameful and bloody affair," Eric Love (2004: 198) writes, "awful in all its details." And yet, the U.S. government would celebrate the Spanish-American War as "a splendid little war" which lasted all of four months, while denigrating the more brutal and costly Philippine-American War with the simple moniker of "insurrection." [3]

Some of the vocabulary and images of the Philippine-American War would re-appear in America's later wars: The term *gugu* – from *gago*, the Tagalog word for stupid – would morph to *gook* to accommodate Koreans and Vietnamese. The Spanish practice of *reconcentrado* would be repeated in herding Filipinos into concentration camps, and in the policy of hamletting during the Vietnam War. The "amigo warfare" – friend by day, enemy by night – frustrated U.S. soldiers in the Philippines, as well as in Vietnam. General Jacob Smith who ordered his men to turn the province of Samar into a "howling wilderness," telling his men, "I want no prisoners, I wish you to kill and burn; the more you kill and burn, the more you will please me," would be incarnated in Lieutenant William Calley, accused of the massacre of women and children at My Lai in 1968. Both were court-martialed and found guilty, but the punishment for the former was an admonition and forced retirement, the latter's original life sentence was reduced to house arrest and later voided by presidential pardon. The favored method of torture was the so-called "water-cure" in which the detainee is thrown upon the ground, his arms and legs pinioned, his nose pinched or a bamboo stick inserted to keep his mouth open, and water is poured which he must swallow or else he strangles. After pouring in as much as five gallons, the stomach swells and is about to burst; his body is a frightful object to contemplate and in an agony of pure hell. The water is squeezed out by kneeling on his stomach or pummeled and kicked, blood issuing out from his mouth and nostrils. The process is repeated until he talks or dies. This cannot compare in brutality and barbarity with the "water-boarding" of the War on Terror.

After the brutal pacification campaign, the U.S. launched a policy of "benevolent assimilation, substituting the mild sway of justice and right for arbitrary rule," in the words of McKinley (Miller 1982), whose ultimate aim was the height of social engineering presumptuousness: to remake the Philippines, borrowing from Genesis, "in our image" (Karnow 1989; May 1980). That would mean the benign transformation of the Philippines into a capitalist economy fast growing to be industrial, into a society marked by the association of free and equal citizens, and into a political system that was subject to fair and democratic elections, all after the model of the exceptional state and society of the conquering country. It was to make the Philippines, as it was usually said in the 1950s, the "showcase of democracy in Asia." Its contemporary hubristic resonance is George W. Bush's promise "to rid the world of evil" and to plant democracy in the Middle East by the military conquest of Iraq. But the project, for all its good intentions and beneficent results, had two fatal flaws: racism and colonialism. How can you create another in your own image if the other is viewed as inferior and alien? How can you make another country in your own likeness if you are the master race and the other is a subjugated slave?

What Ruth Paredes (1989: 65-66) writes with powerful clarity about colonial democracy is true of the entire racist, however clothed in religious garb, colonial project.

> The whole American effort to develop democracy under colonialism was flawed by an organic contradiction. . . . In short, sovereignty is external to the colonized territory and in such a circumstance, there can be no democracy. Any attempt at the development of democratic institutions in circumstances so constitutionally antithetical to their prosperity can only produce a distorted experience for the colonized. . . . Not only are institutions distorted but political leadership is inevitably compromised. Elections and public service do not create titans legendary for their bold, commanding leadership, but pygmies stunted by the constraints of collaboration. . . . [N]ative politicians are forced to operate within assigned political boundaries and, more importantly, to curry favor with colonial officials to win their patronage. . . . [N]ative leaders quickly learn a duplicitous political craft of manipulation and dissimulation.

I limit myself to four deformations in Philippine society and culture wrought by racist colonial policies that have disfigured Philippine history since the American colonial period and beyond the inauguration of the Second Philippine Republic on July 4, 1946. The first concerned the disposition of the friar estates (Roth 1977), which had been a most contentious issue in the Philippine revolution against Spain. More than 420,000 acres of the finest agricultural lands were involved, owned by three religious orders, the Dominicans, the Augustinians, and the Augustinian Recollects, who, during the revolution, had transferred titles to secular promoting companies in which they retained a controlling interest. The American authorities had to deal with these corporations as well as with the friars. The problem was complicated by the fact that 60,000 tenants lived on the lands. Negotiations by the Philippine Commission, headed by Gov. William Taft, were finally reached for the purchase of 410,000 acres (167,127 hectares, to be precise) of friars' lands for $7,239,784.66. The contracts were signed on December 22, 1903.

The question then became, to whom should these lands be sold? Instead of selling them to the tenants who had tilled them and resided in them and needed them most, and thus helping to solve the land-reform problem, the commission allowed wealthy elite families and a few corporations to purchase these choice estates. For instance, the Spanish-owned Tabacalera company expanded its holdings to more than 30,000 acres by 1913. The United States forced Japan, Taiwan, and South Korea when the latter were under American control to implement drastic land reform programs, which cut the power of large landowners and installed a mass of smallholders. These major structural reforms would set the stage for their economic takeoff as the "dragons" of Asia (Litonjua 1994). In the Philippines, however, the land policy of the United States augmented the power of the landed elite, the *ilustrado* (educated) class of the Spanish regime, whom "the United States decided to govern the Philippines through" (Salamanca 1984: 2; also Culinane 2003). They will parlay those resources into economic and political power, thus making the Philippine economy and politics "an anarchy of families" (McCoy 1993), violently competing with each other for spoils. Tony Smith (1994) maintains that the American experiment in democracy in the Philippines had effects similar to those in the American South after Reconstruction: the United States handed control of the state to the oligarchs who had control of society. And land reform continues to be a festering sore in the Philippine body politic.

As far as the economy was concerned, the Philippine economy under the Americans was a typical colonial dependency that served the needs of the colonizer country, with specific policies that facilitated the exploitation of the natural resources of the islands, at the same time that they protected business and investment enterprises in the mother country. William Taft took office as Civil Governor in 1901 and inaugurated a policy of "the Philippines for the Filipinos" to promote the material and intellectual welfare of the population, which, in his own words, is "the one course which can create a market here among the people for American goods and supplies that will make the relation of the United States to the Philippines a profitable one for our merchants and manufacturers" (Constantino 1975: 291). A year after he took office, the U.S. Congress passed the Organic Act, which is best remembered for the creation of the Philippine Assembly with limited powers. But the act also set up a legal framework with a marked emphasis on the colonial economy that would facilitate the operation of U.S. businesses and investment enterprises. A high tariff wall was erected to restrain entry of Philippine products to the United States, while tariffs were adjusted in the Philippines to allow the entry of American goods on a preferential basis. Taft wanted landholdings to be allowed a maximum of 25,000 acres for the development of plantations, but the act sided with U.S. agricultural interests to limit acreage for individuals to 16 acres and for corporations to 1,024 acres, thus eliminating competition from Philippine large-scale agricultural production. Thus, the policy of "the Philippines for the Filipinos" would produce contented colonials and the continued retention and exploitation of the country by Americans.

After the destruction of the Second World War, which left Manila, after Warsaw, the most devastated city, and with its imminent departure from the country, the U.S. passed legislation that would ensure the neocolonial status of the Philippines (Shalom 1981). Philippine independence and rehabilitation were tied to the acceptance of the Philippine or Bell Trade Act which instituted nonreciprocal free trade, permitting American goods to enter the country free of duty and in unlimited quantities, but with absolute quotas imposed on the entry of Philippine goods to the American market. It was a curious kind of "benevolence" by the richest nation in the world on a war-torn and backward colony, which stood shoulder to shoulder with the colonizer in the war against Japan. But the most onerous provision was the "parity" clause which gave American citizens and corporations equal rights with Filipinos in the exploitation of natural resources and the operation of public utilities in the Philippines. It contravened the 1935 Philippine Constitution, drafted under American auspices. Its passage by the Philippine Congress and its ratification in a national plebiscite were made possible by the refusal of the American-installed Roxas administration to seat elected members of the opposition, which, in turn, led to the bloody peasant Huk rebellion. George Taylor

(1964: 133) asserted that the United States did not lay "the foundations for the development for a strong and independent Philippines. The Filipinos got off to a very bad start on the road to independence." It is doubly ironic since the end of the war was welcomed by Filipinos as their "liberation" by the Americans, whereas the rest of Southeast Asia decried their European "reoccupation."

American colonial rule was supposed to be a tutelage in democracy. But colonial democracy is a contradiction in terms. What resulted was a corrupted democracy, characterized by Benedict Anderson (1995) as "cacique democracy," essentially an oligarchical democracy and ilustrado politics, captured and imprisoned by wealth and power (Litonjua 2001). Filipino politics has often been described as enmeshed in patron-client networks (Lande 1965; also Culinane 2003), lacking therefore the structural differentiation and functional specialization of American politics. But as Julian Go (2003: 26-27) points out, "the nature of colonial rule itself led to the collaborative patterns. Colonial rule, categorically antithetical to democracy, necessitated patron-client relations among elite segments." David Steinberg (1990: 66) is more emphatic: "The Americans . . . naturally allied with the *ilustrados*, giving them access to power and wealth in exchange for collaboration. The *ilustrados*, in turn, quickly saw the advantages of such an arrangement. Neither side ever regretted this decision to collaborate." In particular, cacique democracy is the outgrowth of the "compadre colonialism" (Owen 1971) of the American period, a model of clientelist politics in which "a senior American colonial official like Cameron Forbes is simultaneously a client of a Washington bureaucrat, perhaps a client or competitor of the incumbent American Governor General, an ally or competitor of another American colonial official, the patron or rival of senior Filipino politicians in Manila, and the patron of American provincial officials with their Filipino clients" (Paredes 1989: 45). In fact, clientelist politics constituted what Stanley (1984: 5; also 1974) calls "the cynically manipulative underside of the collaborative empire," with the following consequence:

> For the Philippines and the Filipinos, the cost has been substantial. Not in terms of lives, to be sure, and not really in economic terms, either, but in terms of the integrity of the polity and the social fabric. Once in office, conservative Filipino politicians became, in effect, the fulcrum of Filipino-American relations and used their position between the two major power blocs, the Americans and the mass of their own people, for narrow self-serving ends.

On the one hand, they arrested the few significant reform programs contemplated by the American government that might have narrowed the gap between rich and poor. On the other, as the political leaders of the country, they took over the campaign for Philippine independence and used nationalist fervor to deflect criticism of their social and economic power.

One of the early acts of the Philippine Commission, chaired by William Taft, even while the fighting between Americans and Filipinos was still going on, was to direct that free primary education in English be provided to the public. On August 21, 1901, some 500 young men and women arrived on the ship *USS Thomas,* hence are known as Thomasites, to establish the Philippine educational system, patterned after that of the United States, with English as the medium of instruction. It was a stroke of colonial genius, especially as it stood in contrast to the Spanish who refused to teach their language to Indios. Education was the perfect tool of cultural colonialism, and compulsory English was the best medium for the colonized to be made in the image of the colonizer. Filipinos today glory in the fact that most Filipinos know and can speak English, unlike their counterparts in Asia, and that this English fluency makes it easier to adjust to American life and society. That I am writing this in English attests to that fact. But what we know now of language is that it is not a mere means of communication; it is a tool for the construction of social identity and social reality. Humans reached consciousness in the evolutionary ladder almost at the same time that they developed the ability to symbolize. Language as a system of conventional symbols is a powerful tool in the creation of colonial consciousness, colonial identity, colonial mentality, and colonial culture. It enables the colonizer, in the graphic imagery of Paulo Freire (1971, 1973), to inhabit the mind of the colonized, for the colonized to "house" the colonizer in his mind.

Renato Constantino (Shaw and Francia 2002: 177-92; also Constantino 1978) wrote an eye-opener of an article in 1966 in the *Weekly Graphic Magazine* with the title "The Miseducation of the Filipino." He reminded his Filipino readers that "the educational system introduced by the Americans had to correspond, and was designed to correspond, to the economic and political reality of the American conquest.... The molding of men's minds is the best means of conquest. Education, therefore, serves as a weapon in wars of colonial conquest.... The primary reason for the rapid introduction, on a large scale, of the American public educational system in the Philippines was the conviction of the military leaders that no measure could so quickly promote the pacification of the islands as education." He continued:

> The first and perhaps the master stroke in the plan to use education as an instrument of colonial policy was the decision to use English as the medium of instruction. English became the wedge that separated Filipinos from their past and later was to separate educated Filipinos from the masses of their countrymen. English introduced Filipinos to a strange, new world. With American textbooks, Filipinos started learning not only a new language but also a new way of life, alien to their traditions and yet a caricature of their model. This was the beginning of their education. At the same time, it was the beginning of their miseducation, for they learned no longer as Filipinos but as colonials. The ideal colonial was the carbon copy of his conqueror, the conformist follower of the new dispensation. He had to forget his past and unlearn the nationalist virtues in order to live peacefully, if not comfortably, under the colonial order. The new Filipino generation learned of the lives of American heroes, sang American songs, and dreamed of snow and Santa Claus. . . . Spain was the villain, America was the savior.

In a similar vein, and in an article, whose title is a perversely ironic linguistic dig, "English Is Your Mother Tongue/And Ingles Ay ang Tongue ng Ina Mo," Eric Gamalinda (Shaw and Francia 2002: 247-59) stated that "English became a mark of social standing. The more proficient one was in it, the more education one was presumed to have. This perception was important in controlling the islands. When the United States organized the Philippine Assembly shortly after the Philippine-American War, it restricted voting to Filipinos whose incomes were above a certain level and who had considerable American education."

Perhaps the most devastating and lasting effect of colonial education in a colonial language is what Filipinos themselves call "colonial mentality." It is a mentality that considers all things American as superior, and all things Filipino as inferior: books, clothes, films, TV shows, fast food, cigarettes. American goods – stateside, they are labeled – are valued and desired; Filipino products are inferior in quality and disdained. This is the main element of the "damaged culture" of the Philippines that James Fallows

(1987) wrote about, but which was criticized and attacked by a number of Filipinos, a signal itself of the colonial mentality whose continued influence is so painful to admit honestly. U.S. colonialism deformed the land, the economy, and the politics of the Philippines, as well as, its culture. Colonialism involved also cultural power, exercised by colonial rulers to impose its preferred cultural values, forms, and practices, and to marginalize, manipulate, and control cultural meanings. Cultural power worked alongside coercive power to remake colonies, and while it met resistance and clashed with local cultures, was accommodated or domesticated or transformed, colonialism's cultural impact is undeniable and critical (Go 2008). America's intent was to remake the Philippines in its own image. The end result was a distorted and damaged image.

More recent studies emphasize that colonialism was not a one-way street, but had repercussions on the colonizer. Colonialism was a multilayered process which reshaped both colonized and colonizer, affecting them in various ways and with similar effects.

Paul Kramer (2006: 2-3) has written a transnational history of race and empire in Philippine-American encounters of the early twentieth century, a history of the racial politics of empire in the United States and a history of the imperial politics of race in the Philippines: "It is, on the one hand, a history of the racial politics of empire, of the way in which racial hierarchies of difference were generated and mobilized in order to legitimate and to organize invasion, conquest, and colonial administration. . . . It is, on the other hand, a history of the imperial politics of race, of the way that empire-building interacted with, and transformed, the process of racial formation. . . .[T]hese two histories – of the racial remaking of empire and the imperial remaking of race – are not separable. It is not simply that difference made empire possible; empire remade difference in the process."

Alfred W. McCoy (2009: 8-14) also studies how "empire proved mutually transformative in ways that have arguably damaged democracy in both the Philippines and the United States."

> Both modern states were forged after 1898 in the same crucible of colonial conquest that unleashed powerful forces of mutual transformation, particularly in the sub rosa realm of internal security. . . . [America] created a colonial surveillance state that transformed the character of Philippine politics by repressing radical nationalism and replacing it with conservative patronage politics. . . . [In return,] Washington repatriated the personnel and policies of colonial rule during World War I and used

them to conduct what may have been the most systematic surveillance of its citizens ever undertaken by a modern government, producing institutional innovations that helped establish a nascent national security state. . . . [Again, there was] a reverse flow of security doctrines through the periodic dispatch of U.S. military aid and advisory teams to support the Philippine state against internal threats, from counterinsurgency against communist-led peasant guerillas in the 1950s through the antiterrorist campaign against Islamic insurgents since 2001. . . . [T]his study attempts to explore the hidden costs of this march to modernity in both America and the Philippines, arguing that progress toward democracy has also unleashed countervailing forces: a strong state security apparatus, intrusive surveillance, and an empowered executive inclined to use both.

Religion and Colonialism

The twin goals of Spain for the Philippines were the colonization of the islands and the Christianization of its people. But with the Spanish expatriate community primarily residing in the walled city of Intramuros, waiting for the departure and arrival of galleons to and from Acapulco, the transshipment point to Spain and the rest of Europe, the Spanish friars became in effect the colonizers. They went to the hinterlands, congregated the scattered native population into *reducciones* (settlements), *bajo las campanas*, underneath the church bells and as far as the church bells could be heard. They also owned large tracts of land, *latifundias*, in which tenants tilled the land and for whose material and spiritual welfare the friars were responsible. Leon Ma. Guerrero (1963) begins his biography of Jose Rizal, the national hero, with a prologue, "The Last Spaniard," who is the Catholic friar, and ends it with an epilogue, "The First Filipino," Rizal. His first sentence is a fairly accurate summation: "The Spanish history of the Philippines begins and ends with the friar." In fact, the fires of nationalism and revolution were lit by the garroting of the Filipino secular priests, Mariano Gomez, Jose Burgos, and Jacinto Zamora – popularly referred to as Gomburza – who championed the Filipinization of the clergy, and to whom Rizal will dedicate his subversive novel, *El Filibusterismo*.

Like the Spaniards, the Americans arrived in the Philippines with the sword or, better, the krag rifle for colonization and the cross for evangelization. Andrew Preston (2016: 181), however, observes:

Religion featured consistently in the nation's foreign policy between the Revolutionary War and 1898, but it was not until the Spanish-American War, the conquest of the Philippines, and World War I that religious ideologies played a key, sometimes predominant, role. Not coincidentally, these were America's first major wars that were truly foreign. They were not justified in the name of self-defense, national security, or the protection of US sovereignty, as in 1812; they were not propelled by territorial expansion, as in 1846; and they were fought either partly or entirely outside the Western Hemisphere. Once separated from the North American continent, where the imperatives of defense and territorial expansion were obvious (although still contested and controversial), US foreign policy needed strong and compelling ideological justification to pursue national objectives that were often ephemeral and tangential to the nation's actual security needs. Few aspects of American political culture were as ideally suited to the task as religion.

Already expansionists at heart, most American Protestants supported the war against Spain, and lobbied for the annexation of the Philippines. They saw the acquisition of the Philippines as saving Filipinos from Spanish misrule. They held the conviction that the Catholic religion was a corrupt form of Christianity. They saw the annexation of the Philippines as providing a God-given opportunity to expand their missionary activities, to send laborers to reap a great harvest for Christ. Convinced of the righteousness of their calling and of the superiority of their national culture, most Protestant missionaries believed that Catholic Filipino society was backward and debased. Combining Enlightenment values with evangelical zeal, they were convinced in their ability to create a new Filipino and to reform Filipino society in their own image and likeness. Methodists, Presbyterians, Episcopalians, Baptists, other missionary societies and alliances, bible societies and Christian associations soon began fielding missionaries into the fields of ripening harvest. "The Methodist mission soon became the largest mission in the Philippines. By 1916 at least fifty missionaries had served in the mission, and the church claimed about 45,000 members. By 1925 the figure was over 65,000" (Clymer 1986: 5).

At the same time, something curious was happening with the American Catholic Church. Mary Dorita Clifford (1969: 301-02) noted: "The failure of the Catholic Church in the United States to assume responsibility for the religious development of the Philippines when the sovereignty of those islands passed from Spain to the United States has never been honestly admitted by American Catholics. . . . The lack of American response was due, at least in part, to the feeling that sending missionaries to the islands might imply that American Catholics accepted as true the charges of scandal, negligence, and tyranny leveled against the friars. But after Rome refused to expel the friars and sent an American archbishop and three American bishops to the archipelago, this excuse was no longer tenable, yet the response did not improve. The age was one of competitive Christianity, and American Catholics seemed willing to fight Protestant efforts to proselytize, but not to assume the burden. And when, as frequently happened, bigotry raised its ugly head, it was likely to be a Catholic as a Protestant one." Put simply, the American bishops were concerned about the disposition of the friar lands, but they were as racist and supremacist toward a benighted and inferior race as every American of their time was.

The discussion of two issues, where "the Filipino reaction to American rule was most enthusiastic, and institutional change greatest" (Salamanca 1984: 181), will suffice to underlie the role of religion, primarily American Protestant in this case, under American rule in the Philippines: the separation of Church and state, and religion in public schools. One characteristic of Spanish rule in the Philippines was the close alliance between the Roman Catholic Church and the Spanish colonial government. The Philippine Revolution broke out in 1896, one of whose causes was the abuses of the Spanish friars, although it should be pointed out that Filipinos in general were antifriar without being antichurch or anti-Catholic. Title III, Article 5, of the Malolos Constitution read: "The State recognizes the liberty and equality of all religious worship, as well as the separation of Church and State." From the moment of its arrival, the United States became involved in the religious situation in the islands. The terms of capitulation of the city of Manila by Spanish forces in August 1898 stipulated that churches and places of worship and their private property were placed under the safeguard of the American army. It made the U.S. army the protector of the Catholic Church in Manila against attack or seizure by Filipino revolutionaries. Under the Philippine Commission headed by Taft and with instructions by President McKinley, the basic policy of the American regime respecting religion became complete separation of Church and State. This was confirmed in the Organic Act of 1902 and the Jones Law of 1916.

American Roman Catholics generally favored the principle of separation of church and state and of religious liberty as applied to the

Philippines. The policy was also endorsed by Protestant missionaries and helped ease the mind of those Filipinos who were most concerned to see the Catholic Church, especially the friars, disestablished. But Roman Catholic authorities in the Philippines considered religious liberty adverse to public peace, fearing the influx of Protestant missionaries and their freedom to proselytize Filipinos. Peter Gowing (1969: 221) judged that "it took time for the real meaning of religious liberty to impress itself on the minds of the Filipino people... The Roman Catholic Church, stripped of direct power in the government of the Philippines, was left to concentrate on its religious and social ministry far more than before. The coming of American and various European Catholic missionaries helped to liberalize the general nature of Hispanic-Philippine Catholicism. New emphases emerged in church life and Roman Catholics adjusted to the climate of democracy and pluralism fostered during the American regime."

One of the major problems to emerge from the policy of the separation of church and state was that of religion in public education. Under Spain, schools had been almost wholly directed by the church, and remained very largely in the hands of friars. The Americans sought to establish a secular public school system patterned after that of the United States. This brought the American civil and military authorities in conflict with Catholic Church representatives who feared the emergence of a "godless" education. The issue was complicated by "the deeper issue of competitive Christianity [which] found no avenue of communication open with each other. Government officials charged with the obligation of absolute impartiality had no easy task and no assurance that anyone would credit them with acting in good faith.... [E]ven men who acted honestly and impartially were subject to attack, usually most severe from their own coreligionists" (Clifford 1969: 304). Taft had hoped to avoid friction in critical areas, such as education, by making all concessions possible within the constitutional framework of separation of church and state.

In December 1900, a school bill was ready for public hearings and a final vote. But the provision for the use of school buildings after school hours for religious instruction drew a great deal of fire. Another provision for 1,000 American teachers of English brought forth charges of proselytism and favoritism, and led directly to the adoption of a civil service examination as a method for selecting teachers for the schools. On January 21, 1901, the school bill was passed. But recriminations and attacks did not stop which now centered on secretaries of education. Two other problems cropped up: the use of biased textbooks in the schools and the placing of Filipino exchange students to the United States in Protestant colleges and universities. James F. Smith as Secretary of Education successfully established a civil service for the selection, promotion, and dismissal of teachers and superintendents, took a courageous stand on the textbook issue, and completely reorganized the Department of Education. When Smith accepted the governorship in 1906, his continued interest in the Department of Education ensured that David Prescott Barrows, responsible for the reorganization, stayed on as a general superintendent until1909 and that the measures which had been adopted to eliminate discriminatory practices were continued.

"Thus, the foundations of a modern, secular educational system [were established and] were readily and warmly accepted" by both American colonial administrators and Filipino educational elite (Salamanca 1984: 161).

Kenton Clymer (1986: 7-8) gives an overall assessment of the Protestant role in the American colonization of the Philippines:

> The missionaries constituted an important and articulate segment of the American colonial population. They helped shape attitudes in the Philippines and in the United States about Filipino culture and about the American presence in the islands; on occasion they helped shaped policy as well. They helped reconcile Filipinos to their new fate and were allies with the government in what both perceived as "civilizing" mission. At the same time, they viewed themselves as the conscience of the American experiment and did not hesitate to judge other Americans harshly for not living up to what they believed was the best in the American tradition. An examination of their ideas, attitudes, and perceptions [which he does in his volume], then, helps us understand better the American colonial experience and the colonial mentality.

But as far as the specifically religious Protestant mission, i.e. the conversion of natives and the establishment of churches, Clymer (1986: 3) asserts: "Spain succeeded admirably in her task. The tenacious Moros in the south held fast to Islam, and many Igorots and other mountain and forest people retained their traditional animistic faiths. But the rest of the population (the great majority) adopted Spanish Catholicism, though with distinctly Filipino nuances. Here, as elsewhere, a syncretic Catholicism emerged." American Protestant missionary activity did not do much to change the religious picture.

Clymer (1986: 194-95) adds:

> [M]ost missionaries, reflecting the intellectual milieu of the late nineteenth century, displayed condescending, paternalistic, and sometimes racist attitudes toward Filipinos. Though their attitudes in this regard were no worse (and perhaps were more enlightened) than those of other American colonialists, their openly expressed skepticism of the Filipino capacity may well have hindered their efforts to convert the people. Such attitudes were especially noticeable in the missionary response to expressions of Filipino nationalism. Although most missionaries hoped eventually to produce self-governing and self-supporting churches, they could, at first, scarcely imagine Filipinos in leadership positions anytime soon. Thus they deplored Filipino-led schisms, which they blamed on ambitious, immature, and corrupt men. . . . [M]any were suspicious of a Filipino-controlled church of any description and considered the self-proclaimed bishop of the Independent Church a radical nationalist and something of a charlatan.
>
> In any event, only about three percent of the present-day population traces its religious roots directly to Protestant missionaries.

This is surely connected with the *anthropological poverty* which, with economic and political exploitation, was a legacy of colonialism. As John Parratt (2004: 5) explained it in the context of emerging Third World theologies:

> What is being identified here is the denigration of integrity, humanness and culture. Perhaps the most obvious way was the imposition of an alien language upon colonised peoples. . . . [L]anguage speaks of personal and cultural identity. Allied to this went the denigration of aspects of culture, and in particular of indigenous religions. If economic and political disruption resulted from Western imperialism, the demonisation of indigenous cultures was more likely to be the result of [Western] Christian missions. This happened most dramatically with "traditional" or folk

cultures from which the majority of Christian converts came. . . . In the process of description these forms of religiosity were demonised by the use of emotive and pejorative terminology. Little attempt was made to understand the kind of spirituality which gave rise to these religious forms. While colonial administrators were on the whole less likely to be concerned with value judgments on traditional religion, Christian missions usually pursued a policy of seeking to wipe the slate clean of "paganism" so that the true faith could be written afresh on the mind of the native – a theory of "displacement."

Conclusion

"The Philippines was indelibly marked by the DNA of colonialism," Luis Francia (2010: 10) writes. "The country's very name encapsulates its colonial history. The Anglicized 'Philippines' or the Spanish 'Filipinas' is forever a reminder that this Southeast Asian archipelago was named in 1543 by Ruy Lopez de Villalobos in honor of the sixteenth century Spanish crown prince who would in 1556 become King Felipe II." Not only is the name of the country and its citizens of colonial origin, but the identity of the country and its citizens bear a colonial imprint. Three and a half centuries of Spanish colonialism, a half century of American imperialism, and three years of Japanese occupation cannot but affect the trajectory of Philippine history and the shape of Filipino identity, society, and culture.

The trouble is that memory has played tricks, the remembrance of things past is not fully accurate, and so the present is damaged, and the future looks dim. In the Filipino mind's historical eye, the remote Spanish past was tyrannical and villainous, the American colonial regime was benevolent and beneficent, and the Japanese occupation was simply brutal. Filipino memory has been deflected especially by the partnership between the United States and the Philippine against the Japanese during the Second World War, which has grown to mythic propositions, by the bravery at Bataan and Corregidor and the horror of the Death March, by the promise of General Douglas MacArthur: "I shall return." Renato Constantino attributes it to the miseducation of the Filipino. According to Karl Marx, where you stand (on an issue) depends on where you sit (your interests). For W.I. Thomas whatever is perceived as real has real consequences. Whatever the case may be, there is the need for reexamination, reevaluation, and revision.

Nobody, as afar as I know, has suggested a reexamination of the Japanese occupation, unless it is to determine the claim of the Marcoses that they discovered the treasure of Yamashita to explain their unexplained and unexplainable wealth!

Different and various aspects of the American colonial regime have been the subject of intense, ongoing, and fruitful study and research, and they have been and continue to be published in books and articles. This article simply shares an aspect of that reevaluation.

Is it time for restudying and reexamining the long demonized Spanish past in the Philippines? The thought enters my mind as I finish this article, as the United States prepares for the visit of Pope Francis this September 2015, and as controversy swirls over the canonization of Fray Junipero Serra. Serra was a Spanish Franciscan friar who is considered the father of California for having founded missions from Baja California to San Francisco in the latter part of the eighteenth century. Some Americans of Native American extraction have criticized the proposed canonization because they accuse Serra of mistreating their ancestors and for being associated with the suppression of their culture. My thought has nothing to do with condoning the genocide perpetrated against Native Americans, nor with erasing the sinful complicity of the Church in that crime against humanity, but with a deeply respectful acknowledgment of original Indian life which, after all, Junipero Serra served up to the moment of his death.

My thought is occasioned by an article by Serra's biographer, Gregory Orfalea (2015), who confronts accusations of what happened to the Indians of the Americas in what has been called the first "world war," certainly the original sin of the nation: the spread of smallpox, American violence, genocide, and enslavement. During the French and Indian War of 1760s, a British officer suggested to his officers that they inoculate the Indians with smallpox by means of blankets. This was not the only case. In the following century at least forty smallpox and measles epidemics would ravage the native population. Disease was responsible for the majority of Indians deaths, but American violence was also pervasive. At Sand Creek, at Wounded Knee, during the Modoc War of 1872, Indians were massacred, including, if not mostly, women and children. The arrival of Europeans on the continent saw the decline of 93 percent of the native population. There is no evidence, Orfalea asserts, that Serra was implicated in any such crimes.

There is another distinction to be made between Spanish and Anglo colonists, according to Orfalea. In Spanish America, numerous indigenous peoples were incorporated, rather than eliminated. In California under Spain, there were no large-scale massacres like at Wounded Knee. Under American rule, the loss of indigenous lives was catastrophic, 80 percent died, due not to disease but to murder. "What the Americans did in all but extirpating Indians from the continent was genocide," Orfalea declares, "What the Spanish did, at least in California, was not."

There also was the accusation of slavery, which accusation had its roots in the misunderstanding or ignorance of how the missions worked. No Indians were forced to enter a mission. For a native population, undergoing a disorienting invasion, the missions offered considerable enticements: food, shelter, clothing, the beauty of the churches, and the transfixing display of Spanish power. But there was catch. Once one entered the mission, one was forbidden to leave without permission, and those who did, unless they voluntarily returned, were punished. Indians were hunted down and lashed for leaving. It is estimated that the desertion rate was ten percent, which means that ninety percent stayed. It is also important to note that the majority of California Indians never came to the missions in the first place. At any rate, nothing in the record suggests, Orfalea points out, that Serra was a cruel and vindictive overlord.

Bu I also need to point out that Orfalea's biography is itself scathingly criticized for his manipulation of facts and elaborate use of florid language, thus perpetuating the myths that deny the violence that Junipero Serra brought to indigenous peoples (Abeyta 2015).

"The current puzzlement and anger over the Serra canonization," Orfalea rightly indicates, "is motivated by an entirely justified revulsion over the historic crimes committed against the Indians." There is still much that needs to be confronted with and repented of in the colonization of native peoples, not least by the Christian churches. William Faulkner famously said that "the past is never dead; it is not even past." The past continues to haunt the present, as well as, to cloud the future. Thus, it is necessary to continue to study and research the past, and to make reevaluations and revisions when deemed necessary – for the sake of the present and the future.

In the conclusion of his three-volume masterwork on the Spanish Empire of Carlos V and Felipe II, Hugh Thomas (2014: 293) acknowledges that "the Spanish Empire has been consistently denigrated in the rest of the world." But he then adduces considerations that soften the blows. For one thing, "the Spaniards went to great lengths to analyse the moral basis of their conquests" (Thomas 2014: 287), in which disputations towered the heroic figure of Bartolome de las Casas, and which questionings previous and subsequent empires never undertook. Across the landscape of their empire, great architects carried the ideas behind Spanish churches and palaces in a creative outburst comparable to what occurred in Europe in the Middle Ages. After the building of churches, another remarkable achievement was the policy of congregating the indigenous population in medium-sized towns, where they could be more easily cared for but also supervised, and which became their present urban infrastructure. A string of feasts, processions, and celebrations held the empire spiritually together, facilitated the transmission of the message of Christianity, and continues to enliven the cultures of the peoples up to the present. The Spanish empire lasted three centuries, left behind a Catholic religion and innumerable monuments, a tradition and much literature, and, above all, created dependencies which matured into new independent countries. "Wars in this region are rare. In comparison with the rest of the world, Latin American now seems an oasis of peace" (Thomas 2014: 296).

"Perhaps the greatest achievement of Philip was his inspiration which created a new Christian world in the Americas [and in the Philippines]. Can one imagine in any other age the creative novelty which led to the construction of so many convents, monasteries, and churches? . . . Old Europe had had similar monuments of faith, but in the New World they were an astonishing innovation which articulated the good life for several hundred years," so Hugh Thomas (2014: 298-99) ends his trilogy. Food for thought in the continuing task of studying the past for the sake of the present and the future. After all, the whole of our past has made us who we are.

NOTES

[1] It is worth noting that Reinhold Niebuhr (1932), the most influential American theologian in the 1930's through the 1950s, in his now classic *Moral Man and Immoral Society*, elaborated "that a sharp distinction must be drawn between the moral and social behavior of individuals and social groups, national, racial, and economic." The moral behavior of individuals can be brought about through reason, persuasion, and education, but "when collective behavior, whether in the form of imperialism or class domination, exploits weakness, it can never be dislodged unless power is raised against it. . . . [P]ower must be challenged by power."

In his chapter. "The Morality of Nations," he pointed out that "perhaps the most significant moral characteristic of a nation is hypocrisy. . . . Hardly any war of history has been the occasion of more hypocrisy and sentimentality than the Spanish-American War. . . . The Spanish-American War offers some of the most striking illustrations of the hypocrisy of governments as well as the self-deception of intellectuals. . . . The war was launched on a wave of patriotic sentimentality in which both the religious idealists and the humanitarians went into ecstasies over our heroic defense of the Cuban people . . . Since no promises were made in regard to the Philippines, the hypocrisy of a nation could express itself most unrestrainedly in the policies dealing with them. Though the little junta, of which Theodore Roosevelt and Senator Lodge were the leaders, had carefully planned the campaign of war so that the Philippines would be ours, the fiction that the fortunes of war had made us unwilling recipients and custodians of the Philippine Islands was quickly fabricated and exists to this day. We decided to keep the Philippines against their will at the conclusion of a war ostensibly begun to free the Cubans. . . . The instructions to the army, after Spain finally ceded the islands and the peace treaty was signed, complete the chapter in hypocrisy with an almost perfect touch of dishonesty: 'It will be the duty of the commander of the forces of occupation to announce and proclaim in the most public manner possible that we have come not as invaders or as conquerors but as friends.'"

[2] Aside from sources referenced in the text, elements of this narrative can be found, to name a few, in Abaya (1967), Beisner (1968), Stanley (1974), Constantino (1975), Agoncillo and Guerrero (1977), Healy (1970), Welch (1979), May (1980), Miller (1982), Bain (1984), Karnow (1989).

More recent sources include: Brands (1992), Golay (1997), Musicant (1998), Nugent (2008), Thomas (2010), Miller (2011), Jones (2012).

[3] American history has generally ignored the ignominy and enormity of the Philippine-American War. The classic treatment is Wolff (1960), which was reissued by History Book Club in 2006. More recent treatments are Roth (1981), Linn (2000), Silbey (2007).

6

RELIGION AND VIOLENCE: THE PRIME ANALOGATE OF THE HUMAN

9/11 ignited the current debate on whether or not religion is inherently prone to divisiveness and violence. The butchery of the self-designated Islamic State has only inflamed passions on both sides of the question. One the one side, the so-called New Atheists – Richard Dawkins, Christopher Hitchens, Sam Harris, and Daniel Dennett who embrace their reputation as the "Four Horsemen" – vociferously proclaim that religion is inherently destructive and violent; it clings like a bad seed, it is a relic from the past, and it's time is over. On the other hand, Michael Cavanaugh and Karen Armstrong, one a theologian and the other a historian of religion, have argued that inherent religious violence is a myth, that religion is a construct in the making of modernity to separate rational from irrational, public from private, state from church; anything associated with this construct does not have a transhistorical and transultural reality imputed to it.

This essay seeks to address the myth and reality of religious violence. The traditional liberal narrative of modernity will serve as the background and context of the discussion. Then the arguments of Michael Cavanaugh and Karen Armstrong regarding the myth of religious violence will be laid out. Secularism seems to underlay the arguments against religions violence, so a brief discussion of secularism and its discontents will follow. Finally, I present the prime analogate of the human as an overall template in discussing the issue of violence in religion, which especially applies to the fundamentalism and extremism of Wahhabism.

Modernity and the Liberal Narrative

Charles Taylor (2007: 3), in his masterwork *A Secular Age*, sought to study the titanic shift that happened in Western civilization. "The change I want to define and trace is one which takes us from a society in which it was virtually impossible not to believe in God, to one in which faith, even for the staunchest believer is one human possibility among others," to one, in other words, in which it is possible not to believe in God. He juxtaposed 1500 and 2000, specifically the "porous self" of 1500 to the "buffered self" of 2000. The porous self lived in a divine, enchanted world in which the fullness of life shone through from the outside and from above, from nature and from God, while the buffered self – opaque, bounded, roughened, cushioned, shielded – is rendered impervious to an enchanted cosmos, lives in a disenchanted place, a disciplined and free agent, confronted by a multiplicity of choices for the fullness of life which he alone can choose. It is the difference between contemplating a stained-glass window from inside the church, with the sunlight shining through it, and looking at the stained-glass window from outside. It constitutes "the epochal shift from finding our place in the cosmos to constructing an order within the universe" (Taylor 2007: 114). In other words, it is the rise of modernity, the emergence of a secular age.

There is general agreement that this epochal shift from faith to reason, from authority to liberty, from hierarchy to equality, and from church to civil society happened during the Enlightenment, the period in the seventeenth and eighteenth centuries, when the philosophical ideas of Thomas Hobbes and John Locke and the political system that emerged from them toppled the *ancien regime* of throne and altar.

James MacGregor Burns(2013: 9) sets the stage:

> A century after Martin Luther unleashed the Reformation in Wittenberg, strife between Catholics and Protestants was reaching a terrible climax. The Thirty Years' War engulfed Europe in brutal and chaotic conflict. Mercenary armies of competing emperors and popes, princes, dukes, and archbishops roamed Europe, pillaging towns and villages and slaughtering civilians. They destroyed food stocks and spread plague. Some regions lost more than half of their population. And even as the frenzy of all-against-all conflict gripped the continent, bloody civil war mounted in England that would end in a king's execution and rule by Protestant zealots. Many Europeans despaired that the Apocalypse was at hand.

It was in this world of violence and fear that the first, frail lamps of the Enlightenment were lit. The early philosophers witnessed the devastation, testimony to the desperate need for new thinking, for a revolution in ideas about humankind. The question was simple and stark: How could people be secure in their lives, empowered to make choices conducive to their peace and liberty and happiness?

Amid the devastation, MacGregor Burns identifies five personalities who led the way in the revolution of ideas. For Thomas Hobbes, "there was only the eternal struggle against the darkness and disorder that were the work not of the devil but of men themselves, written in their nature. Yet his justification of civil society and his account of its formation by the consent of the governed became cornerstones of Enlightenment thought, adopted by such thinkers as Spinoza and Locke and Rousseau as well as American and French revolutionaries" (Burns 2013: 12-13). The Enlightenment was the triumph of reason: the highest quality of human beings was not their resemblance to God but their capacity to reason. "Francis Bacon, whose proposal for a new empirical science to replace the arid abstractions of medieval scholasticism gave the Enlightenment its characteristic methods of inquiry and reason. . . . [H]e had the revolutionary idea that the search for truth began with the humble station of a *fact*. . . . Fact was reason's raw material, from which the scientist or philosopher could reach more and more general truths . . . Ultimately, they would arrive at what Bacon considered the grand prize, knowledge of the laws that govern the physical world" (Burns 2013: 13). And knowledge was power which kings could not buy or command.

For Rene Descartes, the first criterion and test of truth was the individual mind: *cogito, ergo sum* – I think, therefore I am – no skepticism could shake the certainty of his own existence. "But the stark rejection of any authority except the mind, with all certainty built up from the new *cogito*, was revolutionary. Just as Copernicus had replaced Earth with the sun at the center of the cosmos, so with the *cogito*, as the authority of God yielded to the thought of man, an idea that would become the first principle of the Enlightenment" (Burns 2013: 19). Baruch Spinoza would weave a wide fabric of thought more radical than any philosopher of the Enlightenment. "He passionately believed that religion was the greatest impediment to enlightenment. . . . [H]is example of biblical criticism would become a powerful weapon in the Enlightenment's long struggle to come to terms with religion. . . . Enlightenment was the key – the use of reason to fulfill the injunction that Descartes had planted as the root of modern thought: Know thyself. . . . No philosopher would make so intoxicating a claim for enlightenment, nor make enlightenment so central to human salvation" (Burns 2013: 23-27).

John Locke was the most consequential of Enlightenment philosophers. "Like most other philosophers of the Enlightenment, he gave a central place to the glowing idea of reason, but his account of it was more qualified, better grounded in empiricism. Though Descartes helped introduce him to the power of rational thought, the Englishman was alive to its limitations, that it would approach the truth only when combined with experience, which included the factor of education" (Burns 2013: 33). "Locke's model was of a radical equality – all human beings born with equally unfurnished but equally-potential-laden minds. . . . No single idea of the Enlightenment was so laden and sweeping as this. . . . Locke wiped the slate clean; he gave people the possibility of starting the world anew" (Burns 2013: 35). "In Locke's state of nature, the insecurity and fear that would drive people together centered directly not on life or liberty, but on property . . . [Thus,] in liberal doctrine, property was the third great value of the trinity, with life and liberty; it became identified with the pursuit of happiness" (Burns 2013: 36, 257). "Locke struck blows at the pillars of absolutism. . . . [But] for Locke, liberty was not a mere negative value, defined by an absence of infringement by government or other people. As a natural right possessed by all, it obliged government to create conditions for its enjoyment and enlargement, though what that meant in practice would be debated for centuries. Still, liberty was a means, not an end. The greatest good, Locke thought, was *happiness*" (Burns 2013: 37). After the Glorious Revolution, Locke attended to the publication of his major works, for which he is better known today.

These revolutionary ideas would be commented upon and debated, elaborated and expanded, and would constitute the Enlightenment's original contribution to politics and economics – liberalism, liberal individualism, individual liberty. They would be at the center of the three great revolutions of the West – British, American, and French – and would be the ideological forces in the making of the modern world. These ideas would lead to the concepts of human rights and religious liberty, the separation of church and state, the differentiation between public and private spheres, the equality of all peoples, regardless of race, color, religion, national origins, gender, sexual orientation, and sexual identity. It would not be, however, a straight and direct line of descent, but would take a long and winding road (Casanova 2007), that would include religious and medieval antecedents, confessionalization of states and territorialization of religions and peoples – *cuius regio eius religio* – the emergence of the nation-state, modern nationalism, colonialism in which race and religion figured, and post-World War II secularization until it results in modern Western secularism. What has been called "the great separation" (Lilla 2007; Litonjua 2007) was not only a long-term historical process, but the entanglement of religion and politics continues to inform modern history and politics, as well as, the movements for social and political reforms – abolition and civil rights, women's suffrage and sexual liberations – in modern liberal societies.

But it is equally true that Enlightenment ideas posed the greatest threat to religious ideas, based as the latter are on faith, tradition, hierarchy, ontological inequality, and scriptural inerrancy. This is especially true in the areas of sexuality, marriage, the family and the home, and women's equality and rights. Thus, the phenomenon of religious fundamentalism has arisen in all religions, which is fundamentally a protest against modernity and the modern world (Lawrence 1990). The Catholic Church, for one, which at Vatican II was said to have made a *rapprochement* with modernity, continues to resist change in the areas of women's rights and human sexuality. What is worse is that the religious impulse is seen as basically apocalyptic, the imposition of God's justice by violence. *Deus vult!* – God wills it! – was the rallying cry of the Crusaders, and religion can be the ultimate, because divine, legitimation of violence. It is a short distance to the allegation that religion is inherently violent.

The Myth of Religious Violence

It is this claim of the inherent violent nature of religion that Michael Cavanaugh vigorously argues against, although it is disconcerting to pick up and read a book entitled *The Myth of Religious Violence* only to find out that the argument is *not* that religion is not violent at all, because, as he himself puts it, that would be like "denying that the world is round." What then is the argument all about? Cavanaugh helpfully summarizes his book (Cavanaugh 2009) in a later article (Cavanaugh 2016).

First, "the idea that religion has a peculiar tendency to promote violence depends on the ability to distinguish religion from what is not religion – the secular, in other words.... What interests me is the way that religion is treated in all the arguments as a transhistorical and transcultural phenomenon that is essentially distinct from secular phenomena. That is, religion is thought to exist in all times and places, and it is essentially absolutist, divisive, and nonrational in ways that secular phenomena are not" (Cavanaugh 2016: 179). There is no coherent distinction between religious and secular. Many definitions of religion are substantivist, others are functionalist. "I think a more satisfactory approach is neither substantivist nor functionalist but constructivist. That is, there is no once-and-for-all definition of religion or the secular. The religious/secular distinction is a modern Western construction that arose as an adjunct to the rise of the modern state and the triumph of civil over ecclesiastical authorities in early modern Europe" (Cavanaugh 2016: 181).

Granted that religion is a social construction of reality, as all social institutions are, are Christianity, Catholicism, Protestant and its various denominations, Judaism, and Islam, therefore, not transhistorical and transcultural religions in their own right?

Second, Cavanaugh traces the genealogy of the distinction between religious and secular. "It is only with the birth of the modern sovereign state that the concept of religion as it is now generally understood was born. . . . It is more accurate to see that the new concept of 'religion' as a separate pursuit from 'secular' was born as a product of the long medieval struggle for predominance between ecclesiastical and civil authorities in Europe. The religious/secular distinction should be seen as reflecting a contingent and local set of political arrangements" (Cavanaugh 2016: 182-83).

Granted that the modern concept of religion was born with the modern sovereign state, are they both bastards, not worthy to be credibly believed and legitimately recognized? Is religion merely a by-product of state formation?

Third, Cavanaugh then applies his genealogy of religion to the so-called Wars of Religion in Europe in the sixteenth and seventeenth centuries, which are commonly used to justify the necessity of the Western secular state. "Something more than doctrinal zealotry was clearly going on, but I do not argue that the wars were really political or economic and not religious. The very distinction between religious and political or religious and economic was what was at stake in the wars; those distinctions were being invented as a consequence of the so-called Wars of Religion, which Jose Casanova says are more accurately called 'the wars of early modern European state formation.' . . . [T]he rise of the state was a primary cause of – not solution to – the so-called Wars of Religion" (Cavanaugh 2016: 185).

Granted that the wars of religion were wars of early modern European state formation, do they make them less wars of religion? Are the wars of religion to be subordinated to the wars of state formation in importance and vehemence? Cause or solution? Chicken or egg?

Finally, Cavanaugh (2016: 186) himself ends: "If there is a simple way to sum up the thesis of the book, it is this: people kill for all sorts of things that they treat as gods, including supposedly 'secular' things like 'freedom.' . . . The point is not at all to deny that Christians and Muslims, for example, use their faith as justification for violence; the point is to level the playing field, so that we examine not just violence on behalf of *jihad* or Jesus, but violence on behalf of free markets and free elections."

Is that what it all boils down to? Well and good! But did he have to write a book whose title dismisses religious violence, which, in turn, leads to the dismissal of his book? I think Cavanaugh overstates his case, and in doing so undermines his own indictment.

Karen Armstrong (2014b) wrote *Fields of Blood: Religion and the History of Violence* which starts with the depiction of the annual ceremony in ancient Israel in which the high priest brought two goats into the Jerusalem temple on the Day of Atonement. He sacrificed one to expiate the sins of the community and then laid his hands on the other, transferring all the people's misdeeds onto its head, and sent the sin-laden animal out of the city, literally placing the blame elsewhere. In this way, Moses explained, "the goat will bear all their faults away with it into the desert place." In his classic study of religion and violence, Rene Girard argued that the scapegoat ritual defused rivalries among groups within the community. In a similar way, Karen Armstrong lays down the principal argument of her book: Modern society has made a scapegoat of faith. Religion has been made a scapegoat of society's violence.

"But [her book] reminds us also that religion can be used, manipulated, and corrupted to rationalize, justify, and legitimate base economic, political, racial, and other issues, especially if they are conjoined with political power and to political purposes. Or that religious bodies, under the cloak of religious liberty and in a misguided recourse to politics, would try to impose their beliefs on the whole of society. Most of all, it should allow us to discern what true religion is so that its prophetic voice for justice and peace can more easily be heard. And not be made a scapegoat for society's violence" (Litonjua 2015a).

In an article in *The Guardian*, Armstrong (2014a) also attacks "the myth of religious violence," "that there is a violent essence inherent in religion, which inevitably radicalizes any conflict – because once combatants are convinced that God is on their side, compromise becomes impossible and cruelty knows no bounds." Similar to Cavanaugh, Armstrong also points out that it was the European Wars, in the 16th an 17th centuries, that helped create this myth, since "before the modern period, religion was not a separate activity, hermetically sealed off from all others; rather it permeated all human undertakings, including economics, state-building, politics and warfare." But she admits that "the Crusades were certainly inspired by religious passion, but they were also deeply political. . . . that Protestants and Catholics certainly experienced [the European wars of religion] as a life-and-death religious struggle, this was also a conflict between two sets of state-builders." Can we separate religions apart as a cause of these conflicts? Or relegate them to a subordinate position?

But in her account of the rise of the liberal secular state, she writes that "all too often an aggressive secularism has pushed religion into a violent riposte. Every fundamentalist movement that I have studied in Judaism, Christianity and Islam is rooted in a profound fear of annihilation, convinced that the liberal and secular establishment is determined to destroy their way of life. This has been tragically apparent in the Middle East." In her peroration, Armstrong ends by saying that "secularism has undoubtedly been valuable to the west, but . . . when secularization has been applied by force, it has provoked a fundamentalist reaction – and history shows that fundamentalist movements which come under attack invariably grow ever more extreme. The fruits of this error are on display across the Middle East: when we look with horror upon the travesty of Isis, we would be wise to acknowledge that its barbaric violence may be, at least in part, the offspring of policies guided by our disdain."

Both Cavanaugh and Armstrong raise important valid points. But as in any other argument, there is a tendency to emphasize where you are right and where the other is wrong, and in doing so, instead of righting the imbalance, you create your own imbalance. Religion is inherently violent, says one side. No, that is a myth, answers the other side. It is secularism and secular ideologies that are equally violent. And so the debate goes on without end.

Secularism and Its Discontents

It would appear that Cavanaugh's and Armstrong's strictures against religious violence have as an underlying aim to discredit the generally positive and beneficial view of secularism, especially as it is presented as an antidote against the supposedly violent tendencies of religion while ignoring or eliding the equally violent proclivities of secular ideologies. This is especially pointed out by Stephen Law (2014) in his response to Karen Armstrong. There are various meanings of "secular" and "secularism." Secular does not necessarily mean not religious, and secularism is not always opposition to religion. "Contemporary political secularists are concerned with religious *neutrality*. They want the state to be neutral on matters of religion. They want church/state separation. They believe the state should not endorse one religion over another, or indeed endorse atheism over religion. They suppose the state should not fund religious schools, or automatically put religious people into positions of political power (any more than the state should be doing this for atheists). This secular neutrality extends to the law. There should not be one law for the religious and another for everyone else. Secularists say, 'One law for all'. . . . Secondly, secularists, in this contemporary sense, emphasize the importance of *religious thought and expression*. People should be free to express their religious beliefs. Religious practice should be protected. Of course the same goes for atheists and secular humanists: they should be no less free to express their views, organise themselves, and publicly argue against religion if they wish. "

Law adds: "Many religious people are Secularists. . . . Still, plenty of religious conservatives and fundamentalists oppose Secularism. Why? Because they do, in fact, want their religion privileged. They want their faith schools state-funded. They want their church leaders undemocratically placed into positions of political power. And they want the legal system to exempt them, on religious ground, from the equal rights protection that applies to everyone else."

Charles Taylor (2007, 2011) has effectively argued that secularization does not mean the privatization of religion, its reduction to the private sphere, nor does it result in the evacuation of religion from the public square, its irrelevance in public affairs. Much less does secularization culminate in the decline and eventual disappearance of religion. Taylor calls these views as constituting the subtraction theory of secularization. Instead, he has convincingly shown that secularization is the gradual explosion over centuries of the galloping pluralism of styles, forms, ways of human flourishing, of the plurality of human choices for human fullness: from the construction of a purely humanistic account of a meaningful life without explicit reference to God, to continued adherence to traditional religiosity and spirituality, centered on God, church, prayer, and sacraments – to no religion at all.

It is well to remember that the world of created reality, the *saeculum*, was granted its integrity and autonomy when the ancient Hebrews conceptualized Yahweh as "wholly other," differentiated from but not opposed to secular reality. In Christianity, the doctrine of the Incarnation also warrants and affirms the integrity and autonomy of the world. But because most sociologists adhered to the subtraction theory of secularization, most notably Peter Berger (1969, 1999) but who has, however, since recanted, secularism was seen as opposed to, if not as actively destined to eliminate religion. A less loaded term like secularity, instead of secularism, could lead to a better understanding of the secular age, its relationship to and need for the sacred, in light of secularism and its discontents, exemplified by the emergence of postmodernism and calls for a post-secular society (Habermas 2008).

John Thornhill (2000: vii-ix) lays down the achievement of and the discontent with secular modernity:

> Modernity's reaction against late medievalism was entirely justified and necessary. The effort to replace the dead hand of tradition with a genuine accountability was, in fact, an outstanding example of the quest for excellence and truth – with deep roots in the Judeo-Christian and Hellenistic traditions – which has been an outstanding characteristic of Western civilization. . . .
>
> The culture of modernity has been forced by the accelerated developments and upheavals of the twentieth century to look more closely at the intellectual assumptions it has long taken for granted. Today, these assumptions are coming under criticism from two opposing directions. The proponents of "postmodernism," on the one hand, would argue that the project of modernity has manifestly failed; it stands condemned of having replaced the "meta-narratives" of the mythologies and religions of past cultures with what were really perspectives of group (class, race, gender) interest and dominance. On the other hand, . . . a growing number of Western thinkers argu[e] that the project of modernity, far from being abandoned, must be carried forward upon the basis of a critical review of the assumptions of the "scientific" methodology which has so powerfully dominated its development. . . . [O]ur Western tradition must not turn away from a job half done. . . .
>
> Central to these problems [affecting the crisis of self-confidence of Western culture] is the lack of any fundamental agreement concerning the nature of reality and the meaning of human existence. If the intellectual principles upon which the project of modernity is built are no more than a shared ideology and the in-house discussions of a philosophy which has become so esoteric that it has no concern to make itself intelligible to ordinary people, then our cultural tradition is forced to live with an emptiness at its core which breeds boredom, frustrations, and self-destructive violence which has come to be all-too

familiar problems in the Western world [and the world as a whole].

It will be remembered that Max Weber (1958), the great sociologist of modernity who identified "instrumental rationality" as its core, already warned of "an iron cage of bureaucratic rationality that permeates every aspect of modern existence." In his own words:

> No one knows who will live in this cage in the future, or whether at the end of this tremendous development entirely new prophets will arise, or there will be a great rebirth of old ideas and ideals, or if neither, mechanized petrification, embellished with a sort of convulsive self-importance. For the last stage of this cultural development, it might well be said: "Specialists without spirit, sensualists without heart; this nullity imagines that it has attained a level of civilization never before achieved."

This is not to deny or evacuate modernity's immense achievements that have transformed irreversibly the human situation of virtually every inhabitant of the planet. But, as John Thornhill (2000: 38) rightly asserts, "our Western tradition's capacity for self-criticism has begun to reassert itself in a recognition of the inadequacy of the 'scientific" outlook of early modernity." This is especially so, since the ideology of modernity is essentially a reactionary movement to the shortcomings of the intellectual climate of medievalism. As such, Enlightenment thinkers tended to ignore, if not dismiss, everything that went before them, everything outside their rationalistic purview, everything that did not meet their stringent criteria. Thornhill (2000: 55) writes:

> The crisis of modernity now faces may well be interpreted as signaling the end of the first phase of modernity as a revolutionary cultural movement, heavily ideological in its cognitive content. At the same time, this crisis constitutes an invitation to embark upon the second phase of modernity as a reactionary movement. The Enlightenment's demand that *all* claims of truth and wisdom be weighed before the bar of human reason's "scientific" spirit was itself unreasonable, in that it failed to be sufficiently open to the full range of sapiential and existential truth. Modernity's first phase must now be followed by a phase in which its

undoubted achievements are balanced by cultural elements neglected by the ideology of the reactionary phase.

Accordingly, John Thornhill examines and discusses some contemporary reactions to modernity, specifically those of the historian J.M. Roberts, the philosopher Alasdair MacIntyre, the economists Paul Omerod and Robert Heilbroner, the statesman Vaclav Havel, and the theologian Johann Baptist Metz, all of whom offer a critical assessment of modernity and propose a reappropriation of the historical and cultural resources of the Western tradition. The essential genius of the Enlightenment was the acceptance of a critical spirit, giving the human agent the freedom to make public use of his reason. But the Enlightenment's reaction against the constraints of tradition was excessive, depriving the new critical spirit of resources essential to the fostering of an authentic human existence. This is especially the case with modernity's insistence on the exclusivity of "instrumental" reason, as Weber foresaw.

Against "postmodernist" critiques, Thornhill further argues that modernity's project is flawed but it should not be abandoned. Modernity, rightly conceived, retains the rational force to carry society forward. A renewed openness to "sapiential" as opposed to "instrumental" reason makes it possible for modernity's valid concerns to be realized. He especially rejects the view that the spirit of modernity is incompatible with Christian, therefore religious, ideas and ideals. A healthy dialogue between a properly autonomous secular order and the principles of Christianity can produce the consensus needed to move Western society and culture forward past crisis. Because as Thornhill puts it in his title, modernity is Christianity's estranged child reconstructed.

Thornhill was writing after the Second Vatican Council, which was often interpreted as Catholicism's rapprochement with the modern world, past therefore religion's tortured confrontation with the secular order as it laid claim to its proper autonomy. Since then, however, especially under the papacies of John Paul II and Benedict XVI, there has been a retrogression into a nostalgia of past triumphalism, a restoration of the claims of "religious liberty" based on the possession of ultimate truths, the continued insistence on traditional sexual morality and on the subordinate status of women, and, worst, a global pedophilia crisis that undermined the moral authority of an ontological hierarchical structure. Thornhill (2000: 223) was not unaware of this even back then: "The church too must heed the warning of Max Weber: if our concerns are shaped by institutional values rather than the values essential to the gospel truth itself, the church of history runs the danger of finding itself more and more imprisoned in an 'iron cage of bureaucratic rationality.' The only overarching plan for the world is that which is in keeping with the divine mystery. It will never be contained in any doctrinal system."

However the wished-for relationship, the worked-out synthesis, the interaction between modernity and religion will be reconstructed, the question of religion and violence occupies a sore point in the dialogue, and must be adequately addressed.

The Prime Analogate of the Human

I start with a basic **sociological datum**. When people gather together in groups and interact with each other on the basis of common norms, they construct two emergent phenomena: social structures and cultures. A group, therefore, is not a mere collection of people. A group is *more* than the individuals who make up the group. The *more* is social structures and cultures. I attend only to the first. Social structures allow people to solve problems that are common to them as groups; they are social arrangements that enable people to live together in a society. If social structures have existed for a long time because they have been found to be good solutions to group problems, they are called social institutions. If they are found in all societies because they solve the basic problems endemic to all groups, they are labeled basic social institutions.

Sociology identifies five basic institutions: marriage and the family, education, economy, government or political institutions, and religion. These institutions before the modern period were structurally undifferentiated and functionally unspecialized. Before the industrial period, for example, the functions of procreating and bringing new members into society, and that of rearing and educating children, plus that of working to meet the basic necessities of life: food, shelter, and clothing, were all "housed" under the social institution of the family. The major sociological contribution of modernity, in fact, Talcott Parsons considered them the essence of modernization, is the structural differentiation and functional specialization of society. (He also added the cultural secularization of society which today is disputed.) We can now identify what are the functions specific to each institution and, therefore, differentiate one from the other. It is a growth in knowledge and analysis, the ability to distinguish, differentiate, and categorize social phenomena.

Two things, I believe, flow from the above development. Because social institutions today are structurally differentiated and functionally specialized, we can now specify what activities properly belong to what institution. It is true that names and labels can expand in meaning and can be metaphorically applied, but that does not negate the original meaning and application of the term. "Family" now does not refer only to the nuclear family of father, mother, and children, but to its various forms: step-family, blended family, single-parent family, gay family. Religion primarily means the social institution that deals with beliefs, commandments, and rituals related to the sacred which bind a community together as church – the four c's of religion: creed, code, cult, and church. But it is metaphorically applied also to passionate commitments and practices, Communism, consumerism, nationalism, Marxism, capitalism, liberalism, and the like. The heart is the human organ of life, but Graham Greene narrates the adultery of Scobie as *The Heart of the Matter*, Nat King Cole sings: "If I give my heart to you, will you handle it with care?" Such uses do not detract from the original meaning of the human heart.

Second, social structures in the premodern era were undifferentialed, their functions unspecialized. But from the vantage point of the modern era, these premodern undifferentiated social structures and their unspecialized functions could still be analyzed and understood, however imperfectly, as if they were differentiated and specialized. To the question: Why is medicine not a basic social institution found in all societies? Are not sickness and death common features of the human condition found as group problems in all societies? The answer: medicine and death were subsumed under the basic institution of religion, because they were mysterious, unexplainable phenomena in those times. Thus, the shaman and the medicine man offered sacrifices to the deity, as well as, to cure diseases. It was only with the discovery of the biological roots of health and sickness by science that medicine emerged as social institution, separate from religion; it is not therefore a basic institution. What was undifferentiated and unspecialized in an earlier era can become differentiated and specialized in our understanding and analysis. That is part of what is meant by growth in knowledge and maturity: the ability to distinguish, to differentiate, to categorize, and to analyze. The child only knows Spot the dog and Blackie the cat. As he grows in knowledge, he learns to categorize that these animals are all dogs, while those animals are cats.

Similarly with religion. Karen Armstrong (2014b) has shown that in the pre-modern world, religion was not a separate sphere of life with its own specific object. Before the modern period, what we now call religion permeated all aspects of life, including politics and warfare. The main reason for this is that people wanted to see meaning in everything that they did. This is the function of what we now call religion. What we now call the religious aspect of people's lives was implicated in and permeated the totality of people's lives, their relationships, their society and world. Myth and ritual made people's lives meaningful, including the violence they experienced in their brutal lives as peasants and the violence they meted out to others as warriors. But Armstrong contends, religion also gave them the resources to question the form of life they lived, the kind of society they supported, to challenge the economic injustice of agrarian society and the systemic violence that ruled their lives. "No myth ever had a single definitive meaning; rather it was constantly recast and its meaning changed. The same stories, rituals, and set of symbols that could be used to advocate an ethic of war could also advocate an ethic of peace."

In Armstrong's account, Judaism, Christianity, and Islam, in the personages of the Hebrew prophets, Jesus, and Muhammad, started as alternatives to the economic injustice and systemic violence of empires. The pristine messages of these monotheistic religions were radically ones of equality and community, of justice and economic well-being for all, and of peace with one another and in society. When they tried to bring to fruition the messages of their religious traditions, as they moved from the margins of society to the mainstream, it could be said that the social structures of religion came to be differentiated, their functions specialized, from the agrarian empires. The subsequent entanglement of religion with the Roman Empire, the outright use of violence in empire-building, colonization, destruction of peoples and their cultures, which have marked the history of Christendom, for example, show how religion can be manipulated and corrupted, its differentiation from political power, for example, can be diminished, if not obliterated, to the detriment of religion itself.

I continue with a **basic moral datum**. Nothing human is totally evil; nothing human is wholly good; everything human is a mixture of good and bad. This also applies to everything socially constructed by humans: social institutions, values, symbols, attitudes, social actions, society. Thus, the human is the supreme analogate in understanding what is happening in the world, the world of humans. Specifically, the human is the template with which to understand religious violence. An analogate is a thing, term, or concept against which we compare, understand, and analyze something else. A template is a framework, an overview within which we place something the better to grasp it, to understand it, and to analyze it. Is religion violent in itself? Well, religion is an institution constructed by humans. Within the framework of what is human and what is constructed by humans, is religion inherently violent? It is not. It can be both good or bad, peaceful or violent, life-giving or death-dealing. Religion can be the best of humanity, but it can also be the worst of humanity.

Oliva Blanchette (2003) and Jeremy Wilkins (2005) have written about the human being as the primary analogate of being in metaphysics. I prefer to look at evolutionary biology to understand the human as primary analogate, the methodological focal point in understanding, in this case, religion and violence. Karen Armstrong (2014b: 7) summarizes an important part of the research:

> Each of us has not one but three brains that coexist uneasily. In the deepest recesses of our gray matter we have an "old brain" that we inherited from the reptiles that struggled out of the primal slime 500 million years ago. Intent on their own survival, with absolutely no altruistic impulses, these creatures were solely motivated by mechanisms urging them to feed, fight, flee (when necessary), and reproduce. Those best equipped to compete mercilessly for food, ward off any threat, dominate territory, and seek safety naturally passed along their genes, so these self-centered impulses could only intensify. But sometime after mammals appeared, they evolved what neuroscientists call the limbic system, perhaps about 120 million years ago. Formed over the core brain derived from the reptiles, the limbic system motivated all sorts of new behaviors, including the protection and nurture of the young as well as the formation of alliances with other individuals that were invaluable in the struggle to survive. And so, for the first time, sentient beings possessed the capacity to cherish and care for creatures other than themselves. . . . About twenty thousand years ago, during the Paleolithic Age, humans evolved a "new brain," the neocortex, home of the reasoning powers and self-awareness that enable us to stand back from the instinctive primitive passions. Humans thus became roughly as they are today, subject to the impulses of their three distinct brains, [also known as reptilian, emotional, and thinking brains].

The traditional explanation of this human situation was the Christian doctrine of original sin. Original sin, the most easily proven doctrine of Christianity according to G.K. Chesterton because we experience it every day, was, in the original telling, the primal sin of pride and disobedience of our first parents, Adam and Eve, that has been transmitted to all human generations descended from them. Because of this sin, St. Paul told us, we desire what is good but in the end we do what is bad; we are torn, conflicted, between following the path of righteousness and walking the road to perdition. Not only that, St. Paul exclaimed that God's entire creation has been affected by it; the whole world groans in pain and suffering, and awaits in anticipation Christ's redemption. Theological debate and controversy have surrounded the doctrine of original sin: In what exactly does original sin consist? How specifically is it transmitted to future generations? How is the entirety of God's creation affected by it?

In the light of what is now the accepted fact of evolution, perhaps the doctrine of original sin can best be understood and explained in evolutionary terms (Litonjua 2015b). Evolutionary science tells us that evolution through mutation, variation, and natural selection is not a perfect process nor does it lead to perfect results, only to the most adaptable results. Kenneth Miller (1999: 101) explains:

> Because evolution can work only on the organisms, structures, and genes that already exist, it seldom finds the perfect solution for any problem. Instead, evolution tinkers, improvises, and cobbles together new organs out of old parts. . . .
>
> The many imperfections of the human backbone . ., regrettably, become increasingly apparent as we age. . . . They are easy to understand if we appreciate the fact that our upright position is a recent evolutionary development. Evolution has taken a spinal column well adapted for horizontal, four-footed locomotion and pressed it into a vertical bipedal service. It works pretty well, but every now and then the stresses and the strains of this new orientation are too much for the new structure.

Our appendix seems only to make us sick; our feet are poorly constructed to bear the brunt of walking and running; our eyes are prone to optical errors and lose their ability for close focus as we age. Plague, pestilence, and parasite, as well as, typhoons, hurricanes, and tornadoes are all indications of the imperfections of the evolutionary process and show the limitations inherent in an evolutionary universe. This could well be the meaning of what St. Paul wrote in Romans 8:22-23: "We know that all creation is groaning in labor pains even until now; and not only that, but we ourselves, who have the firstfruits of the Spirit, we also groan within ourselves as we wait for adoption, the redemption of our bodies."

More to the point, Daryl Domning (2001) addressed the central issue in theodicy, the vindication of the justice of God with regard to moral evil, which in turn lies at the heart of the tug of war between human goodness and human evil. Domning looked at scientific studies of animal behavior: "The picture is not altogether pretty. From ants to apes, the animal world is awash in intraspecific [intraspecies] aggression, deceit, theft, exploitation, infanticide and cannibalism. Our cousins the great apes are adept at political intrigue and quite capable of serial murder and lethal warfare.... The inescapable fact is that there is no virtually human behavior that we call 'sin' that is also not found among nonhuman animals. Even pride, the deadliest sin of all, is not absent.... This is not to say that these animals are guilty of sin; they are simply doing things that would be sinful if done by morally reflective human beings. They also do many things that we can applaud, such as peacemaking and reconciliation, but it is their less admirable actions that are most relevant in the present context."

Domning derives two conclusions. First, "these patterns of behavior are displayed in common by humans and other animals *because they have been inherited from a common ancestor which also possessed them.* In biologists' jargon, these behaviors are homologous." Second, "these behaviors exist because they promote the survival and reproduction of those individuals that perform them. Having once originated (ultimately through mutation), they persist because they are favored by natural selection for survival in the organisms' natural environments. Since these behaviors are directed to self-perpetuation and succeed in a world of finite resources only at the expense of others, it is accurate to call them, in an entirely objective, non-psychological and non-pejorative sense, selfish. Natural selection enforces selfish behavior as the price of survival and self-perpetuation in all living things, even the simplest imaginable. Where cooperative and outwardly altruistic behavior has evolved, it seems always (at least in nonhuman creatures) to be explainable in terms of selfishness and individual advantage, but the reverse is not true. Hence selfish behavior must be the more primitive and fundamental condition."

From an evolutionary perspective, therefore, the reality of original sin manifesting itself in actual sin owes its universality to natural descent from a common ancestor, placed not at the origin of the human race but at the origin of life itself. We all sin because we have inherited from the very first living things on earth a powerful tendency to act selfishly, no matter what the cost to others. But these overt acts of selfishness as the means of natural selection in the evolutionary struggle for competition, adaptation, and survival did not acquire their moral character until the evolution of human intelligence allowed them to be performed by morally responsible beings.

As humans evolved consciousness, thought, language, as they learned to relate to others and live in communities, as they constructed social institutions and cultural systems, as they acquired the capacity to reach out to the transcendent that Robert Bellah (2011) has depicted, they also acquired the moral sense, the moral sensibility, and the moral consciousness to distinguish between right and wrong in their actions, in their relationships to each other, and in their actuations toward the transcendent. That is why history shows that there is growth in morality across spans of time, and there are also reversals that result in the heinous crimes that characterized the twentieth century.

Human beings, in other words, and everything constructed by them are subject to the limitations, contradictions, physical anomalies, and moral transgressions derived from our common evolutionary biological process and human development. We are, and our institutions are, dualities in nature, bundles of good and bad, of right and wrong, of peace and violence, of life and death. It is within these confines and parameters, between these oscillations and swings of the pendulum that human morality, human conscience, and human responsibility must struggle to be able to reach out to become the better angels of our nature.

Thus, the family is a haven of love and care, shelter and protection, but it can be a most violent place where domestic cruelty and child abuse happen. Education provides the knowledge and skills to young people for them to succeed in the world, but it can be a segregated and discriminatory place that benefits only the children of the well-to-do. The economy enables people to meet the basic necessities of life, but it can be controlled by the rich and the powerful only for their own benefit. The political system, in this case democracy, allows people to govern themselves to pursue their common good, but it could be flooded with money that it becomes a plutocracy of the 1%, by the 1%, and for the 1%. Religion empowers people to reach out to their innermost selves, to their neighbors, especially the poor and the downtrodden, and to the sacred, the supernatural, and the transcendent, but it could also motivate people to maim, to destroy, and to kill. Everything human, everything humanly constructed can become evil, can be used for evil purposes, can be manipulated in the pursuit of evil ends, and can be made into a scapegoat for the violence of others. The human and all human creations possess an ineradicable finitude and inevitable fragility. The line dividing good and evil cuts through the heart of every human being, Aleksandr Solzhenitsyn once stated, and through the core of every human institution.

I limit myself to Christianity, the religion I belong to and am most familiar with, to point out some of the sources of the ambivalence, contradictions, and opposing tendencies in all human and social realities, in this case, in religion that lead its practitioners to do good, as well as to practice evil, to wage peace, as well as to inflict violence, to create life, as well as to destroy it. I focus on the incitements to violence of religion. The point of this, as Philip Jenkins (2011: jacket) puts it, is that "Christians cannot engage with neighbors and critics of other traditions – nor enjoy the deepest, most mature embodiment of their own faith – until they confront the texts of terror in their heritage, [as well as, in their teachings and institutional history.]" Again: "The more honestly believers comprehend their faith, including its most unsettling components, the better they can engage constructively with other religions, and with the enemies of all religions" (Jenkins 2011: 227).

Violence in Sacred Writings. In his biogeography of humankind, Alexander Hartcourt (2015: 230, 261-62) concludes that humans "are bad for many species even if we help a few;" "humans are bad for each other, even if we occasionally help one another;" and adds: "Starting with Exodus and the flight of the Israelites from Egypt, and the Israelite god's promise in Exodus to 'deliver the inhabitants of the land into your hand; and thou shalt drive them out before thee,' through the next twelve books of the bible to 2 Chronicles we get a nonstop account of war, rape, looting, and genocide as Middle Eastern peoples compete for land. Only the book of Ruth provides a break from the slaughter and mayhem."

Jenkins (2011: 73) adds: "In terms of its bloodthirsty and intolerant passages, the Bible raises more issues than does the Qur'an. Some Bible passages justify genocide and multigenerational race war; the Qur'an does nothing comparable. While many Qur'anic texts undoubtedly call for warfare or bloodshed, these are hedged around with more restrictions than their biblical equivalents, with more opportunities for the defeated to make peace and survive. Furthermore, any of the defenses that can be offered for biblical violence – for instance, that these passages are unrepresentative of the overall message of the text – apply equally to the Qur'an."

The biblical scenario of the Canaanite conquest is repeated as the Catholic countries of Spain and Portugal went on to colonize Latin America and the Philippines with the sword and the cross, in the *reconquista* of the Iberian peninsula, in the forging of a New Jerusalem in North America with the construction of "a city upon a hill," built upon the genocide of one race and the enslavement of another, and in the scramble for and dismemberment of Africa by Western European powers. "Manifest destiny" it was called by the Americans, *mission civilisatrice* by the French, but it meant the destruction and disappearance of peoples and their cultures. Which raises a disturbing question. Latin American liberation theology has given a new prominence to the Exodus as the central act of liberation by God of oppressed peoples. But there is absolutely no mention of the peoples that were "ethnically cleansed," to use a contemporary term, in the land of Canaan to make room for the Chosen People of Yahweh. What gives?

An interesting twist is offered by current scholarship. The archaeologists Israel Finkelstein and Neil Asher Silberman (2001) argue that instead of the Israelites conquering Canaan after the Exodus, most of them in fact had always been there. The Israelites were simply Canaanites who developed into a distinct culture. A dramatic social transformation took place in the central hill country of Canaan around 1200 BCE. The collapse of the Canaanite political system forced its inhabitants to adapt to new conditions and to fully utilize the region's agricultural potential. What resulted was a revolution in lifestyle from which emerged a distinctive ethnic identity and way of life, and a special relationship to God that have been identified as Israelite. The highpoint was in the eight century BCE when King Josiah enacted a large religious reform, ordered renovations to the temple of Jerusalem, during which the High Priest allegedly found a *scroll of the law*, which insisted on monotheism with sacrifice at a single temple, that in Jerusalem. Finkelstein and Silberman contend, with other scholars, that the core of Deuteronomy is the "scroll of the law" in question, whose author reworked older legends, texts, and histories into a single national history, a "myth" of biblical origins. But don't tell that to Christian religious fundamentalists for whom the bible is literally true and unfailingly inerrant.

Violence in Teachings. Christian churches have also been guilty of condoning, if not actually legitimating and advocating, slavery, racial segregation, and the inferior and subordinate status of women which today goes by the names of sexism and patriarchy, all of which have been lethal. I will concentrate on the social sin of anti-semitism which has infected Churches for so long, thus making them sinful Churches – their doctrinal pronouncements, moral teachings, liturgical celebrations, and ecclesial governance – and which served as the taproot of Hitler's Holocaust (Carroll 2001). In the Gospels, the responsibility for the crucifixion and death of Jesus is attributed to Jews, not Romans. Jews were accused of deicide. Beginning with Constantine and under the aegis of sword and cross, the alliance of throne and altar resulted in the elimination of groups deemed heretical. The Jews would also have disappeared from the face of the earth, were it not for St. Augustine's injunction: Let them survive, but do not let them thrive! As an eternal testament to their perfidy.

It is said today that the transmogrification of polemical anti-Judaism into racial anti-semitism was based on a mistake. The conflict between Pharisees and the Jesus Movement after the destruction of the Temple Jerusalem, reflected in the Gospels, was not about racial superiority and inferiority, not about blood purity and impurity, but about who was the legitimate and faithful successor to whom the law and the prophets of the Torah would be entrusted. It was a polemical and fraternal argumentation between the remaining Jewish groups after Rome had destroyed Jerusalem. But tell that to Mel Gibson – that anti-semitism was based on a contemporary misunderstanding – and to the athletes and celebrities who become born-again Christians and begin spewing anti-semitic remarks once they start reading the New Testament.

Violence in History. It is almost a tired reiteration to mention that the history of Christianity, like the histories of most religions, I suppose, is marred by violence: Crusades, Inquisition, Spain's *reconquista*, imperialism, colonization, to mention a few. Cavanaugh and Armstrong insist that they were not primarily religious, but political. But does that make them less violent, less destructive of peoples and cultures, less matters of life and death for oppressed populations? Does that affirmation absolve religion of complicity, of being manipulated, of being used for nefarious purposes?

What is shocking in recent history is the involvement of Buddhism and Hinduism, long known for their pacificism, in the decades-long, bitter, violent, and deadly conflict in Sri Lanka. The Hindu Tamil Tigers even gained the notoriety of pioneering suicide bombing as a tactic in their war for an independent homeland against the Buddhist Sinhalese, which ultimately failed. No religious motivation here? Simply a struggle between ethnic groups for power, dominance, and territory?

This is not to ignore, much less forget, as Jose Casanova (2007) emphasizes – *pace* Cavanaugh and Armstrong – that "the European short century, from 1914 to 1989, using Eric Hobsbawm's apt characterization, was indeed one of the most violent, bloody, and genocidal centuries in the history of humanity. But none of the horrible massacres – neither the senseless slaughter of millions of young Europeans in the trenches of World War I, not the countless millions of victims of Bolshevik and communist terror, nor the most unfathomable of all, the Nazi Holocaust [?] and the global conflagration of World War II, culminating in the nuclear bombing of Hiroshima and Nagasaki – none of those terrible conflicts can be said to have been caused by religious fanaticism and intolerance. All of them were rather the product of modern secular ideologies and of very secular 'passions.'"

Violent Individuals. Hitler, Stalin, Mao, Pol Pot, and a host of tin-pot dictators epitomize the violence of secular ideologies. Without in any way indicating any moral equivalence, honesty dictates that there are also violent individuals who represent the violence of religions: Yahweh in the Hebrew Scriptures was a god of wrath, Joshua and the judges, Constantine and his fellow Christian Kings, some of whom had to do public penance for their violent crimes, the papal legate who ordered the burning of 7,000 inhabitants inside the Church of the Madeleine in Beziers, France, asking God to recognize his own from the Cathars he was trying to eliminate, Ferdinand and Isabella who created the Spanish Inquisition as an instrument of the ethnic cleansing of the Iberian peninsula of Jews and Muslims, Tomas Torquemada, the "hammer of heretics" of the self-same Inquisition, who spread a reign of terror across Iberia, and, most recently, the eminent clerics, exemplified by Bernard Law of Boston, who "allowed" the spread of the clerical abuse of minors, doing violence, therefore, to them personally and to their families.

Violent Ideologies. Secular ideologies, it has been said, are as violent as religious ideologies. But often they go together – Colonization and Christianization, *Mission Civilisatrice* and Baptize All Nations – reinforcing each other, strengthening each other's tendencies, each other ferocities, and each other lethalities. Spain came to the Philippines, we used to say, with the sword and the cross, followed by the United States with its cross and krag rifle. Both secular and religious ideologies are often complicit in imperialism, colonialism, proselytisim, evangelism, questioning the humanity of native populations, exploiting their natural resources, sexually assaulting their women folk, and destroying their cultures.

Violent Institutions. Thomas O'Dea had pointed out sometime ago that religion needs most, but suffers most from institutionalization. Religion has to formulate its teachings into a creed, its commandments into a code, its liturgical practices into a cult, and organize its followers into a community. These institutional features are a means to an end, to secure the stability and expansion and future of the religion. But soon, however, the means become the ends, offices become sacrosanct, rules are rules, and people are sacrificed for the good of the institution. When that occurs, an inversion of values happens, and the institution has become dysfunctional, pathological, and even lethal, and therefore sinful (Litonjua 2013). Children were abused by priests, and bishops, supposed to be Good Shepherds who tended the most vulnerable of their flocks, sacrificed the children on the altar of the reputation of priests and of the church.

Islamic Fundamentalism and Extremism

To write on religion and violence today without touching on what is raging on in the contemporary Muslim world, on Islamic fundamentalism and extremism that are wreaking terrorism on the world, would be the height of irrelevancy. Besides, it is a topic that lends itself to clarifying the question of the myth and the reality of religion and violence.

Like most religions, Islam is a religion of peace, justice, reconciliation, and brotherhood. Islam means "submission," that is, to Allah, his precepts, laws, ways, and way of life. The "greater Jihad" was first used by Muhammad to refer to the individual Muslim's struggle to conform his life to the tenets of Islam, only secondarily, the "lesser Jihad," to the struggle against the enemies of Islam. Islam in the past, in its glory days, was considered a liberal religion, a liberating force, of intellectual progress and scientific knowledge. Some of the achievements of Islamic scholars in mathematics and astronomy were the building stones of today's sciences. The works of Aristotle, for one, were saved and commented upon by Islamic philosophers, which Thomas Aquinas would use to construct his magnificent *summas* of theological understanding and explanation.

Today, Muslim is associated in the minds of many with terrorist. It is well to remember that even if most terrorists that we know of are Muslims, most of their victims are also Muslims. In other words, fundamentalism and terrorism affect all religions in their struggle and protest against modernity. They affect especially Islam for a variety of historical reasons – the demise of the Ottoman Empire, the fracturing of the Middle East into unviable nations by England and France, the rise of authoritarian states, instead of democracy, and the failure of the promise of economic development – which means that the struggle is not only of Islam against the West but, more critically, of Islam within itself, with factions forming themselves against each other. This is especially the case with the most stringent form of Islam, Wahhabi Islam.

Mohammed ibn Abdul-Wahhab was an early 18th century sheikh who called for a religious reformation in Central Arabia. Feeling that Islam had been corrupted by practices like the veneration of saints and tombs, he called for the stripping away of "innovations" and a return to what he considered the pure religion. He formed an alliance with a chieftain named Mohammed ibn Saud that has underpinned the area's history since then. The Saud family assumed political leadership while Abdul-Wahhab and his descendants gave legitimacy to their rule and controlled religious affairs.

For more than two centuries now, Wahhabism has been the dominant form of Islam in Saudi Arabia. First, there is the big break between Sunni and Shia Islam. Wahhabism is a form of Sunni Islam, but there are also differences between Wahhabism and Sunni Islam. Wahhabism is an austere form of Islam that insists on a literal interpretation of the Quran. Some of the prohibited practices are: listening to music, praying to God while visiting tombs, celebrating the birthday of the prophet Muhammad, adhering to schools of Islamic thought. Wahhabis hold that those who do not practice their form of Islam are heathen and enemies. People are basically of two kinds: Salafis or Wahhabis are the winners, the chosen ones who will go to heaven. The rest are kafirs, the deniers of God, and musraks, who worship false gods. All these people are not accepted by Salafis or Wahhabis as Muslims; they are supposed to be hated, persecuted, and even killed. They are particularly vehement toward the Sufis, the Islam mystics. And of course, they are opposed to the Shiites so that the Middle East today faces the confrontation between Sunni/Wahhabi Saudi Arabia and Shiite Iran.

With the oil bonanza of the 1970s, "exact numbers are not known, but it is thought that more than $100 billion have been spent [by the Saudis] on exporting fanatical Wahhabism to various much poorer Muslim nations worldwide over the past three decades. It might well be twice that number. By comparison, the Soviets spent about $7 billion spreading communism worldwide in the seventy years between 1921 and 1991." Thus, Yousaf Butt (2015) of the National Defense University, declares that "Saudi Wahhabism Is the Fountainhead of Islamist Terrorism." Carol Choksy and Jamsheed Choksy (2015) agree that "the Saudis have been the most persistent source of support for global jihad by spreading Wahhabism abroad to radicalize foreign Muslims and then giving financial support to their violent struggles in countries as far-flung as Afghanistan, Syria, and Libya." In fact, Alastair Crooke (2016), former MI 6 agent, contends that "You Can't Understand ISIS If You Don't Know the History of Wahhabism in Saudi Arabia." Crooke (2014) earlier warned of a "Middle East Time Bomb: The Real Aim of ISIS Is to Replace the Saudi Family as the New Emirs of Arabia."

What has happened to Kosovo (Gall 2016; Kristof 2016) and what is happening in Indonesia (Scott 2016) are instructive, worrisome, and threatening. Kosovo has a statue of Bill Clinton with an arm aloft in a cheery wave in recognition of the American-led intervention that wrested it from Serbian oppression. But 17 years after that event, Kosovo has had more citizens go abroad to fight for ISIS per capita than any other in Europe. Saudi money and influence has transformed this once-tolerant Muslim country into a font of Islamic extremism and a pipeline for jihadists. So what is the greater threat? Al Qaeda, ISIS, Taliban or our so-called ally, Saudi Arabia, whose ideology, schools, and money cultivate fertile soil for terrorists?

Indonesia, home to the greatest number of Muslims in the world, has presented itself as a moderate Muslim democracy that is tolerant and pluralist. Its officials love to say that more than any other country, Indonesia has shown that Islam and democracy are compatible. In 1980,

Saudi Arabia started an all-expenses-paid university in Jakarta, where tens of thousands of graduates trained in strict, puritanical Salafi Islam are produced. "Wahhabi" has become pejorative and linked to violence and terrorism so Saudis and Indonesians prefer the term "Salafi." Now Saudi Arabia intends to dramatically expand the university, from 3,500 graduates to ten thousand graduates a year. It will sponsor a brand-new campus in Jakarta as well as branches in other Indonesian cities. "This decision," writes Scott (2016), "goes to the core of the fight over the definition of Indonesian Islam. It is a religious battle as well as a political one," i.e. between Sunni Saudi Arabia and Shia Iran. It is one more example of the "Arabization" of Islam (Rabasa 2004), on which the fortunes of democracy and pluralism or the future of violence and terrorism hang on the outcome.

Conclusion

Human beings are flawed, broken, self-conflicted, and sinful creatures. So are the institutions they construct for them to be able to live in society. Social constructions, like religion and the state, can produced the heights of glory and grandeur in spirituality, freedom, human fulfillment, and community well-being. They can likewise result in the depths of violence, degradation, enslavement, and death. This is true of religious and secular ideologies, of religious and secular utopias. To argue which ones are more violent and destructive of life, values, property, and societies is a futile exercise and does not benefit the victims who have succumbed to their blindness, arrogance, corruption, and evil. Better to note that while religion has mitigated the violence of humans and their institutions, the democratic state has also tamed the violence that religion has been prone to or has been made a scapegoat of.

So the question is: How will the violence of the fundamentalist and extremist forms of Islam be alleviated? Not of Islam itself, because Wahhabism, for example, is not the totality of Islam. The usual answer is that Islam must undergo its own Reformation as had happened with Christianity in the West, with church and state separated, with public and private spheres delineated from each other, with human dignity and human equality accorded to all, with religious liberty respected of all religions. It is usually added that Islam has its own resources in its sacred writings and teachings, in its scholars and teachers, in its various schools and institutes, and in its traditions and history to achieve its own reformation.

In an interesting book, Shadi Hamid (2016), a senior fellow at the Brookings Institution, argues that the Muslim world is unlikely to witness a replay of the West's journey toward democratic liberalism. In his view, politics is far more integral to Islam than to Christianity, which has traditionally relied on the God/Caesar distinction to separate the holy from the worldly, and therefore to justify separating church and state. Hamid explores the provenance of Enlightenment ideals and questions their claim to universality. Islam is fundamentally different from Christianity, he argues, and this difference has profound implications for the future. Taking his cue from the relative success of the Ennahda movement in Tunisia, Hamid posits that the basic project is to reconcile premodern Islamic law with the modern nation-state. The very process of state-building, buttressed by the international system of state recognition, is inherently secularizing and forces Islamists to limit their ambitions, without, in so many words, the latter undergoing the wrenching process of reformation that tears into shreds any semblance of premodern Islamic life, law, and society. But Hamid claims that Shia Iran falls outside the scope of his study and he is concerned only with the Sunni world. Such a disclaimer immediately puts a cloud on his assertion that political Islam on its own can evolve into Muslim democracy if the world's most prominent Islamist country is exempted from his Muslim exceptionalism.

A quite different perspective emerges from a review of the Arab Spring that swept through Tunisia, Egypt, Syria, Libya, and Yemen in 2010-12. "What all these countries except Tunisia did share in the twentieth century," Gerard Russell (2016) writes, "was the melancholy and ironic fate of Arab nationalist revolutions – against British-backed monarchy or French direct rule – for the most resulting in regimes that were more authoritarian, and in certain ways more self-seeking, than the ones they replaced." But he also identifies that "a problem with secular revolution in much of the contemporary Arab world is that religion, usually of a rather intolerant kind, is often popular. . . . The power of religious extremism and the damage it did to protest movements is a theme that comes across in [surveys] of the Arab uprisings. . . . It might be that in order for democracy to succeed in the Middle East, the nature of religion there must change as well. Intolerant Islamism may have to weaken before democracy can take root. A sense of national loyalty must take precedence over religious solidarity."

At any rate, whether political Islam will follow the West in its journey towards liberal democracy or whether it will embark on its own exceptional path, is a matter for Muslims themselves to discuss among themselves, to argue about and debate with, to wrestle with and to fight over. Ultimately, it should and will be decided upon of, by, and for Muslims themselves.

7

HANS KUNG'S LAST HURRAH?

Can We Save the Catholic Church?/We Can Save the Catholic Church! by Hans Kung.

London: William Collins, 2013, 350 pages.

Hans Kung was one of the first, if not the first, to respond at length and in detail to the call of Pope John XXIII for renewal and reform of the Catholic Church in an ecumenical council, soon to be known as the Second Vatican Ecumenical Council (1962-65) or, simply, Vatican II, with his book, *The Council: Reform and Reunion* (1961).

I think it was Karl Lehmann, assistant of Karl Rahner, who listed Hans Kung as one of five theological *periti* who contributed the most to Vatican II, a list that included Karl Rahner, Yves Congar, Edward Schillebeeckx, and Joseph Ratzinger. But as Lehman climbed the hierarchical ladder of power, unsurprisingly, if not necessarily, he became more conservative, disavowing Rahner's theology. He became Bishop of Mainz, received a Cardinal's hat, was Chairman of the Conference of German Bishops, a member of the International Theological Commission, and co-editor of the conservative theological journal *Communio*.

Two years after the end of the Council in 1965 and five years after its inception in 1962, Hans Kung came out with a volume of 515 pages, simply titled *The Church* (1967). "The problem of God is more important that the problem of the Church;" Kung starts his book, "but the latter often stands in the way of the former." Following the advice of Vatican II in its Decree on Priestly Formation, *Optatam Totius*, no. 16, that "Dogmatic theology should be so arranged that the biblical themes should be presented first," Kung makes this the starting-point of his ecclesiology, from which it passes to historical research and thence to the systematic penetration of ecclesial topics. Taking a cue from Paul VI's pilgrimage to Palestine, Kung wrote that "the Church must return to the place from which it proceeded; it must return to its origins, to Jesus, to the Gospel. And as a direct consequence, this can only mean forward to a new future, the future God has in mind for mankind." *The Church* was the first ecclesiological treatise to develop and elucidate Vatican II's Dogmatic Constitution on the Church, *Lumen Gentium*, and thus became the first text in ecclesiology that departed from Bellarmine's *societas perfecta*.

It did not take long for Hans Kung to express disappointment, dismay, and disapproval at what he saw as betrayals on the part of high authorities in the Catholic Church of the vision, promise, and hope of Vatican II. The gathering storm of discontent erupted in 1968 with the decision of Paul VI to confirm the Church's ban on artificial contraception. National conferences of bishops and moral theologians responded in different ways to *Humanae Vitae*, a significant number of whom were in dissent. Hans Kung's answer was research into and publication of *Infallible? An Inquiry* (1971), on the anniversary of the dogmatic definition of infallibility in 1870. He showed how historically, intellectually, linguistically, and theologically untenable are infallible doctrinal propositions. It was an unhealthy response of Pius IX to his dispossession of temporal power over the Papal States; it was a power grab for a substitute (Hasler 1981). It will be remembered that in connection with the debate on papal infallibility at Vatican I which he opposed, Lord Acton uttered his famous aphorism: "Power tends to corrupt, and absolute power corrupts absolutely." Lord Acton, in fact, therefore, was speaking of absolute papal power. The pope is not infallible, Kung asserted, but the Church is indefectible in the truth because of the gift of the Holy Spirit. It was a very controversial stand, for which he was penalized by Rome, which removed his license to teach as a Catholic theologian. His priestly faculties have never been revoked, however. He had to leave the Catholic faculty, but remained at the University of Tubingen as a professor of ecumenical theology, serving as an emeritus professor since his retirement in 1996.

One criticism of Hans Kung was that he did not pay sufficient attention to the strict and stringent conditions laid down by Vatican I in its definition of the dogma of papal infallibility, namely, that the pope is infallible only if and when in virtue of his office as supreme pastor by a definitive act, i.e., *ex cathedra*, he proclaims a doctrine pertaining to faith and morals as infallible. Vatican II, in *Lumen Gentium,* no. 25, added that the prerogative of infallibility is also present in the body of bishops when, together with the Pope, they exercise the supreme magisterium, above all when gathered together in an ecumenical council. Most of all, Kung is wrong, it was said, in attributing infallibility to Paul IV's teaching on contraception, and in making it the basis of his dissent, since when the encyclical *Humanae Vitae* was presented to the public in 1968, Msgr. Lamberto Lambruschini, the spokesman of the original legislator, made it clear that the teaching on artificial contraception contained therein was not infallible teaching.

Under the pontificate of John Paul II, with Joseph Ratzinger as the Cardinal-Prefect of the Congregation for the Doctrine of the Faith, the aura of infallibility was extended to his pronouncements. John Paul II exercised a dictatorship of absolutism in the Church, while his enforcer of doctrine decried the dictatorship of relativism in modern culture. He was confident and sure, without a shadow of a doubt, in everything that he did, most especially when he spoke of "abortion, abortion, abortion, and Poland" (Breslin 2004: 1). He brooked no dissent from any member of the Church, whom he treated as immature children, even in non-infallible matters, as if there were no non-infallible teachings of his. He emasculated the authority of National Conferences of Bishops, shriveled to insignificance Vatican II's doctrine of collegiality, brought to heel any cleric who opposed him. John Paul II strode the world stage as a colossus in defense of human rights, but reduced the rest of the People of God into an unhealthy dependency and dysfunctionality with his authoritarian and patriarchal rule.

What happened to artificial contraception and women priests, as examples, under John Paul and Joseph Ratzinger is instructive and illustrative of the exercise of ecclesiastical power under them. The ban on artificial contraception was treated as infallible for all practical purposes. With Charles Curran having been expelled from the Catholic University of America, no dissent was allowed on contraception, notwithstanding the fact that the majority of moral theologians and of the faithful did not accept it, but was made into a litmus test for being promoted to the episcopacy. Catholic theologians began to ask: Was Hans Kung right after all? The Catholic hierarchy in both the United States and the Philippines utilized its might and resources to oppose artificial contraception in the Affordable Care Act and the legislation proposed by President Benigno Aquino III.

The official Catholic stand on the possibility of women priests is more adamant. The Doctrinal Congregation under Paul VI declared its impossibility in *Inter Insigniores.* John Paul II in *Ordinatio Sacerdotalis* reinforced the teaching by declaring that it was not within the power of the

Church to change the law. Ratzinger tried to declare the teaching infallible retroactively, an *ex post facto* act whose validity was questioned. He then came up with a new type of teaching called "definitive but not infallible," which created more confusion because traditionally what was definitive was infallible, and what was infallible was definitive. At any rate, bishops who so much as raised the question of women priests were removed and priests who promoted the idea of women priests were excommunicated.

Eamon Duffy (2015: 11) summarizes the criticisms:

> Critics of *Ordinatio Sacerdotalis* pointed out that popes do not have a hotline to God. "Definitive" papal statements are not oracles providing new information, but adjudications at the end of a wider and longer process of doctrinal reflection, consultation, and debate, often extending over centuries. There are procedures to be followed if such adjudications are to command obedience. But the question of female ordination has never been subjected to this kind of extended theological scrutiny, and a properly theological basis for the prohibition remains therefore to be tested. So, it was asked, how did Papa Wojtyla know that the ordination of women was impossible, and what was meant by describing his preemptive strike as "definitive"?

The prohibition was simply an act of routine infallible papal power. Hans Kung was prophetic in his discussion and rejection of papal infallibility. As Herbert Haag (Kung 1994: xvii-xviii) pointed out in his preface to a new expanded edition of Kung's book, "Hans Kung has reproduced the Roman teaching precisely." In fact, he adds: "Pope Wojtyla in his statements has not only endorsed the *de facto* infallibility of the doctrine of *Humane Vitae*, ... he is now declaring specifically that the ordinary magisterium of the Church must be understood and accepted as 'the usual expression of the Church's infallibility.'"

A question has to be raised, therefore, not only regarding the extraordinary exercise of infallibility by the pope alone, but also regarding the ordinary exercise of infallibility by the college of bishops, dispersed throughout the world, but supposedly in union with the pope. The latter is usually pressed to buttress the infallible authority of the pope when he declares a doctrinal and moral teaching of his, i.e., it is not only the pope's teaching but the teaching of all bishops in the world in union with him. How could that be? Bishops are appointed for their loyalty to the pope and for their adherence to the prohibition of artificial birth control. Bishops who so much as raise the possibility of women priests are removed as bishops, while priests who do so are excommunicated. The cards, in other words, are stacked! They are maneuvers reminiscent of the administration of George W. Bush, which concocted intelligence that Saddam Hussein had weapons of mass destruction, and then used that very concocted intelligence to justify its preventive attack against Iraq. In other words, therefore, the ordinary exercise of infallibility of the worldwide bishops in union with the pope is deceitfully used to justify the routine, ordinary, and everyday infallible magisterium of the pope alone. It is a false, because concocted, unanimity, enforced by a reign of fear. It is a far cry from both Vatican I and Vatican II.

For his part, consider what Joseph Ratzinger wrote in his 1986 disciplining of Charles Curran (cited by Sullivan 2013: 11): "The faithful must accept not only the infallible magisterium. They are to give a religious submission of intellect and will to the teaching which the supreme pontiff or the college of bishops enunciate on faith and morals when they exercise the authentic magisterium, even if they do not intend to proclaim it with a definitive act." Infallibility has crept far, wide, and deep. It is authoritarian thought-control worthy of George Orwell's *1984*.

In an interesting article in *Theological Studies*, Francis Sullivan (2014) does three things. First, Sullivan studies the pronouncements of John Paul II on the inadmissibility of women to the priesthood, and finds that his teaching is definitive. Secondly, he analyzes the grounds on which John Paul II based his judgment, and concludes that they do not provide the certainty that the doctrine must have for a pope to declare it infallibly. Third, he finds himself in a pickle as a Catholic theologian. It is none other than Joseph Ratzinger who provides the solution in his essay on the possibility that a seemingly definitive papal pronouncement could be criticized if it lacked the grounds a definitive statement would have to be based on:

> Criticism of papal pronouncements will be possible and even necessary to the degree that they lack support in Scripture and the Creed, that is, in the faith of the whole Church. When neither the consensus of the Church is had, nor is clear evidence from the sources available, a definitive decision is not possible. Were one formally to take place, while conditions for such act were lacking, the question would have to be raised concerning its legitimacy.

Ratzinger wrote this as a young theologian. He has turned his back on the theological positions he stood and fought for at Vatican II. Specifically, he has retracted his former position that divorced and remarried Catholics under some conditions can be admitted to the Eucharist, and this against the background of the efforts of Pope Francis to find out a pastoral solution to the pain and anguish of well-meaning divorced and remarried Catholics. I would not be surprised if he will also disavow this position if and when he finds out that it is being used to "get around" theological positions that he considers infallibly resolved.

The tight grip on infallible authoritarian papal power under John Paul II and Joseph Ratzinger/Benedict XVI imploded in the Catholic Church with the pedophilia crisis that started in Boston under Cardinal Bernard Law and has continued to go global. There was no tool in the infallibility kit of the Vatican with which to deal with the torrent of accusations of priests abusing and raping children and of bishops complicit in and spreading the crimes of their pedophile priests. John Paul II turned a tin ear to the scandal and was himself accused of enabling Marcial Maciel, the priest founder of the religious order of the Legionaries of Christ and the worst predator of them all. Joseph Ratzinger, in the end, "punished" Maciel with a slap on the wrist, by ordering him to retire to a life of "prayer and penitence." Infallible papal power appeared to be restricted to sterile obsession with doctrinal and liturgical niceties, preoccupation with bureaucratic obscurantism and obstructionism, and the shameful protection of institutional and episcopal interests.

Joseph Ratzinger ascends the throne of Peter as Benedict XVI ready to do battle with the dictatorship of relativism. He soon finds himself engulfed with the pedophilia scandal worsening and going global, a festering financial scandal that threatened the Vatican's very fiscal stability, a dysfunctional bureaucracy rife with petty, back-biting turf battles and beset with cronyism, corruption, and waste, aggravated by his own administrative incompetence and his misplaced loyalty to close associates whom he was unable to fire. His and John Paul II's project of a centralized church to restore moral authority and doctrinal orthodoxy, where all roads lead to the Vatican, and where every bishop is elevated primarily for their loyalty had reached an impasse. "[H]is project had failed," Andrew Sullivan (2013: 20) wrote, "the levers he continued to pull – more and more insistent doctrinal orthodoxy, more political conflict with every aspect of the modern world, more fastidious control of liturgy – simply had no impact any more. You can see how, in the maintenance of order, Benedict had become lost in rules and categories that Jesus warned against. His great encyclical, *Deus Caritas Est*, reads like an intellectual brilliantly expressing the love of God – but not a pastor who has easily breathed that love into the church and the world." With all the infallible power that he and his predecessor exercised in an ordinary, routine, and everyday manner, they could not efficiently and effectively administer the clerical bureaucracy that had gone dysfunctionl and pathological precisely because they arrogated unto themselves the ordinary, routine and everyday exercise of infallible power. Benedict resigns. He has had enough of the mess that he contributed to. Let somebody else take care of it.

***

Now, back to Hans Kung. Hans Kung will be remembered as a Church reformer, who fought for freedom and truth *in* the Church. Outspoken, fearless, daring, he addressed issues that remain open but are controversial, which many theologians were afraid to confront. While he continuously called for renewal and reform of the Catholic Church, believing that Vatican II was betrayed by the Roman Curia (Faggioli 2012), he devoted himself to studying, researching into, and writing on important theological topics that instructed, enlightened, encouraged, and motivated people to live a more fully human and Christian life. His writing is a model of clarity, organized systematically to the point of using bullets, a pleasure to read and a joy to understand. His was a critical loyalty to truth, faith, and Church which manifested itself in loyal criticism. As he (Kung 1994: 222) himself put it: "Loyalty and criticism, obligation and freedom, sympathy and absence of prejudice, faith and understanding, are not mutually exclusive, but inclusive."

His trilogy on the Christian life remains a powerful and inspiring read. In *On Being a Christian* (1976), he presented a historical-critical interpretation of the historical Jesus and his message which make them highly relevant existentially to the individual and socially to the community. It is a monumental work that has become a landmark of modern Christian thought. *Does God Exist?* (1980) tackled the perennial question of the existence of God, and sought to answer and redefine this age-old question for today's Christian and world. It is, he said, "an account not of a history of ideas but of concrete human beings made up of flesh and blood, with their doubts struggling, and suffering, with all the questions that still stir us today." Kung in *Eternal Life?* (1984) posed the question that has plagued the human mind in contexts that are congenial to the modern mind. He then approached the religious mind, explored the Resurrection of Jesus, and showed the difference that faith in him makes.

In Thomas Kuhn's (1970) *The Structure of Scientific Revolutions*, which develops the idea of paradigm changes as responsible for scientific revolutions, which became a landmark event in the history, philosophy, and sociology of scientific knowledge, and which triggered reactions and assessments worldwide in scholarly communities, Hans Kung saw in the theory of paradigm changes a viable and useful tool in mapping and understanding the succession of developments in theology. Accordingly, with David Tracy of the University of Chicago, he (Kung and Tracy 1989) organized an international, ecumenical, and interdisciplinary symposium to study and discuss paradigm change in theology.

In his new position as professor of ecumenical theology at Tubingen, Kung (with van Ess, von Stietencron, and Berchert 1986) also organized lecture-dialogues in which three professors lectured on Islam, Hinduism, and Buddhism, after each of which Kung responded as a Catholic theologian, seeking to provide two things: Christian self-criticism in the light of the other religions, and Christian criticism of the other religions in the light of the Gospel. It was, as he put it, "reciprocal information, reciprocal discussion, and reciprocal transformation. Thus we can slowly arrive not at an uncritical mismash, but at a *mutual critical enlightenment, stimulation, penetration, and enrichment* of the various religious traditions." In a similar fashion, Kung and Julia Ching (1989) conducted a dialogue on the interaction of Christianity with Chinese religions, "this third great world religious 'river system' besides the Semitic-prophetic and the Indian-mystic." They show how explosive, like the Taiping Rebellion, how corrupting, like Christian colonialism and imperial trade, and how enlightening, like the approach of Matteo Ricci and colleagues, were these interactions over the centuries.

These two concerns, interreligious dialogue and paradigm change, combined to produce Kung's (1988) proposal for a theology for the third millennium. Kung first reviewed and clarified the classical conflicts so that an ecumenical or interreligious theology will not be caught in cross fires from these old conflicts, but a new beginning can be made in theology, analogous to the paradigm shift in world view brought by scientific revolutions. Future perspectives for theology, new shores for the theological task are demanded in light of the demise of old theological paradigms and the emergence of postmodern theological hermeneutics. The crisis of contemporary theology, for Kung, is not only a matter of isolated symptoms, but a foundational crisis, a crisis that shakes the very foundations of theology. The world is undergoing a long term complex sociocultural upheaval, marked by a farewell to modernity and in transition to postmodernity, the future of theology must equally be altered to reflect the changes in the world around us, especially those altering the face of contemporary world religion.

For me personally, I consider Kung's (1992, 1995, 2007b) massive trilogy on the Abrahamic religions to be masterpieces (Litonjua 2011). He traces the historical development of each of these religious traditions and the paradigm changes they have gone through against the background of what is the abiding substance of their faiths. He identifies three elements in the abiding substance of each faith and six paradigms for each of them. This enables Kung to do three things. "First, it allows him to point out that some historical changes are in historical fidelity to what is abiding and constant, while some historical changes are in radical discontinuity with and even perhaps perversions of the original message, the decisive revelation event, and the distinguishing feature of the faith. Paradigm change always involves gains and losses. Kung evaluates what is gained and what is lost against the constant center and abiding substance of the faith. Second, it enables him to show that some historical forms of the faith have become absolutized, rendered immutable because declared to be of the abiding substance when in reality they are contingent. He emphasizes the relativity of historical developments and therefore the need to contextualize developments alleged to have been ordained with divine sanction. Third, it permits him to raise questions about the possibility of changes in historical forms to meet new challenges, to answer different questions, to inculturate in indigenous cultures, to continue to be relevant in postmodern times. . . . At strategic places in his paradigmatic narrative of the theological histories of the three religions, he offers critical and self-critical questions and reflections based on the paradigmatic change in historical forms he had just discussed" (Litonjua 2011: 289-90). The trilogy is a brilliant application of Thomas Kuhn's theory of scientific revolutions.

"The course of Hans Kung's thought can be described as an ever-widening theological incorporation of increasingly complex fields of thought, without his ever abandoning the centre of his own faith," Karl-Josef Kuschel and Hermannn Haring (1993: ix-x) write. "This immediately suggests the image of concentric circles. The centre is and remains a convinced being, a Christian, reflecting on the significance of Christian existence in today's world." Around this centre, in the 1960s, is a circle of ecclesiological and ecumenical renewal, beginning with *Justification* (1964), his 1957 doctoral dissertation on Karl Barth, Vatican II, renewal and reform of the Church in the light of the Council, the most controversial of which is his book on papal infallibility. To the second circle in the 1970s belong questions to Christianity in general, the question of Jesus as the Christ, and the question of God in the face of the challenge of historical criticism and modern atheism. In the 1980s, a third circle was added, the circle of world ecumenism, dialogue with non-Christian religions, and the question of world ethic.

In the early 1990s, Kung initiated a project called *Global Ethic*, which was an effort to describe what was common to the world religions, and to draw up a minimal code of conduct that everyone can accept. This he explained in *Global Responsibility: In Search of a New World Ethic* (1991), whose three main parts were titled: A. No Survival without a World Ethic; B. No Peace without Religious Peace, and C. No Religious Peace without Religious Dialogue. His vision of a global ethic was embodied in a document for which he wrote the initial draft, *Towards a Global Ethic: An Initial Declaration*, which was signed at the 1993 Parliament of the World's Religions by religious and spiritual leaders from around the world. His project would culminate in the United Nations' *Dialogue among Civilizations* to which Kung was assigned as one of nineteen "eminent persons." He followed this up with his *A Global Ethic for Global Politics and Economics* (1998), where in the rush to globalization he raises and explores vital ethical questions in politics and economics about the coming global society and the shape of our future. He, alone of major Christian theologians, has had the courage to expand his vision beyond narrow church issues to encompass the plight of the global community as it careens in the midst of tremendous global changes and challenges.

Three other publications show the theological width and depth of Hans Kung's knowledge and heft. With Walter Jens, he published *Dying with Dignity* (1996), in which they, with contributions from a medical doctor and a doctor of law, explored, studied, and affirmed the acceptance of euthanasia from a Christian viewpoint. In *The Beginning of All Things* (2007a), he addressed the relationship between religion and science at a time when they seem constantly to clash, eschewed a confrontational model between them as out of date, and accepted evolution. At the same time, he also showed that science raises questions it cannot answer, and therefore he maintained a role for God in founding the laws of nature by which life and humans evolved. Kung has written two volumes of his memoirs, but *What I Believe* (2010) beautifully complements them. He does not interpret "believe" in a narrow ecclesiastical sense or as an intellectualist believing, but "believing is what moves a person's reason, heart and hand, and it embraces thinking, willing, feeling and acting." Also "what" is more than a creed in the traditional sense. "'What' I believe means the fundamental convictions and attitudes which have been and are important to me in my life, and which I hope can also help others to find their way in life: help towards orientation in life." It is a view of life and world as a whole, a kind of *summa* for believers of all faiths.

On Hans Kung's sixty-first birthday, Karl-Josef Kuschel and Herman Haring (1993) offered a kind of workbook, devoted to his career, his work, and his influence. More than twenty contributions move in seven concentric circles to analyze Kung's theology, to describe the state of worldwide Christian theology, and reflect on its effects in a variety of language areas. It ends with a call for the rehabilitation of Kung, whose theology is Catholic to the core, and a critical discussion with whom should be carried on in the context of a legitimate Catholic pluralism. Nothing is more true than what Kuschel and Haring (1993: 8) wrote:

> Unmistakably, it is critical figures like Kung in particular who have made it possible again for countless people to remain or become Christians or even Catholics; in particular, it is theologians like Kung who are open to the world who are again commanding respect for theology and the faith by the standards of a science which argues in a matter-of-fact way; it is Christians like Kung, ready for dialogue and ready to learn, who are gaining a worldwide hearing with Jews and Muslims, with Buddhists and representatives of Hindu and Chinese religions. Here at last we have the practice of what evangelization must mean on the threshold of the twenty-first century, both within and outside the church.

Now, in the twilight of his career and life, the final volume of his memoirs, which has not yet been translated into English, appeared in October 2013, and caused shock (Wilkins 2014). In it, he revealed that he was suffering from Parkinson's disease and macular degeneration which leads to blindness. If he could not write by hand anymore, he asked, and could not read, what was left for him? He considered hastening his life. "Where is it written that in the last phase of their lives human beings lose the responsibility for their lives? You can't read anywhere in the Bible that human beings have to persevere right up to the very end of their lives. . . . The right to life in no way means an obligation to continue living."

He then took it further, according to Wilkins (2014): "As far as I am concerned, the unsatisfactory legal situation in Germany under which so many people suffer, forces me (and as a Swiss citizen with dual citizenship I have the possibility) to join an assisted suicide organization in Switzerland." If and when that happens, I think, it will produce a shock wave far greater than what resulted from the infallibility debate. I just hope that it will not simply be accusations and condemnations of suicide, but will elicit conscientious and responsible discussions of dying with dignity, as Kung had done with Walter Jens, at a time when people are living longer and longer and medical science has discovered new and radical methods for extending life, with all the human, aging, financial, and pain and suffering dilemmas and conundrums they bring with them.

I wish to devote the last part of this paper to what may be Hans Kung's final *cri de coeur* for his beloved Church, a renewed and reformed Church. Before that, in the tenth year of the revocation of his license to teach as a Catholic theologian, and amidst declarations from theologians decrying the state of the Church and calling for its renewal and reform, the most famous of which was the Cologne Declaration – to all of which Papa Wojtyla and Cardinal Ratzinger were deaf and mute – he put together *Reforming the Church* (1990), consisting of articles which did not directly criticize the current course of the Vatican, but articles that addressed pastoral problems and issues that afflicted pastors and laity, currently experiencing, in the words of Karl Rahner, "faith in a wintry season." In an age of *perestroika, glasnost,* and *solidarnocz*, a period of political freedom, human rights, pluralism, and democracy in the East bloc, Kung sought to provide grounds for remaining Catholic, for keeping hope alive, for fidelity to the vision of a future revitalized church.

Kung wrote *Can We Save the Catholic Church?* before Benedict XVI abdicated in 2011 and meant it to be a critical diagnosis of the centralized Roman system. He expressed joy at Pope Francis' different style, and felt he could add a second, affirmative title to the English edition. If you turn the face of the book around, the second title reads *We Can Save the Catholic Church!* Impressed by the decision of Pope Francis in May 2013 to appoint a committee of eight cardinals, most of whom from outside the Roman Curia, to help him introduce reforms to the Church institution, Kung sent copies of his book to all the cardinals on the committee. On May 13, 2013, Kung wrote to the Pope personally, expressing his joy over the pope's bold decision, and enclosed a copy of the Spanish edition of his book. Pope Francis responded in a personal, handwritten note thanking Kung for sending the book and indicating his interest in reading it. He closed the letter with the unpretentious friendly greeting *Fraternamente, Francisco*. Kung then asked Pope Francis for permission to reproduce the warm, handwritten note.

In this book, Kung casts himself in the role of a physician, diagnosing a sick patient and prescribing needed remedies. He identifies the three outstanding features, started by Gregory VII and known as the Gregorian Reform, that mark the Roman System to this day: a centralist-absolutist papacy, clericalist juridicism, and obligatory celibacy for the clergy. Vatican

II, from 1962 to 1965, addressed many concerns of reformers and critics, but was effectively thwarted by the power of the papal Curia. "To this day the Curia – in its current form a creature of the eleventh century – is the chief obstacle to any thorough-going reform of the Catholic Church, to any honest ecumenical reconciliation with the other Christian Churches and the world religions, and to any critical, constructive coming-to-terms with the modern world. To make thing worse there has been a fatal return to old absolutist attitudes and practices" (Kung 2013: xiv).

What Hans Kung is doing here reminds me of Jose P. Rizal, the national hero of the Philippines, who wrote *Noli Me Tangere* (Do Not Touch Me) in 1886, a novel that ignited the first nationalist revolution in Asia, and for which he was executed by the Spanish colonial regime. Rizal saw his beloved country afflicted with a social cancer so malignant that the least contact exacerbates it and stirs in it the sharpest pain. In the Preface "To My Motherland," he wrote:

> Desiring your well-being, which is our own, and searching for the best cure, I will do with you as the ancients of old did with their afflicted: expose them on the steps of the temple so that each one who would come to invoke the Divine, would propose a cure for them.
>
> And to this end, I will attempt to faithfully reproduce your condition without much ado. I will lift part of the shroud that conceals your illness, sacrificing to the truth everything, even my own self-respect, for, as your son, I also suffer in your defects and failings.

In a review of the original German edition of the book, Thomas O'Meara (2012: 466) points out that "the originality of *Can the Church Still be Saved?* lies first in a consideration of church leadership today as a system and second in the use of a therapeutic framework." The opening three chapters examine the illness afflicting the institutional church and how extensive it is, analyze the role of the papacy in this sickness, and identify the seeds of the chronic malady. From Rahner's "faith in a wintry season," the church is now gravely, even terminally, ill, Kung diagnoses, experiencing attacks of fever as symptoms. The sickness is embedded in the "Roman system of rule characterized by a monopoly of truth and power, by legalism and clericalism, by hostility to sexuality, by misogyny and by clerical pressure on the laity" (Kung 2013: 4). Kung expands on this diagnosis by taking up seven myths and the problems they have caused. He dissects these seven myths, seeds of the chronic illness, shares his findings and the therapies necessary to combat them. The role of the papacy is central, because it has become monarchical and absolutist, exercising not a Petrine ministry and primacy of love and service, but a Roman medieval system of governance, control, and domination.

In the fourth chapter, Kung attends to forces driving and opposing reform, efforts at rehabilitation and setbacks into relapse, that include Charles Darwin, the pill, democracy, the Index of Forbidden Books, in which the Roman system mounted frontal attacks on the modern age. Chapter five is entitled The Great Rescue Operation, in which Kung discusses efforts of popes, from Leo XIII on, at reformation and modernity, culminating with John XXIII and Vatican II, only to fall into relapse at a pre-conciliar constellation with John Paul II and Benedict XVI. The last chapter is Kung's proposal for an ecumenical therapy. The system he diagnosed is a dysfunctional and pathological system with its own ideology, psychology, and sociology. Only a deep structural renewal that draws from the social nature of the human person and from the revelation and grace of God will cure the sickness. In all of these, the vision of the Church, revitalized by reforms marked by Christian radicalness, constancy and perseverance of efforts, and coherence of proposals and programs, remains.

***

In *Reforming the Church Today*, Hans Kung (1990: 64-71) had a chapter, entitled "Longing for John XXIV: In Memory of Pope John XXIII," which was his loving tribute to Good Pope John. His words reveal his admiration and affection for "the greatest pope of our century." He recalls the Pope's humanity, simplicity, generosity, and openness, as well as his epochal achievement and his legacy that has been wasted and betrayed by his two successors, and leaves us with the question: "Do we need to come up with any more reasons why today more than ever we long for John XXIV?"

In the original edition of *Infallible?* Hans Kung (1971: 247-253; also Kung 1969) drew a kind of model pope, the pope as he might be, after the pattern suggested by Cardinal Suenens in his interview with several publications, under the heading "Portrait of a Pope." I quote the paragraph that goes to the core of Kung's criticism of the Papal Roman System of authority of the Catholic Church.

> This pope would not regard the centralization of power as a dangerous prelude to a possible schism. He would not prevent, but would foster legitimate diversity: diversity in the fields of spirituality, liturgy, theology, canon law and

pastoral ministry. His aim would be, not to concentrate power permanently at the center, but unpretentiously to serve the local churches in their rich diversity in the one Church; not to suppress differences of opinion among theologians with inquisitorial sanctions from past centuries, but to encourage them in their freedom and service to the Church; not jealously to hold on to powers and prerogatives or to exercise authority in the spirit of the old order, but to make authority felt as service in the spirit of the New Testament and in response to the needs of the present time: fraternal partnership and co-operation, especially with bishops and theologians of the whole Church, opportunity for those concerned to take part in the process of making decisions, and full scope for the exercise of co-responsibility.

On March 13, 2013, a new pope, Cardinal Jorge Mario Bergoglio, was elected. He is the first Jesuit to be elected pope, the first non-European, the first from a Third World country, Argentina, and the first to take the name Francis. He has shown humility, simplicity, and frugality of life. He is open, merciful and non-judgmental. He has a collegial style of governance. He prefers to be called the Bishop of Rome. He is not afraid to consider change. He has aroused much admiration, joy, and hope. He is hailed as Pope of the People of God.

Pope Francis has been full of surprises. It is no wonder because for him (Spadaro 2013), "God is always a surprise, so you never know where and how you will find him. You are not setting the time and place of the encounter with him." The point here is not to catalogue all the indicators and signs of a new papacy and the possible directions toward renewal and reform of the institutional church that the papacy might guide and take us. It is simply to take note of steps taken by Pope Francis – soundings of what might be – that give us hope for a renewed Catholicism *ad intra*, in its governance, its pastoral life and practices, and *ad extra*, in its relationship to other Christians, to other religions, and to the world at large.

On the day he was elected, he appeared on the balcony to introduce himself: "You all know that the duty of the conclave was to give a bishop to Rome. It seems that my brother Cardinals have gone almost to the ends of the earth to get him, but here we are. The diocesan community of Rome now has its Bishop." Note: *a* bishop *to* Rome. Not lording it over the church as an absolute monarch. But one with his fellow bishops of the Church. Bishop of Rome, not Supreme Pontiff.

Before he gives his first blessing as Pope Francis *Urbi et Orbi,* "first I ask a favor of you: before the Bishop blesses his people, I ask you to pray to the Lord that he will bless me: the prayer of the people asking the blessing for their Bishop. Let us make, in silence, this prayer: your prayer for me." Unprecedented, it was not only grace and power from above, but first grace and power from below, from the people, from the People of God, in Vatican II's preferred appellation.

He returned to the guesthouse Casa Santa Marta, where he stayed as cardinal before the conclave, returned after his election to pay his bill, and took up residence there, instead of at the sumptuous papal apartments where his predecessors lived. A sign of simple living and of the need for daily interactions and fellowship with fellow boarders.

Regarding the first question asked "Who is Jorge Mario Bergoglio?" in the now famous interview, published in English in *America,* Antonio Spadaro (2013: 3) writes:

> The pope stares at me in silence. I ask him if this is a question that I am allowed to ask.... He nods that it is, and he tells me: "I do not know what might be the most fitting description.... I am a sinner. This is the most accurate description. It is not a figure of speech, a literary genre. I am a sinner."

One is immediately reminded of Jesus' words: "Let him who is without sin throw the first stone" (John 8:7). It recalls for me also Nelson Mandela's response to an overenthusiastic supporter who called him a "saint." "No," Mandela answered, "just a sinner who keeps trying." Or the words: "Amazing Grace! . . . That saved a wretch like me."

As Andrew Sullivan (2013: 6) takes note:

> Every Pope is a sinner, just as every human being is. But not every Pope has immediately and instinctively *defined* himself as such. Not every Pope introduces himself by abandoning every trace of inherited, acquired authority that comes with the office itself and begins from scratch, as a human being, as a sinner.

Francis convened a Council of Cardinals, representative of the entire Church, to help him reform and restructure the institutional Church, which has become dysfunctional, to say the least. It is his first concrete act of collegiality. He also formed a Council for the Economy, to root out financial corruption in the Church, to correct abuses connected with money, and to stabilize the Vatican's financial resources and standing. He set up a Commission for the Protection of Minors to deal with the clerical abuse of children and the episcopal cover-ups that continue to fester, but which has been criticized for its slowness and lack of action.

Most importantly, Pope Francis has convoked a Synod of the Family to meet in a two-stage process, in October 2014 and in October 2015. Prior to both of these dates, the Vatican issued questionnaires to be discussed and answered by the whole Church – "at all levels" – for feedback to the Synod regarding issues, problems, and pastoral challenges confronting modern families in the context of evangelization, most conspicuously, the pastoral care of homosexual persons and of divorced and remarried Catholics, their broken and fragile families. It was an unprecedented collegial outreach to the entire church. Indian Catholic ethicist Shaji George Kochuthara (cited by Keenan 2015: 131-2) states that "the process undertaken by the Synod is in that way an affirmation of the dignity and role of the conscience, in the day-to-day life of the faithful, in the life of the Church and its teachings." It is sad and shameful, therefore, that the American Catholic bishops decided not to send to the American laity the synod's preparatory consultation of the laity questionnaire that other episcopal conferences sent out. It shows, points out American ethicist James Keenan (2015: 132), their lack of explicit interest in the laity's consciences, the *sensus fidelium*.

Pope Francis' image of the church is very memorable, captivating, and challenging: "I see clearly that the thing the church needs most today is the ability to heal wounds and to warm the hearts of the faithful; it needs nearness, proximity. I see the church as a field hospital after battle. It is useless to ask a seriously injured person if he has high cholesterol and about the level of his blood sugars! You have to heal his wounds. Then we can talk about everything else. Heal the wounds, heal the wounds.... And you have to start from the ground up" (Spadaro 2013: 12). What a relief from sterile doctrinal disputations, moralistic rigidity and condemnations, liturgical literalism and punctilio!

His apostolic exhortation, *Evangelii Gaudium*, celebrates the joy of the gospel, exalts the virtue of mercy, and insists on the centrality of the poor and the marginalized in the mission and ministry of the church. "I prefer a Church that is bruised, hurting and dirty because it has been out on the streets, rather than a Church which is unhealthy from being confined to its own security. I do not want a Church concerned with being at the centre and which then ends up in a web of obsessions and procedures.... A tomb psychology thus develops and slowly transforms Christians into mummies in a museum. . . . I want a Church which is poor and for the poor" (Pope Francis 2013: nos. 49, 83, 198). No more pink shoes and cappa magna!

True to the poor and universal Church he envisions, Francis has appointed cardinals from diocesan sees considered to be marginal to the centers of power in the church, from remote and poor Third World countries which never had cardinals, and from bishops who, in his own words, "smell like sheep" from tending their flocks in the fields. It is with them that Francis hopes to work in revitalizing the Gospel in people's lives, in restructuring the bureaucracy of the institutional Church to serve the needs of the entire People of God, in collegially governing the Church in its ministry of mercy, justice, love, and peace.

On the second anniversary of his pontificate on March 13, 2015, Pope Francis announced an extraordinary Jubilee or Holy Year of Mercy to commence on December 8, 2015, the fiftieth anniversary of the closing of Vatican II in 1965 – and just over a month of the closing of the Synod on the Family – and to end on November 20, 2016. "It will be a Holy Year of Mercy," he said, "We want to live in the light of the word of the Lord: 'Be merciful as your Father.'" His announcement was a ringing endorsement of the lasting significance of Vatican II for the entire Catholic Church, especially after the doubts sown and the betrayals of its vision made by Ratzinger/Benecict XVI, especially his ill-conceived "reform of the reform" of the liturgy.

In his famous interview with Spadaro (2013: 30), Francis had already forcefully expressed the contemporary impact of Vatican II:

> Vatican II was a re-reading of the Gospel in light of contemporary culture. . . . Vatican II produced a renewal movement that simply comes from the same Gospel. Its fruits are enormous. Just recall the liturgy. The work of liturgical reform has been a service to the people as a re-reading of the Gospel from a concrete historical situation. Yes, there are hermeneutics of continuity and discontinuity, but one thing is clear: the dynamic of reading the Gospel, actualizing its message for today – which was typical of Vatican II – is absolutely irreversible.

In announcing also the beatification of the slain Salvadoran Archbishop Oscar Romero as "martyr of the church of the Second Vatican Council," Pope Francis' Vatican marked a shift toward the acceptance of the progressive changes of Vatican II, especially its emphasis on the church that stands with the poor. In meeting with Gustavo Gutierrez, the acknowledged father of Latin American liberation theology, Francis has also cleared the air of the ideological animus that Ratzinger directed at it.

Most of all, on the eve of Christmas, December 23, 2014, Pope Francis received in audience the Cardinals and Superiors of the Roman Curia for the presentation of Christmas greetings. On the same occasion in 2005, Benedict XVI used his address to sow confusion in the interpretation of Vatican II by unfairly contrasting the hermeneutics of continuity/reform with that of discontinuity/rupture. This time Pope Francis (2014) gave the Roman Curia a fifteen-point examination of their consciences. It is worth reading and perusing in its entirety since it is also a useful examination of conscience for every bureaucrat of whatever stripe and of all Christians at all levels. It is a diagnosis of ills.

1. The sickness of feeling oneself "immortal," "immune" or in fact "indispensable," neglecting the necessary and usual controls.
2. The sickness of "Martha-ism" (which stems from Martha), of excessive business.
3. The sickness of mental and spiritual "petrification": namely those who have a heart of stone and a "stiff-neck."
4. The sickness of excessive planning and functionalism.
5. The sickness of bad coordination: when the members lose communion among themselves.
6. The sickness of spiritual Alzheimer's: namely the forgetfulness of the "history of salvation."
7. The sickness of rivalry and vainglory.
8. The sickness of existential schizophrenia: it is the sickness of those who live a double life.
9. The sickness of gossip, of grumbling and of tittle-tattle.
10. The sickness of divinizing directors: it is the sickness of those who court their superiors, hoping to obtain their benevolence.
11. The sickness of indifference to others.
12. The sickness of the mournful face: namely of brusque and sullen persons.
13. The sickness of accumulating.
14. The sickness of closed circles: where belonging to a little group is more important than that of belonging to the Body.
15. The sickness of worldly profit, of exhibitionism.

Pope Francis adds that "these sicknesses and these temptations are, naturally, a danger for every Christian and for every Curia, Congregation, parish, Ecclesial Movement, etc. and they can strike at the individual as much as the communal level."

The question is whether these sicknesses are failings on the individual level, maybe even sins but in the personal realm. Or whether they are illnesses that have become embedded into ecclesiastical structures, built into positions, orders, ministries that wield power and authority. Have they become part and parcel of ecclesiastical culture such that whoever has climbed the ecclesiastical ladder must necessarily have imbibed its sickly values and attitudes as a precondition and must in turn imbue others with them in a vicious cycle of causation? In that case, might these ill structures better be called structures of injustice, social structural sins, which demand drastic renewal and radical reform? The critique must not remain on the level of individual failings, but must be systemic, of the system itself.

In the preface to the English edition of his book, Hans Kung (2013: xvii) makes this resoundingly clear:

> To use the medical analogy that serves as the leitmotif of this book [and of Pope Francis' address to the Curia], the Church's only alternative to what would amount to assisted suicide is radical cure. That means more than a new style, a new language, a new collegial tone; it means carrying out the long-overdue, radical structural reforms and the urgently needed revision of the obsolete and unfounded theology behind the many problematical dogmatic and ethical positions that his predecessors have attempted to impose upon the Church. If Pope Francis commits himself to such a radical reform, he will not only find broad support within the Church, but he will also win back many of those who, publicly or privately, have long since abandoned the Church. Such a renewed Roman Catholic Church could once again become the witness to the Gospel of Christ that it was meant to be.

I believe Pope Francis recognizes this. But in *Evangelii Gaudium* (2013: no. 26), he also makes a necessary rejoinder:

> There are ecclesiastical structures which can hamper efforts at evangelization, yet even good structures are only helpful when there is life constantly driving, sustaining and assessing them. Without new life and an authentic evangelical spirit, without the Church's "fidelity to her own calling", any new structure will soon prove ineffective.

Eamon Duffy (2015: 13) ends his article on Pope Francis in *The New York Review of Books* with the categorical statement that "whether he will succeed is a moot point." Pope Francis is unlikely to have a long pontificate: he is an old man. He does not have the time to ensure that those around him and after him share his vision. "No pope, however charismatic, can change the church alone; they need the help of their civil servants. For as they say in Rome, popes come and go, but the Curia is immortal."

Jean-Louis de la Vaissiere (2015), for his part, points out on the occasion of Pope Francis' second anniversary that "his opponents are playing a waiting game as they seek to put the brakes on his reform drive." He quotes the Vatican expert Marco Politi who has recently published an essay entitled "Francis among the wolves:" "Politi believes the historic decision of Benedict to retire rather than die in office – and 78-year-old Francis's own hints he could do likewise – have been game-changers inside the Holy See. 'This is a pontificate with a limited timeframe. That means opponents can watch the clock and tell themselves, 'we only have to wait four, five years and it will be over.' That's new and it strengthens."

There is no better indication how dysfunctional and even pathological the Catholic Church institution has become!

David Gibson (2015) has a different take on the matter. He maintains that "contrary to the imaginings of Francis' foes, he doesn't seem to have a platform and agenda he wants to pass – it's more about opening the church to the Spirit, to get closer to Jesus and the Gospels. It's not making an idol of the Second Vatican Council or going 'back' to anything, but moving ahead, always, as the Council envisioned. That's an agenda in itself, of course. Where that will lead, or if such a vision can have a structure to ensure its propagation, or whether it will always need leaders like Francis to push it, is an open question. In American politics we often lament the focus on process over policy. In the Vatican under Francis, that's a virtue. Policies are not the goal. How you get there is as important as where you wind up."

Pope Francis has said as much. In *Evangelii Gaudium* (2013a, no. 22), he exults:

> God's word is unpredictable in its power. The Gospel speaks of a seed which, once sown, grows by itself, even as the farmer sleeps (Mk 4:26-29). The Church has to accept this unruly freedom of the word, which accomplishes what it wills that surpass our calculations and ways of thinking.

Even the papacy cannot control the word of God or the work of Spirit. Cynics will say: *Consuelo de bobo!* Solace of the fool! Pope Francis, the Pope of the People, has definitely sown more than a seed – of joy, of love, of hope. We wait, we pray, we hope that it will bear fruit in a renewed and reformed Church, the pilgrim People of God on its way to its eschatological fulfillment.

***

Since finishing the above article I have read two books that make me realize the more how difficult it will be to reform the structures of authority and governance of the Catholic Church. They make me more pessimistic about the possibilities of changing the culture of the Roman Curia, its adherence to power and privilege, hierarchy and patriarchy.

Peter Heather in *The Restoration of Rome* (2013), the sequel to his *The Fall of Rome* (2005), picks up from when the curtain fell on the Roman Empire in Western Europe, and tells the story of three great imperial pretenders who attempted to revive the Roman inheritance in Western Europe: Theoderic, Justinian, and Charlemagne. In the end the restoration of stable imperial power on a truly Roman scale proved possible only with the reinvention of the papacy in the eleventh century. Under the imperial rulers and pretenders from Constantine to Charlemagne, Heather (2013: 312) writes, "without any doubt, the emperor was the functioning head of the Christian Church. Others, including popes, played a part, but the imperial role in the formulation of correct doctrine, in defining and enforcing expected standards of practice, and in selecting personnel was paramount." Fast forward to November 11, 1215, Heather (2013: 350-51) continues:

> In the Fourth Lateran Council, we finally encounter a papacy which was recognizably functioning as the head of Western Christendom: calling councils of massed clergy, dictating the agenda, setting standards of belief and practice for clergy and laity alike, and attempting to have those standards enforced. . . . Not only did Innocent III claim total authority over the Western Church, and demonstrate the reality of that claim in the extraordinary gathering of churchmen who turned up in Rome for Lateran IV, but he based that claim on the assertion that his authority was of a higher order than any of the worldly rulers of Christendom.

Though that claim was rooted in the forged *Donation of Constantine*, the Pope became in effect the supreme monarch, *pontifex maximus*, of

Christendom and the Catholic Church the restoration of the Roman Empire. Alan Ryan (2012: 188, 194) adds:

> It was the papacy, rather than the barbarian kingdoms that inherited the territory of the empire, that inherited the imperial conception of the state. This was not merely a matter of the papacy's mimicking the outward trappings of imperial office, although it did so. It was rather that the church was the means by which Roman notions of law-governed political community were transmitted to medieval Europe... [T]he papacy copied the thrones, tiaras, and robes of the Roman Empire, and in the course of time, the cardinals, who were originally the assistants of the popes in matters of liturgy and care of the poor, came to form a College of Cardinals that replicated the Roman Senate.

Centralized rule, autocracy, absolutism have become part and parcel of the DNA of the institutional Catholic Church, inherited from the Roman Empire. In his review of Peter Heather's book, Michael Walsh (2014: 31) recalls Edward Gibbon's thought that the pope was the ghost of the Roman emperor seated on the throne of St. Peter, and adds that "perhaps he might have likened the current papal penchant for canonizing their predecessors to a revival of that imperial practice of deifying one's ancestors."

For Massimo Faggioli (2015: 49), the Church "reform," which was an explicit mandate Pope Francis received from the conclave, will mean "the end of the confluence of the Rome of the Caesars with the Rome of Peter, as the confluence of the royal and priestly powers in the person of the pope of Rome ... the end of the confluence between Caesar and Peter in the papacy." Will this be done? Can it be done?

Gerald Posner (2015) in *God's Bankers*, which he had researched into and worked at for ten years, narrates a history of money and power at the Vatican, a toxic combination anywhere else, but most specially in the high corridors of religious and spiritual power. It is a sordid story, at the center of which is the Vatican Bank, officially known as the Institute for the Works of Religion (IOR), which was manipulated and corrupted to pursue ends which had nothing to do with religion and the salvation of souls. Slush funds were established, corrupt money was laundered, bribes were fueled by church money, extortion, blackmail, and embezzlement were rife, dummy foundations were erected, illicit money was channeled for personal aggrandizement, political purposes, and criminal activities.

In the process, the Vatican became complicit in political intrigue, murders and assassinations, and questionable suicides, in illegal and immoral associations, if not partnerships, with the Mafia and Freemasonry. It is a salacious story in which the names and reputations of popes, cardinals, archbishops, bishops, and other high officials of the Catholic Church are implicated and tarnished.

Gerald Posner suggests obliquely that it might not simply be antipathy toward Jews, or love for Germany, or inordinate fear of Communism more than of Nazism that kept Pius XII silent on the Holocaust. It might well be connected with what surfaced decades later about Nazi gold. In 1997, in connection with the demand for restitution to survivors of the Holocaust, the term "Nazi gold" was coined to refer to the wartime loot that disappeared into Swiss banks, never to be seen again. Pressure grew for Switzerland and other nations to declassify documents and to cooperate in determining how much money was involved. Even the Portuguese shrine of Our Lady of Fatima admitted hiding 110 pounds of Nazi gold which was later used to expand the shrine's sanctuary. The Vatican was the only nation that refused to do anything. The director of the Simon Wiesenthal Center, Rabbi Marvin Heir, reported that the gold deposited at the IOR was likely used to fund "the Vatican rat line where basically many leading Nazi war criminals escaped to Latin America with Vatican passports" (Posner 2015: 184). The Vatican stonewalled every request to open its archives for inquiry. The Vatican keeps mum about Nazi gold, just as it did about Nazi atrocities.

One of the very things that Karol Wojtyla did as John Paul II was to instruct Archbishop Paul Marcinkus, the IOR Chief, to find the money to solve the financial scandal of the corrupt Palatine monks that ran the Philadelphia-area shrine Our Lady of Czestochowa, the "Black Madonna" of Poland, after which the new Pope simply ended the investigation and quashed the original findings into the Palatines. John Paul considered Marcinkus a worthy ally, capable of coming up with the money, some from the CIA and the Reagan administration, and channeling it to the Pope's anti-communist allies in Poland, all the while prohibiting priests to engage in politics. No wonder John Paul coddled Marcinkus and shielded him from prosecution for his criminal activities. He was determinedly blind, however, to the depravities of the pedophiles, Marcial Maciel Degollado, founder of the Legion of Christ, and Hans Hermann Groer, Cardinal-Archbishop of Austria, a posture he maintained in the face of the global pedophilia scandal, the greatest internal crisis of the Catholic Church in modern times (Berry and Renner 2004).

Jason Berry (2011: 359) commented on the election of Joseph Ratzinger as "a pope of ironies:" with his years of prosecuting theologians who did not toe his line of moral absolutes, he was now faced with the task of cleaning up the financial mess at the Vatican Bank; as the Grand Inquisitor who stood firm on definitive doctrinal and moral statements, he now entrusted himself to his longtime aide Tarcisio Bertone, whom he appointed Secretary of State out of a misguided sense of loyalty. What followed was a cascade of scandals that showed Benedict, for all his righteous rectitude as the enforcer of belief, to be a weak and incompetent leader: financial problems continued to metastasize and hemorrhage, the pedophilia crisis went global, the discovery of a gay lobby and sexual blackmail inside the Curia, the exile of Archbishop Carlo Maria Vigano to Washington, D.C., for his corruption busting, Vatileaks by Paolo Gabriele, Benedict's butler. The long-entrenched corruption and abuse of power, petty back-biting turf battles, waste, nepotism, and cronyism in the management of departments continued unabated under the unchecked power of Bertone. What was left for the German Rottweiler was to scamper away with his tail between his legs.

The question that was asked of the Roman praetorian guards was: *Quis custodiet custodes?* Who will guard the guardians? The question that is to be asked, in light of Posner's history of money and power at the Vatican, is: *Quis custodiet Papam?* Who will guard the Pope? Who will provide transparency and accountability of an absolutist and autocratic institution that is answerable only to itself? *Prima sedes a nemine iudicatur* (Nobody can judge the see of Rome)! Will the reforms of Pope Francis be enough and lasting?

***

Happily, I did not rely on the disjointed sourpuss of a review by William Portier (2015), but I took it upon myself to read Garry Wills' (2015) latest book, on Pope Francis and the Catholic Church. Portier, for example, titles his review "Just a Gang of Thieves?" This is taken from Will's (2015:135) explication of St. Augustine's City of God and the Earthly City. For Augustine, the City of God is not the Church but the ideal community that does not exist on earth, and the Earthly City is not the state but fallen mankind, whose love of self can lead to hell. We do not inhabit either of these lasting communities, but share for a while a third city, "a mixed bag in both the political and religious spheres. . . . a place of divided loyalties, not only in its social relations but in the individual soul." But this does not free those in either church or state from their duties to just activity. "At whatever level – in the small gang of thieves acting together for efficiency and fairness, or the larger gang of thieves called the government trying to enforce justice, or the large gang of sinners called the church trying to remind one another of the love of God – we are bound to moral duty, however we fail to achieve it." Is this what Portier disapproves in Wills' characterizations, by adding the word "just"? Does he also dislike, therefore, the current Pope who says that the most accurate description of him is that he is a sinner? Is he also "just" a sinner?

Wills (2015: 136-37) does these characterizations to contrast them against "the antisocial pathology of doing business only with those who judge as you do, think as you do, feel as you do, and act as you do," which was "the intellectual unanimity [that] Pope Leo XIII yearned for as he looked back on the thirteenth century as an ideal 'age of faith,' [but which] harmony of church and state was achieved by interdicts, assassinations, and enslavements."

In 1972, Garry Wills published *Bare Ruined Choirs*, recently reprinted by Paulist Press (Wills 2014), his take on Vatican II and its aftermath. His main contention was that the Council "let out the dirty secret . . . that the church changes." In view of the intransigent opposition, based on the immutability of doctrinal and moral teachings, to possible changes, even pastoral ones, under Pope Francis, Wills (2015) undertakes another worthwhile effort to show "how change – far from being an enemy of Catholicism – is its means of respiration, its way of breathing in and out." Change is the lifeblood of the Church that Vatican II described and that Pope Francis has brought back to salience as the People of God.

First, Wills points out that for those who fear change, it helps not to know much history. One begins with the certitude that the church is today what it has always been, retrojecting the present backward into the past, extrapolating therefore current forms into a fictive immutability. But instead of reading history backward, history should be read forward, from the origins of what was thought, taught, and practiced to their current forms. And if this is done as G.K. Chesterton did and as John Henry Newman proposed, there is change, development, mistakes, errors, remission, and progression.

This Wills does in five areas of concern: from the tyranny of Latin to a new Pentocost of freed tongues, from church without states to a church monarchy with state and as state, to churches and states in a pluralist world – the longest section of the book, which has the most implication for church reform and governance – from anti-Judaism and anti-Semitism to interreligious respect, dialogue, and cooperation, from religious pronouncements on sex, the maleness of Christ, and the right to life based on natural law to their loss of legitimacy and acceptance, and finally from the rigid obligation for auricular confession to its practical disappearance. Wills guides the reader through two thousand years of history, often long stretches of error, but often, too, corrected from the original springs of faith. "The church can live," Wills declares, "because it can learn, correct, and change under God's direction."

Last but not least, Wills pointedly reminds us, that "the papacy is not a prophetic office . . . the man at the center cannot rebel against himself. The pope must, by his office, care for continuity and minimize disruption." At the same time, Pope Francis (2013a: nos. 114, 113), in his apostolic exhortation, *Evangelii Gaudium*, has made the church as the people of God a leitmotiv of his papacy: "Being Church means being God's people . . . God has found a way to unite himself to very human being in every age. He has chosen to call them together as a people and not as isolated individuals." He (Pope Francis 2013a: nos. 111, 119) emphasizes that the church exists concretely in history as a people of pilgrims and evangelizers, whom he has constantly urged to go out to the periphery, the margins, the frontiers, to take God's love to them. God, for Pope Francis, furnishes the totality of the faithful, his pilgrim people, with an instinct of faith – *sensus fidei* – which helps them discern what is truly of God. "A pope who believes in *that* church," Garry Wills concludes his introduction, "will not try to change it all by himself – which is the best way to change it."

8

A NEW WORLD ORDER MADE IN THE IMAGE AND LIKENESS OF CHINA

When China Rules the World: The End of the Western World and the Birth of a New World Order, by Martin Jacques. New York: Penguin Press, 2009, 550 pages.

Asia's Cauldron: The South China Sea and the End of a Stable Pacific, by Robert D. Kaplan. New York: Random House, 2014, 225 pages.

The Devouring Dragon: How China's Rise Threatens Our Natural World, by Craig Simons. New York: St. Martin's Press, 2013, 289 pages.

The rise of China, it has been assumed, will replicate the rise of the West; it will follow the trajectory that the West had initiated to become a modern nation. First, the rise of China will be primarily economic: it will grow in economic strength and, because of its size, will become the biggest economy in the world; it will create a large middle class; it will raise the standard of living of its people; it will create the most expansive consumer class in the world; it will lower its poverty rate. Second, it will become a modern nation, much like other Western nations; its social and political culture will be not much different from those of the West: an emphasis on individual, human, and citizenship rights, a system of governance that is based on law, equality and democracy. Thus, third, China will eventually occupy its proper place in the community of sovereign nations, a community that adheres to a liberal world order, created and maintained by the West since World War II and especially led by the United States. John Ikenberry (2008, 2011, 2014) is a foremost proponent of these views. Francis Fukuyama (1989, 1992) categorically declared "the end of history" as a clash of ideologies because capitalism and democracy have definitely triumphed.

Not so fast, argues Martin Jacques, co-founder of the UK think tank Demos, who writes a regular column for *The Guardian* and has been a visiting senior fellow and professor at various institutions and universities. I admit that I considered his book as just one more in the flood of books on China, until I belatedly opened its first pages and found the names of Eric Hobsbawm, Niall Ferguson, and Arne Westad, historians from whom I have learned much, in his acknowledgements. If Jacques is half correct in his analysis and predictions, his book is revisionist and radically different from other books on China and will be the most consequential among the prognostications on China's future.

Before all else, the rise of China calls into question the rise of the West itself. Not industrialization as the take-off for economic growth. Not the fact that the industrial revolution started in England. Not the fact that "once Britain embarked on its Industrial Revolution, investment in capital- and energy-intensive processes rapidly raised productivity levels and created a virtuous circle of technology, innovation and growth that was able to draw on an ever-growing body of science in which Britain enjoyed a significant lead over China." Nor the fact that Britain, because of its economic prowess, became a world empire, to be followed by the United States with its economic, military, and imperial outreach. Nor the fact that "Europe was the birthplace of modernity.... Modernity and Europe became inseparable, seemingly fused, the one inconceivable without the other: they appeared synonymous."

What the rise of China calls into question are, first, the characteristics of the West that it derives from its cultural legacy of Greek democracy, Roman law, and Judeo-Christian religion which are posited as preconditions for take-off, industrialization, and economic dominance. The West is made, therefore, the defining model of a modern society, the template against which every subsequent transformation should conform to and be measured by, which is simply Eurocentric and ethnocentric.

Second, the hindsight thinking that because of the dazzling success and extraordinary domination of Europe from the beginning of the 19th century, the roots of that success must date back longer than they actually did, that they were the product of a very long historical process that took place over several centuries. The decisive period of change was the 19th

century. Before that, in the late 18th century, Adam Smith pointed out, China enjoyed a more developed and sophisticated market than Europe because of its absence of feudalism. Paul Bairoch has calculated figures for per capita income that put China ahead of Western Europe in 1800, with Asia as a whole behind Western Europe but in advance of Europe. The most advanced regions of China, notably the Yangzi Delta, were more or less on par with the most prosperous parts of northwest Europe, in particular Britain, at the end of the 18th century.

Third, while modernity is made possible by industrialization and economic take-off, and while Europe was the birthplace of modernity so that modernity has been indelibly linked with Europe and the West, the rise of China and other non-Western nations to economic prominence means that they are also spawning their own distinctive ideas, values, institutions, and ideologies, shaped by their own histories and cultures, prising apart in the process the relationship between the West and modernity. Japan, for example, is modern but hardly Western. We are witnessing a world with multiple, competing, and contested modernities, in which the particularism and exceptionalism of the Western experience are becoming more apparent. In fact, the West itself, in debates about postmodernity, has expressed qualms about its own modernity.

The experience of the West cannot be universalized as historical law. The explanation for the economic breakthrough achieved by Britain was due to two short-term contingent and conjunctural, highly specific and particular factors, as Kenneth Pomeranz (2000) had elucidated. First, England discovered large quantities of coal which eased the growing shortage of wood, fueled the Industrial Revolution, and enabled England to break the crucial constraint of land which had become increasingly exhausted through overuse. Second, much more importantly, the colonization of the New World, namely the Caribbean and North America, provided huge tracts of land, a massive and very cheap source of labor in the form of slaves, and an abundant flow of food and raw materials. Manchester would not have been possible without the land to raise sheep and to grow cotton and the cheap and plentiful supplies of cotton, sugar, and timber from British slave plantations. "The role played by colonization, in this context," notes Jacques, "is a reminder that European industrialization was far from an endogenous process." Jacques sums up by quoting Christopher Bayly's (2004: 469) conclusion: "If, in terms of economic growth, what distinguished Europe from China before 1800 was only its intensive use of coal and the existence of a vast American hinterland to Europe, then a lot of cultural baggage about inherent European political superiorities looks ready to be jettisoned."

Martin Jacques contends that Europe and the West are a poor template for understanding the rise of China in particular and of Japan and East Asia in general. In fact, the modernity which has been a Western monopoly, has been decidedly broken and is ineluctably being transformed into diverse and plural non-Western forms. Of course, the airports, the shopping malls, the high-rise buildings, and busy urban centers of the non-Western world, which constitute the hardware of modernity, are all too familiar to any Western traveler. But dig deeper into their cultural software and you will find combinations of pre-modern and modern ways of thinking, of mixtures of past and future, alternative and convincing concepts, theories, and frameworks. This Jacques interestingly explores with regard to language, the body, food, and politics. This leads Jacques also to declare that the Age of the West, which marked the 19th and 20th centuries, is coming to an end. The West is no longer the exclusive home of modernity, which threatens Western countries with an existential crisis of the first order. The bearer of this change will be China.

Martin Jacques starts the second part of his book, the Age of China, with China's economic transformation, "surely the most extraordinary in human history, notwithstanding the sheer novelty of Britain's as the first." We all know that beginning with the four modernizations of Deng Xiaoping in 1978, the economy of China has grown to be the second biggest in the world and is expected to overtake that of the United before the middle of the century. The most significant fact for me is that the number of people living in poverty in China fell from 250 million in 1978 to 80 million in 1993 and 29.7 million in 2001, thus accounting for three-quarters of global poverty reduction during this period. It has been the greatest poverty-reduction program ever seen.

But the continuing economic success of China is not guaranteed. Jacques catalogues the most severe economic challenges China faces. Is China's economic growth sustainable? A serious and sustained drop below 8 percent carries the threat of serious social unrest. The priority given to breakneck economic growth has moved China from being a highly egalitarian society to becoming one of the most unequal in the world. The inequality is threefold: between coastal and interior provinces, between urban and rural areas, and between those in the formal economy and those dependent on informal economic activities. The sense of insecurity of many Chinese is compounded by China's lack of a decent social safety net and the threadbare character of key public goods. China's growth has been extremely resource-intensive, rapidly exhausting what limited resources it has. As a result, China has become dependent on the rest of the world for huge quantities of raw materials, with levels of demand that are unsustainable in terms of the world's available resources. Another more ominous result is the huge ecological deficit that China has accumulated in just a few decades, especially its use of coal which fired up its hypergrowth: water shortages, lack of drinking water, and polluted groundwater, rampant deforestation, vanished rivers if they have not become industrial sewers, polluted cities, acid rain affecting a third of Chinese territory, deserts covering a quarter of the country, 58 percent of land classified as arid or semi-arid. The picture of people with masks against a backdrop of a hazy, smoke-filled sky sums up the environmental destruction that China has wrought upon itself with its breakneck economic growth. China has overtaken in 2007 the U.S. as the biggest emitter of CO_2, although not in per capita terms. "If the world's biggest polluter doesn't radically reduce the amount of coal it burns," Jeff Goodell (2014) writes, "nothing anyone does to stabilize the climate will matter." Yet he also shows how difficult it is to move China to take any meaningful action as the nations of the world prepare to gather in Paris in December 2015 to try to hammer out a global climate agreement.

This is equally true of the United States. As I finish this review essay, there is late breaking news that the U.S. and China have reached a climate accord, in which the United States would emit 26 to 28 percent less carbon in 2025, while China pledged to reach peak carbon emissions by 2030, if not sooner. Immediately, however, Republicans, who will control both houses of Congress, denounced the accord and vowed to derail it (Landler 2014).

But, Jacques insists, much more is needed to understand China's rise and its implications. "China, by the standards of every other country, is a most peculiar animal. Apart from size, it possesses two other exceptional, even unique, characteristics. China is not just a nation-state; it is also a civilization *and* a continent." China as civilization refers to "its history, dynasties, Confucius, the ways of thinking, their relationships and customs, the *guanxi* (the network of personal connections), the family, filial piety, ancestral worship, the values, and distinctive philosophy." This self-awareness and continuity of being a civilization remains the primary point of reference for the Chinese people amidst all the huge and revolutionary disruptions and discontinuities they have undergone. "There are no other people in the world," Jacques writes, "who are so connected to their past and for whom the past – not so much the recent past but the long-ago past – is so relevant and meaningful." The most influential writer who shaped China with his arguments and moral precepts is Confucius. Two of the most obvious continuities in Chinese civilization, those that concern the state and education, can be traced back to Confucius. The state is the embodiment and guardian of Chinese civilization, whose most important task is maintaining its unity. Education is vested with the authority and reverence of Chinese civilization, with teachers the transmitters and bearers of wisdom.

"The fact that [China] is a continent in size and diversity," Jacques affirms, "is critical to understanding how the country functions in practice." Instead of seeing China through the prism of a conventional nation-state, it is better to think of it as a continental system containing many semi-autonomous provinces with distinctive political, economic, and social systems. The provinces are akin to nation-states that enjoy great autonomy. The fundamental importance of the relationship between Beijing and the provinces revolves around the question of centralization and decentralization which constitutes the fundamental fault line of Chinese politics. One of the key reforms of Deng Xiaoping was to grant more freedom to provincial and local governments as a means of encouraging greater economic initiative. But this major shift in power soon became a concern for the central government, and it was largely reversed.

Although politics is the most impoverished area of debate in China, its most fundamental feature is the overriding emphasis on the country's unity, whose reverse is the pathological fear of division and instability. It is here that Martin Jacques introduces his discussion of democracy, communist rule, and state capitalism. "Whatever democratic political system evolves in China," Jacques opines, "will bear the heavy imprint of its Confucian past.... It would be wrong, moreover, to regard Confucianism as entirely inimical to democratic ideas.... The mandate of Heaven, in recognizing the right of the people to rebel if the emperor failed them, was certainly a more democratic idea than its European counterpart, the divine right of kings." Democracy in China, therefore, might emphasize more the importance of accountability with regard to the conduct of officials than the issue of elections. During the reform era, there has been a steady process of depoliticization, which in effect resulted in a new kind of compact: the task of the Communist Party is to govern, while the people are left free to make money. Thus, the Party has been transformed from a revolutionary organization into a ruling administrative party. But the state has consistently been seen as the apogee of society, enjoying sovereignty over all else. The developmental state in East Asia and China has been instrumental in their economic success. So it will not be a surprise that the capitalism with Chinese characteristics will not be the neoliberal kind of market economy, but will have the state as an integral functioning partner. And if this century will increasingly belong to China and India, in conjunction with the United States, it will be the Age of the Megastate, looking very different from the Westphalian system that we have been accustomed to.

China's civilization-state serves as a constant reminder that China is the Middle Kingdom, occupying as the center of the world a different position from all other states. Every society in some way thinks of itself as racially superior to all others, sees the world in terms of its own history, values, and mindset, and seeks to shape the world according to its experiences and perceptions. Race and ethnicity always enter into a country's sense of origins and destiny. For China, this means two things. China was once populated by a multitude of races, but today projects itself as a homogeneous nation, sharing a common origin and a natural affinity as Han Chinese. And while the racial superiority of the United States and Israel, for example, arises from the belief that they are God's chosen people, the racial chauvinism of China rests on the conviction of "an innate, almost visceral Han sense of superiority." China's utterly Sinocentric view of its place in the global order brings with it a belief in its universalism, the relevance and application of its culture to all peoples and societies, and its inherent superiority to all others. What does this Middle Kingdom mentality imply for China as a great power? "White racism has had a far greater and more profound – and deleterious – effect on the modern world than any other," Jacques points out. Do we expect that China as a global superpower will be less informed by yellow racism and sense of superiority?

China's regard of itself as being at the summit of the global hierarchy of race is already evident in its own backyard as East and South East Asia are being reconfigured by China's rise. The past is prefiguring the present and the future. Until the latter decades of the 19th century, China enjoyed regional dominance in Asia, which dominance took the form of a tributary system. Korea, part of Japan, Vietnam, and Myanmar paid tributes to China, while a large number of South East Asian states either paid tribute or acknowledged Chinese suzerainty. From the second half of the 19th century, the European-conceived Westphalian system, with its colonial subsystem, steadily replaced the tributary system as the organizing principle of interstate relations in the region. Today, everywhere in East and South East Asia, China has become the locomotive of growth by serving as a market for regional states and a provider of investment and technology. Even Australia with its huge deposits of raw materials, especially iron ore, has not escaped the attention of China's voracious appetite. But China's economic power does not translate into an interdependence of equality with its neighbors; it is a tributary relationship of dominance and dependence. It also means the effective exclusion of the United States from economic diplomacy in the region.

China has also begun to flex its military muscle. Robert Kaplan, who has written volumes on foreign affairs and political conflicts all over the world, and who was named by *Foreign Policy* as one of the world's Top 100 Global Thinkers in 2011 and 2012, contends that China has made the South China Sea *Asia's Cauldron*, effectively putting an end to a stable Pacific. The South China Sea is the location of the Spratly and Paracel Islands, a collection of uninhabited rocks, under which is believed to be precious mineral deposits. The Spratly are to the north of East Malaysia and Brunei and to the west of the Philippines, and the Paracels are to the east of Vietnam, over both of which China claims sovereignty, but which is contested by the aforementioned countries. There is also the dispute between Japan and China over the Diaoyu/Senkaku Islands in the East China Sea, and over Taiwan. All of these countries, except Japan and Taiwan, do not have the military capability to thwart China's claims, and China has, until now, not shown any intentions of using military force. And even if and when it does, it is doubtful that the United States will militarily engage China over these islands. In the meantime, tension abounds and skirmishes ensue as China slowly squeezes the resolve of the concerned countries into submission.

Kaplan points out that the South China Sea connects the maritime world of the Middle East and Indian Subcontinent to that of Northeast Asia. It is as central to Asia as the Mediterranean is to Europe. It is arguably the most critical geographical juncture of the non-Western world. If the dominance of Great Britain in the 19th century demanded the control of the Mediterranean Sea, and if the ascendancy of the United States in the 20th century necessitated the control of the Great Caribbean, stretching from Florida to Venezuela, together with the Gulf of Mexico, and uniting North and South America into a single coherent geopolitical system, the rise of China is leading it to dominate the maritime passage of the South China Sea. It will be remembered that the Monroe Doctrine of 1823 was primarily about the political consolidation of the American home continent, within whose geopolitical sphere of interest fell the Great Caribbean. Eliminating Europe from the New World was the foreign policy cornerstone that was the Monroe Doctrine, so the question is: Will China have as a goal of grand, long-term strategy the elimination of America from Asia? "That is why," Kaplan foresees, "the South China Sea will be among the most salient political and moral registers of any future U.S. defense retrenchment. Here is where everyone is arming to the teeth, even as China's military is pulling further and further ahead of every other in the region."

China's global power is being driven by its voracious need for raw materials of which it does not have enough. "In 2001," Martin Jacques takes note, "China officially launched its 'Going Global' strategy, which was primarily intended to foster a closer relationship with commodity-producing countries and thereby secure the raw materials the country urgently required for its economic growth. The effects of this policy have been dramatic. . . . [I]n fact China's changing relationship with the developing world is of rather greater import in China's emergence as a nascent global power." The most dramatic example is Africa. Chinese imports from, and Chinese investments in, sub-Saharan Africa have dramatically risen, and this without regard to the African country's dictatorial rule and human rights record. China's impact on Africa has so far been positive, increasing the latter's strategic importance in the world economy. "There is little evidence that China's record in Africa is any worse – and in fact is almost certainly far better – than the West's own miserable catalogue of support for corrupt dictatorial regimes on the continent, not to mention its colonial legacy." According to Stefan Halper (2010), this has led to the growing discussion and resonance in the developing world of what is called the "Beijing Consensus," as opposed to the neoliberal "Washington Consensus," which emphasizes strong government, state-led investments, and controlled markets for economic growth and development.

The Devouring Dragon that is China's economy, however, has not had equally beneficial effects on the global environment. Craig Simons, former Peace Corps China Volunteer, Knight Science Journalism Fellow, and reporter on the environment for various publications, categorically states that China's rise threatens our natural world, assaulting it at an alarming rate. "The problems that are obvious across China – millions of pollution-related deaths, plunging water tables, the eradication of wildlife – are beginning to stretch far beyond its borders to reshape the physical planet: the air we breathe, the health of the oceans and the last remaining tracts of untouched forests, the diversity of plants and animals, the climates that shape where and how we live – the very metabolism of our rapidly crowding planet."

Simons also points out, as if people still needed to know, that scientific study after scientific study show that "humanity is using natural resources unsustainably – in ways that deplete them faster than they can be replenished or their wastes safely dealt. Since the beginning of the Industrial Revolution, for example, we have cleared more than one quarter of the world's original forests and an even larger fraction of its wetlands and plains; set off the world's sixth great era of extinctions – with losses occurring at a rate scientists consider between one hundred and one thousand times greater than before humans dominated the Earth; pumped enough carbon dioxide and other greenhouse gases into the atmosphere to heat the planet by more than 1 degree Fahrenheit; depleted the oceans to the point that the UN Food and Agricultural Organization classifies more than one-quarter of fish species as 'overexploited' or 'depleted'; and released billions of toxic and hazardous materials into the air and water."

Simons, however, is honest to admit that "the Western world is largely responsible. The impact of today's wealthy states was to some extent a direct result of colonization and resource exploitation – the slaughter of species for profit and sport. But it also grew from a ratcheting up of the planet's economic metabolism: as people in London, Paris, and New York demanded tropical products, for example, land was cleared, roads were built, animals were hunted, and communities were pulled into the modern world, initiating additional sets of cascading change. Writing about the United States, Richard Tucker, a historian at the University of Michigan, argues that demands for imported products have constituted a dimension of American power that while 'almost totally ignored . . . has surpassed all others in its grasp of Nature's global resources and thus in its worldwide ecological impact.'"

To put things into proper perspective, Simons also compares the ecological footprint of an average Chinese citizen with the typical American:

> The average American is responsible for 13,647 kilowatt-hours of electricity each year – enough to run 136,470 one-hundred-watt lightbulbs simultaneously for an hour. He (or she) uses 933 gallons of crude oil and 2,156 cubic meters of natural gas. He is responsible for roughly 18 metric tons of carbon dioxide emissions and eats 238 pounds of meat. He almost certainly owns a car. Every day, he throws away four and a half pounds of trash.
>
> The average Chinese citizen, by comparison, looks as green as a Vermont wind farm. She (or he) uses just 18 percent of the American's electricity demand, one-tenth of his oil demand, and less than 5 percent of his natural gas demand. She is responsible for less than one-third of the American's carbon dioxide emissions and – even though Chinese demand has more than doubled in recent years – eats half as much meat as her American counterpart. China surpassed the United States as the world's largest

auto market in 2010, but odds are high that she does not own a car. (In 2008, only one in twenty-eight Chinese owned a motor vehicle.)

But today as Western countries have passed the reins of economic growth to the developing world, among developing nations, "China by dint of its rapidly growing needs, its ancient belief in natural cures, and its nascent environmental awareness, stands above all others in the damage it is causing to biodiversity. . . . [G]rowing Chinese desires have pushed resource exploitation into the Earth's last untouched places."

A most tragic aspect of the ecological catastrophe we are facing is the rate at which plants, animals, and fishes are going extinct. Whereas earlier episodes were caused by massive natural disruptions of the earth's ecological processes, like collisions with asteroids and volcanic eruptions, the current episode of mass extinction is one in which one species, the human species, has pushed the others over the cliff to oblivion. A large share of responsibility for the multiplication of endangered species, of their extinction or near-extinction lies with the increasing prosperity of a growing number of people in China, who can afford their every whim and fancy, like home décor and ornaments of ivory. There is also the impact of traditional Chinese medicine, which continues to utilize various animal and plant parts to allegedly cure any and every ailment, the most infamous of which are tiger bone and rhino horn. Then there is the world's most open-minded culinary appetite, where almost everything that moves is considered edible, where exotic meats are enjoyed, often of poached and smuggled wildlife. In China, it is said, people eat everything on four legs except tables, everything that flies except planes and everything in the water except boats. China's culinary taste is rooted in its belief in traditional medicines: because every animal part has medicinal benefits, they eat everything.

Simons notes that "it took Europe a couple of centuries to destroy its environment. It took the U.S. about a century to get from a frontier mentality to where we are now. China is doing this whole process at breakneck speed. It's doing it in just a few decades." It will be a sad day when the most lasting legacy of China's epic tale ends with the destruction of the natural world.

The future shape of a new world order being driven by China's emergence as a global power remains as yet unclear. Martin Jacques lays down eight characteristics of Chinese modernity that will impact the processes of its transformation. One, China is not a nation-state in the traditional sense, but a civilization-state. Most of what China is today

– its social relations and customs, its ways of being, its sense of superiority, its belief in the state, its commitment to unity – are products of its long history as a civilization. Two, China increasingly conceives its relationship with East Asia in terms of a tributary state. Could the same kind of hierarchical system be repeated elsewhere? Could there even be a global tributary system? Three, because of the distinctively Chinese attitude towards race and ethnicity, it will mean that as China interacts with the rest of the world, it will remain aloof, ensconced in a hierarchical view of humanity, its sense of superiority resting on a combination of cultural and racial hubris. Four, China operates, and will continue to operate, on a quite different continent-sized canvas from other nation-states. For one thing, the democratic systems that we associate with the West have never taken root on such a vast scale as China, with the single exception of India. The fact that China's true Western counterpart, the European Union, is similarly without democracy serves to reinforce the point. Five, the Chinese state is venerated, above society, possessed of great prestige, regarded as an embodiment of what China is, and the guarantor of the country's stability and unity. The legitimacy of the Chinese state does not depend on electoral mandate, but on that of Heaven. Six, Chinese modernity, like other East Asian modernities, is distinguished by the speed of the country's transformation. It combines, in a way quite different from the Western experience of modernity, the past and the future at once and the same time in the present. Seven, since 1949 China has been ruled by a Communist regime. Negative Western attitudes toward China continue to be highly influenced by the fact that it is ruled by a Communist Party. But the Chinese Communist Party has created and re-created the modern Chinese state: it reunited China after a century of disunity; it defeated Japanese colonialism; it played a critical role in the rise of China; it now manages China as a global power. Whatever the longer term may hold, the Chinese Communist Party must be viewed in a more pluralistic manner than was previously the case. It is certainly different from its Soviet counterpart. Eight, China for some time to come combines the characteristics of a developed and developing country. It will continue to display the interests and characteristics of both. But China is the first great power that comes from the "wrong" side of the divide between First and Third Worlds.

But if and when China becomes a major global power, what will a globally hegemonic China look like? What would a *Pax Sinica* mean? Martin Jacques catalogs 14 characteristics of America's global hegemony and speculates how these characteristics would change "when China rules the world." It is a very interesting exercise, at the end of which, Jacques does not speculate that "the most traumatic consequences will be felt by the West because it is the West that will find its historic position being usurped by China.... If Europe will suffer, that is nothing to the material and existential crisis that will be faced by the United States. It is almost completely unprepared for a life where it is not globally dominant.... The United States remain[s] largely blind to what the future might hold, still basking in the glory of its past and present, and preferring to believe that it would continue in the future.... The turning point in the United States may well prove to have been the financial meltdown in September 2008, with the near collapse of the financial system and the demise of neo-liberalism."

Jacques issues a cautionary warning: "The biggest danger facing the world is that the United States will at some point adopt an aggressive stance that treats China as the enemy and seeks to isolate it. A relatively benign example of this was the proposal of the Republican presidential candidate Senator John McCain for a 'league of democracies', designed to exclude China and Russia (which he also wanted to expel from the G8) and thereby create a new global division. The longer-term fear must be that the U.S. engages China in military competition and an arms race in something akin to a rerun of the Cold War."

Jacques' peroration is worth quoting:

> The emergence of China as a global power in effect relativizes everything. The West is habituated to the idea that the world is *its* world, the international community *its* community, the international institutions *its* institutions, the world currency – namely the dollar – *its* currency, and the world's language – namely English – *its* language. The assumption has been that the adjective 'Western' naturally and implicitly belongs in front of each important noun. The West will progressively discover, to its acute discomfort, that the world is no longer Western. Furthermore it will increasingly find itself in the same position as the rest of the world during the West's long era of supremacy, namely being obliged to learn from and live on the terms of the West. For the first time, a declining West will be required to engage with other cultures and countries and learn from their strengths. The United States is entering a protracted period of economic, political and military trauma. It finds itself on the eve of a psychological, emotional and

existential crisis. Its medium-term reaction is unlikely to be pretty: the world must hope it is not too ugly.

In the meantime, President Xi Jinping has consolidated power and established himself as the paramount leader of China, has articulated a simple and powerful vision of the rejuvenation of the Chinese nation under the mantra "Chinese Dream," and has proposed to reform, if not revolutionize, political and economic relations with the rest of the world that will propel China to the top of the world order (Economy 2014; Beech 2014). The West, on the other hand, is confronted with an entrenched political paralysis. The European Union cannot get its act together to solve its enormous problems, and is in danger of dismemberment and dissolution (*Foreign Affairs* 2012). In the broken American system, Republicans and Democrats, the former more than the latter, assiduously pursue brute partisanship that renders impossible consensus on the common good. They are American Neros fiddling while American Rome burns (*Foreign Affairs* 2014). And yet, as Thomas Mann and Norman Ornstein (2013) declare, "It's Even Worse Than It Looks," and it will get worse before it gets any better. Napoleon is supposed to have said: "China is a sleeping giant. Let her sleep, for when she wakes she will move the world." China has awakened, but the world awaits in trepidation whether it will be for good or ill of all of humanity and the planet.

9

DEMOCRATIC DECAY IN THE WEST AND THE GLOBAL RACE TO REINVENT GOVERNMENT

The Origins of Political Order: From Prehuman Times to the French Revolution, by Francis Fukuyama. New York: Farrar, Straus and Giroux, 2011, 585 pages.

Political Order and Political Decay: From the Industrial Revolution to the Globalization of Democracy, by Francis Fukuyama. New York: Farrar, Straus and Giroux, 2014, 658 pages.

The Fourth Revolution: The Global Race to Reinvent the State, John Micklethwait and Adrian Wooldridge. New York: Penguin Press, 2014, 305 pages.

    I start with two misgivings. Francis Fukuyama (1989) is a Stanford political scientist. He is forever associated with the triumphalistic thesis: "the end of history." His argument: The implosion of the Soviet Union marked the end of history, not history as the chronological unfolding and progression of events, but history as the locus of the clash of civilizations. With end of the Soviet Union, the ultimate transformation of world politics has arrived with the triumph of liberal democracy. Liberal democracy, therefore, constitutes the "end point of mankind's ideological evolution" and the "final form of human government," thus the end of history. Henceforth, chronological history means the inevitable march and spread of democracy.

But then Fukuyama ignored what is true and just about liberal democracy as he supported the unjust aggression against Saddam Hussein's Iraq, which was masterminded by his mentor, Paul Wolfowitz. Not only was the intelligence manipulated to justify the attack, not only was it quixotic to plant the seeds of democracy at the point of bayonets, but the result has been unmitigated disaster. It set in motion a catastrophic chain of events: immense suffering for the Iraqi people, a huge deterioration in Western and Muslim relations, greater political instability in an already unsettled region. It has given rise to the Shia Crescent that stretches across Iraq, Iran, Syria, and Lebanon, and has made Iran a power, possibly nuclear, to contend with in the Middle East. In retaliation, the Sunni-dominated and self-designated Islamic State leaves a human wreckage of its own brand of barbarism and nihilism across Iraq and Syria. Fukuyama has since distanced himself from the hubris of neoconservatism but he cannot take back the severe damage done to liberal democracy at home and the tainted reputation of liberal democracy abroad that he was party to.

Francis Fukuyama attributes the origins and inspiration of his massive two-volume work to Samuel Huntington's (1968) *Political Order in Changing Societies*. In fact, he considers it a classic which needed serious updating which he now provides. In graduate school, I had a different reading. Huntington posited that "the most important political distinction among nations concerns not their form of government but their degree of government." For modernizing Third World countries that are no longer traditional but are not yet modern, Huntington proposed strong governments as the key to political order and stability. He asserted that "the Kremlin may well be the most relevant model for many modernizing countries in this century . . . The primary need their countries face is the accumulation and concentration of power, not its dispersion, and it is in Moscow and Peking and not in Washington that this lesson is to be learned." He therefore extolled Lenin over Marx, "a political primitive," in that "Lenin elevated a political institution, the party, over social classes and social forces" as the organizational principle of modern society."

For Donal Cruise O'Brien (1979), Huntington's politics of order marked the erosion of the democratic ideal in American political science. Mark Kesselman (1973) considered Huntington "assigned reading in Silone's school of dictators." This was the period in which, after the 1964 installation of a military regime in Brazil, a wave of authoritarianism swept across Third World countries. Indeed, when I left the Philippines, the country was no longer "the showcase of democracy in Asia," but was in the grip of the conjugal dictatorship of Ferdinand and Imelda Marcos. And in justifying his "democratic revolution," Marcos (1974) quoted and referenced Huntington's *Political Order in Changing Societies*.

Fukuyama's first volume seeks to trace the origins of political order from prehuman times to the French Revolution. The main contention that underlies his study of the development of political institutions is that "the kinds of minimal or no-government societies envisioned by dreamers of the Left and Right are not fantasies; they actually exist in the contemporary developing world." They exist as tax-free libertarian paradises of poverty and misery in sub-Saharan Africa, as lawless individuals and groups in Somalia, armed with assault rifles and rocket-propelled grenades, as the corrupt, disastrous, and ineffective government of Nigeria, incapable of guaranteeing intellectual property rights, much less a decent standard of living for its citizens.

"Political institutions are necessary and cannot be taken for granted," Fukuyama affirms. "A market economy and high levels of wealth don't magically appear when you 'get government out of the way'; they rest on a hidden institutional foundation of property rights, rule of law, and basic political order." He cannot emphasize enough that "'institutions matter': poor countries are poor not because they lack resources, but because they lack effective political institutions." The three categories of institutions in question are 1) the state, 2) the rule of law, and 3) accountable government. He considers China as a paradigm of state formation, religion as key to the origins of the rule of law, and the story of accountable government as largely a European one. "Once this combination state, law, and accountability appeared, it proved to be a highly powerful and attractive form of government that subsequently spread to all corners of the world."

At the start, Fukuyama looks at "the overarching framework of evolutionary biology" to discern the important biological building blocks out of which we can construct a theory of political development. He identifies natural characteristics, not unique to human beings, but shared among many animal species, that are the basis for the evolution of increasingly complex forms of social organization. Evolved human nature provides certain structured paths toward sociability that give human politics its peculiar character. The all-important point is that, contrary to Thomas Hobbes and modern neoclassical economists, human beings did not start out as solitary individuals who gradually came to form societies over the course of historical time. "The behaviorally modern human beings who emerged somewhere in Africa fifty thousand years ago were socially organized from the start, just like their primitive forbears."

Humans were first organized into band-level societies, consisting of small groups of individuals, mostly composed of genetic relatives, who subsisted off hunting and gathering. The first major institutional transition was the shift to tribal-level societies, organized around the belief in the power of dead ancestors and unborn descendants. They prevailed over band-level societies because they were capable of achieving enormous wealth by pushing back the dating of common ancestry. The shift also required the emergence of a religious idea, belief in the ability of dead ancestors and unborn descendants to affect health and happiness. This is also an early example of ideas playing a critical independent role in development.

The next important political transition is that to a state-level society, Hobbes' Leviathan, which possesses a monopoly on legitimate coercion over a defined territory. Max Weber distinguished two kinds: the patrimonial state is considered the personal property of the ruler and the administration of it is an extension of the ruler's household, whereas the modern state is impersonal, in which a citizen's relationship to the ruler does not depend on personal ties but simply as one's status as a citizen. For Fukuyama, "China was the first world civilization to establish a nonpatrimonial, modern state, which it did some eighteen centuries before similar political units appeared in Europe. State building in China was driven by the same circumstances that necessitated centralized states in early modern Europe: prolonged and pervasive competition." Thus, the truism enunciated by Charles Tilly: "War made the state and the state made war."

Before leaving the discussion on state formation, Fukuyama makes three detours: how India's early development diverged from China's due to the rise of Brahmanic religion; how tribalism was the main obstacle to political development among the Arabs, and how the European exit from kinship was due to religion, with the Catholic Church destroying extended kinship groups.

The second category of institutions, the rule of law, understood as the rules that are binding even on the most powerful actors in society, has its origins in religion. It is only religious authority that was capable of creating rules that warriors needed to respect. The rule of law was most deeply institutionalized in Western Europe, due to the Roman Catholic Church. The central event marking the autonomy of church was the investiture conflict that began in the eleventh century, which pitted the church against the Holy Roman Emperor over the latter's interference in religious matters. Thus, in Western Europe, law was the first of the three major institutions to emerge. China never developed a transcendental religion, the state emerged first, and law has never existed as a constraint on political power.

The result was that European monarchs never acquired the concentrated powers of the Chinese state. Only in Russia, where the Eastern Church was subordinated to the state, did such a regime emerge.

Democratic accountability was the last of the three sets of institutions to emerge. The main mechanism of accountability went by different names, the most famous of which was Parliament, in England. They were originally feudal estates representing elites in society. Ambitious monarchs sought to undermine the powers of these estates, but only in England was there a relatively even contest between king and estates. With the Glorious Revolution of 1688-89, a new monarch, William of Orange, agreed to the constitutional settlement embodying the principle of "no taxation without representation." These principles – no taxation without representation, and consent of the governed – would become the rallying cry of the American colonists against British authority in 1776. Thomas Jefferson would incorporate John Locke's ideas of natural rights into the American Declaration of Independence, and the idea of popular sovereignty would become the basis of the Constitution, ratified in 1789.

But Fukuyama is clear: "Neither the Glorious Revolution nor the American Revolution produced anything like a genuine social revolution." The contradictions between founding principle and social reality came to a head in the Civil War over slavery. Abraham Lincoln would make the decisive argument that harked back to the founding. A country based on natural rights and political equality cannot survive if it tolerated so blatantly contradictory an institution as slavery. Other conflicts would emerge in later years, whose resolution would expand the circle of people protected by the Constitution "But the basic political order established by the Glorious Revolution and the American Revolution – an executive accountable to a representative legislature and to the whole society more broadly – would prove durable. . . . [L]ater debates and conflicts revolved entirely around the question of who counted as a full human being whose dignity was marked by the ability to participate in the democratic system."

Fukuyama ends his first volume by pointing out the two major accomplishments of the other great revolution of the late 18th century, the French Revolution. It led to the development and promulgation in 1804 of Europe's first modern law code, the Civil Code or Code of Napoleon, and to the creation of a modern administrative state, through which the code was implemented and enforced. These revolutions traced in the first volume marked the point at which all three categories of institutions – state, rule of law, and democratic accountability – came into being and resulted in what we now call liberal or constitutional democracy.

Two monumental developments were unfolding during the moments of political upheaval: the Industrial Revolution, whose enormous consequences began to change the underlying nature of societies; and the second wave of colonialism which set Europe on a collision course with the rest of the world. In his second volume, Fukuyama continues his account of how state, law, and democracy developed over the last two centuries, interacting with one another and with the new economic and social dimensions of global development, specifically of industrialization in the West and of colonialism in the non-West.

The Industrial Revolution brought about vastly increased rates of economic growth of per capita output that resulted in increased rates of change in all dimensions of development, especially in its enormous social and political consequences. Europe and America first experienced this revolution and were also where the first liberal democracies appeared. As far as state formation and democracy are concerned, the most modern contemporary bureaucracies were those established by authoritarian states in their pursuit of national security. This was true of ancient China, as well as, of Prussia, the preeminent example of modern bureaucratic rule, later to become Germany. On the other hand, countries that democratized early, before they established modern institutions, found themselves developing clientelistic public sectors. This was the fate of the United States – which was overcomed by a coalition of new social actors and strong political leadership – and of Greece and Italy as well. Sequencing is most important. If democracy precedes state-building, high-quality governance is more difficult to achieve than inherited modern states from absolutist ones.

Another potential tension between state-building and democracy is that between state-building and nation-building. As is the case with modern bureaucracies, strong national identity is most effectively formed under authoritarian conditions. Democratic societies lacking strong national identity have grave difficulties agreeing on an overarching national narrative, but are often riven by racial, ethnic, and religious divisions. Many peaceful democratic societies today built on an accepted national identity and commonly held values are in fact the beneficiaries of prolonged violence and authoritarian rule, which they have conveniently forgotten. But violence is not the only route to national identity; it can be forged by political elites to fit the realities of power, or established around expansive ideas like that of democracy itself.

The emergence or non-emergence of modern states in the non-Western world, colonized and overwhelmed by European powers, is a different story. Generally, European colonizers destroyed the legitimacy of traditional institutions, which like in sub-Saharan Africa were already weak at the start. The policies undertaken by colonial powers, the length of time they remained in control, and the resources they invested had consequences for postcolonial institutions. But the most successful non-Western countries today are those that had the most developed indigenous institutions before contact with the West and were not therefore fully undermined by colonialism. The contrast between sub-Saharan Africa and East Asia make this very clear. Latin America lies between these extremes. Despite their large pre-Columbian empires, the region never developed powerful state-level institutions. Existing political structures were destroyed by conquest and disease, and replaced by settler communities that brought with them the authoritarian and mercantilist institutions then prevailing in Spain and Portugal. Thus, the nature of the indigenous state institutions prior to colonialism makes for the differences in political development between sub-Saharan Africa, Latin America, and East Asia.

Fukuyama limits his discussion of democratic accountability not to the Third Wave of democratization which began in the early 1970s, but to the First Wave, the period of democratic expansion in Europe in the wake of the American and French Revolutions. 1898 saw the outbreak of revolutions in Europe, which has been compared to the 2011 Arab Spring. Within less than a year, however, the old authoritarian orders have been restored everywhere, which shows how difficult the road to democracy is. The spread of democracy depends on the legitimacy of the idea of democracy itself. For most of the 19th century, elites did not believe that the masses had the capacity to exercise the franchise responsibly. The rise of democracy therefore has much to do with the spreading views of human and political equality.

The Industrial Revolution brought about profound changes that resulted in a world we live today, of expanding and globalized democracy. Explosive economic growth mobilized new classes of people, specifically the bourgeoisie or middle class and the new industrial working class. In almost all cases the rise and growth of middle-class groups was critical to the spread of democracy, a thesis that had been expounded by Seymour Lipset and Barrington Moore (Litonjua 2011).

Fukuyama concludes his section on democratic accountability with a view toward the future. "If a broad middle class is indeed important to the survival of democracy, what will be the implication of the disappearance of middle-class jobs as a result of advancing technology and globalization?" Put differently, at a time of yawning economic inequality, can there be a democracy of the 1%, by the 1%, and for the 1% (Litonjua 2015)?

Fukuyama ends his massive work with a section on political decay, the rise and decline of democracy in the West, specifically in the United

States. One has the feeling that the entire work had for its final purpose and destination the ills of the American, hence Western, democratic governance. Samuel Huntington (1965) had written that institutions are created to meet certain needs of society, but they can grow rigid and fail to adapt when circumstances that brought them into being in the first place change. Fukuyama identifies a second source of decay, that is, when elites "capture" the state, when they use the apparatus of the state to protect and promote their interests, and those of their kin and allies. Following Weber, Fukuyama calls this "repatrimonialization," the capture of ostensibly impersonal state institutions by powerful elites to buttress their positions.

There is much to learn from the scope and sweep of Fukuyama's historical survey of democratic political development. There are interesting nuggets and enlightening insights on many and various aspects of political order in diverse geographical locations, which can only be appreciated by going through the two volumes, in themselves quite organized and readable. A few of these from his section on political decay can be mentioned.

Democracy itself can be and has become the source of political decay, Fukuyama writes. The presidential constitutional system of American democracy of checks and balances between executive, legislative, and judicial branches on the federal and state levels, unlike the union of legislative and executive in the parliamentary system, has become polarized and dysfunctional, which polarization and dysfunctionality are aggravated by a twenty-four hour cycle of news by media that are equally ideologically polarized. This is being replicated in the governance structure of the European Union, exemplified by the euro debacle and the Greek crisis, so that people do not have much confidence, are losing trust in, are questioning the legitimacy of what is happening in both Washington and Brussels. But with the almost divine worship of the Constitution by Americans, it is impossible even to raise the question.

Many institutional rigidities result from this system of checks and balances. Democratic government has become a highly dysfunctional bureaucracy, beholden to many different constituencies, producing poorly-drafted legislation, beginning with budgets, and ill-designed delegation of authority between legislative committees and executive departments. The entire legacy of congressional mandates – poorly crafted, poorly funded, and poorly administered – has produced a sprawling government that nonetheless fails to perform many basic functions – think Veterans Administration. Fukuyama repeats the contention that American politics has degenerated into a "state of parties and courts" that has usurped the functions of the executive. Political parties run on the aggregation of rigid and extreme ideological interests, concentrated in gerrymandered congressional districts. Courts which have also become polarized along extreme and rigid ideological lines insert themselves into either policy making or routine administration. American democracy has become America the vetocracy, a system of veto players. "Virtually all features of [the] constitution – presidentialism, bicameralism, federalism, judicial review – while functionally different from one another can be thought of as potential veto points in the process of reaching a collective decision. . . . A veto player is simply political science lingo for what Americans have traditionally called checks and balances."

The second mechanism of democratic decay is evident in the capture of large parts of the government by well-organized interest groups, who conduct their business and influence through well-financed lobbies. This is called by Fukuyama "a system of legalized gift exchange, in which politicians respond to organized interest groups that are collectively unrepresentative of the public as a whole." Fukuyama does not explicitly address it, but the U.S. Supreme Court has been complicit in this "repatrimonialization" of the American state by declaring that corporations are people and that money is free speech. With *Buckley v. Valeo* and *Citizens United* the democratic process is drowning in a flood of money, on which politicians must stay afloat but through which ordinary citizens cannot traverse. It is no longer "one person, one vote;" it has become "one dollar, and many dollars at that, and one vote." This strikes at the very systemic roots of democracy, because it leads to "a crisis of representation, in which ordinary people feel their supposedly democratic government no longer truly reflects their interests but is under the control of a variety of shadowy elites."

Some scholars have argued that democracy has self-correcting mechanisms to prevent decay. But Fukuyama writes: "But there is no guarantee that this self-correction will occur . . . The conservatism of institutions [and the venality of oligarchies] often make reform prohibitively difficult. [Both] kinds of political decay lead either to slowly increasing levels of corruption, with correspondingly lower levels of government effectiveness, or to violent populist reactions to perceived elite manipulation." His prognosis is dire: "[T]he United States, as the world's first and most advanced liberal democracy, suffers from the problem of political decay in a more acute form than other democratic political systems. . . . While the American economy remains a source of miraculous innovation, American government is hardly a source of inspiration around the world at the present moment."

Fukuyama ends by expressing his conviction that "a political system resting on a balance among state, law, and accountability is both a practical and a moral necessity for all societies. . . . [T]he development of these three sets of institutions becomes a universal requirement for all human societies over time." Is liberal democracy therefore a political universal? Fukuyama recognizes that there have emerged "principled alternatives to liberal democracy," most notably that of China, but he is not optimistic about them. At one time, he was triumphalistic about liberal democracy. This time he is more sober and cautious and fretful – in light of the decay of democracy in the West, led by the United States.

***

At this juncture, John Micklethwait and Adrian Wooldridge, editor-in-chief and management-editor respectively of *The Economist*, pick up the thread of the argument and continue the political narrative, arguing that we are in the midst of a "fourth revolution," the global race to fix government and reinvent the state. The first three revolutions were the rise of the nation-state, the liberal state, and the welfare state, each discussed and analyzed through the lens of a single political author each – British manifestations – on whom Micklethwait and Wooldridge focus as representing, without distractions, the three revolutions: Thomas Hobbes, John Stuart Mill, and Beatrice Webb. There was also a half, unfinished and unfulfilled, revolution: Milton Friedman's paradise lost.

"The main political challenge of the next decade," Micklethwait and Wooldridge announce, "will be fixing government." This need arises from the failure of the Western democratic state which is bloated, polarized, paralyzed, and dysfunctional. The ills of the Western state are encapsulated in the seven deadly sins of California government: it is out of date, useless in making its public sector efficient, captive of special interests, is overactive in producing complex regulations, fuzzy in its finances and liabilities, is no longer progressive in that the young are the losers from generational struggles, and suffers from partisan paralysis and gridlock. (This is not exactly a fair characterization of California, unless you completely disregard, as the authors do, that the California state is a pioneer in, among other things, dealing with environmental problems.) The most worrying thing about all this gridlock, buffoonery, and bile is that they are the result of giving power to the people. "Democracy is being disfigured by unrealistic expectations and contradictory demands. California is the ultimate example of the perils of democracy."

But democracy in California offers also a glimmer of hope. Under Jerry Brown, "the Greece of America is beginning to fix itself. It has taken the most important step for all substance abusers: admitting that it has a problem." There is even a rebirth of centrist pragmatism as the design faults in California's structure – two-thirds majority no longer needed to pass budgets in the legislature, open primaries, redistricting reforms – have begun to be fixed. It is indeed possible to find more flickers of hope as across the West people are probing questions about the size and scope of government.

Failure is not the only prod to change, competition is also. The direct challenge of "the Asian alternative" has taken concrete historical form in Lee Kwan Yew's Singaporean model of authoritarian modernization. Singapore is often ridiculed as Disneyland with the death penalty, a supersized shopping paradise where chewing gum is banned and litterbugs are given a trashing. But with rising China's leadership sharing three of Lee's convictions: that Western democracy is not efficient; that both capitalism and society need to be directed; and that getting government right is the key to their regime's success and survival, the emerging Beijing consensus has become a formidable alternative to the crisis of the Western model of democracy and free-market capitalism.

Micklethwait and Wooldridge assess two parts of the Asian alternative that China has most obviously tried to follow Singapore, but on a grander scale: state capitalism and its reliance on a cadre of meritocratic planners rather than democratically elected politicians. China's new model of state-directed capitalism has done wonders in creating wealth and lifting millions from poverty, but it also comes with weaknesses, the most serious of which is its scope for corruption. When copied by weak and incompetent states, like those in the Arab world and sub-Saharan Africa, state capitalism simply becomes colossal crony capitalism.

As for meritocracy as an alternative to democracy, this is a new version of an ancient faith in an educated mandarinate. Micklethwait and Wooldridge open their book with a description of the China Executive Leadership Academy in Pudong, a huge compound spread across some forty-acres, where China trains its Platonic guardians for the future. The Chinese system of meritocracy can claim two victories: the circulation of elites and a long-term approach, but elitism without democracy comes with a lot of problems which are beginning to show up, particularly at the lower levels: unresponsiveness to the complaints of ordinary Chinese citizens. Besides the emperor's court is not as meritocratic as claimed. The Party elite are "red princelings," and all of China's leaders systematically use their power to accumulate wealth and privilege.

Failure and competition also provide opportunity. Sweden took the opportunity of the near-collapse of its "all you can eat" state to do most of the things politicians know they ought to do but have seldom the courage to attempt. It has reduced public spending as a proportion of GDP, put its pension system on a sound foundation, used educational vouchers to send children to independent schools, and "Swedish health care is now arguably the most efficient in the rich world." The other three Nordic societies, Norway, Denmark, and Finland, to a lesser degree, have also followed the new Nordic model, by extending the market into state, rather than extending the state into the market. Micklethwait and Wooldridge then show examples of how the Leviathan of the corporate world and of government are being fixed, the former prodded by technology, globalization, and consumer choice, and the latter by the fact that it is running out of cash. They focus on the part of Leviathan that is both most associated with government sluggishness and is most likely to bankrupt it: health care. Their example is Devi Shetty, India's most celebrated heart surgeon, who has built a medical empire by applying mass production to health care. They also mention the Internet as the biggest change maker of all, the idea of breaking the state down into smaller and more innovative units, and the importance of diversity and pluralism in governmental forms and the need to experiment and be pragmatic.

In all of these, however, there is no mention of 9/11 – except for the growth of the security state – and the asymmetric violence, conflict, and war that are being conducted by religious terrorists, leaving the wreckage of human lives and human societies in their wake. It is as if the Great Recession of 2008 never happened, caused by free wheeling financial markets, that wreaked havoc on the global economy and from which many have not yet recovered. There is no inkling of the ecological catastrophe that hangs over planet earth and threatens life itself, nor of nuclear proliferation, arms race, drone warfare, and internet hacking. I don't think, and I do not know if Micklethwait and Wooldridge think, that such problems can be solved by Milton Friedman's paradise regained, however technological and global it can become. As far as I know, it is only the noisy cabal of libertarians, free market fundamentalists, oil and gas industry vested interests, and climate change denialists who think and applaud so.

The answer lies in the chapter entitled "What Is the State For?" but whose answer Micklethwait and Wooldridge preempt by laying down their ideological leanings: "We want the state to be smaller and individuals to be freer." No surprise here from the editors of *The Economist*. For them, the state is stuck in a paradox: "Government, backed by the general democratic will, has never been more powerful; but in this bloated, overburdened condition, it also has seldom been as unloved or inefficient." The overfeeding is the work of both the Left and the Right, but "the main culprit is the Left (as we have argued throughout this book) . . ." One can certainly agree with many of their proposals in lightening the burden on Leviathan, especially on the American one: privatization, elimination of subsidies for the wealthy – farm subsidies, subsidizing the financial-services industry and the production of fossil fuels – and trimming entitlements. But in the end, as President Barack Obama has said, the question is not whether government is big or small but whether the state is effective and efficient. What is big and what is small depends on the necessary tasks the people has set the state for. Even Micklethwait and Wooldridge themselves – surprise! surprise! – opine that "a truly radical America would leapfrog over the muddle of Obamacare and pluck . . . the European idea [of] a single-payer system, broadly along the Swedish model."

Having earlier debunked the Asian alternative of government and refusing to see any value in it, having damned the bloat, gridlock, buffoonery, and bile of the American democratic political system, Micklethwait and Wooldridge wistfully conclude, after another plethora of proposals to complete "the half success of the Reagan-Thatcher reforms" in a Fourth Revolution, that "the West has been the world's most creative region because it has repeatedly reinvented the state. We have every confidence that it can do so again, even in these difficult times."

10

IN THE WRECKAGE OF AN IMPERIOUS AND IMPERIAL PAPACY: SEEDS OF HOPE UNDER POPE FRANCIS

A Still and Quiet Conscience: The Archbishop Who Challenged a Pope, a President, and a Church, by John A. McCoy. Maryknoll, NY: Orbis Books, 2015, 344 pp.

The Francis Effect: A Radical Pope's Challenge to the American Catholic Church, by John Gehring. Lanham, MD: Rowman and Littlefield, 2015, 267 pp.

Pope Francis among the Wolves: The Inside Story of a Revolution, by Marco Politi. New York: Columbia University Press, 2015, 270 pages.

    Karol Wojtyla was elected Pope in 1978, took the name of John Paul II, ruled the Church for 27 years until his death in 2005. He appointed Joseph Ratzinger Cardinal-Prefect of the Congregation for the Doctrine of the Faith in 1981, which he led for twenty-four years, after which he himself was elected Pope in 2005, took the name of Benedict XVI until his resignation in 2013. There was much continuity – long and close association – between the two papacies, much overlap in orientation, policy, and governance so that for the practical purposes of this paper, they will be considered one continuous papacy. I characterize this papacy as imperious, marked by arrogant assurance, because it eliminated without much ado all aspirations, manifestations, and instrumentalities of collegiality, a core doctrine in the governance of the Church that was taught by Vatican II. It therefore is also imperial, characteristic of an empire or an emperor, which befits the Roman Catholic Church as the restoration of Rome (Heather 2013), but again which Vatican II tried to correct with its image of the Church as the entire Pilgrim People of God. The wreckage from the imperious and imperial Woytyla-Ratzinger papacy is what now confronts Pope Francis, especially as it presents itself and afflicts the Catholic Church in the United States.

Archbishop Raymond Hunthausen

In the wreckage left in the Catholic Church by the Wojtyla-Ratzinger papacy, the case of Archbishop Raymond G. Hunthausen, archbishop of Seattle from 1975 to 1991, stands out because of the reasons his life and career were destroyed, for the tactics used in his persecution, and for the purposes he was sacrificed. It happened, Kenneth Briggs (1992) told us, in "the year that shook Catholic America," between the notification to Rev. Charles E. Curran in August 1986 that he was being stripped of his right to each as a Catholic theologian to Pope John Paul II's visit, hailed as a "superstar," to the United States in September 1987. It included, among other things, the dismissal of Rev. John J. McNeill from the Jesuit order for speaking out against the Church's stand on homosexuality and the issuance of arrest warrants for American Archbishop Paul C. Marcinkus for his role in the collapse of Banco Ambrosiano. He, however, flourished under John Paul II.

One feels the heaviness of heart as ecclesiastical authoritarianism imposes its will on a Church most recently declared to be the People of God. This is the feeling I get from reading this immensely interesting, painfully researched, and very well written book by John McCoy who first followed this story as a reporter for the *Seattle Post-Intelligencer*, and headed the communications departments of the Catholic Archdiocese of Seattle and World Vision International, which sheds enormous light on the recent shameful past of the Catholic Church. I just hope that it bodes as a lesson and a challenge as well in the age of Pope Francis for the pilgrim People of God in the present and for the future.

Archbishop Hunthausen was "the quintessential Vatican II bishop," writes John McCoy. He was the last U.S. bishop appointed before the Council opened on October 11, 1962, and, at forty-one, the youngest of the American bishops. Hunthausen imbibed the then prevalent disciplined, traditionalist Catholicism from his parents in his youth and, later on, in his seminary training from the Sulpician Fathers. "It was all book learning. We didn't have any practice. We didn't go out to parishes – hardly at all," he would recall, "At the seminary it was so unreal." Vatican II was a revelation to him of the true liberty of the children of God. He vowed to make the pastoral care of his priests, religious, and laity a priority. His was a very open and welcoming ministry. He was willing to listen and support gay and lesbian Catholics in their efforts to remain true to their sexual identities as Catholics. He advocated for the increased roles of women, he participated in interfaith social justice and liturgical efforts, he allowed former priests to participate fully and publicly as laymen in parish life.

But more than anything else, it was his peace advocacy against nuclear weapons that led to his long, dark night, and his public humiliation by the Wojtyla-Ratzinger papacy. McCoy devotes his first two chapters to Hunthausen's prophetic witness, which was nourished by the writings of Jesuit Fr. Richard McSorley and conversations with the peace activist Jim Douglass. Chapter 1, titled "Trident," recalls the U.S. Navy's plan to make Bangor the home of the world's most lethal nuclear weapon. The Trident submarine, the most effective limb of the three-legged nuclear defense strategy of the U.S., carries twenty-four Trident II missiles, each equipped with eight warheads for a total of 192 on board each vessel. The Trident II missile travels at 250 miles a minute and can land within three hundred feet of targets up to six thousand miles away. Each warhead packs six times the destructive power of the atomic bomb dropped at Hiroshima. Hunthausen's ecclesial jurisdiction was already one of the most militarized regions in the nation. The *USS Ohio*, the first Trident submarine, was scheduled to arrive at Bangor in August 1982. The *USS Ohio*, the Navy boasted, has more explosive power than what was fired by all the world's navies in all the wars of history. Archbishop Hunthausen called it "the Auschwitz of Puget Sound."

Hunthausen not only participated in protests and demonstrations, he not only gave talks against nuclear weapons and for peace, he not only supported the anti-nuclear movement, he also shared a vision of another action, that of refusing to pay the 50% of taxes that goes to military spending and thus use the IRS Form 1040 to vote for life. Thus, as McCoy puts it in his Chapter 2, titled "Tax Protest:" "A Catholic archbishop, a citizen of the United States, the country that regards itself as the global champion of freedom and democracy, he invited all Americans – especially his fellow Christians – to revolt against their government's investment in nuclear arms by refusing to pay their federal income tax."

It will be remembered that at this time "the Reagan administration, preaching 'peace through strength,' had embarked on the biggest nuclear arms buildup in history. The USSR was responding in kind, beefing up its already superior ballistic missile numbers with yet more missiles. There was serious talk of first strikes with tactical or 'surgical' nuclear weapons. Anxiety and apprehension stalked the land." Books were published narrating the horrors of nuclear war, movies were showing the destruction of humanity and the end of civilization, the anti-nuclear movement grew in numbers, protests and demonstrations were held all over the country, the Doomsday Clock of the Bulletin of Atomic Scientists had inched closer to midnight, and the U.S. Catholic bishops were debating issuing their *The Challenge of Peace: God's Promise and Our Response*.

(As I write this, Wiiliam J. Perry, Secretary of Defense from 1994 to1997, perhaps the most knowledgeable person on the science and politics of modern weaponry, writes: "Today, the danger of some sort of nuclear catastrophe is greater than it was during the Cold War and most people are blissfully unaware of this danger." He also says that the nuclear danger is "growing greater every year" and that even a single nuclear detonation "could destroy our way of life" [Brown 2016].)

At the very same time, Papa Karol Wojtyla, while prohibiting and condemning political activism among his clergy, was himself deeply involved in the life and politics of Poland. In his visits to his native land, he aroused his audiences to have no fear and stand up to the atheistic Communist regime that ruled the land. The Wojtyla-Ratzinger papacy established an alliance with the Reagan administration to oppose Communism, to liberate Poland and Eastern Europe and defeat Communism as their final goals, which they eventually successfully achieved. Intelligence, money, resources, and materiel were exchanged and channeled. Nothing in the eyes of the Vatican could and should endanger and upset this relationship.

Basing itself on clandestine charges from mean-spirited critics – contained in a folder of newspaper clippings and letters of the "apostolic visitator," Archbishop James Hickey of Washington, DC – the Vatican targeted Hunthausen and opened an investigation into practices of the Seattle diocese that ostensibly violated liturgical rules and ecclesiastical discipline, that failed to enforce Catholic teaching and to heed church law. It is a riveting story, told by a masterful journalist, of how the Vatican mandated an official visitation of the bishop and the diocese, how Donald Wuerl was appointed auxiliary bishop with extraordinary powers which in the end did not work out, the bafflement and resentment of Hunthausen, the clergy and the people with him, at how he was being undermined and humiliated in such a public way, while the specific evidence against him remained a closely guarded secret with Ratzinger. McCoy ably guides the reader into understanding the intricacies, trivialities, and hypocrisies of

Vatican politics, into appraising the personal costs to Hunthausen, which also affected his colleagues and people, and to grasping the profound institutional harm done to the American church by an autocratic papacy and its bureaucrats.

One gets the feeling that Hunthausen was selected to send a powerful warning. He was not a celebrity among his colleagues, but a humble pastor of a bishop of a small, perhaps insignificant, diocese, so that targeting him would not arouse the ire of the entire American church and nation but would succeed as a shot over the bow. Two incidents narrated by McCoy caught my attention.

The first incident happened at the end of the interview of Father Larry Reilly, the seminary theology professor who was Archbishop Hunthausen's previous theological adviser, when Archbishop Hickey turned off the tape recorder and turned to Reilly:

"Well, Larry," he said. "I guess we both know why I'm really here, don't we?"

"Yes, Archbishop," Reilly replied. "You're here because of Ronald Reagan and the archbishop's position on nuclear disarmament."

"That's right," Hickey said. "That's right, Larry."

Nothing more was said.

The second incident occurred at the end of their *ad limina* visit when Archbishop Hunthausen and his agreed-upon Coadjutor Archbishop Thomas Murphy were invited to concelebrate mass with John Paul II and to assist him in distributing communion. Among the guests were the author James Michener who was a Quaker.

Hunthausen and Murphy were in a cab on their way home to the airport and their flight back to Seattle. Murphy asked Hunthausen if he had noticed that the Holy Father had given communion to Michener.

"You're kidding," said Hunthausen, who began to chuckle.

"Murph," he said, "it seems we ought to turn this car around right now, head back to Ratzinger's office, and demand a visitation of the Holy See."

Archbishop Hunthausen was a Good Shepherd before his time, a time of imperial ecclesiastical rule and servile episcopal leadership, of faith as intellectual acceptance of doctrinal propositional truths, of morality as rigid adherence to sexual rules and liturgical practices in a church institution that considered itself the refuge of the pure remnant and the bulwark against the modern world. He would be a Good Shepherd today who smelled of his sheep in a church that is a field hospital where the poor and suffering are taken cared of, the grieving and sorrowing are consoled, the marginalized and the migrant are welcomed, where the joy of the Gospel and the happiness of married love are proclaimed and the care of the earth is preached and pursued. Because it is the time of Pope Francis who intends to bring to fruition the vision of Good Pope John and Vatican II. It is for this very same reason that John McCoy set aside his notes for twenty years and returned to them only after Pope Francis became Bishop of Rome, the successor of St. Peter, to restore the reputation of a still and quite conscience, to tell his story of courage, fidelity, and perseverance, and to inspire those who suffer not for the church, but because of the church.

Archbishop Hunthausen joins the list of recent prelates who were punished by the Wojtyla-Ratzinger papacy because they did not toe the autocratic line nor fit the mold of a subservient bureaucrat: Archbishop Jean Jadot, Apostolic Delegate to the United States, who selected pastors as bishops, not doctrinaire bureaucrats, but who after his tenure was relegated to obscurity; Archbishop Francis Quinn of Sacramento, CA, who dared raise the issue of birth control at the 1980 Synod on the Family and who wrote a book on the reform of the papacy, even though it was in response to John Paul II's encyclical, *Ut Unum Sint*; Australian Bishop William Morris who was forced to retire from his rural diocese of Toowoomba simply for suggesting the possibility of ordaining women; Australian Auxiliary Bishop Patrick Power who was critical of the church's response to the clergy abuse scandal; Cardinal Loris Capovilla, secretary to John XXIII, who was forgotten by John Paul II and Benedict XVI – to minimize the fond memory and promise, rendered empty by them, of John XXIII and Vatican II? – and only made a cardinal by Pope Francis in 2014 at the age of 98. He has since died on May 25, 2016 (Faggioli 2016).

Patrick Howell (2016) of Seattle University objects to the subtitle of McCoy's book, because Archbishop Hunthausen never sought to challenge pope, president, or church. But his "still and quiet conscience" and witness were a challenge to the powers that be, both ecclesiastical and secular, as do the conscience and witness of any saint, even with a small s, as Howell himself describes "the saintly and prophetic archbishop of Seattle, Washington."

Amidst the Ecclesiastical Rubble

During his tenure John Paul II strode the world stage as a colossus for human dignity, human rights, and religious freedom, especially against Communism. But like many autocratic priests and bishops who treat their parishes and dioceses respectively as their personal fiefdoms, it must truthfully be said that John Paul II also ruled over the entire Church institution as an imperious feudal lord. He appointed bishops to be his bureaucratic branch managers in their dioceses, considered priests as obedient foot soldiers in his war against the so-called culture of death, and reduced lay people once more to passive pray, pay, and obey automatons. He brooked no dissent of any kind, and his Cardinal-Secretary of enforcement dutifully swatted down thoughts and actions not to their liking. John Paul II and his Cardinal-Secretary sought to remake the Church into their own imperial image and likeness. Such an irony for a Pope who was credited with contributing to the downfall of the Soviet Empire to erect his own ecclesiastical facsimile of an empire.

Very early in his papacy, there was an incident that revealed Wojtyla's attitude toward his office and the church. It had to do with a simmering financial scandal about a group of Pauline monks that ran a Philadelphia-area shrine to Our Lady of Czestochowa, the "Black Madonna" revered by Polish Catholics (Posner 2015: 280-82). The committee established to investigate the matter found that the monks had not only squandered nearly $20 million in charitable contributions, but there was evidence of "mismanagement, dubious business practices and what Vatican investigators described as 'chaotic' and 'immoral' life styles." Shades of Boccaccio! The Paulines had raised $400,000 for bronze plaques for the shrine but never made a single one. Donors gave $250,000 for Masses that the priests never celebrated. Sixty-four thousand dollars went to cemetery upkeep that was never performed. Making matters worse, the monks violated their poverty vows. The Pauline defaulted on $4.3 million in church bonds bought mostly by Polish American Catholics. They ran their 130-acre hill-top monastery "more like a resort hotel than a monastic institution." A majority of the thirty monks had their own cars, paid for by contributions from the faithful, and all had credit cards that were charged against donations.

Seventeen days after assuming the papacy, John Paul reversed the recommendations of the investigating committee. He then issued a Papal Decree ending all investigation into the Paulines, vacating the original findings. He worked out a backroom deal with Archbishop Paul Marcinkus, head of the Vatican Bank, who directed more than $5 million to Cardinal John Krol of Philadelphia to settle financial liabilities. (It will be this same Vatican Bank, officially called Institute for the Works of Religion [IOR in Italian], which under Cardinal Tarcisio Bertone, favorite ecclesiastic and Secretary of State of Benedict XVI, will become a site for money laundering, embezzlement, and other shady financial dealings that will drive Benedict XVI to resign.) It was as if Karol Wojtyla now Supreme Pontiff of the Roman Catholic Church "owned" the church and could do anything he wanted with it. A little pesky financial scandal could simply be dealt with and disappear.

As his papal tenure stretched out in years and decades, John Paul II grew in international political stature, power, and influence. Having worked out an alliance with the Reagan administration, he was credited with freeing his beloved Poland from Communist rule, with contributing to the downfall of the Soviet Union and to the liberation of Eastern Europe. He was riding on the crest of international popularity and adulation. As far as the Catholic Church was concerned, he was in total control. His Cardinal-Prefect of enforcement has squashed all dissent, eviscerated the power of subordinate governing institutions, imposed his interpretation of Vatican II, and ruled with an iron fist in a velvet glove on the whole Church. To crown it all, John Paul II had also issued his own updated version of the Syllabus of Errors, *Evangelium Vitae*, in which he lists what he considered "intrinsic evils," and denounces them one after the other without further ado. The institutional church was humming along splendidly in imperial calm or so it seemed.

Thus, it was no wonder that when the pedophilia crisis erupted in the Diocese of Boston, the Vatican was caught off guard and tried to dismiss it as one more instance of media sensationalism in the United States. John Paul II was said to be tone-deaf toward the crisis. But it would be more accurate to say that he did not believe it and did not care. He did not believe that it could happen to the church he had ruled with an iron fist, and it was just another pesky scandal that could easily be dealt with and dismiss. But then, the founder of the religious order of priests, beloved of John Paul II, turned out to be the worst of the worse: a drug addict, a bigamist, a sexual pervert, and child predator (Guillermoprieto 2010). And the clerical sexual abuse crisis was soon rocking other Catholic Churches in other countries. The Wojtyla-Ratzinger papacy, resting as it was, on authoritarian grains of sand, was soon engulfed by it worldwide. Two reactions showed the arrogant sense of shameless impunity. The resignation of Cardinal Bernard Law of Boston was accepted, but then he was assigned to the plush position of St. Mary Major and membership in several dicasteries. Miguel Maciel of the Legionaries of Christ was asked to retire and spent his years of retirement in prayer and penance. They were less than slaps on their wrists, but they were slaps in the faces of the victims of the clerical sex abuse scandal and their families.

John Paul II has been officially canonized, together with John XXIII, in a move by Pope Francis to bring Catholic liberals and conservatives together. John Paul was especially admired for not being afraid and ashamed to be seen growing old and physically debilitated, a witness to the human dignity of the elderly. But then the governance of the church was left to competing factions, to corrupt lobbies, to administrative mismanagement and financial shenanigans. Besides, an officially canonized saint is not meant only to highlight one's personal holiness, but to serve as a saintly model for those who are still living and struggling. What sort of leadership does John Paul II model? Saint Pius X, himself an autocratic pope, responsible for years of repression against the so-called evils of Modernism and for decades of the dearth of scholarship in Catholic theology, is now the patron saint of the schismatic Pius X Society which opposes Vatican II. Saint John Paul II, the second coming of Pius X, is extolled as the beacon of clarity and purity of inflexible doctrinal and moral pronouncements against the culture of death of the modern world. Like Pius X, John Paul II is a model of authoritarian, not servant, leadership.

Now it has been revealed that Karol Wojtyla has had a long and secret love story with a married woman (Luxmoore 2016). I am happy for him that he, even as archbishop, cardinal, and pope, experienced loving and being loved by a woman, an experience he denied the rest of his fellow clerical caste. There is an agreement that their love for each was a truly, deeply, and really intense love of a committed couple with shared interests and memories, short, however, of its genital expression. I just hope that when the dynamism of their love pressed for physical expression, he did not let his beloved simply twist in the wind, as strong celibate men are wont to do, because such "safe" relationships, according to Eamon Duffy in the PBS special, *The Secrets of Saint John Paul*, are often exploitative of women and unjust to them. It would have been a similarly twisted version of having your cake and eating it too, of having and enjoying the best of both worlds. But it is simply dishonest and unjust that the crucial role and contribution that Anna-Teresa Tymieniecka played in the scholarship and life of Karl Wojtyla would not be acknowledged, but instead consciously hidden and hopefully buried. It is unconscionable that her name and presence in the biography and history of John Paul II would simply vanish, having been deliberately erased and obliterated by his closest allies and associates. Shades of Stalin's Soviet Union! But then again, it is in keeping with a papacy that carries a secret love interest but has patriarchal attitudes towards and issues patriarchal pronouncements on women.

During the thirty-five years of the autocratic Wojtyla-Ratzinger reign – twenty-five years of John Paul II, the twenty-four concurrent years of Joseph Ratzinger as doctrinal watchdog, and eight years of Benedict XVI – the Catholic faith became entombed in concrete propositions – abortion is murder, contraception is morally wrong, homosexuality is disordered, women cannot be priests – Catholic moral practice was reduced to intellectual acquiescence to these doctrinal beliefs, liturgical life was restricted to participation in literal translations from Latin, spirituality was strict and rigid submission to the papal magisterium.

Joseph Ratzinger was the hatchet man in policing the autocratic church. This is harsh, but truth has to be told to power. Ecclesial careers were destroyed, reputations besmirched, theological scholarship and movements condemned, ecumenism and interreligious dialogue brought to a halt, condemnations and bannings rampant, discouragement and disillusion among the laity rife, membership lost, and fear stalked the church. Ratzinger participated in Vatican II and contributed much to the formulation of its vision and teachings, which contributions he completely repudiated as he climbed the ecclesiastical ladder. He was *peritus* to Cardinal Josef Frings of Cologne who, early on in the Council, condemned the "medieval" practices of the Holy Office, successor to the Inquisition. As Cardinal-Prefect of the Congregation for the Doctrine of the Faith, successor to the Holy Office, Ratzinger precisely replicated the tactics that Cardinal Frings condemned. When Thomas Reese, S.J., editor of *America*, repeated the same accusations years later, one of the first actions of Benedict XVI was to have Reese removed as editor.

Ratzinger was a professional theologian and he, more than anybody else, knew that there is a hierarchy of truths in doctrine, that there are unresolved questions in the life, teachings, and governance of the church, but instead of providing space for the free discussion and scholarship of controverted issues, he clamped down on dissenting opinions and imposed his own theological preferences. Even now bishops and theologians are asking for reform of the inquisitorial procedures of the Vatican's chief doctrinal office which was headed by Ratzinger for twenty-four years (McElwee 2016). The worst example of Ratzinger's draconian measures was his condemnation of Latin American liberation theology which left the Latin American church and continent open to the scourge and ravages of neoliberalism.

Ratzinger envisioned the church as a prophetic remnant of pure, undefiled, devoted, and faithful witnesses, Augustine's City of God on earth, in confrontation with the secularism and relativism of the City of Man. I suppose he saw himself as the ruler of this remnant, wielding the dictatorship of absolutism to wage cultural war on the dictatorship of relativism, egging on his faithful cultural warriors, as he strode the ramparts of the Vatican, clad in the fur-lined hat of the eighth century, the elaborately embroidered stole from the 18th century, and the fashionable red-pink shoes. Would he have restored the triple papal crown and the *sedia gestatoria*? Even in ecclesiastical circles, if not more, as Lord Acton originally intended, absolute power corrupts absolutely.

Perhaps nothing captures more graphically the corrupt depths – the arrogance, the sense of ownership of the church, and the impunity – the institutional Catholic Church had sunk to under the Wojtyla-Ratzinger papacy than the colored photograph published in *The New York Review of Books* to accompany an article on Cardinal Tarcisio Bertone, Ratzinger's favorite ecclesiastic, by Ingrid Rowland (2014). This is Rowland's description:

> A photograph taken in Argentina in 2007 shows two cardinals, Jorge Mario Bergoglio and Tarcisio Bertone, sitting side by side, although their chairs are on two different levels. At the time, Bertone was the Vatican's Secretary of State, having traveled to a village in northern Pentagonia "in the name of His Holiness Benedict XVI" to preside over the beatification of a turn-of-the century religious student.
>
> Bertone's wooden armchair sits on a dais that puts him a good six inches higher than Bergoglio, the Archbishop of Buenos Aires, who perches uncomfortably on his metal-and-plastic seat, and the man known to many as the "vice-pope" occupies his virtual throne with kingly complacency, clad in yards of fine Italian filetto lace beneath his golden chasuble, with a sporty pair of aviator sunglasses to complement his gold-embroidered miter (and is that a Rolex on his wrist?). Next to him, in Jesuit black under plain white robes, Cardinal Bergoglio, with his iron cross and his horn-rimmed spectacles, looks open-mouthed upon the radiant spectacle, his famously mobile face providing the perfect caption to the picture. Six years later, Bergoglio became Pope Francis, and things have not been the same since.

The American Catholic Church

John Gehring (2015: 19, 27), who is program director at the Faith in Public Life, an advocacy group in Washington, DC, and was former associate director for media relations at the U.S. Conference of Catholic Bishops, in his chapter on the making of a culture of warrior church in the United States, writes:

> During the thirty-five years that Pope John Paul II and Pope Benedict XVI led the Catholic Church, influential American Catholics baptized the Iraq War, made an idol

of unfettered markets, and narrowed Catholic identity to a checklist that aligned neatly with the Republican Party. Quick to challenge a U.S. bishops' conference they perceived as too liberal and enjoying access to the top levels of the Vatican under the papacy of John Paul II, Catholic conservatives with intellectual chops and culture warriors with sharp elbows rose to prominence. . . .

Buoyed by a generation of more conservative bishops appointed by Pope John Paul II, these Catholic activists, intellectuals, and media figures spoke loudly, organized strategically, and played a key role in influencing the American Catholic narrative. . . . Once at the forefront of moral debates in the 1980s, moderate bishops and a handful of progressives in the hierarchy lost the steering wheel. The sharp turn came with a cost. An embattled posture and a politicized theology of "non-negotiables" have failed the church's broad pro-life mission, and it is in danger of marginalizing Catholic leaders who once operated at the center of American and moral discourse.

It is painful to read how the Catholic Church in the United States, a progressive force for ordinary Americans from the New Deal to Vatican II, became "an increasingly tribal American Catholic Church during the John Paul era;" how its episcopal leadership fought for the rights of labor, the promotion of health care for everyone, the protection of immigrants, and the succor for the poor, but became obsessed in denouncing abortion, contraception, homosexuality, and feminism; how they shifted their attention and focus from the aspirations and needs of the common faithful to cater to their right-wing sponsors for power, privilege, and largesse; how, having disconnected themselves from their flocks in the pews, they grew more autocratic and ultimately lost their moral credibility and legitimacy as they were engulfed in the scandals of their own making. It all started with how abortion reconfigured American politics, Gehring argues, and gave rise to the Religious Right.

It is important to make clear, however, that the Religious Right, typified by Jerry Falwell and his organization, Moral Majority, did not emerge primarily due to abortion, but to race. In the wake of the *Brown v. Board of Education* decision of the Supreme Court in 1954 which outlawed school segregation, new whites-only schools appeared in the south as a response to the desegregation of public schools, while still claiming tax-exempt status as charitable institutions. In May of 1969, a group of African American parents in Holmes Country, Mississippi, sued the Treasury Department to prevent three new whites-only K-12 private academies from securing tax-exempt status because of their discriminatory practices. In *Green v. Kennedy* (David Kennedy at that time was secretary of the treasury), decided in 1970, the plaintiffs won a preliminary injunction against the "segregation academies." On June 30, 1971, the United States District Court for the District of Columbia issued its ruling, *Green v. Connally* (John Connally replaced David Kennedy as secretary of the Treasury), which upheld the new IRS policy that racially discriminatory private schools are not entitled to Federal tax exemption.

"The *Green v. Connally* ruling provided a necessary first step," Randall Balmer (2014) wrote. "It captured the attention of evangelical leaders." Bob Jones University in Greenville, South Carolina, was especially obdurate, arguing that racial segregation was mandated by the Bible, until the IRS rescinded the school's tax exemption. For many evangelical leaders, Bob Jones University was the final straw. But Paul Weyrich, a religious conservative, political activist, and co-founder of the Heritage Foundation, saw an opening and the beginnings of a religious conservative political movement. Several years in Jimmy Carter's term, he and the leaders of the nascent religious right blamed the Democratic president for the IRS actions – even though the policy was mandated by Nixon and Bob Jones lost its tax exemption a year and a day before Carter was inaugurated as president. "[E]vangelical leaders, at the behest of conservative activist Paul Weyrich," Balmer (2014; see also Prothero 2016: 188-194) pointed out, "seized on abortion not for moral reason, but as a rallying-cry to deny President Jimmy Carter a second term. Why? Because the anti-abortion crusade was more palatable than the religious right's real motive: protecting segregated schools. So much for the new abolitionism."

Balmer (2014) issued a postscript:

> The Bob Jones University case merits a postscript. When the school's appeal finally reached the Supreme Court in 1982, the Reagan administration announced that it planned to argue in defense of Bob Jones University and its racial policies. A public outcry forced the administration to reconsider; Reagan backpedaled by saying that the legislature should determine such matters, not the courts. The Supreme Court's decision in the case, handed down on May 24, 1983, ruled against Bob Jones University in an 8-1 decision. Three years later Reagan elevated the

sole dissenter, William Rehnquist, to chief justice of the Supreme Court.

With the political strength of their racist allies of the evangelical right on their side – "Falwell did not preach his first anti-abortion sermon until 1978, and the Southern Baptist Convention did not oppose abortion until 1980" (Prothero 2016: 193). – American Catholic prelates proclaimed as their battle-cry that anti-abortion advocacy is the lynchpin of Catholic identity, waded into the mud and muck of partisan politics, and waged public battles against Catholic pro-choice politicians, banning them from giving public speeches and commencement addresses at Catholic schools, and, in the case of elected and elective Catholic officials – Mario Cuomo, Geraldine Ferraro, and John Kerry, most prominently – shamefully utilized the Eucharist as their weapon, by declaring pro-choice Democrats as unfit to receive Communion. When Barack Obama became the first African American to become President of the United States, instead of celebrating it as an event that could happen only in these United States, key members of the hierarchy led the public denunciations, abetted the personal attacks, and contributed to delegitimizing his presidency. When Notre Dame University decided to grant Obama an honorary degree, hate groups gathered at the Catholic university to denounce the President of the United States and the President of Notre Dame. It was short of a lynching party instigated by mitered heads of the American Catholic Church.

The wall of hypocrisy, arrogance, and self-righteousness that the American Catholic episcopate erected around their ecclesiastical fiefdom soon imploded with the explosion of the clerical pedophilia crisis. It revealed that hundreds of priests for decades had been abusing, exploiting, and raping children for their sexual gratification, that many bishops knew about the abuse of children by their priests, that, instead of punishing them and reporting them to the proper authorities, hid their crimes and transferred them from parish to parish to parish, thus spreading the rot throughout the church. Their behavior was shameful and criminal and was not worthy of good shepherds who took care of their flocks, but was characteristic of wolves who preyed on the most vulnerable of their flocks. Cardinal Bernard Law of Boston, who was the foremost champion of doctrinal and moral clarity in the culture wars, was forced to resign in disgrace. It was the American Catholic Church's Watergate. At the latest count, the Catholic Church in the United States has incurred nearly $4 billion in costs related to the clerical abuse crisis during the past 65 years (Ruhl and Ruhl 2015). This is the least of its costs, which includes dioceses filing for bankruptcy, ministries underfunded, families lastingly wounded and scarred, young lives forever damaged and truncated, an increasing number of Catholics disaffiliating themselves from the institution to become, one in ten, ex-Catholics, the largest "denomination," if it were a denomination, after that of Catholics.

The U.S. bishops, reeling from the child abuse scandal, have not learned anything, and they forged on with their culture wars. This time, the target was the Affordable Care Act, derisively labeled as Obamacare. Instead of accepting it as a fulfillment, however flawed, of universal health care that the U.S. Catholic Church had been fighting for from its origins, as the majority of Catholic nuns did, the U.S. bishops rejected it for its contraception coverage, even after the Obama administration had made an accommodation which most people praised. Under the banner of religious liberty, the U.S. bishops now declared war against Obamacare, using the Little Sisters of the Poor as pawns in their court challenges. They held rallies, which they titled "Fortnight for Freedom," to urge the faithful to decry the loss of religious freedom in these United States and to fight for its restoration. To draft the Mother of God into the campaign, the official paper of the Brooklyn, New York, diocese featured an offensive front-page image of the Blessed Mother wrapped in an American flag. It is the irony of ironies. The Catholic Church for most of its existence denied the validity of religious liberty, except for itself, until at Vatican II, under the scholarship of John Courtney Murray, S.J., the doctrine of religious liberty was validated as a universal human right. It is a perverted reversal, therefore, for the American Catholic hierarchy to claim religious freedom for its rejection of the contraception coverage in the Affordable Care Act in their institutions that employed non-Catholics and served non-Catholic clients. And this for a teaching that the majority of Catholic moral theologians do not accept and the majority of Catholic women simply ignore – including the women relatives of the bishops? The campaign fizzled out. I suppose most Catholics and most Americans find the claim that religious freedom is endangered in the United States absurd, compared, for example, with the situation of Christians in the Middle East. And yet, that is exactly what the Catholic bishops shamelessly postulate. They have even made a slick video to propagate their contemptuous take on American religious liberty (*Commonweal* 2016). They are on a path of corrupting religious liberty (Gehring 2016).

An earthquake shook the foundations under the feet of the extreme right of the American Catholic Church with the resignation of Pope Benedict XVI, its stalwart defender and himself an inflexible culture warrior, and the election of Pope Francis, the first pope from a Third World country, Argentina, and the first Jesuit to boot. The American bishops were taken aback. The priorities of the new Pope did not align with the objectives they were pursuing. In fact, in many ways, their obsessions were opposed to the vision of Pope Francis of what the Church should be and should do. They were confused, bothered, and bewildered. Some of them began to speak out against Pope Francis. But for most of them, I suppose, their hope is that the tenure of Pope Francis will be short.

The Challenge of Pope Francis

Much has been written about Pope Francis since his ascension to the chair of Peter, Bishop of Rome, on March 13, 2013, regarding his simple lifestyle, his vision of the Church as a field hospital, his outreach to the poor and migrants, his emphasis on mercy as the soul of the Gospel, his efforts to proclaim the joy of the Gospel, the happiness of married love, and the care we should all have for the earth, our Mother, all of which were prefigured in his short contribution to the pre-conclave General Congregation (Vallely 2015: 151-52):

> The only purpose of the Church is to go out to tell the world the good news about Jesus Christ. It needs to "surge forth to the peripheries," not just geographically but to "the existential peripheries" where people grapple with "sin, pain, injustice, ignorance, indifference to religion and misery."
>
> Instead the Church has got too wrapped out in itself. It is too navel-gazing. It has become "self-referential" which made it sick. It is suffering a "kind of theological narcissism." When Jesus said: "Behold I stand at the door and knock" people assumed he was outside, wanting to come in. But sometimes Jesus knocks from within, asking us to let him out into the wider world. "A self-referential Church wants to keep Jesus to itself, instead of letting him" out to others.
>
> The Church is supposed to be "the *mysterium lunae*" – the mystery of the moon is that it has no light but simply reflects the light of the sun, and the mystery of the Church is that it reflects the light of Christ. The Church must not fool itself that it has a light of its own; if it does that it gives in to "spiritual worldliness" which is what Henri De Lubac in *The Splendour of the Church* called "the worst evil

that can befall the Church." That is what happens with a self-referential Church, it believes it has its own light.

Put simply, there are two images of the Church: a Church which evangelizes and comes out of herself or a worldly Church, living with herself, of herself, for herself. The next Pope should be someone who helps the Church surge forth to the peripheries, like a sweet and comforting mother who offers the joy of Jesus to the world, bringing "changes and reforms" for the salvation of souls.

I cannot add any more to that. I simply want to point out some of the things Pope Francis has said and done that I find appealing and that makes me hopeful in moving the Church to become more the Church envisioned by Vatican II. Pope Francis is the first pope not to have participated in Vatican II and, therefore, he is free from the ideological entanglements that have ensnared and polarized Catholics, especially in the United States. He has fully embraced Vatican II as a true ecclesial event, without reservations, restrictions, conditions, and qualifications, and he has said that he intends to implement and realize the vision of Vatican II of a Church that is collegial in its governance, understandable in its doctrines, merciful in its practice, and in friendly collaboration with, and faithful service to, all faiths and peoples, including the care of Mother Earth.

Pope Francis adheres to the core image, enunciated at Vatican II, of the Church as the People of God on a pilgrimage. Before there is office, power, privilege, and hierarchy, there is first of all the fundamental dignity, unity, and solidarity of the entire people of God. Office, power, privilege, and hierarchy are not for the personal aggrandizement of the office-holder, but for service to the entire People of God, especially those who disadvantaged in life. Pope Francis (2013a: 9) pointed out: "Belonging to a people has a strong theological value. In the history of salvation, God has saved a people. There is no full identity without belonging to a people. No one is saved alone, as an isolated individual, but God attracts us looking at the complex web of relationships that take place in the human community. God enters into this dynamic, this participation in the web of human relationships."

He has also compared the Church to a "field hospital." "It is useless," Pope Francis (2013a: 11-12) states, "to ask a seriously injured person if he has high cholesterol and about the level of his blood sugars! You have to heal his wounds. Then we can talk about everything else. Heal the wounds, heal the wounds. . . . And you have to start from the ground up. The

Church sometimes has locked itself up in small things, in small-minded rules. The most important thing is the first proclamation: Jesus Christ has saved you. And the ministers of the church must be ministers of mercy above all." While clergy might be ontologically different, such difference does not mean superiority, much less lording it over the laity, but always in servant leadership to the entire *laos* or people of God. Bishops and priests as shepherds and pastors, he put it graphically, should have the "smell of sheep," *their* sheep of the poor, the marginalized, the disadvantaged, the destitute.

Pope Francis (2013a: 13-14) has advised us not to be obsessed with abortion, contraception, and homosexuality. "The church's pastoral ministry cannot be obsessed with the transmission of a disjointed multitude of doctrines to be imposed insistently. . . . We have to find a new balance; otherwise even the moral edifice of the church is likely to fall like a house of cards, losing the freshness and fragrance of the Gospel." Nor should – I think I am not deviating from him – the intellectual and propositional adherence to these "pelvic issues" be made the litmus test of orthodoxy and fidelity. One sister of mine, who has had too much of Mother Angelica of the Eternal Word Television Network, pointed out to me once that Cardinal Bernard Law was a *summa cum laude* graduate as, I suppose, many of the priests, who abused children, were proficient in theological doctrine and knowledge. But they were precisely the ones who loved doctrinal truths, Pope Francis (2016b: no. 305) harshly suggests, "as if they were stones to throw at people's lives," while "sitting on the chair of Moses and judging at times with superiority and superficiality difficult cases and wounded families." Gabriel Moran (2016: 11) writes that "the richness of the Catholic tradition is not found in a series of truths," a set of doctrines. Nor should religious faith be reduced to the intellectual adherence to such propositional truths and doctrines.

"Jesus Christ is the face of the Father's mercy," is Pope Francis' (2016a: 105) first sentence in his Bull of Indiction of the Extraordinary Jubilee of Mercy. The name of God is mercy, he has repeatedly proclaimed. Mercy is the divine attitude that embraces. It is God's self-giving that welcomes. It is God's loving face that leans down to forgive. What a difference from condemnations, anathemas, inquisitions, excommunications. Mercy, not cruelty, not casting off. Forgiveness, not hardness of heart, not harshness of tone, not ugliness of words. Inclusion, not exclusion, not banishment. But this is what Jesus was all about: "He who is without sin cast the first stone." When the Scribes and the Pharisees heard this, they went away one by one, starting with the elders. "Neither do I condemn you. Go, and sin no more" (John 8: 3-11). Jesus was all about doing the will of God, going and doing likewise (like the Good Samaritan), loving God and neighbor, healing the sick, exorcising evil, having mercy, and forgiving sins. It was all about following Jesus, then it became all about worshipping Christ. At the Council of Nicaea, convoked by Emperor Constantine, to unify the faith and the empire, it became all about beliefs: I believe in God . . . I believe in Jesus Christ . . . I believe in the Holy Spirit . . . etc. Gone was discipleship, gone were the Beatitudes, gone was loving God and neighbor.

It seems to me that, at the deepest level, Pope Francis is calling us back to the basics of the faith, to the fundamentals of the Gospel, to the discipleship of Jesus, to the practice of the Beatitudes. Reality is more important than ideas, he says. Oxthopraxis is of more consequence than orthodoxy, Latin American liberation theologians pointed out. Justice, mercy, fidelity are weightier matters of the law than tithes of mint and dill and cummin, Jesus taught. For too long, the public face of the Catholic Church has been one of doctrinal rigidity and moral restrictions, especially on sexuality. It was one of condemnations and penalties on what it considered dissent and disloyalty, while it ignored clerical abuse and episcopal dereliction and financial shenanigans. It was one, therefore, that aroused fear, anger, and disdain. In his first apostolic exhortation, Pope Francis (2013b: no. 1) shared his reform program of proclaiming and spreading *Evangelii Gaudium*, the joy of the Gospel of Jesus. The primary reality for the Christian is not God's commands, but God's love and presence through Jesus in our lives. This is the joy of the Gospel that fills hearts and minds who encounter Jesus. Pope Francis encourages "the Christian faithful to embark upon a new chapter of evangelization marked by this joy, while pointing out new paths for the Church's journey in years to come."

This is at the heart of the challenge of Pope Francis that confronts the American Catholic Church. John Gehring argues that it is a difficult challenge for a church that was once known as a towering force for social justice – specifically in defense of labor rights, for the protection of immigrants and the poor, and in the promotion of universal health care – but has become an anti-abortion, anti-contraception, anti-gay, and anti-feminist conservative bastion aligned with the Republican Party. Its hierarchy and clergy, put into place by the Wojtyla-Ratzinger papacy, glory in their designation as JPII bishops and priests and are comfortably safe and secure, clear and certain in the absolutism of their doctrinaire positions. Supported by well-funded and well-equipped foundations and buttressed by conservative theological advisers, this church of culture warriors constitutes a wall of resistance to the pastoral initiatives of Pope Francis.

Marco Politi (2015: 54-55), a veteran journalist on Vatican issues, situates the opposition to Pope Francis by some members of the worldwide episcopate by providing the basic context of his reform program which is:

> a coherent design to dismantle the imperial character of the papacy, its Caesarian absolutism, semidivine and fed by the aura of infallibility that has clung to the papal court. The formal title of the successors of Peter is itself pagan, for the *pontifex maximus* was the chief priest of ancient Rome. . . . The "sacred" and grandiloquent character that has become attached to the bishopric of Rome does not derive from Christianity, much less from the Gospel, but from the later Roman Empire. "Everything having to do [with] the Emperor Diocletian was defined as 'sacred': his edicts, his bedchamber, his bodyguard, the papal chancellery," writes the historian Giovanni Filoramo, evoking the heightened rituality of the late imperial court. "Those granted an audience with the emperor were admitted to the 'adoration of the purple,' the hem of the imperial mantle."
>
> This is the origin of the red shoes and red shoulder cape of the popes. It has nothing to do with the redness of blood or with any symbolic readiness for martyrdom. It is the red of absolute power. The custom of prostration before the pope and cardinals corresponds to the self-effacement of subjects in the presence of the Roman emperor and his great imperial counterpart and model, the Persian king of kings. The "Sacred Rota," the "Holy Inquisition," the "sacred palaces" of the Vatican, the "audience of kissing the hand," the "sacred congregations," the "kissing of the pope's slipper" – all are descended from the practices of the absolute oriental monarchies, where the sovereign's mere nod was the supreme law.
>
> "Heads of the church have often been narcissists, flattered and thrilled by their courtiers. The court is the leprosy of the papacy," Francis confided to Eugenio Scalfari, founder of the newspaper *La Repubblicca*.

This is the underlying reason why Pope Francis is fighting against daunting opposition. Politi rightly titles his book *Pope Francis among the*

Wolves. According to legend, Saint Francis of Assisi once met a wolf, to which he addressed a mild sermon. Won over by the saint's words, the fierce animal grew gentle and submissive, lowered his head, and followed. The enemies of Pope Francis are not so quick to yield. Within the curia especially, there are nests of criticism and dislike, often bitter, contemptuous, and condescending, ravenous wolves. In the ranks of the Catholic hierarchy worldwide, there are obstacles arising from inertia and nostalgia, from a refusal to abandon comfortable habits of the past, from attachment to rigid dogmatic and moral structures, and from the enjoyment of the appurtenances of power and privilege. Compare them to "the smell of the sheep," Politi's first chapter on the pastoral care and ministry Jorge Mario Bergoglio exercised in the *villas miserias*, the shantytowns of Buenos Aires.

A quotation from Politi (2015: 175) is pointed:

> The ecclesiastical historian Alberto Melloni uses very severe terms to describe the arena that Francis has entered. The personnel of the curia "have inherited the notion of being the center and the whole at the same time." In this environment careerism prospers, with its sorry train of adulation and backbiting, thanks to "inflated egos that disdain the very institutional setting they exploit." The degradation worsened, according to Melloni, in the third of the century that ran from the election of Wojtyla to the resignation of Ratzinger.

But there is also a groundswell of support for Pope Francis. They are ordinary Catholics, imbued with the spirit of Vatican II and led by a diminishing number of Vatican II bishops and priests, who are tired of a church mired in sex and financial scandals and devastated by culture wars. They long for a church promised by Vatican II, open to and inclusive of all, for pastors who exercise a servant leadership of the People of God, for an ecclesial institution that is humble and merciful and free of the trappings of worldly power. They are inspired and energized by what they see in and hear from Pope Francis (2013b: no. 49): "I prefer a Church which is bruised, hurting and dirty because it has been on the streets, rather than a Church which is unhealthy from being confined and from clinging to its own security. I do not want a Church concerned with being at the centre and which then ends by being caught up in a web of obsessions and procedures." They hope that his reforms of the Roman Curia and bureaucracy will result in a more collegial governance of the church, in the ordination of more compassionate and pastoral bishops and priests. They want to follow where Pope Francis leads them in the joy of the Gospel, in the happiness of love, and in the care for our common home, the earth.

The big question is whether or not we, the entire People of God, will take advantage of this providential moment – surely a biblical *kairos* – and put our efforts in the remaking of a church in the image and likeness of the Church of Christ, *Lumen Gentium*. What Francis is doing is important and consequential to and for the Church. What we do with Francis is equally important and consequential.

Conclusion

I started this review essay as the dysfunctionality and polarization of the American political system came to a head in the 2016 Republican presidential primary elections. Thomas Mann of the Brookings Institution and Norman Ornstein of the American Enterprise Institute (2016a, 2012) came out with a new and expanded edition of their searing analysis of the hyperpartisanship of the political parties that has gridlocked the American government and has brought it to the brink of institutional failure. They repeat their contention that political paralysis is largely because of the transformation of the Republican Party into an ideological force of radical right extremism and their "unified strategy of opposing, obstructing, discrediting, and nullifying" the important initiatives of the Democratic and first African American President, Barack Obama.

The most quoted line is from the introduction of their first book: "The Republican Party has become an insurgent outlier – ideologically extreme; contemptuous of the inherited social and economic policy regime; scornful of compromise; unpersuaded by conventional understanding of facts, evidence, and science; and dismissive of the legitimacy of its political opposition. When one party moves this far from the center of American politics, it is extremely difficult to enact policies responsive to the country's most pressing challenges" (Mann and Ornstein 2013: xxiv).

The indictment is repeated in the afterword of the paperback edition: "[T]he Republican Party continuous to demonstrate that it is an insurgent force in our politics, one that aspires to rewrite the social contract and role of government developed and affirmed over a century by both major political parties. The old conservative GOP has been transformed into a political party beholden to ideological zealots, one that sees little need to balance individualism with community, freedom with equality, markets with regulation, state with national power, or policy commitments with respect for facts, evidence, science, and a willingness to compromise" (Mann and Ornstein 2013: 216).

Prior to the release of their new and expanded edition and in the midst of the presidential primaries, Mann and Ornstein (2016b) wondered that "incredibly, Republican destructiveness is even worse than it was four years ago – and the party is paying for it with a surge of anti-establishment populism that is tearing its coalitional base." They (Mann and Ornstein 2016a: 204) maintain that "the main problem remains an insurgent outlier Republican Party, in the midst of an existential struggle for its soul." It is no longer *It's Even Worse Than It Looks*, but *It's Even Worse Than It Was*.

And to erase all doubt, conservative Daniel Henninger (2016), writing in *The Wall Street Journal*, declared that "Barack Obama will retire a happy man. He is now close to destroying his political enemies – the Republican Party, the American conservative movement and the public-policy legacy of Ronald Reagan." To which Fareed Zakaria (2016) replied, "Obama's success in this regard, if it can be called that, is a passive one. He has let his opponents self-destruct and never overplayed his hand. . . . [M]any Republicans' rhetoric about Obama quickly became personal – with insinuations about his origins, race, religion, faith and loyalty to the country. . . As Obama kept his cool, the Republican Party descended deeper into the politics of identity, flirting with racial, religious and ethnic grievances . . . The result has been an ideological implosion, and it's unclear what will emerge from the debris."

This is the Republican Party that Bishop Thomas Tobin of Providence, Rhode Island, publicly switched allegiance to and affiliation with as a registered member, out of discomfort with and disaffection from Pope Francis (Desmond 2013). Stupid and shameful move!

Thus, the contagion of political craziness that has infected the GOP with Donald Trump and Ted Cruz leading the pack of Republican presidential contenders has now even spread to the leadership and ranks of Catholic Republican conservatives. After a gaggle of conservative Republicans labeled Trump as a threat to conservatism and decided to take a stand against him, a similar flock of Catholic conservative Republications followed suit and issued an urgent appeal to their fellow Catholics to oppose Trump in his bid to become the Republican presidential nominee. "The problem is," Anthony Annett (2016b) points out, "these Catholic Republicans are directly implicated in Trump's meteoric rise. They actively supported economic policies that fed the beast of insecurity, and they actively undermined the values embedded in the Catholic social tradition that might have acted as a bulwark against this narcissistic blowhard."

In their desperate effort to stop Trump, to find an acceptable alternative to Trump, or, at least, to keep the nomination process open till their national convention, conservative Republicans began to tout Ted

Cruz. "[T]he most hated Senator in Washington . . . deriding his own party's leadership as a criminal cartel of bloodsuckers," Michael Scherer (2016) of *Time* paints him. "He stands for ideological purity. Obstruction over compromise. Confrontation despite the odds." He is, perhaps, more dangerous than Trump in his rigidity and inflexibility as an ideologue and true believer. He is "Lucifer in the flesh," former Speaker John Boehner called him, a "jackass," "the most miserable son of a bitch I have worked with," and a "wacko bird," by John McCain. Soon, however, the self-same group of prominent Catholic Republican conservatives who opposed the candidacy of Trump, decided to endorse Ted Cruz for president. "He will foster a culture, from the top down, that honors the Constitution," they trumped him over Trump. "No word about a culture that honors the gospel or the common good," Anthony Annett (2016a) rightly argued, using the contemporary relevance of the four Americans – Abraham Lincoln, Martin Luther King, Jr., Dorothy Day, and Thomas Merton – Pope Francis (2015b) used as a yardstick in his address to the U.S. Congress.

The problem now, as Patricia Miller (2016) asks is: Who will Catholic Bishops turn to in the Republican Party during the Age of Trump? It is a problem that was created by the Wojtyla-Ratzinger papacy itself. John Paul II banned the political participation of the clergy in partisan politics while he himself was neck deep in Polish politics and in political alliance with the Reagan administration. Cardinal Jaime Sin of Manila reported that he was treated like dirt in the Vatican after he took part in bringing the downfall of the Marcos dictatorship in the Philippines. The American episcopate did not heed the admonition to eschew partisan politics, but instead carefully cultivated power and influence with the Republican Party and got accustomed to them. Will they continue to nurture such a relationship with the Republican Party of Donald Trump and will they continue to derive and exercise power and influence in it?

What has become of the Republican Party of Abraham Lincoln and Theodore Roosevelt and Dwight Eisenhower? What will happen to prominent American Catholic leaders, both ecclesiastical and lay, who have lashed their vision, their values, and their political fortunes to the extreme right of the political spectrum? This is a large part of the wreckage left behind by the Wojtyla-Ratzinger papacy, from which the Catholic Church under Pope Francis has to extricate itself.

11

A MORAL QUESTION FOR THE DISMAL SCIENCE: CAPITALISM FOR THE FEW, BUT NOT FOR THE MANY?

The Making of Global Capitalism: The Political Economy of the American Empire, by Leo Panitch and Sam Gindin. London: Verso, 2012, 456 pp.

Seven Bad Ideas: How Mainstream Economists Have Damaged America and the World, by Jeff Madrick. New York: Knopf, 2014, 254 pp.

Economics: The User's Guide, Ha-Joon Chang. New York: Bloomsbury Press, 2014, 365 pp.

Misbehaving: The Making of Behavioral Economics, by Richard H. Thaler. New York: W.W. Norton, 2015, 415 pp.

Animal Spirits: How Human Psychology Drives the Economy, and Why It Matters for Global Capitalism, by George A. Akerlof and Robert J. Shiller. Princeton, NJ: Princeton University Press, 2009, 230 pp.

Phising for Phools: The Economics of Manipulation and Deception, by George A. Akerlof and Robert J. Shiller. Princeton, NJ: Princeton University Press, 2015, 272 pp.

Saving Capitalism: For the Many, Not for the Few, by Robert B. Reich. New York: Knopf, 2015, 279 pp.

Just Money: How Catholic Social Teaching Can Redeem Capitalism, by Clifford Longley. London: Theos, 2014, 92 pp. www.theosthinktank.co.uk

In his Apostolic Exhortation on the Proclamation of the Gospel in Today's World, *Evangelii Gaudium,* The Joy of the Gospel, Pope Francis (2013a: nos. 50-60) punctuated his analysis of the contemporary "signs of the times" with successive "nos:" "no to an economy of exclusion," "no to the new idolatry of money," "no to a financial system which rules rather than serves," and "no to inequality that spawns violence." The Pope elaborated by pointing out that "such an economy [of exclusion] kills," that in the new idolatry of money "man is reduced to one of his needs alone: consumption," that financial experts and political leaders need to ponder the words of St. John Chrysostom: "Not to share one's wealth with the poor is to steal from them and to take away their livelihood," and that "unbridled consumerism combined with inequality proves doubly damaging to the social fabric; inequality inevitably engenders a violence which recourse to arms cannot and never will be able to resolve."

Many conservative American Catholics refused, resisted, and rejected these papal denunciations of their beloved economic system of capitalism. They rationalized that the Pope did not know what he was excoriating, that he did not have the competence to pass judgment on the American economic system, that what the Pope knew and experienced was the corrupt kind of capitalism of Argentina. In an opinion piece for *The Wall Street Journal,* written with CNBC's Larry Kudlow, Cardinal Timothy Dolan of New York, the financial center of global capitalism, echoed these criticisms of Pope Francis' views of capitalism, arguing that the Pope's negative views do not apply to America's "virtuous capitalism," but to the "exploitative racket for the benefit of the few powerful and wealthy" which passes as capitalism in developing or newly industrialized countries. The Cardinal then himself became the object of a barrage of criticisms from theologians who specialize in Catholic social teaching. A couple of examples: "It wasn't Argentinean populist economics, Eastern European crony capitalism, or African kleptocracy that threatened the world economy with the worst recession since the 1930s. It was no-holds-barred American capitalism that did it," Drew Christiansen pointed out. "One does not need to travel to a developing nation to see a system that is functioning as 'an exploitative system.' The signs are all around us in the United States," added Joseph McCartin (Reese: 2014: 23-24).

I start this review essay with moral judgments because I hold that economics and the economy are not only about making money and reaping profits, not only about productivity and efficiency, not only about entrepreneurship and marketing, nor only about factories and corporations. Economics and the economy are about people and the common good, about the livelihood and survival of ordinary citizens, about life and death for the poor and the marginalized. They are about the moral issues of justice, fairness, and equity. The great economist John Maynard Keynes ultimately saw economics not as a natural science but as a moral one, Robert Skidelsky (2009: xvii, 133) reminds us:

> Keynes was a moralist. There was always, at the back of his mind, the question: What is economics for? How does economic activity relate to the 'good life'? How much prosperity do we need to live 'wisely, agreeably, and well'? This concern was grounded in the ethics of G.E. Moore, and the shared life of the Bloomsbury Group. Broadly, Keynes saw economic progress as freeing people from physical toil, so they could learn to live like the 'lilies of the field', valuing today over tomorrow, taking pleasure in the fleeting moment. . . . He was a philosopher and moralist as well as an economist, and he never ceased to question the purposes of economic activity. Briefly stated, his conclusion was that the pursuit of money – what he called 'love of money' – was justified only to the extent that it led to a 'good life'. And a good life was not what made people better off: it was what made them good. To make the world ethically better was the only justifiable purpose of economic striving.

The economy, because it has the most immediate impact on other social institutions, has become the most important social institution in modern society and, in fact, in the world that has become globalized. The economy is the basic institution found in all societies that deals with the use of land, labor, capital, and technology for the production, distribution and consumption of goods and services. Basically, the economy answers the most fundamental question asked by humans formed in groups: How shall we provide ourselves with food, shelter, and clothing? Economics, on the other hand, studies the actual workings of the economy, how goods and services are actually produced, distributed, and consumed in an efficient, productive, and profitable manner. It studies empirically the consequences of economic policies, and from the conclusions of those empirical studies suggests and prescribes courses of economic action for the future. The trouble with the dominant form of economics today, the rational expectations theory in macroeconomics and the efficient market hypothesis in financial economics of the neoclassical school, see economics as defined by its theoretical approach, that of rational choice; its basic assumption is the rationality of actors, it bases its understanding of the economy from abstract and theoretical models, and it proceeds in its prescriptions from the logical consequences of those theories.

In the modern world, there are two ways of organizing and managing an economy: via the mechanism of the market or through the power of the state. The economic system that relies on the market is usually called capitalism, while the one that uses the power of the state is designated as socialism. In the modern world, however, there is no pure capitalism nor pure socialism; all economies are mixed economies, using a combination of state interventions and market operations. These combinations vary across nations and across the history of a particular nation. To illustrate: imagine a straight line, on which to array all economies in world, with the left end of the line indicating socialism, and the right end pointing to capitalism. No economy is placed at either extreme. The United States is nearest the right end, China is nearest the left end,

and the Scandinavian countries are located somewhere in the middle. In the history of a particular country, the pendulum also swings between the left and the right. Put differently, there are gradations in the ways market and state combine not only across countries, but also within countries. The Great Depression was due to the pendulum having swung too much to the right, the market became practically totally unfettered without oversight from the state. As a result of the Great Depression, the economic pendulum in the United States swung more to the left, to greater regulation by the state. The stagnation of the 1970s moved the pendulum to the right, and further to the right under neoliberal globalization.

The Great Recession of 2008, the worst since the Great Depression, has been explained as the pendulum having swung too much to the right again. Under the aegis of the ideology of neoliberalism, the state retreated and unfettered markets swept across the economy, now gone global, with the mantra: liberalization, privatization, and deregulation. Any country that wanted to participate in the global economy had to be integrated into it, by accepting and implementing the demands of neoliberalism: welfare programs had to be curbed, education and poverty subsidies eliminated, labor unions restrained, regulations of all kinds lifted, free trade established, free flow of finance encouraged. In other words, the state had to be circumscribed, its activities constricted – all to allow unfettered freedom to markets. Put differently, American-style capitalism had to become globalized, for globalization to work across the porous borders of the global economy, to work, it was alleged, for the benefit of all countries, societies, and cultures. This is the mainstream justification for neoliberal globalization, the defining concept of the time (Litonjua 2008).

Global Capitalism and the State

Leo Panitch, Canada Research Chair in Comparative Political Economy in the Department of Political Science at York University, Toronto, and his colleague, Sam Gindin, former Research Director of the Canadian Auto Workers' Union and Parker Chair in Social Justice at York University, dissent from the mainstream view. From the very start they make clear that their "book is about globalization and the state. It shows that the spread of capitalist markets, values and social relationships around the world, far from being an inevitable outcome of inherently expansionist economic tendencies, has depended on the agency of states – and of one state in particular: America. Indeed, insofar as the relationship between the American state and the changing dynamics of production and finance was inscribed in the very process that came to be known as globalization, this book is devoted to understanding how it came to be that the American state developed the interest and capacity to superintend the making of global capitalism. In this respect, this is emphatically *not* another book on US military interventions; it is about the political economy of the American empire."

Put differently and to emphasize, globalization is not a force of nature, as President Bill Clinton famously put it. Globalization is a socio-political construction (Litonjua 2008), pushed forward by vested interests in governments and businesses. Globalization is not a contentless phenomenon; it is not a simple overwhelming process erasing borders between nations and encompassing the globe; globalization is the global spread of capitalism; it is global capitalism. "[T]he making of global capitalism ... transcend[s] the false dichotomy between states and markets ... [S]tates need to be placed at the center for the search for an explanation of the making of global capitalism. The role of states in maintaining property rights, overseeing contracts, stabilizing currencies, reproducing class relations, and overcoming crises has always been central to the operation of capitalism. Far from multinational corporations (MNCs) finding it most convenient to have a world 'populated by dwarf states at all,' they depend on *many* states to see to it that these things are done" (Panitch and Gindin 2012: 1).

There is more: "The American state has played an exceptional role in the creation of a fully global capitalism and in coordinating its management, as well as restructuring other states to these ends. . . . [I]t was the immense strength of US capitalism which made globalization possible, and what continued to make the American state distinctive was its vital role in managing and superintending capitalism on a worldwide plane" (Panitch and Gindin 2012: 1). The contention, therefore, that globalization is in reality Americanization is true and right.

The first thing the authors do is to examine the DNA of American capitalism. "The role that the United States came to play in the making of global capitalism," Panitch and Gindin (2012: 25) point out, "was not inevitable, but nor was it accidental." From its earliest days, the United States had been expansionist. Throughout the first half of the nineteenth century, as the population grew and pressed westward, the government continually acquired new territory: the trans-Appalachian West, the Louisiana Territory, Florida, Texas, Oregon, California, New Mexico, Alaska, and more. This territorial expansion came at the expense of the genocide of Native Americans and the enslavement, later the segregation, of African Americans. It was the nation's "Manifest Destiny," underpinned by racial superiority and religious mission, to do so, it was believed. Herein lie the roots of the uniquely dynamic and expansionist nature of American capitalist development.

This territorial expansion took place alongside the dynamic development of the economy, fast becoming a great industrial power, in both of which the state played a very active role. In the absence of traditional state bureaucracies that oversaw capitalist development in Europe and Japan, Morton Horwitz (1977, 1994) showed that law became the dynamic element in the economic growth of the U.S. American law was transformed to favor economic growth and development; it shielded the very rich and protected entrenched interests. In turn, "the legal profession came to play an especially active role in the modernization of the American state. The large law firms that rose alongside the new corporations acted as broker-dealers not only with Wall Street and London investment houses, but also with governments at all levels – even to the point of drafting 'the documents they needed to build governance and capital structures to settle the rights, duties, and discretionary authority of the participants in the enterprise and (having) them approved by a legislature or a court.'. . . What above all drove the modernization of the state was the remarkable political coalescence of business and political elites in response to intense and widespread class conflict. . . . The most important expression of this regrouping was the new alliance between business and the Republican

Party that was forged in the run-up to the 1896 election" (Panitch and Gindin 2012: 33-34).

But it was in 1898, with the Spanish-American War, that the nation expanded overseas, embarked on a new course of imperialism. Cuba, Puerto Rico, Hawaii, Guam, and the Philippines fell under the sway of the American state and the American economy and resulted in the internationalization of the American capitalist state. The United States sought to remake the Philippines "in our image" (Karnow 1989). It was not, however, an altogether successful and pleasant imperial venture. A three-year pacification campaign that saw 4,000 American soldiers and about 200,000 Filipino revolutionaries fall in combat soured imperial dreams. Theodore Roosevelt, when he decided to built the Panama Canal, no longer wanted to occupy the entire country, but only a slice of the land needed for the construction, operation, and management of the canal. Formal empire gave way to informal empire in the same way that the British Empire became the "imperialism of free trade" (Gallagher and Robinson 1953). The notions of racial superiority and religious mission in the "benevolent assimilation" of inferior and pagan races were recast in explicitly economic and capitalist terms. In fact, the original economic justification underlying the occupation of the Philippines, that it would be the stepping-stone to the vast markets of China, was transformed into a capitalist informal empire as the means of penetrating China, to be done collectively by the United States, Europe, and Japan. The linkage between territorial expansion and colonial occupation had been broken.

The Great Depression, FDR's New Deal, and World War II tremendously expanded the capacities and reach of the American state. "The most important novelty of the relationship between capitalism and imperialism," Panitch and Gindin (2012: 7-8) write, "that World War II set in train was that the densest imperial networks and institutional linkages, which had earlier run North-South between imperial states and their formal and informal colonies, now ran between the US and other major capitalist states. The creation of stable conditions for globalized capital accumulation, which Britain had been unable to achieve (indeed hardly even to contemplate), was now accomplished by the American informal empire, which succeeded in integrating all the other capitalist powers into an effective system of coordination under its aegis." The Bretton Woods System – The World Bank, The International Monetary Fund, and the General Agreement on Tariffs and Trade, later to become the World Trade Organization – played a central controlling and coordinating role in the administration of global capitalism. "This was the crucial moment in the historical differentiation between the economic and political in the making of global capitalism. In the passage from Britain's only partially informal empire to the predominantly informal American empire, something much more distinctive had emerged than Pax Americana replacing Pax Britannica. The American state, in the very process of supporting the export of capital and the expansion of multinational corporations, increasingly took responsibility for creating the political and juridical conditions for the general extension and reproduction of capitalism internationally" (Panitch and Gindin 2012: 6).

Domestically, however, between 1945 to the 1970s, what thrived in the United States was a managed capitalism in which capital, labor, and government worked together to bring about the golden age of capitalism. This was also true, to a certain extent, on the international level, as Barry Eichengreen and Peter Kenen (1994) pointed out. But this "golden age of capitalism," writes Thomas Piketty (2014), was an anomaly in the long historical stretch of unequal capitalism, primarily made possible by the destruction of capital due to depression and war. The U.S.-led postwar order is usually called "embedded liberalism." Panitch and Gindin (2012: 9) agree with a reservation: "The social reforms of the welfare state were extremely important in terms of employment and income security, education and social mobility, and they strengthened working classes in many respects; but at the same time these reforms were limited by the way they were linked to the spreading and deepening of markets amid the relaunching of global capitalism."

The new relationship between capitalism and informal American empire constituted also a distinctively new form of political rule. Instead of aiming for territorial expansion along the lines of the old empires, informal rule took the form of the growth and maintenance of military installations around the globe, mostly on the territory of independent states. Chalmers Johnson (2004) has given a trenchant expose of the string of U.S. military bases – an empire of bases – that encircles the globe to maintain the supremacy of the United States. With this strategically placed line of more than 800 military bases, "the American state arrogated to itself the sole right to intervene against other sovereign states (which it repeatedly did around the world), and largely reserved to its own discretion the interpretation of international rules and norms. Its global each and responsibilities made it not so much *primus inter pares* as qualitatively distinct from other advanced capitalist states" (Panitch and Gindin 2012: 12). For Johnson, global capitalism is the name of the reconstituted American empire.

With stagflation of the 1970s, the American state was now uniquely placed and uniquely capable to spread the globalization project, which it was totally freed to do with the collapse of the Soviet Union in 1991. Under the aegis of neoliberalism, a no-holds-barred laissez-faire raw capitalism, to triplicate the adjectives, was promoted by the "Washington Consensus" of the U.S. Treasury Department, the International Organizations of the World Bank, the International Monetary Fund, and the World Trade Organization, and business corporations. Neoliberal globalization of class power and inequality swept across the globe, erasing borders between nations for the production and trade of goods and services, steamrolling welfare programs and labor unions, as well as, nationalities and cultures, and manufacturing a McWorld of superficial and artificial consumption. In chapter after illuminating chapter, Panitch and Gindin (2012) trace the realization of global capitalism as it created the path to discipline the new age of finance and integrated both Europe and Japan. They examine the rule of global capitalism, its laws of free trade, global investment, and disciplinary internationalism, the integration of China, the globalized economy with the U.S. as chief financial architect. The United States had created a capitalist world in it own image and likeness.

Panitch and Gindin (2012: 21) observe:

> In true imperial fashion, the US fully shared its problems with the rest of the world. Given the role of the US financial assets and consumer spending in global capitalism, illusions that other regions might be able to avoid the crisis [i.e., the financial crisis that started with the bursting of the housing bubble in the United States and became the Great Recession of 2008, the worst economic debacle since the Great Depression of the 1920s] were quickly dispelled. But the centrality of the American state was at the same time made clearer than ever. Its key role in global crisis management was confirmed as the crisis unfolded, with the US Federal Reserve directly bailing out foreign banks and providing other central banks with much-needed dollars, to the Treasury's coordination of stimulus policies with other states. The enormous demand for US Treasury bonds right through the crisis reflected the extent to which the American state continued to be regarded as the ultimate guarantor of value, and demonstrated how much the world remained on the dollar standard. Even while international tensions surfaced, what was so striking when

the G20 leaders were gathered together to meet for the first time in late 2008 in Washington, DC was consensus on avoiding protectionist measures [i.e., consensus on maintaining American-style global capitalism].

Panitch and Gindin (2012: 331) repeat that "it took an empire of a new kind, founded on US capitalism's great economic strength and centered on the capacities of the American state, to make global capitalism a reality. Yet no sooner did the task look to be more or less complete when the fourth great crisis of global capitalism (after those of the 1870s, the 1930s, and the 1970s) spread quickly across the world. . . . [I]t is especially important to recognize the central role which the American state continues to play in reproducing global capitalism. The current crisis has amply demonstrated the many challenges and contradictions it faces in doing this; but it has also demonstrated that, while the American empire is certainly not always able to control the spirits it has called from the deep, it nevertheless remains critical to the system's survival."

Panitch and Gindin once more deconstruct the alleged dichotomy between state and market. State and market are misplaced polarities. Of course, states can be overpowering and suffocating, while markets can be manipulated and corrupted. But, state and market are enmeshed with each other in the making of capitalism, hence in the construction of global capitalism. In truth, markets do not exist without states. In fact, markets are created by states. States provide the infrastructure, physical, legislative, and juridical, that enable markets to function efficiently, productively, and profitably. States also dictate what goods and services can be exchanged in the market, what rules govern transactions for them to be just and fair, what penalties will be exacted to prevent and punish fraud and corruption. Thus, Panitch and Gindin (2012: 340) emphasize that the "secular struggle between classes is ultimately resolved at the *political* – not the economic or cultural – level of society. . . . [T]oday's revived demands for social justice and genuine democracy could only be realized through a fundamental shift of political power, enabling fundamental changes in state as well as class structures. This would need to begin with turning the financial institutions that are the life-blood of global capitalism into public utilities that would facilitate, within each state, the democratization of the decisions that govern investment and employment. . . . Advancing such radical politics requires a sober perspective on what currently exists, and how we got here, so as to understand more clearly the nature and scale of the task involved in getting somewhere better. This has been our goal in writing this account of the making of global capitalism. Its unmaking will only be possible if the states that have made it are themselves transformed – and that applies, above all, to the American state."

This is the capitalist economy of exclusion that kills, according to Pope Francis, the capitalist economy that worships the idols of profit, the financial capitalist system that rules instead of serves, the economy the reduces the human person to a unit of consumption, that creates inequality which in turn spawns violence. The existential problem is that capitalism's irrationalities in which we are all enveloped now threaten earth's carrying capacity and sustainability and, thereby, our own lives and existence. This Pope Francis (2015a) also warns us about in his encyclical, *Laudato Si'*, on care for the earth, our common home.

The Failure of Economics

Nobel laureate in economic science Paul Krugman (2009) has declared that it is not just the American economy that is bankrupt, but the economics profession as well. The Great Recession, the most serious economic crisis since the Great Depression, marks the intellectual collapse of the ideology of the rational free market, especially as applied to the financial sector. He writes:

> As I see it, the economics profession went astray because economists, as a group, mistook beauty, clad in impressive-looking mathematics, for truth. . . . Unfortunately, this romanticized and sanitized vision of the economy led most economists to ignore all the things that can go wrong. They turned a blind eye to the limitations of human rationality that often led to bubbles and busts; to the problems of institutions that run amok; to the imperfections of markets – especially financial markets – that can cause the system's operating system to undergo sudden, unpredictable crashes; and to the dangers created when regulators don't believe in regulation. . . . Economics, as a field, got in trouble because economists were seduced by the vision of a perfect, frictionless market system.

Even now, as James Galbraith (2014: 189-205) points out, "the crackpot counterrevolution" is being waged that would blame FDR and the New Deal for failing to promote economic recovery after the Great Depression, and consequently that would accuse the government of causing the subprime mortgage crisis that precipitated the Great Recession. It would upend the historical sequence between government size and economic growth, arguing that the size of government retards economic growth, that therefore to have higher rates of growth, you have to starve government spending. Galbraith calls what is involved "the method of crackpot reasoning," reflecting "the crackpot worldview," with the disgraced Alan Greenspan assuming a new mantle: "crackpot-in-chief."

The intention, of course, is to advance the crackpot reasoning that if you want to stimulate, cut taxes; if you want to get growth, cut spending. All of which boils down to demonizing government and idolizing the market, the most disastrous conclusions of what Pius XI called the "poisoned spring" of the economic libertarianism of Menger, Mises, Hayek, and Rothbard of the Austrian school of economics (Sibley 2011), which includes extolling deracinated individualism, misconceives freedom as simply the absence of constraints imposed by other people, rejects the notion of common good, simply treats labor as a disutility and a commodity, promotes unrestrained competition and consumption, and considers inequality as never unjust. Economic life, therefore, has no moral or social character, and economics is only beholden to the idols of the market.

It is worth noting that the American Economic Association, now the bulwark of the economic ideology of the rational market, once had a radical past. The original draft of the organization's 1885 "platform" read:

> We regard the state as an educational and critical agency whose positive aid is an indispensable condition of human progress. While we recognize the necessity of individual initiative in industrial life, we hold that the doctrine of *laissez-faire* is unsafe in politics and unsound in morals; and that it suggests an inadequate explanation of the relations between the state and the citizens.
>
> We do not accept the final statements which characterized the political economy of a past generation [regarding the laissez-faire economic orthodoxy of the Gilded Age]. . . . We hold that the conflict of labor and capital has brought to the front a vast number of social problems whose solution is impossible without the united efforts of Church, state, and science.

Bernard Weisberger and Marshall Steinbaum (2016) bring to light this little-known radical past of the American Economic Association, how the "implication clashed with the political bulwark against so-called 'class legislation,' namely any attempt to alter the social hierarchy through collective action or public policy. At all levels, therefore, this approach defied the intellectual foundations of classical economics." They unfold a story of how the drafters were marginalized, some hounded out of the academy and the government, accused of advocating socialism under the guise of sympathy for the oppressed, and made to hew to "the rule for what could be advocated by professional economists was simply that which was not far outside the political mainstream or threatening to incumbent wealth and power." Weisberger and Steinbaum conclude that "it is hard to imagine that in exiling radicalism from the AEA and from mainstream economics, its practitioners attained enormous intellectual prestige by sacrificing the disinterested search for answers to the most controversial questions in economics to the professional imperative of gaining the approval of the elite."

Jeff Madrick, former economics columnist for *Harper's* and *The New York Times* and author of several books on economic issues, among other things, expands on Krugman's indictment by critically examining seven ideas of what are now mainstream economic theories that have been wrongly applied such as to cause lasting harm to America and the world. These seven bad economic ideas are at the root of why capitalism is wreaking havoc on lives, societies, and the planet. These ideas, understood and practiced in their proper historical, social, and economic contexts, are good economic ideas, contributing great insights and suggesting practical applications. But used in their extreme, exclusivistic, and doctrinaire sense, these "ideas contributed to or justified much of the financial behavior that caused the [2008] crash and the deep recession that followed."

One, The Invisible Hand. This core idea constitutes the focus of the worship of the market. This is suppose to refer to the automatic and almost magical functioning of the market in which demand, supply, and price interact with each other to produce and maintain equilibrium in the economy. The original understanding by Adam Smith of the metaphor is itself contested. Edward Kleinbard (2015: 31-37) points out that Adam Smith used the metaphor only three times in his voluminous writing, was a professor of moral philosophy at Glasgow University, and had just completed at the time of his death a revised sixth edition of his *The Theory of Moral Sentiments*. Adam's basic moral point is that we are social animals, and our happiness and prosperity are inextricably bound up with the happiness and prosperity of society. In *The Theory of Moral Sentiments*, Smith is concerned with how we become better persons, such that we achieve the good life which consists in our personal happiness and the happiness of society. Smith promotes the inculcation of a strong internal ethical compass through education and socialization, and the development and exercise of our moral faculties in and through which we cooperate with God. *"The Wealth of Nations,"* writes Kleinbard (2015: 35), "assumes the importance of the inculcation of internal virtue to all those individuals trucking, bartering, and purchasing to their hearts' contents, just as *The Theory of Moral Sentiments* assumes that there will be a whole lot of trucking, bartering, and purchasing going on." Here is where the metaphor of "invisible hand" enters. The invisible hand connects the internal moral virtues and values of individuals with their trucking, bartering, and purchasing such that the market promotes an end, their happiness and prosperity and society's, which was no explicit part of their intentions. Kleinbard (2015: 36) concludes that "the hand in question is rendered invisible, not because it belongs to Mr. Marketplace but because it is the hand of God, who wishes for the happiness of His people." Kleinbard (2015: 36) adds that "this connection between the invisible hand and Providence is made explicit in Smith's third use of the term, in *The Theory of Moral Sentiments.*"

In modern economic discourse, the "invisible hand" is uprooted from Smith's context, rendered autonomous, and is idolized. It is only the invisible hand that should rule the economy, it is only the invisible hand that should be the be-all and end-all of all economy activity. Therefore, there should be no interference with the untrammeled market, much less by the visible hand of government. The market cannot be manipulated by the powerful; it cannot be perverted by fraud and criminality; it cannot be corrupted for nefarious ends.

Second, Say's Law. In the aftermath of the Great Depression of the 1930s, John Maynard Keynes proposed fiscal stimulus to promote aggregate demand even to the extent of the government incurring budget deficits. In the wake of the Great Recession of 2008, however, free market economists dictated austerity economics as the solution to the extent of balancing budgets, cutting spending, and paying off debts. This was based on the law of French economist Jean Baptiste-Say that supply creates its own demand. Keynes had long discredited Say's law, saying that it did not belong to the contemporary economy, it clearly had failed, and the Great Depression was the result. Ronald Reagan promoted it, convinced of the validity and credibility of Laffer's curve, although his running mate, George H.W. Bush labeled it "voodoo economics." It made a comeback after the Great Recession. Its return was built on the assumption of a self-regulating economy where there are no gluts of production, savings, and labor, where there are no uncertainty and no "animal spirits," concepts introduced by Keynes but are inconvenient concerns for market fundamentalists. Keynes' adage to save during boom times and to spend during bust times was upended, and the result was a prolonged recession that caused more unnecessary suffering.

Third, Friedman's Folly. This is the label Madrick attaches to the belief, whose most rigorous defender is Milton Friedman, that a free market without government interference provides all the governance and all the protection the liberty of a nation needs. This flows directly from the fundamentalist conviction that the market, and the market alone, should rule not only the economy by society as well. It completely ignores the role of government in the building of infrastructure necessary for economic exchanges, in the enforcement of contracts and the prevention of fraud, in the laying down of regulations that govern the market. It is usually said that liberals favor big government while conservatives prefer small government. I beg to disagree. Conservatives also want big government, but one that meets their opulent needs and caters to their moneyed interests – the rest of the citizenry be damned! Friedman's is less of a folly than a dangerous delusion foisted on unsuspecting adherents.

Fourth, It's All about Inflation. It was usually pointed out that there are two macroeconomic problems: those of unemployment and of inflation. In the now not too famous Phillips' Curve, they are presented as two problems that work against each other, that can only be solved at the expense of the other. But inflation and unemployment are not of equal importance, certainly not of equal severity. Inflation is a problem but at least you have the wherewithal, although of declining buying power. Unemployment is a problem, especially if you and your family are dependent on what you earn while working. But the new orthodoxy of mainstream economic thought is all about targeting inflation, not primarily about promoting growth and employment. Targeting inflation fits the ideological goal of limiting government and extolling free markets, which is another indication, if you still need one, of an economy biased, tilted mightily in favor of the rich and the powerful.

Fifth, No Speculative Bubbles. With the ideology of the unfettered market that came to reign in the economics profession came also the efficient markets theory (EMT) that began to rule the financial sector. Stock prices accurately reflect the value of companies; there cannot be speculative bubbles of any kind of financial instrument; trying to control derivatives did more harm than good; the only objective of executives should be to maximize the value of their companies' stock. The rationality of the market was pushed to the extreme with the creation of newfangled financial instruments that resulted in the enormous bubble of the housing market which, when it burst, brought about the Great Recession of 2008. EMT turned out to be a destructive set of ideas, whose trail of damages included jobs lost, incomes gone, rising inequality, lives damaged, wealth squandered that spread across families, communities, nations, and the globe. And yet, none of the EMT proponents and practitioners, whether in the academy, think thank, banking institution, corporate office, or regulatory agency suffered any dent in reputation, loss of prestige and influence, much less faced serious penalties for fraud, injustice, and corruption.

Sixth, Another Friedman's Folly. Globalization came to be governed by the mantra of liberalization, privatization, and deregulation of the so-called "Washington Consensus," whose ardent "phrasemaker" is the *New York Times* columnist Thomas Friedman, a true believer in the earlier Friedman, but whose folly is writ large. He is riding on a Japanese bullet train, eating a sushi lunch box, on his way to visit a Toyota manufacturing plant where the Lexus is built. He is dazzled by the speed and the smoothness of the ride on the bullet train, and marvels at the efficiency and productivity of the Lexus plant. But he does not betray any hint that he recognizes that the bullet train and the Lexus plant are not the products of the laissez-faire capitalism he is promoting but of the "developmental state" that made Japan an economic superpower. On another trip, this time, to Infosys Technologies Limited, one of the jewels of the Indian information technology world at Bangalore, he passes by potholes, sacred cows, horse-drawn carts, motorized rickshaws, and women trying to balance water jars on their heads. But once he enters the totally different world of Infosys and sees the glass-and-steel buildings, the massive swimming pool nestling amid manicured boulders and lawns, the multiple restaurants, and the fabulous health club, he forgets – or deliberately ignores? – what he had just passed by and declares that *The World Is Flat* in the twenty-first century. Such are Friedman's follies as he celebrates a globalized economy being torn apart between the 1% and the 99%.

Seventh, Economics is Science. One last bad idea that has damaged America and the world is the belief that economics is a science no different from, or at least the closest to, the hard sciences of physics, chemistry, and biology. It is a bad idea because it gives economic theories and predictions the credibility that it does not have and can never have. Economics, as practiced by most economists today, is mainly assumptions and deductions logically deduced from such assumptions. They are not even empirical scientists in that they do not conduct observation, experiment, and research on their own, but rely for their studies and conclusions on data sets collected mostly by government agencies. Besides, the basic assumption is preposterous: that the human agents in the economy are totally rational actors, who in their economic activities are engaged in completely optimizing the results of their behaviors, choosing only the best, the best good, the best service, the best price. Think of Mr. Spock in *Star Trek* who decides solely on the basis of reason, not emotion or passion. And in competitive markets where these Spock-like economic agents operate, prices are free to move up and down so that supply equals demand, and you always have equilibrium. Thus, economics is not only a dismal science, but a dangerous one, imposing its unrealities on the real world.

This being the case, it is time to relearn basic economics once more, not the economics based on unfounded assumptions about human nature and human behavior, not the economics of theoretical models and abstract reasoning keyed to political and business interests, but the economics that is the empirical study of the actual workings of real economies. This Ha-Joon Chang, professor of economics at Cambridge University, offers in his very accessible user's guide.

First of all, he decries the currently dominant school of economics, the so-called Neoclassical School, for exercising "economics imperialism," applying its so-called economic approach to everything. He emphasizes that "economics should not be defined in terms of its methodology, or its theoretical approach, but in terms of its subject matter, as is the case with all other disciplines. The subject matter of economics should be the economy – which involves money, work, technology, international trade, taxes and other things that have to do with the ways we produce goods and services, distribute the income generated in the process and consume the things thus produced . . ." He highlights the fact, therefore, that "there are many different ways of doing economics, each with its own emphases, blind spots, strengths and weaknesses. After all, what we want from economics is the best possible explanation of various economic phenomena rather than a constant 'proof' that a particular economic theory can explain not just the economy but everything."

But before he examines the diversity of approaches to economics, he discusses a brief history of capitalism, how economically we have gotten here, the teaching of which neoclassical economists simply disdain and no longer tackle in their courses. He discusses a wide range of economic theories – from Classical to Behavioral economics, from the Marxists to the Austrians – to reveal how a hundred flowers bloom in the field of economics, contrary to the imperialistic pretensions of rational expectations theory and efficient market theory. He demonstrates how to use economics to understand the real world economy: output and income, production, finance, inequality and poverty, work and unemployment, the role of the state – which mainstream economic theory has no use – and the international dimension.

Lastly, Chang makes clear that "economics is a political argument. It is not – and can never be – a science; there are no objective truths in economics that can be established independently of political, and frequently moral, judgments. Therefore, when faced with an economic argument, you must ask the age-old question 'Cui bono?' (Who benefits?), first made famous by the Roman statesman and orator Marcus Tullius Cicero?" I believe this is simply what Pope Francis is asking: Is the present economy working for the common good? What is the present economy doing to the poor? What is the present economy making of the earth, our common home?

Behavioral Economics

The most interesting and consequential change currently happening in the economics profession is the ongoing paradigm shift to behavioral economics. No guide could be better in understanding what is involved in behavioral economics than one of the creative geniuses who was at the beginning and the center of the most important revolution to happen in the field of economics in the last thirty years than Richard Thaler, professor of behavioral science and economics at the University of Chicago Booth School of Business, in the very bastion of laissez-faire economics. The all-important starting point in understanding the behavioral economic revolution, Thaler (2015: 5-6) explains at the outset, is to grasp the fundamental assumption of the regnant unfettered market economics.

> The core premise of economic theory is that people choose by optimizing. Of all the goods and services a family could buy, the family chooses the best one that it can afford. Furthermore, the beliefs upon which Econs make choices are assumed to be unbiased. That is, we choose on the basis of what economists call "rational expectations." If people starting new businesses on average believe that their choice of succeeding is 75%, then that should be a good estimate of the actual number that do succeed. Econs are not overconfident.
>
> This premise of *constrained optimization*, that is, choosing the best from a limited budget, is combined with the other workhorse of economic theory, that of *equilibrium*. In competitive markets where prices are free to move up and down, those fluctuate in such a way that supply equals demand. To simplify somewhat, we can say that Optimization + Equilibrium = Economics. This is a

powerful combination, nothing that other social sciences can match.

People who inhabit the fictional world of neoclassical economics, who hew therefore to the model of completely rational *homo economicus*, Thaler calls for short Econs, while the species of homo sapiens that we are, Humans, do a lot of misbehaving, often buying what we please or what pleases us, doing impulse shopping and buying, consuming what is not good for us and even what is bad for us. The Nobel laureate Herbert Simon, decades ago, already pointed out that people do not optimize, they "satisfice:" they do not go through every piece of research and information to buy a car, they do not have the time, energy, and resources to do that, they act with the information that satisfies them. I wonder even why that is not evident, unless you are blind to your own behavior, the behavior of the members of your family, the behavior of your friends and acquaintances. You do not need a dose of psychology to know and experience that, although Thaler uses as epigram Vilfredo Pareto: "The foundation of political economy and, in general, of every social science, is evidently psychology." We are not all Vulcans of *Star Trek;* even the ever logical Mr. Spock occasionally shows glimpses of his humanity.

Richard Thaler helpfully divides his book in chronological stages, from the beginnings in the 1970s when he and his colleagues conducted small experiments that showed biases in human conduct – buying a clock radio, selling basketball tickets, applying for a mortgage – and that therefore deviated from the model of human rationality. From there, they went into larger and more sophisticated experiments that showed so-called factors considered irrelevant or anomalous by free-market economists have important consequences. They practically looked at everything: household finance, assigning faculty offices in a new building, TV games, the NFL draft, and businesses like Uber, to mention a few. The practical understanding of people's actions, their miscalculations, their misbehaviors, human incentives and foibles, led people and will lead readers how to make better decisions in an increasingly complex world, where pure rationality after all does not rule. Thaler narrates the spirited battles and the struggles, often laced with antic and humorous stories, he and his colleagues waged to bring an academic discipline down to earth in the face of the opposition of its practitioners who considered what they were doing a sideshow.

By the 1990s, behavioral economics had two primary goals: the first was empirical, finding and documenting anomalies, and the second was developing theory. But a third goal was lurking: the use of public policy to make lives and societies and the world better. Three chapters discuss how behavioral economists came up with suggestions on how to make people save more for tomorrow, and how to make people achieve their goals without restricting choices. This is where the notion of *nudge*, trying "to influence choices in a way that will make choosers better off, *as judged by themselves*," came about, resulting in a book co-authored with Cass Sunstein. Two examples drive home the point: the use of bumpy lane markers that reflect light to decrease accidents, especially during the night, and painting the etched image of a housefly near the drain of a urinal to reduce "spillage." But the most interesting chapter of the three is on the formation of the Behavioural Insights Team (BIT) in the U.K., whose most basic idea was to use the insights of behavioural science to improve the workings of the government, followed by the formation of the White House Social and Behavioral Sciences Team (SBST). It is worth emphasizing that when anyone asks Thaler to sign a copy of *Nudge*, he always adds: "Nudge for good."

Before looking forward to what behavioral economics might become, Richard Thaler looks back and takes stock. Behavioral economics is no longer a fringe operation. Surprisingly, Thaler states that the behavioral approach to economics has had its greatest impact in finance. But it in no way mitigated the wreckage of the Great Recession of 2008 that the rational expectations theory and the efficient market hypothesis left behind; in fact, they continue to ply their destructive wares. The field where the behaviorally realistic approaches have had the least impact is macroeconomics, and yet fiscal and monetary policies are vitally important to any country's welfare and an understanding of Humans is essential in choosing them wisely. It is therefore in that area that Thaler is most anxious to see adopt them. At any rate he (Thaler 2015: 357-58) is hopeful:

> I am entirely optimistic about the future of economics. One sign that I find particularly encouraging is that economists who do not identify themselves as "behavioral" wrote some of the best behavioral economics papers published in recent years. These economists simply do solid empirical work and let the chips fall where they may. . . .
>
> When all economists are equally open-minded and are willing to incorporate important variables in their work, even if the rational model says those variables are supposedly irrelevant, the field of behavioral economics will disappear. All economics will be as behavioral as it needs to be. And those who have been stubbornly clinging

to an imaginary world that consists only of Econs will be waving a white flag, rather than an invisible hand.

George Akerlof and Robert Shiller, Professors of Economics at the University of California, Berkeley, and Yale University respectively, published their book earlier than Richard Thaler but they touch on topics, not particular emphasized by Thaler, but are part and parcel of rational expectations theory and efficient market hypothesis of the dominant laissez-faire economics. Thaler emphasized the false ideas of the totally rational actor and of the automatic equilibrium of competitive markets. Akerlof and Shiller focus on the presence of animal spirits among actors in the global economy and the necessity of government in the neoliberal order of unfettered markets and raw capitalism. And they wrote at a difficult juncture, to say the least, in macroeconomic theory, the start of the Great Recession which, at that point, was on the precipice toward another Great Depression.

"Animal spirits" is a term used by John Maynard Keynes to explain the workings of the economy and the role of the government in it. The economy is not just governed by rational actors, who "as if by an invisible hand" engage in economic transactions to their mutual economic benefit. Nor do private markets, of their own accord and with no government interference, "as if by an invisible hand," assure full employment. As Akerlof and Shiller put it: "*Left to their own devices*, capitalist economies will pursue excess, as current times bear witness, There will be *manias*. The manias will be followed by *panics*. There will be joblessness. People will consume too much and save too little. Minorities will be mistreated and will suffer. House prices, stock prices, and even the price of oil will be boom and then bust. . . . Speaking of excesses, the current economic crisis has been astutely explained by George W. Bush: 'Wall Street got drunk.'"

But why did it get drunk, in the first place? Because it dismissed the existence of animal spirits and the necessary role of the government in taming and disciplining them, in dousing the fires that they ignite. "In the original sense of the term, in its ancient and medieval Latin form *spiritus animalis*, the word *animal* means 'of the mind' or 'animating.' It refers to a basic mental energy and life force. But in modern economics *animal spirits* has acquired a somewhat different meaning; it is now an economic term, referring to a restless and inconsistent element in the economy. It refers to our peculiar relationship with ambiguity and uncertainty. Sometimes we are paralyzed by it. Yet at other times it refreshes and energizes us, overcoming our fears and indecisions." The authors add: "Just as Adam Smith's invisible hand is the keynote of classical economics, Keynes' animal spirits are a keynote to a different view of the economy – a view that explains the underlying instabilities of capitalism."

Their book draws on the emerging field of behavioral economics, which describes how the economy works in the real world, not through abstract mathematical formulas. For it describes how the economy works when people are really *human*, that is of all-too-human animal spirits. The first part of the book describes five different aspects of animal spirits and how they affect economic decisions: *confidence, fairness, corruption and antisocial behavior, money illusion,* and *stories.* The second part describes how they these five animal spirits affect economic decisions, demonstrating how they play a crucial role in answering eight questions:

1. Why do economies fall into recession?
2. Why do central bankers have power over the economy, insofar as they do?
3. Why are there people who can't find a job?
4. Why is there a tradeoff between inflation and unemployment in the long run?
5. Why is saving for the future so arbitrary?
6. Why are financial profits and corporate investments so volatile?
7. Why do real estate markets go through cycles?
8. Why does poverty persist for generations among disadvantaged minorities?

In answering these questions, Akerlof and Shiller succeed in telling how the economy really works and why the world economy has fallen into its current crisis, where existing economic theory fails. They also allow us to understand what needs to be done to extricate ourselves from the crisis, while mainstream classical economics continue to exist on its flawed assumptions and incomprehensible mathematics.

In *Phising for Phools*, George Akerlof and Robert Shiller continue their disquisition on animal spirits in the economy, but this time on malign ones, thus the economics of manipulation and deception. To "phish" is computerese coined in 1996 as the Web was getting established and is defined by the *Oxford English Dictionary* as "to perpetrate a fraud on the Internet in order to glean personal information from individuals, esp. by impersonating a reputable company; to engage in online fraud by deceptively 'angling' for personal information." Using the computer definition as a metaphor, Akerlof and Shiller present a definition that is much more general and reaches farther back in history. "It is about getting people to do things that are in the interest of the phisherman, but not in the interest of the target. It is about angling, about dropping an artificial lure into the water and sitting and waiting as wary fish swim by, make an error, and get caught. There are so many phishers and they are so ingenious in the variety of their lures that, by the laws of probability, we all get caught sooner or later, however wary we may try to be. No one is exempt." Phishing for phools, thereore, is the economics of profit-making through manipulation and deception.

A *phool* is someone who, for whatever reason, is successfully phished. There a two kinds of phools: psychological and informational. Psychological phools come in two kinds: In one case, the emotions of the psychological phool override the dictates of his common sense. In the other, cognitive biases act like optical illusions, lead him to misinterpret reality, and he acts on the basis of the misinterpretation. Informational phools act on information that is intentionally crafted to mislead them.

The most disturbing thing about phishing is that it is built into the free market system. The most fundamental concept in economics is that of the invisible hand that brings the interaction of supply and demand through the price mechanism into market equilibrium. But there are not only market failures and market externalities beyond the control of the invisible hand of the market. The free market system itself exploits our weaknesses automatically so expect to be deceived and manipulated. In a free market there is not only the freedom to choose, but the freedom to phish and be phished. Both are part and parcel of the natural workings of the free market system. It is the psychological, behavioral tendencies of all actors in the economic system, which are at everybody's peril to ignore.

Akerlof and Shiller start with how phishing for phools played a critical role in the financial bubble and bust of 2008-9. They put it in a nutshell by discussing a kind of phishing that played a central role in the crisis and that they call Reputation Mining. If I have a reputation for selling beautiful, ripe avocados, I have an opportunity. I can sell you a mediocre avocado at a price you would pay for a perfect avocado. I will have mined my reputation. I will also have phished you for a phool.

The reputation mining in question involved the reputations of a variety of financial institutions that they had built up over the years, which they then used to subvert the system for rating securities. The great US credit rating agencies had built up their reputations, and the public had become dependent on these ratings for their investments. The public had no reason not to trust their ratings of the newfangled securities that had come to existence. But they were not able to tell apart the good avocados from the mediocre ones or even from the truly rotten ones produced by growers who were not interested in producing good avocados, but who could package their rotten avocados with good avocados and bring them to the rating agencies that, in turn, mining their reputations, rated them AAA. It was inevitable that the rotten avocados would eventually be discovered, and when they were, the complex, mortgage-based derivatives fell massively in value, perilously bringing the entire financial system to the brink of another great depression, only to be averted by government intervention.

Akerlof and Shiller then consider phishing in many other contexts: how advertisers zoom in on our weaknesses; rip-offs regarding cars, houses, and credit cars; phishing in politics; phood, pharma, and phishing; innovation and phishing; the great phishing opportunities for tobacco and alcohol; bankruptcy for phishes and profit; phishes with junk bonds as bait. They visit phishing for phools in settings ranging from the very general, such as consumer spending and financial markets, to the quite particular, such as congressional elections or the ways that Big Pharma parries its regulators and phishes the doctors who prescribe its medicines. They also narrate stories of resistance heroes, which include those who measure and enforce measurement of quality standards; businessmen of conscience with good products who have moral and economic reasons to fight phishers; government heroes in the evolution of legal standards that protect us; regulatory heroes who resist regulatory capture.

All in all, Akerlof and Shiller give us a new sense about economics: an awareness of phishing for phools as the result of the natural workings of the economic system; a new perspective on where and when it occurs and the how of its practice; the significance of phishing for phools in our lives and of the ways to fight manipulation and deception.

Capitalism for the Many

Saving Capitalism is perhaps the best and most enlightening book coming from the pen of Robert Reich, Chancellor's Professor of Public Policy at the University of California, Berkeley, and former Secretary of Labor under President Bill Clinton. He goes back to the original questions we posed at the beginning of this review: Market or state? Are they separate? Are they opposed? Can the market exist without the state? These are crucially important questions for the country and for the world. The national narrative that animated the country and the world after the New Deal of Franklin Delano Roosevelt rescued us from the Great Depression and fought Fascism and Nazism in the Second World War was that government was good in solving social problems, was helpful in creating a good and prosperous society. In the wake of the stagflation of the 1970s and the accompanying fall of corporate profits, Ronald Reagan announced that government is not the solution to our problems; government is the problem. Since then, the narrative has been that whatever the government does is bad, that the beast of the government must be starved. Instead, the market must be set free to work its magic, it must be unfettered from all kinds of constraints. The free market is extolled to high heavens, while the government is demonized. Thus, the neoliberal ideology of liberalization, privatization, and deregulation became the "Washington Consensus" for the globalized economy.

Going back for a moment to the economics of manipulation and deception, Akerlof and Shiller also acknowledge that a new story has ruled the country for several decades now. The Age of Reform from 1890 to post-World War II – the agrarian Populism led by William Jennings Bryan, the good-government Progressivism led by Theodore Roosevelt, and the New Deal experimentalism led by Franklin Delano Roosevelt – resulted in a more expansive view of government and in a remarkable consensus that government is a useful counterweight to the excesses of free markets. But that story has become Old Story. The New Story is that government is the problem, that markets work perfectly as long as people are free to choose. Akerlof and Shiller (2015: 152-53) write:

> New Story is wrong: because its characterization of the economy is wrong. Its characterization of US history is wrong. Over many years, those years of the Age of Reform, and beyond, we saw a great expansion of governmental activity. By careful trial and error, in response to painful experience, we had implanted government programs and laws that addressed real needs: Social Security, Medicare, securities supervision, deposit insurance, the interstate highway system, aid to the indigent, supervision of food and drugs, environmental protection, auto safety laws, laws against mortgage-gouging, civil rights, and gender equality. Just to name a few. A long, hard-fought history – of nearly a century at the time of Reagan's inauguration – had evolved a system of government that did serve the people.
>
> New story – that government is the problem – is itself a phish for phools. Its appeal then and now has a ring of truth: especially since stories about what goes right are a much tougher sell for reporters than stories about what goes wrong. Reporters with such stories as "SEC employees are excellent hard-working public servants" quickly lose their jobs. So the news about government is mainly about

its faults. Furthermore, the public's dependence on those government programs' working well is further reason why the "news" is: when they don't.

At its most fundamental level, Robert Reich digs deeper to announce that markets need government, that markets cannot exist without government. Markets are exchanges between supply and demand mediated by the mechanism of price. But these exchanges cannot happen unless, first, there is a physical infrastructure of roads and bridges, railways, airports, and ports, which the state builds, maintains, and repairs. The state also provides the necessary juridical framework within which markets operate and without which markets become predatory: law and order, the enforcement of contracts, laws against fraud and corruption, penalties for violations. Markets are governed by rules: what to sell, what is the just price, what are the liabilities for defective products, when is there fraud and corruption. The rules are laid down by the state. Marijuana in the recent past could not be sold in the free market; now it can be in several states. There is no market for human organs, nor for children up for adoption, nor for slaves now. Not everything can or should be for sale, Debra Satz (2010) and Michael Sandel (2012) have argued, there are moral limits of markets. The state agrees by establishing legal limits of markets.

It used to be that the study of economy was called political economy, based on the recognition that the economy cannot be separated from politics. Economics, as Robert Reich puts is, was the study of how society's laws and institutions related to a set of moral ideals, of which fair distribution of income and wealth was a central concern. After World War II, under the powerful influence of Keynesian economics, the focus shifted away from these concerns and toward taxes and transfers as means of both stabilizing the business cycle and helping the poor. With Alfred Marshall, economics became autonomous and sought to identify abstract variables applicable to all systems of production and exchange with no attention to distribution of resources and inequality of outcomes, or to society's legal and political institutions. The shift was from specific moral, political, and institutional contexts to supposedly scientific and universally applicable "laws." But this is another *phish* for *phools* that hides the meretricious, if not incestuous relationship, between economic wealth and political power.

Our elected representatives write the rules for the market, but who are these elected politicians. They have been elected because they themselves have the wealth or have been backed by monied interests. Once elected, they write the rules for the market economy. Whose interests do the rules they write serve? The answer is too obvious to give. But is our democracy not supposed to be a representative democracy? Our democracy has been hijacked by economic and political power. It is sick, and its three ills are congressional gerrymandering, suppression of minority votes, and big money financing, abetted by U.S. Supreme Court decisions. Our democracy has become a plutocracy, a government of the 1%, by the 1%, and for the 1%. Because of the vicious, meretricious, and incestuous cycle between economic wealth and political power, our economy and politics have become a winner-take-all economy and political system.

Robert Reich identifies five building blocks of capitalism, about which decisions and rules must be made: property, monopoly, contract, bankruptcy, and enforcement. Decisions on these matters by public officials and entities do not intrude on the market. They constitute the free market. Without them there is no market. The rules and decisions are how the government organizes the market. This is the invisible hand of the market which is connected to a wealthy and muscular arm. The "free market" is a myth that prevents us from examining the underlying rules, the changes that are made to them, who made those changes, and for whose benefit those changes were made. It helps that the underlying rules are well hidden in the economy where so much that is owned and traded is becoming intangible and complex. In today's economy, which has been globalized and financialized, it is very difficult to tell who owes what to whom, or when, or why. The Great Recession of 2008 is testament to the dark recesses of the economy where even bankers, financiers, mortgage lenders, and money makers could not find their way.

Reich elaborates on the rules governing the five pillars of capitalism on which markets depend but which have been skewed and twisted by economic wealth and political power. Reich points out that "many of the most vocal proponents of the 'free market' – including executives of large corporations and their ubiquitous lawyers and lobbyists, denizens of Wall Street and their political lackeys, and numerous millionaires and billionaires – have for many years been actively reorganizing the market for their own benefit and would prefer these issues not to be examined." There is no better guide in knowing and understanding these issues than Robert Reich, and his writing is organized and clear.

One example will suffice. Private property is the most basic building block of free-market capitalism. The most important property today is intellectual property – new designs, ideas, and inventions. What exactly counts as intellectual property, and for how long can you own it? You can no longer own slaves, but how about the human genome? The genes of a plant or of an animal? An algorithm, or something as simple as a recipe? An entire legal and lobbying industry has developed around defining and promoting property rights, defending patents, or suing for patent infringement. Early on, products from nature could not be patented. But in the 1990s, pharmaceutical companies were allowed to patent processes they used to manufacture vaccines and other products from nature. Many lifesaving drugs continue to be made by only one company after the original patent expires, because patents are renewed on the basis of small and insignificant changes. The TRIPs (Trade-Related Aspects of Intellectual Property Rights) protocol of the World Trade Organization (WTO) was very contentious because what started as an effort to stem intellectual property piracy of Western consumer products became a reverse biological piracy of indigenous resources and natural endowments – the corporate patenting, e.g., of the rosy periwinkle, the neem tree, and basmati rice – that threatens the livelihood of peoples in the Third World/Global South (Litonjua 2010).

Reich uses as epigram a quotation from an 1814 book by John Taylor: "There are two modes of invading private property; the first, by which the poor plunder the rich . . . sudden and violent; the second, by which the rich plunder the poor, slow and legal." This is what is happening to the capitalist economy in the United States, from which it is spreading around the world with scandalous and dangerous outcomes: the 1% is becoming filthy rich, the middle and working classes are shrinking and getting angry, and the poor are left to desperately fend for themselves. The challenge is not to technology and economics. It is to democracy. The critical debate is not about the size of government; it is about whom the government is *for*. Can democracy, will democracy be able to save capitalism – for the many, not for the few?

Since we are asking a moral question, it is worthwhile to take a look at Catholic Social Teaching, the body of principles and teachings of the Catholic Church on social, economic, and political issues. Lord Maurice Glasman pointed out: "There is no more reasonable tradition from which to begin an analysis of the causes of the crisis of capitalism and no more fertile terrain out of which to begin to fashion a politics of the common good than Catholic Social Thought." Cardinal Vincent Nichols, Archbishop of Westminster, explains that "Catholic social teaching seeks to apply the essence of Christian moral principles to life in society. It is not an economic or political programme, but it offers a powerful way of thinking about what the common good requires, and how structures in society can promote or undermine human well being and the requirements of justice." Fortunately there is a Christian think tank in the United Kingdom, *Theos*, working in the area of religion, politics, and society, which was launched in November 2006 with the support of the Archbishop of Canterbury and the Cardinal-Archbishop of Westminster, although it is independent of any denomination. Theos conducts research, publishes reports, and runs debates, seminars, and lectures on the intersection of religion, politics, and society in the contemporary world. In 2014, Theos published a report: *Just Money: How Catholic Social Teaching Can Redeem Capitalism*, by Clifford Longley.

The report starts with an analysis of the banking crash and ensuing global recession. It identifies market fundamentalism, under the label of neoliberalism, as the main culprit that drove the world economy to the edge of the precipice in the crash of 2008. "The basic flaw in the [neoliberal] system is not just about personal greed, but about the idea that free market forces need not be, and should not be, deflected from scruples about their consequences; in other words that economics has no need of morality, that 'the business of business is business', and what matters is the short-term maximization of shareholder value." It adds: "Despite the catastrophe of 2008, neoliberalism remains the default orthodoxy among professional economists. That means that the problems have not been cured, and until they have, another catastrophe is likely." The system is broken and discredited, there must be another and a better way.

Clifford Longley calls on Just War Theory to present an analogous Just Money Theory. Just as there are *antebellum*, *in bello*, and *post bellum* conditions that make the waging of a war just, so, argues Congley, there must also be principles, values, and conditions that make the making of money just, which principle, values, and conditions he draws from Catholic Social Teaching. He enumerates this coherent set of principles at the outset which calls for both structural and personal change in the way the economy functions. These principles confront the false ideology of neoliberalism in the name of sound economics and humanity itself.

i. Prioritizing the common good over profits;
ii. Respect for human dignity and opposition to discrimination;
iii. Sustainability, solidarity, subsidiarity and civil society;
iv. Defence of workers' rights;
v. Recovering a sense of vocation and virtue in pursuit of "excellence" in trade or professional skills;
vi. Priority for the poor and disadvantaged and resistance to unfair inequality;
vii. Importance of reciprocity and unconditional gift (gratuitousness);
viii. Private property held under stewardship;
ix. Dangers of marketisation and commodification;
x. The state's duty to protect and promote the common good.

It suffices for the purposes of this already long review article to dwell on the two key values that are at the core of Catholic Social Teaching: human dignity and common good. It is instructive, in the first place, to remember the pronouncements of two progenitors of market fundamentalism. Ayn Rand extolled "the virtue of selfishness," considered altruism a "basic evil," railed against "parasites," "looters," and "moochers" of government benefits, but in the end, sick and advanced in age, she and her husband applied for Social Security and Medicare. She was the inspiration for Republican Speaker of the House Paul Ryan, himself a Catholic, and mentor to Alan Greenspan, former Chair of the Federal Reserve. Chicago economist Milton Friedman declared that "there is one and only one responsibility of business – to use its resources and engage in activities designed to increase its profits . . ." Corporations do not have responsibilities, only executives do – and their responsibility as agents of their owners is to maximise shareholder returns. Thus, his edict was: "the business of business is business." This is the neoliberal revolution that Ronald Reagan sought to bring about in the United States and Margaret Thatcher in the United Kingdom. But "just as any revolution eats its children," Mark Carney, Governor of the Bank of England, noted, "unchecked market fundamentalism can devour the social capital essential for the long-term dynamism of capitalism itself."

The human person in the neoliberal economic ideology is a deracinated individual, both as a consumer and as a worker. As a consumer, the individual is *homo economicus*, perfectly rational, who knows his interests, utilizes the best information, and thus optimizes his behavior in consuming the products and services offered in the free market. His aggregate demand calibrates aggregate supply to bring the market to equilibrium. As a worker, the individual is a cog in the capitalist machine, a mere means of production, whose labor is reduced to a commodity, subject therefore to the exigencies of the labor market. Workers, the first item in the expense budget, are the first to be sacrificed when economic troubles loom.

Catholic Social Teaching offers a diametrically opposed picture of human dignity and common good. Every human person has an innate human dignity that is derived from the fact that every human being is a creature of God. The human person is an end, not a means, Immanuel Kant laid down as a categorical imperative, and can never be used as a means to an end. The simple translation is that every person is a someone, not a something. Also, every human being is a social being, a political animal, a *zoon politikon*, in the terminology of Aristotle. To be human is to enter into relationships with others founded on true respect for their dignity and for activities which have meaning and purpose because they serve the common good. John XXIII defined the common good as "the sum total of human conditions which allow people, either as groups or as individuals, to reach their fulfillment more fully and more easily." Human flourishing, in other words, can only be achieved in community. Individual flourishing and common good go together. One corollary of common good, therefore, is that persons and communities are also moral actors. Economic choices, whether as producers, sellers, consumers, business leaders, bankers, or policy makers, inescapably have a moral dimension.

Catholic Social Teaching emphasizes that from the Catholic faith no specific and detailed economic or political program can be deduced, nor does the Catholic Church have solutions to technical problems in the economy and polity. What Catholic Social Teaching offers is vision, principles, values, orientations that promote the common good and safeguards the human dignity of every person and of all persons, the human community itself.

Surveying the wreckage of neoliberalism in the aftermath of 2008 and utilizing the perspectives and insights of Catholic Social Teaching, Clifford Longley's analysis addresses the flaws in the neoliberal system and suggests reforms that restore trust, remove sources of instability, and make businesses more sustainable long-term. Markets would function better, the adjustments required in the way business and the economy works are feasible, realistic, and politically do-able. More fundamentally, a post neoliberal market economy as laid down in his report would make for a fairer, more vibrant, and more prosperous economy for a happier and more fulfilled population. It would be a capitalism for the many, not only for the few.

Conclusion

This review essay started with the adverse moral criticisms by Pope Francis of capitalism. It ends with a further reflection on Pope Francis's negative ideas on capitalism. Pope Francis addresses economic issues under the overarching concept of idolatry. The greatest sin in the Bible is not atheism, the denial of God, but idolatry, the worship of false gods. The main point of Pope Francis is that we have come to worship profit over people, we idolize money before poor people's welfare, health, and lives, we reverence consumerism even if it results in inequality and violence, we sacrifice the planet at the altar of the "invisible hand" of the almighty market. "The return of the Golden Calf," William Cavanaugh (2015: 699) notes, marks an important shift from Vatican II's (1965) *Gaudium et Spes*, on theories of secularization, and therefore in Catholic Social Teaching. "Francis virtually never talks about the contemporary economy without leveling the charge of idolatry, a charge absent from the discussion of economics in *GS* and almost entirely absent from Vatican II as a whole." Francis therefore represents another advance in the development of theological ethics.

Secularization in the 1960s was understood as the result of structural differentiation and functional specialization The social structures of society were undergoing a continuing process of differentiation such that they were becoming more autonomous, rational, and neutral in terms of their own specific integrity, values, and norms. It was, in the image of Max Weber, a process of disenchantment: what was once embedded in the sacred realm was coming to exist on its own secular terms. Understood this way, secularization was a positive process; it was giving to the secular, the world, its own God-given integrity, autonomy, and rationality, subject to its own laws, values, and norms. Secularization, at the same time, was concomitantly understood as the displacement of religion from its central, public, and governing place in society, to be relegated to its proper private spiritual sphere, and perhaps eventually – mistakenly, it turned out – to its decline and disappearance in modern society.

This was the situation when Vatican II convened. This was the intellectual atmosphere in which *Gaudium et Spes* was drafted, debated upon, and finally approved. Chapter III of *Gaudium et Spes* is devoted to Socio-Economic Life. The themes touched upon hew to the main lines of papal social pronouncements, with the dignity of the human person as its *leitmotif*. Among its topics: economic development in the service of and under the control of the human person; the elimination of growing inequalities between people, sectors of the economy, and nations; the promotion of the dignity of labor and its participation in profits and decision-making; the proper concept of private property and the common purpose of created things; attention to the needs of underdeveloped nations, support for land reform, no discrimination against immigrants, and the care for the poor. The chapter is marked by the conviction that there are problems of the economy, but they can and should be addressed by sincere and rational persons. The role of the Church was to offer guiding principles that stake out the limits of the moral order. It was by respecting the integrity, autonomy, and rationality of secular society, its laws, norms, and values that religion would retain its relevance in the world. It was also by recognizing its limitations in the secular world that the Catholic Church can continue to play a role in the modern world to which it was establishing a rapprochement. But there are lines in the chapter which are prescient: "Many people, especially in economically advanced areas, seemed to be hypnotized, as it were, by economics, so that almost their entire personal and social life is permeated with a certain economic outlook. These people can be found both in nations which favor a collective economy as well as in others."

The "secularization thesis" of the 1960s has, of course, been abandoned. Jay Tolson (2015) in his editorial on the special issue of *The Hedgehog Review* on Re-Enchantment puts it well: "But facts on the ground, including certain epochal events, defied received ideas and theories. Not only did religions and religious passions reassert themselves around the world (in both inspiring and terrifying ways), but growing doubts about the overly reductive claims of scientific reason opened the door to new understandings of cause and value, and of their possible connections. If the world had been truly disenchanted in the first place, was it now undergoing a kind of re-enchantment? ... At the very least, we appear to have entered a liminal age, poised somewhere between the secular and the postsecular..."

There are many kinds of re-enchantment, as evidenced in the special issue of *The Hedgehog Review*. But I am interested in the re-enchantment involved in the migration of the sacred to areas of life, previously thought of and celebrated as totally secular, specifically to that of neoliberal economics and the neoliberal economy. Because of this economic re-enchantment, commodities, following Karl Marx, are not only the ones fetishized, but so are economic ideas and theories, most especially the "invisible hand" of the market. Not only are they fetishized, re-enchantment ideologizes them, sacralizes them, and idolizes them. They become, as it were, the font of divine economic wisdom, the unquestioned workings of divine economic providence. This enchanted economics and economy have no need of economic history, economic sociology, and political economy, nor are they based on empirical observation, experimentation, and research. Their theoretical justifications and policy prescriptions emanate, I suppose, from the mathematical equations and abstract deductions revealed to their founding fathers from on high. This re-enchanted economics and economy are the "golden calf" of modern society.

In the words of Pope Francis (2013a: no. 55-56):

> We have created new idols. The worship of the ancient golden calf (cf. *Ex* 32:1-35) has returned in a new and ruthless guise in the idolatry of money and the dictatorship of an impersonal economy lacking a true human purpose. The worldwide crisis affecting finance and the economy lays bare their imbalances and, above all, their lack of real concern for human beings; man is reduced to one of his needs alone: consumption.... In this system, which tends to devour everything which stands in the way of increased

profits, whatever is fragile, like the environment, is defenseless before the interests of a deified market, which become the only rule.

This is the background and the basis of Pope Francis' persistent denunciation of economic idolatry. As Cavanaugh (2015: 707, 714) puts it: "Economics is perhaps the area in which the breakdown of the neat distinction between enchanted, sacred religion on the one hand and the disenchanted, profane secular on the other is most apparent. . . .[T]here has been a migration of the holy from the church to the world, such that capitalism, for example is best understood not as devoid of gods but as a new type of – often idolatrous – religion." Cavanaugh (2015: 699) adds: "Francis represents an opportunity to shift Catholic discourse about secularization, an opportunity with implications for the way we look not only at economics but at other secular phenomena as well. Progressive Catholic thought in the period of the Second Vatican Council tended to view the secular world as disenchanted. Francis has suggested, on the contrary, that we are faced not so much with a loss of faith as with a new religion, an idolatrous faith. Such an approach could open up new possibilities for a theological response to secularization. . . . [T]he theological lens of idolatry can be a productive way to approach secularization generally and economy more particularly."

Before I end, it is worth recalling the most trenchant criticism ever made of the capitalist economic system, that of the much-condemned Karl Marx, although Marx himself spoke of capitalism as the most powerful solvent of enchantment: "All that is solid melts into the air; all that is holy is profaned." Moreover, whatever severe criticism he made of capitalism, Marx looked at it kindly and positively as the necessary stage in the historical development towards communism. Still, it is worth understanding once more his acute and resonant analysis of capitalism. First, Marx identified the fetishism of commodities as the central structural problem of capitalism. Man is *homo faber:* he makes products for his use, he controls the products of his own labor. With capitalism, man now produces products for exchange, in exchange for money. The products become commodities; they acquire an independent existence apart from the human labor that made them. They are reified, they are esteemed no longer for their use-value but for their exchange-value. The development of commodities, Marx labeled, as the fetishism of commodities – the attribution of magical power to fabricated things – by which workers forget that it is their labor that gives value to commodities. A person who has a sexual fetish, for example, believes that it is the fetish that has power over him, that arouses and gratifies him.

Marx originally linked fetishism to alienation: people lose control of their own labor and in the process lose the sources of their own selfhood. "The life which he has given to the object sets itself against him as an alien and hostile force;" it confronts him as alien power. Later on, as Eugene McCarraher (2015: 90) puts it, "the *anima* of capitalist animism in Marx's anatomy of [capitalist] enchantment shifted from estranged labor to money ... Marx portrays money as the ontological foundation of a uniquely pecuniary way of being in the world – a metaphysics of money that resembles and supplants traditional forms of enchantment. On one level, money is another marker of alienation: Like divinity, it betokens 'the alienated ability of mankind.' ... Having drowned religious faith in the arctic of pecuniary reason, money becomes 'the almighty being,' the 'truly creative power,' the *de facto* ontological basis of reality in capitalist civilization. 'The power of money in bourgeois society' extends farther and deeper than the market in commodities; like the God of Genesis, it brings things into being from nothing, and consigns all indigent objects and desires to the void of nonexistence." If I don't have money, I am nothing. If I have money, I am everything.

Read the words of Marx (Ritzer 1988: 53) himself:

> That which is for me through the medium of *money* – that for which I can pay (i.e., which money can buy) – that am *I*, the possessor of the money. The extent of the power of money is the extent of my power. Money's properties are my properties and essential powers – the properties and powers of its possessor. Thus, what I *am* and *am capable* is by no means determined by my individuality. I *am* ugly, but I can buy for myself the most *beautiful* of women. Therefore I am not *ugly*, for the effect of *ugliness* – its deterrent power – is nullified by money. I, as an individual, am *lame*, but money furnishes me with twenty-four feet. Therefore, I am not lame. I am bad, dishonest, unscrupulous, stupid; but money is honored, and hence its possessor. Money is the supreme good; therefore its possessor is good. Money, besides, saves me the trouble of being dishonest: I am therefore presumed honest. I am *stupid*, but money is the *real mind* of all things, and how then should its possessor be stupid? Besides, he can buy talented people for himself, and is he who has power over the talented not more talented than the talented? Do not I, who thanks to money am capable of *all* that the human

heart longs for, possess all human capacities? Does not money, therefore, transform all my incapacities into their contrary?

Thus, Eugene McCarraher (2015: 89) argues that, as far as the capitalist economy is concerned, "we have never been disenchanted:" the "waters of pecuniary reason constituted a baptismal font, a consecration of capitalism, as a covert form of enchantment, all the more beguiling on account of its apparent profanity." What Pope Francis is doing, therefore, is disenchanting capitalism, revealing the false worship of the capitalist Golden Calf.

12

THE FINANCIALIZATION OF THE GLOBALIZED ECONOMY AND THE ECONOMIC WAR AGAINST LIFE ON EARTH

Makers and Takers: The Rise of Finance and the Fall of American Business, by Rana Faroohar. New York: Crown Business, 2016, 388 pages.

This Changes Everything: Capitalism vs. The Climate, by Naomi Klein. New York: Simon and Schuster, 2014, 566 pages.

    Human society is presently undergoing a third dramatic and wrenching structural transformation. It is estimated that modern humans – anatomically correct human beings like you and I – appeared on earth some fifty thousand years ago. For forty thousand years, humans lived in small nomadic bands, hunting animals and gathering plants and fruits for food. With the invention of the plow and the domestication of animals, humans began to live in permanent settlements, tilling the land. This first dramatic transformation of human society, the agricultural revolution, resulted in economic surplus which, in turn, led to the erection of cities, the establishment of fulltime service workers, the beginnings of what we now call civilization.

Some two hundred years ago, a second great structural transformation occurred with the industrial revolution. Human and animal sources of energy were replaced by non-animal and non-human sources of energy. The results were hitherto unimaginable increases in efficiency and productivity. The industrial revolution was actually composed of several distinct but interrelated phases of technological breakthroughs. The first phase was the application of steam power to textiles, mining, manufacturing, and transportation. The second phase involved the use of oil and electricity, the invention of the telephone and the telegraph, of the automobile and the airplane. The third phase was marked by the technologies of atomic fission and fusion, supersonic aircraft and missiles, television and computers (Eitzen and Baca, 1989: 1-2). The third phase of the industrial revolution is still in progress and is giving way to a third great structural transformation.

The agricultural revolution took almost ten thousand years to run its course, and the industrial revolution lasted but two hundred years. The third great structural transformation has given rise to what has been variously referred to as an information/knowledge/post-industrial society. Whereas the agricultural evolution was ushered in by the plow, the industrial revolution by the use of steam power, the technological tool of the post-industrial age is the silicon microchip which has been ranked as just behind the wheel and equal to the steam engine among history's technological thresholds. All three mark fundamental turning points in human history, which have brought, and are bringing, fundamental changes to economies and societies, to the relationship of people and work, to family and other social institutions, to nature and the environment, and to planet earth itself. The changes were, and are, wrenching, leaving in their wake human winners and losers.

The most dramatic manifestation of this third fundamental transformation of human society is the globalization of the capitalist economy. Because of the microelectronic revolution, the economy has become global, not merely international. An international economy is characterized by a division of labor between the extraction of raw materials in Third World countries and the manufacture of finished goods in First World countries. A global economy is one single market for capital, commodities, skilled labor, and technical knowledge, all of them crisscrossing boundaries easily through worldwide communications and transportation systems in search for the lowest costs on labor and supplies and the highest returns on investments or profits for products. One result is that First World economies have undergone deindustrialization and are now dominated by their service sectors, whereas some Third World countries are registering higher rates of industrialization than First World countries.

William Greider (1997) was one of the first to write a most compelling narrative of this one world fast coming into existence whether we are ready or not. Whereas the agricultural and industrial transformations were gradual enough to allow for adaptation, the rate of change today is phenomenal and unprecedented that there are marked discontinuities. It is a veritable global revolution. Greider compares it to a huge machine that is reaping tremendous benefits for a few, but wreaking enormous havoc in the lives of the many. It is a wondrous machine whose efficiency churns out excess supplies of goods and services, which exert downward pressures on prices and wages, and which, in turn, reaps enormous wealth for its beneficiaries. Thus, the dynamics of the global economy play out as a human struggle in which peoples and nations, rich and poor alike, face a multiplicity of opportunities and dangers. Some win; more lose.

The manic logic of global capitalism is especially evident in finance capital which Greider (1997: 250) calls "the Robespierre of this revolution." Finance capital is the driving force of expansionary capitalism. It fuels increasing production, starts new ventures and new enterprises, and enables the creation of multiplying new wealth. In the global economy, finance capital has become totally unfettered and completely mobile, besting the best efforts of governments to contain or regulate it. But the most alarming aspect of globalized capital is not its speed or its volume, but its price (Greider 1997: 234). It has become detached from real economic activity, but thrives on debt and speculation. Fortunes are made and lost in financial markets without much reference to productive activities. They have become casino economies. The divergence has become pathological that it is now the financial tail that wags the economy which produces, distributes, and consumes goods, services, and technology. Greider (1997: 227) points out that "finance capital's capacity to become deranged in search of higher returns has played out again and again in different forms of manias and crashes," which disorders, history also informs us, have been corrected in grim and violent ways: economic depressions and great wars.

One reality that became evident with the disappearance of its archenemy, communism, is that there are many kinds of capitalism, different ways of organizing a market economy. East Asia has state capitalism, the alliance of big business and government. Western Europe has social or social-democratic capitalism which provides a generous social safety net of welfare. The United States has liberal capitalism, the most laissez-faire of the three, where the market is the freest. In the global economy, however, as Lester Thurow (1996: 1, 5) puts it, "the market, and the market alone, rules. . . . 'Survival of the fittest' capitalism stands alone." It has destroyed the implicit post-World War II social contract in the United States, has undermined the welfare state in Western Europe, and made untenable East Asian state capitalism.

Global capitalism marks the third stage in the worldwide development of capitalism. First, there was competitive capitalism in which relatively small businesses competed on the basis of price. Then came monopoly or corporate capitalism, which saw large corporations trying to get oligopolistic holds on market share. Now we have global capitalism whose main characteristic is the mobility and volatility of capital on a global scale. It is primarily this "new leviathan" (Ross and Trachte, 1990) of global finance that has devastated economies and societies of less developed countries, exemplified by the Asian financial crisis of 1997. Once foreign capital takes flight and financial panic starts, the value of local currencies takes a precipitous fall despite the sound "fundamentals" of their economies. Thus, globalization significantly augments and spreads the inherent instability of capitalism. The International Monetary Fund, the surrogate government in global financial matters, neither acts to contain its volatility nor cushions the effects of its instability because it has become the main proponent of an unfettered world economy. Under the aegis of the neoliberalism of the so-called "Washington Consensus" – liberalization, privatization, deregulation – the IMF, the World Bank, and the World Trade Orgniazaion, together with top U.S. government bureaucracies, have become the leading cheerleaders of laissez-faire globalization.

Neoliberalism, the unfettered market ideology, is the new fundamentalism sweeping across the one world in the making, commodifying, and commercializing human life and everything it touches – without moral moorings, without human values and considerations, without humane intentions and aspirations. The banner program of this revived Social Darwinism is carried by the Republican Party, starting with Newt Gingrich's Contract with America (Thurow 1996: 249). "In fact," E.J. Dionne (1996: 12) adds, "the new Republican philosophy looks *backward* to the late nineteenth century, seeking to revive the radical, unregulated capitalism of the Gilded Age and that era's belief that material progress depends on the fiercest forms of unchecked competition." The logical end-result of this market fundamentalism was the Great Recession of 2008, from whose devastation we have not yet completely recovered.

Finance Capital

Rana Faroohar, business columnist of *Time* magazine and CNN's global economic analyst, picks up from the greatest market meltdown since the Great Depression to point out that the financial practices and philosophies that nearly toppled the global financial system have infiltrated all American businesses. We have not learned the lessons of the Great Recession of 2008. We are, therefore, on a collision course for another great, if not greater, cataclysmic meltdown.

Faroohar, in conjunction with many other economists, identifies the problem as the "financialization" of the economy:

> a term for the trend by which Wall Street and its way of thinking have come to reign supreme in America, permeating not just the financial industry but all American business. The very type of short-term, risky thinking that nearly toppled the global economy in 2008 is today widening the gap between rich and poor, hampering economic progress, and threatening the future of the American Dream itself. The financialization of America includes everything from the growth in size and scope of finance and financial activity in our economy to the rise of debt-fueled speculation over productive lending, to the ascendancy of shareholder value as a model for corporate governance, to the proliferation of risky, selfish thinking in both our private and public sectors, to the increasing political power of financiers and CEOs they enrich, to the way in which a 'markets know best' ideology remains the status quo, even after it caused the worst financial crisis in seventy-five years. It is a shift that has even affected our language, our civic life, and our way of relating to one another. We speak about human and social 'capital' and securitize everything from education to critical infrastructure to prison terms, a mark of our burgeoning 'portfolio society.'

A few numbers indicate the disproportionate power that finance holds in our society: it represents about 7 percent of our economy but takes around 25 percent of all corporate profits – almost a third at the height of the housing boom, but up from some 10 percent it was taking twenty-five years ago – while creating only 4 percent of all jobs. It used to be that finance was at the service of productive capital, providing investments, and facilitating business. Finance has become an end in and of itself, having been detached from its moorings in the real economy. Corporations are less engaged in making products – cars, refrigerators, computers, electronics

– than in taking money. They have become as, Rana Faroohar's title puts it, no longer *makers,* but *takers,* in a twist on Congressman Paul Ryan's and Presidential candidate Mitt Romney's exaltation of makers, like themselves, and scorn for takers, for the less fortunate of society. The biggest problem is that the ideology that underlies financialization has taken "cognitive capture" not only of the elite of American society, but of ordinary Americans whose eyes are focused on the gains or losses they are making in the stock market where more and more of them have put in their savings.

Rana Faroohar starts her narrative with what Tim Cook, Steve Jobs' successor as CEO of Apple, did in 2013. He decided that the company needed to borrow $17 billion. Not that there was no money sitting in the bank, nor that profits were not flowing in. Apple's financial masters had determined that borrowing was the more cost-effective way to obtain the funds. What was the money for? To buy off investors by repurchasing stock and fattening dividends, which would goose the company's lagging share price. "This was never the Steve Jobs way," Faroohar states. "Jobs focused relentlessly on creating irresistible, life-changing products, and was confident that the money would follow." She adds: "The fact that Apple, probably the best-known company in the world and surely one of the most admired, now spends a large amount of its time and effort thinking about how to make more money via *financial* engineering rather than by the old-fashioned kind, tells us how upside down our biggest corporations' priorities have become, not to mention the politics behind the tax system that encourages it all. This little vignette also demonstrates how detached many of our biggest businesses have become from the needs and desires of their consumers – and from the hearts and minds of the country at large."

The business of America is no longer business, but finance. But the rise of finance has led to the fall of American business. Faroohar looks at the effects of our dysfunctional financial system on *business* itself, and thus moves beyond sound bites into the real analysis of the problem and illustrates how financialization damages the very heart of our economy and thus endangers prosperity for us all.

If there is a Godfather of modern finance, Faroohar states, it must be Sanford Weill, former CEO of Citigroup, whose creation in 1998 was a seismic moment in the story of financialization for it resulted in the planet's biggest-ever financial conglomerate. It would also be the nail in the coffin of Glass-Steagall (1933), the Depression-era banking legislation that prohibited commercial banks from engaging in investment businesses, thus protecting consumers from exploitation. Earlier on, Walter Wriston of First National City Bank had developed ingenious ways to get around

Glass-Steagall, by introducing certificates of deposits (CD) and credit cards. As more and complex financial innovations were created, slowly regulations around interest rates and the price of credit began to fall away, money becoming not a limited commodity but something you could buy – at the right price, of course. Finance was becoming an end in and of itself, rather than a facilitator of real business.

The financialization of the economy was turbocharged in the 1980s, fueled by the laissez-faire policies of the Reagan administration that strongly favored Wall Street. By the October 1987 stock market crash and with Alan Greenspan taking control of the Fed, the government had gotten into the habit of lowering interest rates to jump-start markets each time they weakened. It was kerosene for finance, adding both reward and risk. Bill Clinton, surrounded by advisers from Wall Street, bought into the financialization trend, accelerated the neoliberal globalization of the economy, and finally repealed Glass-Steagall in 1999. The trajectory pointed straight into the Great Recession of 2008.

Faroohar then examines how financial thinking came to dominate American corporate life with the end result that corporations became interested not only in *making* products, but also, if not more, in *taking* money. Robert McNamara and the Whiz Kids at Ford Motor Company figure prominently in this narrative. Their obsession with crunching numbers led to the development of a culture of management by numbers, focused on squeezing pennies out of costs while ignoring the creative and productive sides of business. Key metrics, like body-counts, also determined major decisions in the Vietnam War, not because they were the best, but because they were the easiest to calculate. General Motors had already adopted this financially-driven decision-making and will evolve from a company focused on making cars to one focused on making money and pleasing the financial markets. The decline of the American automotive industry signaled the ultimate spread of financialized thinking into every corner of American business today.

The biggest problem with the financialization of the economy is what is called "cognitive capture." Following FDR's New Deal, the narrative that captured the nation's imagination was that government was good, a savior – from the Great Depression, from the tyrannies of Fascism and Nazism, and from World War II; government was the solution to our social ills. Ronald Reagan famously declared that government is not the solution to our problems; government is the problem. Thus began the exaltation of the free market, the invocation of the magic of the magic, the denigration of government and everything that it stood for and did. In the global economy, the mantra became liberalization, privatization, and deregulation. This emphasis on the market, to the exclusion of everything else, is what now governs people's mindsets. The market, and the market alone, should rule. People have fallen in thrall to the business theology or, better, idolatry of the market as god (Cox 1999, 2016).

How this has come about is best explored by delving into the history of business education and how it came to focus on the prioritization of shareholder interest and balance sheet manipulation to the exclusion of real managerial skills in controlling the quality of products. Faroohar declares that the key factor is that the basic training that business leaders receive is dictated by the needs of Wall Street, not by those of Main Street. MBA education today is basically an education in finance. "Despite the financial crisis of 2008, most top MBA programs in the United States still teach standard 'markets know best' efficiency theory and preach that share price is the best representation of a firm's underlying value, glossing over the fact that the markets tend to brutalize firms for long-term investment and reward them for short-term paybacks to investors." She adds: "One of the scariest trends in business these days is the increased movement of MBAs and finance types into the technology industry. They now are bringing their focus on financial engineering and balance sheet manipulation to firms such as Google, Apple, Facebook, Yahoo, and Snapchat – a shift that, if history is any indicator, doesn't bode well for the future of such firms."

In this connection, it is worth noting the review that Amitai Etzioni (2015) did of dozens of studies that explored the relationship between exposure to neoclassical economics and antisocial behavior. He concluded that both effects – a selection effect that those with antisocial tendencies tend to study economics, and an indoctrination effect that exposure to neoclassical economic theory causes antisocial behavior – play a role in explaining the debased behavior of economists and students of economics.

The one good news that Faroohar narrates is the turnaround of General Electric from being the country's fifth-largest bank under Jack Welch to reclaim its roots in industry under Jeffrey Immelt, although the jury on Wall Street is still out.

The festering bad news is that derivatives – those financial instruments like futures contracts or options which are derived from other forms of assets and whose values are determined from the fluctuations in the underlying asset – continue to dominate the financial market. Derivatives from mortgages, spliced and diced into more complex and esoterically-named instruments, and sold again and again were responsible for the financial meltdown of the financial market in 2008. They continue to play a big role in the uneven recovery of the housing market, but now in the form of private equity, the funds and investors that directly invest in private companies or that engage in the buyouts of public companies, and which are part of the shadow banking sector, operating largely outside of governmental regulation. Private equity investors have become the largest group of buyers in residential housing properties, pricing homes beyond the reach of most middle-class American families and making the American Dream of owning a home an elusive fantasy. Worse, companies are using derivatives to corner commodities, e.g., food and tin, to manipulate commodity markets, and thus to control the natural resources that companies and consumers depend on. They make the markets. They are the markets. Truly, derivatives are, in the description of Warren Buffett, "financial weapons of destruction."

Finance and Wall Street do not only own and control our working lives on Main Street, but have hijacked out lives in retirement. There is therefore a looming crisis in our already fragile retirement system which former Senator Tom Harkin predicted will become a "tsunami." The root cause is the privatization of retirement which has enabled asset management, the fastest-growing sector of finance, to run our retirement savings, to throw them at risky funds that track the market, to grow rich at unnecessary fees, and in the process to gamble away our nest eggs. Our retirement system has become an area of major risk, where the primary goal of funds is not to earn steady returns for clients, but to earn profits for the firm.

Faroohar tells the story of Detroit, the biggest municipal bankruptcy in U.S. history and the high-profile pensions fight at the heart of it. Wall Street came into the picture, selling the city on $1.4 billion of complex and security deals, including pension obligation bonds called certificates of participation. The result was that Detroit's public employee pensioners – hardworking Main Street Americans who had toiled in often thankless jobs, like bus drivers, clerks, sewage workers, and trash collectors – were asked to take huge cuts in their retirement income to pay hundreds of millions of dollars to bankers. Some creditors were even pushing Detroit to mortgage the priceless art in its hallmark museum, including works by Van Gogh, Whistler, and Degas, in order to keep cops and ambulances on the street. The Detroit story has something of a happy ending, Faroohar tells us. Activists and local politicians decided to fight back, federal judge Steven Rhodes approved the city's bankruptcy plan, threw out the initial settlement of $800 million derivatives deal, and made financial institutions settle for a fraction of that amount. The Detroit resolution shows that with enough determination, makers can fight takers, and win.

The financialization of the economy illustrates, more than anything else, the symbiosis of our economic system with our political system. Those who make it big in the economy gain the power to influence our political institutions, what laws to pass that promote their interests, what tax advantages and loopholes that benefit them, what regulations to oppose that hinder their businesses. The elected officials of our political institutions who are so dependent on the monetary contributions of the well-to-do in their all-year-round campaigns reciprocate by meeting their demands for fear of alienating their largesse. It is a vicious cycle that makes for a winner-take-all economics and a winner-take-all politics (Hacker and Pierson 2010), with the rest of society taking the hindmost.

The tax system, for example, privileges corporations over individuals, encourages debt, the lifeblood of finance, over equity, and allows firms to engage in financial engineering as a business strategy. A truly amazing kind of fiscal gymnastics is tax inversions, which are essentially complicated schemes by which American companies avoid paying their fair share in taxes by buying foreign firms in cheaper overseas tax jurisdictions. Thus, globalization and financialization work hand in glove to allow firms to fly thousands of feet above the realities of people on the ground: hard-to-come-by good jobs, stagnant wages, shrinking living standards, poor-quality schools. More perversely, the revolving door between Washington and Wall Street creates the political environment that sustains financialization, strengthens cognitive capture, privileges corporations and financial institutions over the fates of ordinary citizens, and ultimately is destructive of the legitimacy of democracy. The Obama administration's fumbling of the financial crisis by focusing the bail-outs on banks and ignoring the throes of ordinary homeowners is a factor in the rise of the Tea Party and the emergence of right-wing populism.

Debt, deregulation, finance, and money politics grow hand in hand. That is why Rana Faroohar's well-written and very enlightening book on the financialization of the globalized American economy must be read in conjunction with Jane Mayer's (2016) *Dark Money*, her powerful and provocative expose of the hidden history of the billionaires behind the rise of the radical right, whose core beliefs include that taxes are a form of tyranny, that government oversight of business is an assault on freedom, that an unregulated market results in the best of economic worlds, and therefore are primarily responsible for finance to be unmoored from the real economy, thus perverting our society and our democracy.

"The U.S. system of market capitalism itself is broken," Faroohar (2016) asserts in the recap of her book in *Time*. "To understand how we got here, you have to understand the relationship between capital markets – meaning the financial system – and business." This she does ably, clearly, and comprehensively in *Makers and Takers*, which she ends with five suggestions on how to fix it, on what we can do to put our financial system back in service to the real economy that most of us has the fortune to live in: End complexity, cut leverage; Less debt, more equity; Rethink who companies are for; Build a new growth model; and Change the narrative – Empower the makers. This is not to quibble, but after reading her book, one gets the impression of the enormity of the task to turn back the tide of financialization. Even after the Great Recession of 2008, the promised reforms have yet to come to pass. Do we need another Great Depression to wake us all up? It is a small consolation, but Rana Faroohar has made us all understand the great problem and the greater danger.

Climate Change

"Climate scientists agree: climate change is happening here and now," the 2014 Report by the American Association for the Advancement of Science reads. "Based on well-established evidence, about 97 percent of climate scientists have concluded that human-caused climate change is happening. This agreement is documented not just by a single study, but by a converging stream of evidence over the past two decades from surveys of scientists, content analyses of peer-reviewed studies, and public statements issued by virtually every membership organization of experts in this field."

"Climate change has become an existential crisis for the human species," Naomi Klein writes, "Global warming poses a clear and present danger to civilization." In Klein's two earlier books, *No Logo* changed our way of thinking about globalization and became an anti-globalization movement bible, while *The Shock Doctrine* alerted us to the exploitation of natural disasters and man-made events (Iraq War) to push through controversial neoliberal policies while citizens were too emotionally and physically distracted to mount effective resistance. With *This Changes Everything*, she intends to weave all the seemingly disparate issues of the central ideological battle of our time into a coherent narrative about how to protect humanity from the ravages of both a savagely unjust economic system and a destabilized climate system, and hopes that the urgency of the climate crisis can provide a much-needed catalyst for and form the basis of a powerful mass movement.

Klein starts her book with the meeting of the Heartland Institute's Sixth International Conference on Climate Change, held in late June 2011, the premier gathering for those dedicated to denying the overwhelming scientific consensus that human activity is warming the planet. She notes the gists of the various presentations given: "In America today, we are overregulated. If the greens have their way, we will have a $CO2$ budget for every man, woman, and child on the planet, monitored by an international body." "The issue is that no free society would do to itself what the climate change agenda requires. The first thing to doing that is to remove these nagging freedoms that keep getting in the way." Modern environmentalism is compared, among other things, to the Catholic Inquisition, to Nazi Germany, to Stalin's Russia. Barack Obama is likened to Chairman Mao; climate change is a stalking horse for National Socialism; environmentalists are like Aztec priests. But, most of all, Klein points out, she heard versions of "climate change is a Trojan horse designed to abolish capitalism." Klein follows this up with her inconvenient truth: "I think these hard-core ideologues understand the real significance of climate change better that most of the 'warmists' in the political center, the ones who are still insisting that the response can be gradual and painless and that we don't need to go to war with anybody, including the fossil fuel companies."

With these words, I immediately remember L. S. Stavrianos' (1989) innovative new world history in which he draws lifelines – the environment, relations between the sexes, social organization, and war – from our past of kinship, tributary, and capitalist societies. Arriving at the juncture that leads to capitalist societies, Stavrianos (1989: 89) identifies the essence of capitalism in Joseph Schumpeter's memorable characterization of its dynamics as "creative destruction."

> Capitalism's basic competitive drive brings on bursts of technological and institutional innovation, and with these comes increase productivity. So compelling is its creative impulse that capitalism has enveloped the entire globe, overwhelming traditional cultures and economies, while transforming peoples on all continents. This seemingly irresistible process, however, generates the other half of Schumpeter's equation – destruction. Destruction is the inevitable concomitant of relentless creativity. The self-generating technological exuberance and economic expansionism have overrun any institution and any object, animate or inanimate, standing in the way of capitalism's sacred principle: profit or perish. The victims of capitalism's creative drive have included not only overseas food-gathering tribal peoples, but the venerable civilizations of China, India, and the Middle East, and the underdeveloped societies of today's Third World; not only the green valleys of eighteenth century Wales, but the continental expanses of Amazonia, and the entire planetary ecosystem of the late twentieth century. The particular combination of creativity and destruction that

capitalism has generated provides the foundation both for the extraordinary achievements and the appalling setbacks of recent centuries, for the unprecedented promise and peril of our time.

Not only societies, peoples, and cultures, but the entire planet is now at capitalism's mercy. That is why "climate change detonates the ideological scaffolding on which contemporary conservatism rests," whose core beliefs are that the magic of the market should reign supreme, that government intervention is an assault on freedom, that taxes and regulations are a form of tyranny. The threat goes deeper because climate change challenges the very core narratives about what humans are and should be doing on earth, that they are the pinnacle of creation, charged with dominating and subduing the earth. Humans thought that they had ultimately tamed nature by splitting the atom, but now nature is striking back for all the depredations that humans have inflicted upon it. Still, it is easier to deny the reality of climate change than to face the prospect of changing the fundamental, growth-based, profit-seeking logic of capitalism. And yet, Robert Gordon (2016) titles his book, *The Rise and Fall of American Growth*, challenging the idea that the era of unprecedented growth in the century after the Civil War will continue unabated, but instead has come to an end.

Citing Giovanna Ricoveri who said that the origin of the present ecological crisis lies in "the mortal conflict between capital and nature; but people are also part of nature, and the exploitation of nature is therefore also the exploitation of some people by other people. Ecological degradation is also the degradation of human relationships," Martin O'Connor (1998: 9, 1) had edited a collection of articles titled *Is Capitalism Sustainable?* and asked: "First, given what we know about capitalist relations and forces of production, and about the failures of capitalism up until now to ensure regeneration of the social and ecological conditions needed for accumulation, is an *ecologically sustainable* capitalism possible? Second, and more crucial, can one plausibly suggest that capitalism might be reformed to respect the integrity of the social and ecological domains hitherto subject to savage exploitation?"

The very word "sustainable" has been hijacked (Bruno and Karliner (2002). It first came into prominence as "sustainable development" in a report of the United Nations Commission on Environment and Development, *Our Common Future*, chaired by Gro Harlem Brutland, former Prime Minister of Norway, which it defined as "development that meets the needs of the present without compromising the ability of future generations to meet their own needs." But the definition was "vague and diffuse, allowing for many interpretations and eventually giving rise to a dangerous misconception that sustainable development is the same thing as sustainable or sustained growth" (Martens and Schilder 2001: 813). That is why James O'Connor (1998: 154) asks: Is sustainable capitalism possible? "Capitalism is self-destructing and in crisis; the world economy makes more people hungry, poor, and miserable every day; the masses of peasants and workers cannot be expected to endure the crisis indefinitely; and nature, however 'ecological sustainability' is defined, is under attack everywhere."

Naomi Klein in fact shows the distinctly bizarre, because self-defeating, behavior of market fundamentalism that the economic system of capitalism has become that pits, for example, free trade against climate change. Ever since James Hansen, then director of NASA's Goddard Institute of Space Studies, testified before a packed congressional hearing on June 23, 1988, that he had "99 percent confidence" in "a real warning trend" linked to human activity, efforts have been made, however small and haphazard, to confront the problem. In 1992, the first United Nations Summit met in Rio, where the Framework Convention on Climate Change was signed. That same year the North America Free Trade Agreement was passed, and in 1995 the World Trade Organization came into existence. The problem is that green programs that are undertaken to lower global emissions are challenged under the international trade agreements of the WTO. The U.S. challenged China's wind power subsidy programs, China in turn filed complaints against the renewable energy programs of the EU, and Washington again launched attacks on India's large, multiphase solar support program, and so on and so forth in retaliation. Meanwhile large corporations with their large carbon footprints merrily go on their trade routes, plying their products all over the world. Trade trumps climate.

Another self-defeating contradiction of the neoliberal capitalism that has come to dominate the world is the brutal politics of austerity which derives from the neoliberal ideological pillars of no spending, no government, no regulation, no taxes. There is no doubt that climate change has increased the frequency of drought, intense hurricanes, super typhoons, and devastating floods and the intensity and duration of heat waves and other extreme types of weather. At the same time, almost every government in the world has chipped away at the foundations of what makes a society good: its public health and health care system, its public housing and education, its social welfare programs for the poor and disadvantaged, its public transport, and its infrastructure of roads, bridges, canals, airports, seaways, and electric grid. The result is that natural disasters become unnatural catastrophes resulting in the terrific loss of life and property and astronomical costs and damages. Ideology blinds to climate change.

As the two examples above show, climate disputes and climate change solutions hinge on efforts of governments to introduce some measure of industrial planning to their economies. Take the case of renewable energy. "If industrial policy were brought in line with climate science," Klein writes, "the supply of energy through wind, solar, and other forms of renewable energy (geothermal and tidal power, for example) would generate huge numbers of jobs in every country – in manufacturing, installation, maintenance, and operation. . . . They are not, however, the kinds of jobs that the market will create on its own. They will be created on this scale by thoughtful policy and planning." This will also mean that the idea of private ownership will have to be reconceptualized. Instead public utilities, including prisons, are being handed over to notoriously ruthless for-profit corporations. The greatest problem is that long-term rational planning represents a departure from neoliberal orthodoxy; it will involve picking winners in the market, fixing prices, and creating a fair playing field to enter the market.

Any lasting and worthwhile alternative to our climate-change-fueled disaster capitalism must also mean that we stop plundering the earth to promote exponential material growth with no limits on resource exploitation. This is called "extractivism," the mentality that allowed so many of us, and our ancestors, to believe that we could relate to the earth with such violence in the first place – to dig and drill out the substances we desired while thinking little of the trash left behind, whether in the land or water where the extraction takes place, or in the atmosphere, once the extracted material is burned. . . . Though developed under capitalism, governments across the ideological spectrum now embrace this resource-depleting model as the road to development, and it is this logic that climate change calls profoundly into question." This carelessness at the core of our economic model wages war against life on earth and is diametrically opposed to stewardship which involves taking care that regeneration and future life continue.

Naomi Klein devotes three chapters under the heading "magical thinking." First, there is the dangerous merger of big business and big green, exemplified by The Nature Conservancy, renowned for buying ecologically important tracts of land and turning them into preserves, but which it then exploited the land donated by Mobil into its own gas and oil operation, sending millions in revenue flowing directly into its coffers. Second, there are no messiahs, the green billionaires won't save us. The notion that transforming the economy away from fossil fuels is not about confronting the rich and powerful but simply about reaching them with sufficiently persuasive facts and figures and appealing to their sense of humanity is a broken dream. Third, the Pinatubo option of dimming the sun and various methods of geoengineering might turn out to be cures worse than the disease; "bioengineering will certainly monsterize the planet as nothing experienced in human history."

What then needs to be done, if anything can be done? Can there be any expectation for change, if in the end the root cause is the economic system of capitalism? Klein delivers some signs of hope. First, there is "Blockadia," which "is not a specific location on a map but rather a roving transnational conflict zone that is cropping up with increasing frequency and intensity wherever extractive projects are attempting to dig and drill, whether for open-pit mines, or gas fracking, or tar sands oil pipelines." This indicates a fundamental change in perspective, primarily driven by a desire for a deeper form of democracy. The awakening of the sleeping giant of latent ecological outrage is marked by a shared determination to stay in the fight for the long haul, the prominent role played by women, and the widespread awareness of the climate crisis. In Blockadia outposts all over the world, the initials BP act as a kind of mantra and invocation – shorthand for: whatever you do, take no extractive company at its word. Which means that the extractive industries are losing, if they have not yet lost, their credibility and legitimacy.

Second, under the heading, "Love will save this place," Klein points to the power of ferocious love people have for their children, for their customs and identity, for the integrity of their territory, the lands and waters, and the stewardship practices that link them to their landscape that resource companies and their advocates in government inevitably underestimate, precisely because no amount of money can extinguish it. The duty to protect water is especially the animating force behind every single environmental movement fighting extreme extraction. Two solid victories are in the offing. "[T]he country's elites, the wealthy winners in China's embrace of full-throttle capitalism, are increasingly distressed by the costs of industrialization" – ironically a reason "to thank smog." Another is the divestment campaign, led by young people, which puts the fossil fuel companies business model on trial. The eventual goal is to confer on oil companies the same status as tobacco companies, which means to question the legitimacy of their profits and to raise the issue of their reappropriation in solutions to the climate crisis.

Third, the exercise of Indigenous rights has played a central role in the rise of the current wave of fossil fuel resistance. Indigenous land and treaty rights have proved a major barrier for the extractive industries in many of the key Blockadia struggles. They have become the most robust tools available to prevent ecological crisis. This was especially evident when in the 1990s the Supreme Court of Canada handed down a series of landmark decisions designed to test the limits of Aboriginal title and treaty rights. But federal and provincial governments did little or nothing to protect the rights affirmed by the courts, so it fell to Indigenous people to go out on the land and water to assert them. Many of these protests attracted participants from all of the country's ethnic groups such that environmental groups recognized that these were the same rights they were fighting for and formed coalitions and joined solidarity protests with them. Still, the industry can still get its way by raw political power. The positive thing is that battles against specific oil, gas, and coal companies are coalescing into pro-democracy movements, "opening up spaces for a historical reconciliation between Indigenous peoples and non-Natives, who are finally understanding that, at a time when elected officials have open disdain for basic democratic principles, Indigenous rights are not a threat, but a tremendous gift."

Fourth, the most potent weapon in the battle against fossil fuels is the creation of real alternatives. In fact, the fundamental shift in power relations between humanity and the natural world demanded by climate change cannot happen if there are no realistic alternatives. "[T]oday's climate movement does not have the luxury of simply saying no without simultaneously fighting for a series of transformative yeses." The difficulty is that the resources for such a transition must ultimately come from the state, collected from the profits of fossil fuel companies, and from public interest institutions like colleges and municipalities that are willing to divest their fossil fuel holdings and reinvesting them in the clean tech sector. This is already happening, however. Resistance and alternatives are "the twin strands of the DNA of social change. One without the other is useless." Klein comments: "The denizens of Blockadia live and know this. Which is why theirs is neither a movement of negation (no to the miners/ drillers/pipe layers/ heavy haulers), nor solely of protection (defending cherished but static ways of life). Increasingly, it is also a constructive movement, actively building an alternative economy based on very different principles and values."

Fifth, in her last chapter Naomi Klein narrates her own fertility saga as she goes to Louisiana to cover the BP spill. She comes to the realization that "for all the talk about the right to life and the rights of the unborn, our culture pays precious little attention to the particular vulnerabilities of children, let alone developing life." One fisherman worried that when he and his colleagues will be hauling in their lines only to "come up with a handful of nothing." "In species after species, climate change is creating pressures that are depriving life-forms of their most essential survival tool: the ability to create new life and carry on their genetic lines." It dawns on her that we are part of a vast biotic community. And yet "as a culture, we do a very poor job of protecting, valuing, or even noting fertility – not just among humans but across life's spectrum." Because there are no corpses, just an absence – more handfuls of nothing. The hope lies in cultures that have kept alive their alternative way of seeing the world alive in the face of the bulldozers of colonialism and corporate globalization. Such are the cultures of Indigenous Peoples who are increasingly assuming leadership roles in environmental movements and in which nature is Mother Earth, a living organism which must be protected and nourished. What is emerging therefore is a new kind of reproductive rights movement, one fighting not only for the reproductive rights of women, but for the reproductive rights of the planet as a whole.

Naomi Klein begins her conclusion with a talk by Brad Werner, complex systems analyst, whose bottom line was: "global capitalism has made the depletion of resources so rapid, convenient, and barrier-free that 'earth-human systems' are becoming dangerously unstable." In other words, the earth is more or less f**cked. The one dynamic that offered some hope is resistance movements of people who "adopt a certain set of dynamics that does not fit within the capitalist culture."

Klein then reviews past social movements in history that had tremendous influence on how the dominant culture evolved: the human right movements, most prominently civil, women's, and gay and lesbian rights; the labor movement; postcolonial independence movements; the battle against apartheid in South Africa; and the movement for the abolition of slavery. While these movements were mostly, even hugely, successful, the economic side of these struggles was far less successful. But this failure to usher in a more equitable economic system is not a cause for inertia, much less for despair.

Klein suggests another way of looking at the track record: the fight for ecological justice represents "nothing less than the unfinished business of the most powerful liberation movements of the part two centuries, from civil rights to feminism to Indigenous sovereignty. . . . Climate change is our chance to right those festering wrongs at last – the unfinished business of liberation."

Naomi Klein has given us a panoramic view of the ecological crisis: the obstacles that stand in the way of a solution, the local outposts of resistance movements, the bold court challenges by Indigenous groups, the chock points to slow the expansion of fossil fuel companies, and the economic alternatives proposed and the ways of living being mapped out within planetary boundaries. Climate change is an existential threat. It is about changing the world – before the world changes so drastically that life itself is in danger of extinction.

Conclusion

In *A Secular Age,* Charles Taylor (2007) names the secular social imaginary "the immanent frame." It is a worldview that exists within a disenchanted world where supernatural beings and forces do not operate. Everything important is this-worldly, explicable on its own terms; everything fits within time-space-energy-matter dimensions. Social and political orders are constructed by humans for mutual benefit. Society is made up of individuals, and each is charged with finding his or her own way of being human. This "immanent frame" brought about tremendous advances in science and technology.

But the "immanent frame" of our secular age also narrowed our understanding of nature and the environment into products, commodities to be used, consumed, and discarded. There is nothing "sacred" about nature, nothing akin to a living organism about it. Nature is "there" for humans to use, abuse, and misuse for their benefit, for their profit, and even for their amusement.

The ecological crisis and the crisis in capitalism to which it is inseparably connected are not merely economic problems, much less are they simply technological difficulties waiting for technical adjustments. They are moral problems: they raise questions of right and wrong, of good and bad, of intention and malice. They are also spiritual issues: who are we as humans, what is nature in the final analysis, what is our relationship and responsibility as humans to later generations, to nature, and to our future.

To answer these questions, there must be a change in the modern social imaginary. And the change must come from outside the immanent frame. Lynn White (1967) is usually quoted as blaming arrogant Christianity for the ecological crisis, but his last words in the very same article are not:

> More science and technology are not going to get us out of the present ecological crisis until we find a new religion, or rethink our old one. . . . Possibly we should ponder the greatest radical in Christian history since Christ: Saint Francis of Assisi. . . . The key to an understanding of Francis is his belief in the virtue of humility – not merely for the individual but for man as a species. Francis tried to depose man from his monarchy over creation and set

up a democracy of all God's creatures. With him the ant is no longer simply a homily for the lazy, flames a sign of the thrust of the soul toward union with God; now they are Brother Ant and Sister Fire, praising the Creator in their own ways as Brother Man does in his. . . . His view of nature and of man rested on a unique sort of panpsychism of all things animate and inanimate, designed for the glorification of their transcendent Creator, who, in the ultimate gesture of cosmic humility, assumed flesh, lay helpless in a manger, and hung dying on a scaffold.

Today another Francis, Pope Francis, is sounding the call against a predatory capitalism that is worshipped like a sacred calf and for the care of Mother Earth, our sister and common home, in his encyclical *Laudato Si'*. Our responsibilities extend across time and space, and they include the entirety of creation. We are united in solidarity not only within generations but also between generations, not only with our fellow human beings but with the whole earth and all its creatures.

13

FROM POLITICAL THEOLOGY TO POLITICAL PHILOSOPHY, AND BACK

The Stillborn God: Religion, Politics, and the Modern West, by Mark Lilla. New York: Knopf, 2007.

9/11 destroyed the perception of and attitude towards religion as a wholly benign phenomenon, healing the pains and sorrows of the individual, succoring the loneliness and emptiness of life, gathering people to bring about justice and peace in benighted communities, and promising the rewards and happiness of the afterlife. In one fell swoop, religion showed its violent and ugly face, moving the perpetrators of 9/11 to kill and die for God, murdering at least three thousand innocent lives, causing unimaginable pain to husbands, wives, children, and relatives, and wreaking havoc on a city harboring people of different races, religions, and ethnicities.

I have been teaching the anthropology and sociology of religion on and off for the past twenty years. After 9/11, I could sense a palpable urgency on the part of my students to make sense of violence committed in God's name, of terrorism carried out in the name of religion. Is religion inherently violent? What are the causes of religious violence? How do we tame violence committed in the name of God? I picked up Mark Lilla's book in expectation to find some answers to these questions. I found the first chapters engrossing, but I finished the book disappointed.

Mark Lilla's book may well be subtitled "from political theology to political philosophy, and back," although he leaves the return of political theology hanging in the air. Religion being the system of ultimate meaning, it is no wonder that peoples in all societies and cultures appeal to religion for the final explanation of life, its origins and destiny, as well as, of the world, how it should be ruled and governed. From the pervasiveness of political theology, Lilla studies the emergence of political theory, the attempt to explain politics and government, severed from the claims of a deity. Thus ensued what he calls "the Great Separation."

This was a historical breakthrough. Religions, especially those that make universalistic and monopolistic truth claims, are subject to the totalitarian temptation, i.e., to baptize all nations, to make believers of all people. Religions actually become totalitarian when they are wedded to political power. Leviticus tells me that homosexuality is an abomination. If I had the political power to eradicate this abomination, why should I not eliminate all homosexuals from the face of the earth? I limit myself to the history of the Catholic Church. Constantine legalizes Christianity; Theodosius makes it the official religion, and cross and sword become the ideological allies in uniting and maintaining the empire. Heresies and heretics disappear from the face of the earth. The Jews would have, too, were it not for St. Augustine's injunction for them to survive, but not to thrive. The *reconquista* of the Iberian Peninsula, torture and the Inquisition, the Crusades and the sack of Constantinople, colonization by Spain and Portugal became possible through the marriage of religion and political power. It could be said that the loss of the Papal States and, therefore, of the instruments of political power and coercion rendered impotent the totalitarian temptation for the Catholic Church. But it remains true that religious utopias, no less than secular utopias, can only be created through violence and bloodshed.

The accomplishment of Hobbes, Locke, and Hume, therefore, was a historical turning point. Liberal democracy breaks the alliance between religion and political power and, therefore, also the temptation of religion to turn to violence, even if it has happened so far successfully only in the West. Lilla's exposition of the thought of Thomas Hobbes, John Locke, and David Hume is highly interesting and enlightening. I do not have the expertise to quibble with the historical trajectory that he traces. But Lilla does not attend to what liberalism and democracy have become, even in advanced Western liberal and democratic societies. Liberalism extols the deracinated individual, severed from the social ties of family, community, and religion. Liberalism promotes an individualism that subverts commitment and community, and that wallows all too often in moral filth and degradation. Whereas democracy in the recent past tamed the cruelty of the market and distributed the benefits of capitalism, democracy today is subservient to the demands of capital and serves those who have the wherewithal to grease the democratic machine. One arrogance of American foreign policy is the promotion of U.S.-style liberal democracy when half of its citizens is alienated from it.

I am reminded of John Courtney Murray's contention that there are two kinds of liberalism, the Continental and the Anglo-Saxon. The former is the child of the absolutisms of church and state, and is marked by hostility to religion. Its goal is a completely secular society. The latter has a more benevolent attitude toward religion. The First Amendment of the U.S. Constitution forbids the establishment of religion at the same time that it allows its free exercise. The Founding Fathers were men of religious conviction, albeit of the deist kind. The American people, as a whole, are religious and do not find their religious convictions incompatible with the classic liberal values of human dignity and human liberty. It is no wonder that Murray, supported by the American bishops, became the theologian of religious liberty at Vatican II.

However, my impression is that American liberalism has moved to become indistinguishable from Continental liberalism with its deracinated individualism and moral relativism, with tolerance as its most objective value and sincerity its most redeeming quality. I do not very much like Cardinal Joseph Ratzinger giving a campaign speech for the papacy by denouncing contemporary society for "building a dictatorship of relativism that does not recognize anything as definitive and whose ultimate goal exists solely of one's ego and desires," but I think he has a point. Nor do I agree with his solution, which seems to me to be the re-concentration of ecclesiastical power in the Vatican, the denunciation of theological thought that is not in line with his without due process, the continuation and strengthening of an authoritarian and patriarchal church institution. He does not recognize that there is a dictatorship of absolutism that is equally, if not more, pernicious that the dictatorship of relativism. There is much to celebrate about the accomplishments of a liberal and democratic state, but there is also much to mourn about the evils it has spawned.

Lilla of course mentions Rosseau and Kant, and their attempts to restore a religious dimension to politics that is compatible with modernity. He discusses liberal Protestant theology as a response to the Great Separation, which itself was a response to the crisis of Christian political theology. But liberal theology's third way between Christian political theology and the Great Separation turned out to be a dead end, religiously and politically, with the two World Wars. Thus, *The Stillborn God*. Today, the achievement of a politics separate from theology remains a fragile construction, even in the West, and the temptations of political messianism remain strong, even in the West.

It is very frustrating to come to the end of Lilla's book. The preceding chapters prepared me to a satisfying denouement. But it ends with a thud. For one thing, he does not update his discussion of political theology. He does not mention the developments that came after and that were reactions to the "stillborn God" of liberal theology. There are no Niebuhrs, no Paul Tillich, Langdon Gilkey, Jurgen Moltmann, Dorothee Soelle in his narrative. Is he aware of Latin American liberation theology, black liberation theology, European political theology, feminist liberation theology, Asian and African liberation theologies, all political theologies that do not negate the great separation, but build on it to claim a legitimate democratic space in the public square? They are political theologies all right, but they issue the ancient call for biblical justice and reconciliation that is due the poor and oppressed, racial, ethnic and gender minorities, too often ignored even in liberal societies; they announce the tidings of peace amidst the wars and genocides of the twentieth century that have been perpetrated by the other side of the great separation.

For another thing, he does not bring his discussion to the present. He fails to analyze the religious fundamentalism that is sweeping the modern world. In the United States, arguably the most modern of nations, the religious right has captured the Republican Party. Hinduism and Buddhism have sprouted their own fundamentalist sects, and even suicide bombers at that. Needless to say, radical Islam has gone nihilistic. Why this resurgence? Following Lilla, is this not a response to the intended or unintended results of the Great Separation? Is not the reappearance of political theology a reaction to the dire consequences of political philosophy that has replaced it? Because he does not ask these questions, Lilla ends with a not very helpful peroration that those of us who have accepted the heritage of the Great Separation must rely on our own lucidity if our experiment is to work.

To be fair to Lilla, he has written an article, "The Politics of God," in the August 19, 2007, issue of *The New York Times Magazine*. In it, he notes that the twilight of the gods has been postponed with the reappearance of political theology. And we in the West are disturbed and confused. He counsels that we must keep in mind the two schools of thought about religion and politics: a political theology centered on God, and a political philosophy focused on man. We have learned Hobbes' lesson too well, but have failed to heed Rousseau, so we are in an intellectual bind as we encounter political theology today. Our complacent liberalism stands exposed to the passion of revolutionary messianism. He calls for a transformation of biblical faith, a renewal of political theology from within, but not for an examination of the excesses of liberal values, nor for a renewal of liberal faith that connects mundane lives to ultimate meanings. He has not yet gone far enough, I think.

Still and all, Mark Lilla's *The Stillborn God* is a valued read, and a good place to continue the discussion.

14

THE END OF THE DEVELOPMENT PROJECT?

The Global Development Crisis, by Benjamin Selwyn. Cambridge, UK: Polity Press, 2014, 248 pp.

The central paradox of the contemporary world, hence at the heart of the development crisis, is the simultaneous presence of wealth on an unprecedented scale, and mass poverty. Soon after the onset of the current global economic crisis, the World Bank estimated that its effects would generate from 50 million to 90 million more extreme poor in 2009 than expected before the crisis. Since then the crisis has deepened and shows little sign of abating. The plight of the global poor contrasts with the fortunes of the world's 100 richest persons who, in 2012 alone, became $241 billion richer. Oxfam calculates that this $241 billion would be enough to end extreme poverty (those living under US$1.25 a day) four times over.

Whatever happened to the development project? Development as a concept and as a project started soon after World War II when President Harry Truman announced a "fair deal" for the entire world, especially for the poor and suffering peoples of the "underdeveloped areas." With the decolonization of African countries in the 1960s and the formation of the Third World, the United Nations declared the 1960s as the Development Decade and President John F. Kennedy launched the Alliance for Progress. Underlying all these efforts was the Keynesian emphasis, learned from the Great Depression, on the state in both developed and underdeveloped countries as the driver of development: the former would provide the funds and technical expertise, and the latter had the task of undertaking development projects. The state would reappear later as the "developmental state," deemed responsible for the economic success of Japan and East Asia, and for the phenomenal growth of China's economy.

A shift occurred in the 1970s when free market ideas gained ascendancy under the flag of neoliberalism. The "Washington Consensus" soon mandated liberalization, privatization, and deregulation of economies as the surest path to growth and prosperity. The international agencies of Bretton Woods meant to provide stability for the world economy and to prevent another Great Depression were corralled to integrate national economies into an economy now become global and to impose the necessary discipline to maintain such free-market integration. Newly unfettered financial markets began to metastasize with newfangled financial instruments that transformed the global economy into a global casino, where the tidal waves of money were primarily speculation and debt. Neoliberalism met its comeuppance in the United States, home to neoliberalism, with the Great Recession of 2008, which ironically did not become another Great Depression due to government infusions of cash.

These "state-centred" and "capital-centred" approaches to development constitute the background for the global development crisis that Benjamin Selwyn, Senior Lecturer in International Relations at the University of Sussex, studies. What these conceptions of development ignore are the laboring classes which are subordinated to the requirements of state and capital. A "labour-centred" development does not ignore the actions of state and market actors, but views their actions from the perspective of labor, interprets them as processes and outcomes of complex relations between social classes, and thus fosters labor's own vision of development. In this conception, laboring-class struggles are potentially developmental, contributing directly to improvements, both materially and in terms of generating more freedoms, of their lives and of their dependents and communities.

The bulk of Selwyn's volume is devoted to a masterful analysis of key development thinkers, representatives of the non-liberal political economy, scrutinized in light of a "labour-centred" development. Friedrich List, whose central insight was that economic development under capitalism requires an extensive role for the state in generating and directing resources, directly influenced the central strategy of late developing societies, e.g. Japan and the rest, as they attempted economic catch-up with already advanced countries. But catch-up development, even under statist political economy, also required heightened exploitation and hence labor repression. Karl Marx, after the collapse of really-existing socialism in Eastern Europe and the Soviet Union, was adopted, by many on left and right, for his alleged Eurocentrism and claimed as a prophet of capitalist globalization; he after all declared the double mission of England in India: the annihilation of Asiatic society and the laying of the material conditions of Western society in Asia. Selwyn offers an alternative reading, how for Marx global capitalism generated a global laboring class, and how capitalism's continued reproduction generated rival politics – of divide and rule by capital, and of international solidarity by labor. Marx was clear: "The emancipation of the working classes must be conquered by the working classes themselves."

Leon Trotsky and Alexander Gerschenkron advanced the insights and theories formulated by Marx and List respectively. Both men recognized that late developing countries potentially possessed a "privilege" of backwardness which could enable them, under certain circumstances to leap over more advanced nations. Against linear concepts of development, both understood the unevenness of development and therefore utilized a dialectical approach to international development. Gerschenkron identified the role of institutions in realizing the advantages of backwardness, while Trotsky, aware of the disruptions engendered by catch-up strategies, identified how they could be turned to opportunities, not for capitalist industrialization but for socialist revolution. But a more fundamental divergence occurs between them: Labor repression was normatively and prescriptively advocated by the followers of Gerschenkron, while for Trotsky, such repression represented resistance and provided the opportunity to organize workers and peasants into potentially revolutionary movements that could pursue an alternative form of development. For this reason, for Selwyn, Trotsky's conception of development is ultimately superior to Gerschenkron's.

Joseph Schumpeter's concept of creative destruction explains how industrial innovations reshape capitalism. But it strips away two concerns: how capitalism is constituted by exploitative class relations, and how national economies exist in and operate through the capitalist world system. Schumpeter's creative destruction, therefore, is not useful in examining the dynamics of capitalist competition on a global scale and in comprehending the processes of global stratification and inequality. For Karl Polanyi, "to allow the market mechanism to be sole director of the fate of human beings and their natural environment . . . would result in the demolition of society." Human freedoms could only be realized and protected if society was able to subordinate the market to its democratically formed objectives. Selwyn argues that "Polanyi's institutionalist analysis and sharp critique of liberal economics contributes to the endeavour of creating such a society," but "it is most effective when completed by Marx's more fundamental critique of capitalism and vision of socialism.... [O]ne of Polanyi's central concerns, the prevalence of poverty under capitalism, can better be comprehended by conceptualizing commodification and exploitation as two interrelated, rather than mutually exclusive processes and relations."

Amartya Sen proposes a radically different vision of development, understood as a process of human flourishing. Development is expanding human freedoms both as goals and means of development. But Sen undermines his bold alternative route to human development, "by wedding his vision to a conception of capitalist markets as spheres of freedom." Selwyn holds that instead "Marxist political economy bases itself on the self-activity of the masses and the conviction that it is through such activity that capitalism can be transcended – into a system where development really is a process of a continual expansion of freedom for all." I suppose that Selwyn would apply the same critique to Martha Nussbaum who shares with Sen a capabilities approach to human development, with two distinctive traits: she focuses on women in the Third World, and she offers a universal listing of human capabilities. Selwyn's critique would also be true of the Human Development Index (HDI), which Sen helped to formulate, and which comprehends the development process as one based on increases in life expectancy, education, and income of populations.

There is much to learn from Benjamin Selwyn's critical engagement with thinkers who have formulated alternatives to neoliberal development theory and practice, especially as the latter are floundering in the current economic crisis. Except for Marx and Trotsky, Selwyn faults them all for failing to recognize the exploitative nature of capitalism and for subordinating laboring classes to its imperatives. Accordingly, in his last chapter, Selwyn presents the contours of a Marxist, labor-centered conception of development where labor generates its own democratic developmental trajectory against and beyond capital. It entails three steps: first, it understands policies and strategies of state and capital as results of and responses to the dialectic of capital-labor relations; second, it views such actions from the perspective of their impacts on workers' human development; and third, it takes sides with laboring classes, theoretically and politically, by illustrating potential weaknesses of states and capital that could be used by workers to democratically enhance their human developmental potential.

The struggle against capitalist exploitation is long and hard. As Michael Burawoy ("For a Sociological Marxism: The Complementary Convergence of Antonio Gramsci and Karl Polanyi," *Politics and Society*

31:2, June 2003, p. 251) puts it: "The socialist transition [or to a better economic system] can no longer be understood as the collapse of an entire order to be replaced by a completely new one. It no longer springs from the coincidence in time and space, of economic contradiction, class struggle, and the seeds of the new. Nor will the socialist transition of tomorrow be centered on the nation-state alone, but will include local struggles, of disparate kinds, connected across national boundaries . . . This calls for a new type of Marxist, not the legislator of classical Marxism who would formulate the laws of the collapse of capitalism, or the organic intellectuals of a working class revolution, but the ethnographic archeologist who seeks out local experiments, new institutional forms, real utopias if you wish, who places them in their context, translates them into a common language, and links them one to another across the globe."

Similarly, Selwyn writes that labor's struggle against capitalism takes myriad forms and has many outcomes. It often mainly results in "inroads" and "encroachments" into capital's power over labor, as his cases from China, South Korea, Northeast Brazil, Venezuela, Bolivia, Egypt, and Argentina illustrate. But they offer hope that "another world is possible." Selwyn's volume is a welcome, needed, and valuable contribution to international development studies. Besides, it is well-written and organized.

15

POPE FRANCIS, IDOLATRY, AND CAPITALISM: A SUMMATION

In his Apostolic Exhortation on the Proclamation of the Gospel in Today's World, *Evangelii Gaudium,* The Joy of the Gospel, Pope Francis (2013a: nos. 50-60) punctuated his analysis of the contemporary "signs of the times" with successive "nos:" "no to an economy of exclusion," "no to the new idolatry of money," "no to a financial system which rules rather than serves," and "no to inequality that spawns violence." The Pope elaborated by pointing out that "such an economy [of exclusion] kills," that in the new idolatry of money "man is reduced to one of his needs alone: consumption," that financial experts and political leaders need to ponder the words of St. John Chrysostom: "Not to share one's wealth with the poor is to steal from them and to take away their livelihood," and that "unbridled consumerism combined with inequality proves doubly damaging to the social fabric; inequality inevitably engenders a violence which recourse to arms cannot and never will be able to resolve."

Pope Francis addresses economic issues under the overarching concept of idolatry. The greatest sin in the Bible is not atheism, the denial of God, but idolatry, the worship of false gods. The main point of Pope Francis is that we have come to worship profit over people, we idolize money before poor people's welfare, health, and lives, we reverence consumerism even if it results in inequality and violence, we sacrifice the planet at the altar of the "invisible hand" of the almighty market. "The return of the Golden Calf," William Cavanaugh (2015: 699) notes, marks an important shift from Vatican II's (1965) *Gaudium et Spes*, on theories of secularization, and therefore in Catholic social teaching. "Francis virtually never talks about the contemporary economy without leveling the charge of idolatry, a charge absent from the discussion of economics in *GS* and almost entirely absent from Vatican II as a whole." Francis therefore represents another advance in the development of theological ethics.

Secularization in the 1960s was understood as the result of structural differentiation and functional specialization The social structures of society were undergoing a continuing process of differentiation such that they were becoming more autonomous, rational, and neutral in terms of their own specific integrity, values, and norms. It was, in the image of Max Weber, a process of disenchantment: what was once embedded in the sacred realm was coming to exist on its own secular terms. Understood this way, secularization was a positive process; it was giving to the secular, the world, its own God-given integrity, autonomy, and rationality, subject to its own laws, values, and norms. Secularization, at the same time, was concomitantly understood as the displacement of religion from its central, public, and governing place in society, to be relegated to its proper private spiritual sphere, and perhaps eventually – mistakenly, it turned out – to its decline and disappearance in modern society.

This was the situation when Vatican II convened. This was the intellectual atmosphere in which *Gaudium et Spes* was drafted, debated upon, and finally approved. Chapter III of *Gaudium et Spes* is devoted to Socio-Economic Life. The themes touched upon hew to the main lines of papal social pronouncements, with the dignity of the human person as its *leitmotif*. Among its topics: economic development in the service of and under the control of the human person; the elimination of growing inequalities between people, sectors of the economy, and nations; the promotion of the dignity of labor and its participation in profits and decision-making; the proper concept of private property and the common purpose of created things; attention to the needs of underdeveloped nations, support for land reform, no discrimination against immigrants, and the care for the poor. The chapter is marked by the conviction that there are problems of the economy, but they can and should be addressed by sincere and rational persons. The role of the Church was to offer guiding principles that stake out the limits of the moral order. It was by respecting the integrity, autonomy, and rationality of secular society, its laws, norms, and values that religion would retain its relevance in the world. It was also by recognizing its limitations in the secular world that the Catholic Church can continue to play a role in the modern world to which it was establishing a rapprochement. But there are lines in the chapter which are prescient:

"Many people, especially in economically advanced areas, seemed to be hypnotized, as it were, by economics, so that almost their entire personal and social life is permeated with a certain economic outlook. These people can be found both in nations which favor a collective economy as well as in others."

The "secularization thesis" of the 1960s has, of course, been abandoned. Jay Tolson (2015) in his editorial on the special issue of *The Hedgehog Review* on Re-Enchantment puts it well: "But facts on the ground, including certain epochal events, defied received ideas and theories. Not only did religions and religious passions reassert themselves around the world (in both inspiring and terrifying ways), but growing doubts about the overly reductive claims of scientific reason opened the door to new understandings of cause and value, and of their possible connections. If the world had been truly disenchanted in the first place, was it now undergoing a kind of re-enchantment? . . . At the very least, we appear to have entered a liminal age, poised somewhere between the secular and the postsecular . . ."

There are many kinds of re-enchantment, as evidenced in the special issue of *The Hedgehog Review*. But I am interested in the re-enchantment involved in the migration of the sacred to areas of life, previously thought of and celebrated as totally secular, specifically to that of neoliberal economics and the neoliberal economy. Because of this economic re-enchantment, commodities, following Karl Marx, are not only the ones fetishized, but so are economic ideas and theories, most especially the "invisible hand" of the market. Not only are they fetishized, re-enchantment ideologizes them, sacralizes them, and idolizes them. They become, as it were, the font of divine economic wisdom, the unquestioned workings of divine economic providence. This enchanted economics and economy have no need of economic history, economic sociology, and political economy, nor are they based on empirical observation, experimentation, and research. Their theoretical justifications and policy prescriptions emanate, I suppose, from the mathematical equations and abstract deductions revealed to their founding fathers from on high. This re-enchanted economics and economy are the "golden calf" of modern society.

In the words of Pope Francis (2013a: no. 55-56):

> We have created new idols. The worship of the ancient golden calf (cf. *Ex* 32:1-35) has returned in a new and ruthless guise in the idolatry of money and the dictatorship of an impersonal economy lacking a true human purpose. The worldwide crisis affecting finance and the economy lays bare their imbalances and, above all, their lack of real

concern for human beings; man is reduced to one of his needs alone: consumption. . . In this system, which tends to devour everything which stands in the way of increased profits, whatever is fragile, like the environment, is defenseless before the interests of a deified market, which become the only rule.

This is the background and the basis of Pope Francis' persistent denunciation of economic idolatry. As Cavanaugh (2015: 707, 714) puts it: "Economics is perhaps the area in which the breakdown of the neat distinction between enchanted, sacred religion on the one hand and the disenchanted, profane secular on the other is most apparent. . . .[T]here has been a migration of the holy from the church to the world, such that capitalism, for example is best understood not as devoid of gods but as a new type of – often idolatrous – religion." Cavanaugh (2015: 699) adds: "Francis represents an opportunity to shift Catholic discourse about secularization, an opportunity with implications for the way we look not only at economics but at other secular phenomena as well. Progressive Catholic thought in the period of the Second Vatican Council tended to view the secular world as disenchanted. Francis has suggested, on the contrary, that we are faced not so much with a loss of faith as with a new religion, an idolatrous faith. Such an approach could open up new possibilities for a theological response to secularization. . . . [T]he theological lens of idolatry can be a productive way to approach secularization generally and economy more particularly."

Before I end, it is worth recalling the most trenchant criticism ever made of the capitalist economic system, that of the much-condemned Karl Marx, although Marx himself spoke of capitalism as the most powerful solvent of enchantment: "All that is solid melts into the air; all that is holy is profaned." Moreover, whatever severe criticism he made of capitalism, Marx looked at it kindly and positively as the necessary stage in the historical development towards communism. Still, it is worth understanding once more his acute and resonant analysis of capitalism. First, Marx identified the fetishism of commodities as the central structural problem of capitalism. Man is *homo faber:* he makes products for his use, he controls the products of his own labor. With capitalism, man now produces products for exchange, in exchange for money. The products become commodities; they acquire an independent existence apart from the human labor that made them. They are reified, they are esteemed no longer for their use-value but for their exchange-value. The development of commodities, Marx labeled, as the fetishism of commodities – the attribution of magical power to fabricated things – by which workers forget that it is their labor that gives value to commodities. A person who has a sexual fetish, for example, believes that it is the fetish that has power over him, that arouses and gratifies him.

Marx originally linked fetishism to alienation: people lose control of their own labor and in the process lose the sources of their own selfhood. "The life which he has given to the object sets itself against him as an alien and hostile force;" it confronts him as alien power. Later on, as Eugene McCarraher (2015: 90) puts it, "the *anima* of capitalist animism in Marx's anatomy of [capitalist] enchantment shifted from estranged labor to money ... Marx portrays money as the ontological foundation of a uniquely pecuniary way of being in the world – a metaphysics of money that resembles and supplants traditional forms of enchantment. On one level, money is another marker of alienation: Like divinity, it betokens 'the alienated ability of mankind.' . . . Having drowned religious faith in the arctic of pecuniary reason, money becomes 'the almighty being,' the 'truly creative power,' the *de facto* ontological basis of reality in capitalist civilization. 'The power of money in bourgeois society' extends farther and deeper than the market in commodities; like the God of Genesis, it brings things into being from nothing, and consigns all indigent objects and desires to the void of nonexistence." If I don't have money, I am nothing. If I have money, I am everything.

Read the words of Marx (Ritzer 1988: 53) himself:

> That which is for me through the medium of *money* – that for which I can pay (i.e., which money can buy) – that am *I*, the possessor of the money. The extent of the power of money is the extent of my power. Money's properties are my properties and essential powers – the properties and powers of its possessor. Thus, what I *am* and *am capable* is by no means determined by my individuality. I *am* ugly, but I can buy for myself the most *beautiful* of women. Therefore I am not *ugly,* for the effect of *ugliness* – its deterrent power – is nullified by money. I, as an individual, am *lame,* but money furnishes me with twenty-four feet. Therefore, I am not lame. I am bad, dishonest, unscrupulous, stupid; but money is honored, and hence its possessor. Money is the supreme good; therefore its possessor is good. Money, besides, saves me the trouble of being dishonest: I am therefore presumed honest. I am *stupid,* but money is the *real mind* of all things, and how then should its possessor be stupid? Besides, he can buy talented people for himself, and is he who has power over

the talented not more talented than the talented? Do not I, who thanks to money am capable of *all* that the human heart longs for, possess all human capacities? Does not money, therefore, transform all my incapacities into their contrary?

Thus, Eugene McCarraher (2015: 89) argues that, as far as the capitalist economy is concerned, "we have never been disenchanted:" the "waters of pecuniary reason constituted a baptismal font, a consecration of capitalism, as a covert form of enchantment, all the more beguiling on account of its apparent profanity." What Pope Francis is doing, therefore, is disenchanting capitalism, revealing the false worship of the capitalist Golden Calf.

16

THE U.S. PRESIDENTIAL ELECTION OF 2016: INITIAL THOUGHTS

Against the expectations of all and shocking to most, Donald Trump won the presidency of the United States in 2016. It was a victory through the U.S. Constitutional quirk of the Electoral College because he lost the popular vote by 2.9 million. How to explain his wholly surprising victory, given especially his campaign that fed on fear and hate, with his future tenure therefore fraught with uncertainty, apprehension, and dangers. Trump's victory is usually attributed to the wave of populism that is sweeping across the West, which *Foreign Affairs* (2016) featured on its cover even before the elections. It is the revolt of the masses against elites, it is said, who have been disregarded, if not dismissed, by the political powers that be. Trump's constituency, it is pointed out, is the white working class, the quintile in the stratification system who fall between the poor below and the middle class above, who have been disadvantaged by technology and globalization, who have been the losers and victims of the wrenching changes brought about by the twin structural transformations human society is currently undergoing: the change from agricultural to industrial to post-industrial society, and the transformation of capitalism from competitive to corporate to global financial economic system (Litonjua 1999).

They blame government for their economic woes. They rage at government. They accuse government of not only ignoring them, but of coddling the poor, women, immigrants, and ethnic minorities. They are "strangers in their own land," they tell Arlie Hochschild (2016) who interviewed them in Southwest Louisiana. They are nostalgic about the past, when factories dotted the landscape of America, and when manufacturing jobs afforded their families a decent way of life. They despise their political leaders in Washington, and their contempt reached its nadir at the first African American President, egged on by trash-talk radio they listen to.

What they do not realize is that in a global age, corporations, not governments, have become the main economic actors. Governments, if truth be told, are subservient to them, attracting them to invest in their countries through tax cuts and other amenities. Corporations roam the borderless global economy in a relentless search for the lowest costs and the highest profits. This is the main reason for the deindustrialization of America, for the loss of manufacturing jobs, and for the lowering of the standard of living of the working class. The old jobs are not coming back, and if they do come back, they will be different manufacturing jobs. The new manufacturing jobs will demand more skills and education. Structural transformations demand adjustments and accommodations on the part of individuals. And the new manufacturing jobs will need less manpower, because they will involve advanced technology, like computers and robotics. It is a new reality for the working class and, for that matter, for everybody else.

It is well to remember, as Robert Kuttner (2016) reminds us, to know the difference between envy and jealousy. Envy is about two people, jealousy is about three people. In the same spirit, John Judis (2016) draws a useful distinction between right-wing populism and left-wing populism: "Leftwing populists champion the people against an elite or an establishment. Theirs is a vertical politics of the bottom and middle arrayed against the top. Rightwing populists champion the people against the elite that they accuse of coddling a third group, which can consist, for instance, of immigrants, Islamists, or African American militants. Leftwing populism is dyadic. Rightwing populism is triadic. It looks upward, but also down upon an out-group."

The populism that elected Trump was not motivated by envy but fueled by jealousy. People were angry at economic and political elites not for the simple reason that they appropriated the wealth and prosperity of the country for themselves, but that, according to their frenzied vision, part of the loot was siphoned off to help the "undeserving other:" the poor, women, immigrants, minorities, who are for the most part nonwhite, unlike them. Thus, the underlying factor in Trump's victory is the issue of race. Trump's candidacy and victory were explicit reactions to the fact of a black president and could only have followed the tenure of a black president. "Make America great again" was his slogan. It was a dog-whistle for "Make America *white* again" (Young 2016). It was dubbed "white nationalism." It was a cruder and baser rehash of Richard Nixon's "Southern strategy:" emphasize the resentment against the North for its "war of aggression" against the South, harp on punishing Democrats for passing the Civil Rights Act and Voting Rights Act, and stoke the hatred for the black slave, the quintessential "other" in American society and history now become an uppity person.

With the election of Barack Obama in 2008 half of the country went bonkers. With his reelection in 2012, they went "bonkier."

The contrast could not be sharper. As word of Obama's election in 2008 spread across social media, students at Brown University, my alma mater, gathered at the Quad to sing the National Anthem, God Bless America, and I'm Proud To Be An American, if I remember right, after which they quietly slipped back to their dorms. I am sure they were relieved and hopeful that Bush II's disastrous presidency had finally come to an end. "It could happen only in America," people usually said, "A member of a race that we dehumanized, enslaved, and segregated has been elected President of these United States." It was an expression of wonder and amazement and admiration for the country.

In the South, however, where I found myself in 2013, the atmosphere was toxic. "I had not in my wildest dream expected a black man to be elected president in my lifetime," a passing acquaintance told me. Donald Trump and the newly formed Tea Party questioned his birth and therefore his legitimacy. He was portrayed as a monkey, a degenerate black. They compared him to Hitler, labeled him a socialist. They attacked not only his policies but his person. They blamed him personally for their problems and their deteriorating social conditions. Mitch McConnell, Senate Republican leader, with Eric Cantor, Paul Ryan, Jim DeMint, and Newt Gingrich, gathered his minority caucus to plan how to thwart the new president: no cooperation, no compromise, opposition to him at every turn, refusal to give him any legislative victory, determination to make him a one-term president. It was obstruction for the sake of obstruction, a "forever war," Paul Roberts (2014: 193- 224) calls it. They were bent on destroying him even before he started his tenure. It would be an eight-year campaign of racial intransigence against the leader of the free world. It was a far cry from the words of the great President of the Philippine Commonwealth, Manuel Quezon: My loyalty to my party ends where my loyalty to my country begins.

Donald Trump appears on the political stage as a knight in shining armor, ready to do battle for the working class, to make them great again. His supporters and followers lap it up. But in reality he is a buffoon, an egomaniac, a hustler – and a racist, sexist, and homophobic bully, one who seeks to dominate and to erode the victim's sense of self-worth. They do not care if he is a billionaire who does not pay taxes, who ridicules by imitating a journalist with a disability, who gropes women and grabs their pussies, who would ban Muslims from the United States, who would build a wall across the south to stop immigrants, to mention only his most egregious remarks. It was weird, to say the least, the working class reposing its hopes and future on a man who has taken advantage of the opportunities for outsourcing and offshoring his business interests provided by globalization, who has manipulated the loopholes he found in the tax, economic, and political systems to enrich himself and his family – nefarious activities that in the final analysis have impoverished the very working class now rooting for him.

He promised to make America *white* again, and they responded:

58 % of white voters;

67 % of non-college whites;

49 % of whites with college degrees;

63 % of white men;

53 % of white women;

80 % of white evangelicals, and even

60 % of white Catholics.

And now we know that Russia was engaged in hacking the electoral process to damage Clinton and to favor Trump. Was there collusion between Russia and the Trump campaign to thwart the American democratic process? FBI Director James Comey already intervened to announce the reopening of his investigations into Hillary Clinton's emails eleven days before the elections, an intervention reminiscent of Edgar Hoover's many political shenanigans, that was denounced by both Republicans and Democrats. But he refused to say whether there were FBI investigations into Donald Trump, and there were, we now know. Fake news, false claims, so-called "alternative" facts were spread by trash talk radio, and books on alleged improprieties and health issues of Clinton were written by hack authors. So whose presidency can now be marred by the claim of illegitimacy? Trump claims massive voter fraud – without any evidence – to explain his 2.9 million defeat in the popular vote, but considers his narrow Electoral College victory a triumph to crow about.

More importantly, how will the American Catholic Church react? Will its leadership be supportive of or at least be passive before the policy initiatives of the Trump administration, considering that the majority of white Catholics voted for him? Will the bishops, most of whom were appointed during the tenures of John Paul II and Benedict XVI, be content in lieu of the promise of Trump to oppose abortion, to defund Planned Parenthood, to repeal Obamacare with its hated contraception mandate, and to promote religious liberty? Or will the leadership of the American Catholic Church heed the call of Bishop Robert McElroy (2017), appointed Bishop of San Diego by Pope Francis, to become "disruptors" and "rebuilders?"

> We must all become disruptors. We must disrupt those who would seek to send troops into our streets to deport the undocumented, to rip mothers and fathers from their families. We must disrupt those who portray refugees as enemies rather than our brothers and sisters in terrible need. We must disrupt those who train us to see Muslim men, women and children as forces of fear rather than as children of God. We must disrupt those who seek to rob our medical care, especially from the poor. We must disrupt those who would take even food stamps and nutrition assistance from the mouths of children.
>
> But we, as people of faith, as disciples of Jesus Christ, as children of Abraham, as followers of the Prophet Muhammad, as people of all faiths and no faith, we cannot merely be disruptors, we also have to be rebuilders.
>
> We have to rebuild this nation so that we place at its heart the service to the dignity of the human person and assert what the American flag behind us asserts is our heritage: Every man, woman and child is equal in this nation and called to be equal.

We must rebuild a nation in solidarity, what Catholic teaching calls the sense that all of us are the children of the one God, there are no children of a lesser god in our midst. That all of us are called to be cohesive and embrace one another and see ourselves as graced by God. We are called to rebuild our nation which does pay $15 an hour in wages, and provides decent housing, clothing and food for those who are poorest. And we need to rebuild our Earth, which is so much in danger by our own industries.

Most importantly, what is in store for us all and for the country? A trade war with China? Another Great Depression? A new Cold War? A nuclear conflict with North Korea and Iran? God forbid! But we have to remember: He who shows fear, reaps war. He who sows hate, reaps death. He who sows the wind, reaps the whirlwind!

REFERENCES

Abaya, Hernando J. 1967. *The Untold Philippine Story.* Quezon City, Philippines: Malaya Books.
Abbott, Walter M., S.J., ed. 1966. *The Documents of Vatican II.* Piscataway, NJ: New Century Publishers.
Abeyta, Loring. 2015. "Cloying book skirts damage Serra wrought," *National Catholic Reporter,* September 25-October 8.
Agoncillo, Teodoro A., and Milagros C. Guerrero. 1977. *History of the Filipino People,* 5th ed. Quezon City, Philippines: R.P. Garcia Publishing.
Ahern, Kevin. 2015. "Follow the Footnotes," *America,* June 18.
Allen, John, Jr. 2012. "Translated Final Interview with Martini," *National Catholic Reporter,* September 4.
Anderson, Benedict. 1995. "Cacique Democracy in the Philippines." In *Discrepant Histories: Translocal Essays on Philippine Cultures,* ed. by Vicente L. Rafael. Philadelphia, PA: Temple University Press.
Anderson, Gerald H. 1969. "Providence and Politics behind Protestant Missionary Beginnings in the Philippines." In *Studies in Philippine Church History,* ed. by Gerald H. Anderson. Ithaca, NY: Cornell University Press.
Annett, Anthony. 2016a. "Ted Cruz or Pope Francis?" *Commonweal,* March 28.
----------. 2016b. "Catholic Republicans Are Implicated in the Rise of Donald Trump," *Commonweal,* March 9.
----------. 2015. "The Next Step: How Laudato si' Extends Catholic Social Teaching," *Commonweal,* July 7.
Armstrong, Karen. 2014a. "The Myth of Religious Violence," *The Guardian,* September 25.
----------. 2014b. *Fields of Blood: Religion and the History of Violence.* New York: Knopf.

Avram, Wes, ed. 2004. *Anxious about Empire: Theological Essays on the New Global Realities*. Grand Rapids, MI: Brazos Press.

Bain, David Haward. 1984. *Sitting in Darkness: Americans in the Philippines*. Boston: Houghton Mifflin.

Balmer, Randall. 2014. "The Real Origins of the Religious Right," *Politico*, May 27.

Bartlett, W.B. 1999. *God Wills It! An Illustrated History of the Crusades*. Great Britain: Sutton Publishing.

Bayly, C.A. 2004. *The Birth of the Modern World 1870-1914: Global Connections and Comparisons*. Oxford: Blackwell.

Beech, Hannah. 2014. "The Power of One: Xi Jinping, China's strongest leader in years, aims to propel his nation to the top of the world order," *Time*, November 17.

Beisner, Robert L. 1968. *Twelve against Empire: The Anti-Imperialists, 1898-1900*. New York: McGraw-Hill.

Bellah, Robert N. 2012. "The Heritage of the Axial Age." In *The Axial Age and Its Consequences*, ed. by Robert N. Bellah and Hans Jonas. Cambridge, MA: Harvard University Press.

----------. 2011. *Religion in Human Evolution: From the Paleolithic to the Axial Age*. Cambridge, MA: Harvard University Press.

----------. 2004. "The New American Empire: The Likely Consequences of the 'Bush Doctrine.'" In *Anxious about Empire: Theological Essays on the New Global Realities*, ed. by Wes Avram. Grand Rapids, MI: Brazos Press.

Berger, Peter L. 1999. "The Desecularization of the World: A Global Overview." In *The Desecularization of the World: Resurgent Religion and World Politics*, ed. by Peter L. Berger. Washington, DC: Ethics and Public Policy Center.

----------.1969. *The Sacred Canopy: Elements of a Sociological Theory of Religion*. Garden City, NY: Doubleday.

Berger, Peter L., and Thomas Luckmann. 1967. *The Social Construction of Reality: A Treatise in the Sociology of Knowledge*. Garden City, NY: Anchor Books.

Berry, Jason. 2011. *Render unto Rome: The Secret Life of Money in the Catholic Church*. New York: Crown.

Berry, Jason, and Gerald Renner. 2004. *Vows of Silence: The Abuse of Power in the Papacy of John Paul II*. New York: Free Press.

Berry, Thomas. 1992. *The Dream of the Earth*. San Francisco, CA: HarperCollins.

Berry, Wendell. 1978. *The Unsettling of America: Culture and Agriculture*. New York: Avon Books.

Blanchette, Oliva. 2003. *Philosophy of Being: A Reconstructive Essay in Metaphysics.* Washington, DC: Catholic University of America Press, 115-144 Boff, Leonardo. 1997. *Cry of the Earth, Cry of the Poor.* Maryknoll, NY: Orbis Books.

----------. 1995. *Ecology and Liberation: A New Paradigm.* Maryknoll, NY: Orbis Books.

Borg, Marcus J., and John Dominic Crossan. 2007. *The First Christmas: What the Gospels Really Teach about Jesus' Birth.* HarperOne.

Brands, H.W. 1992. *Bound to Empire: The United States and the Philippines.* New York: Oxford University Press.

Breslin, Jimmy. 2004. *The Church That Forgot Christ.* New York: Free Press.

Briggs, Kenneth. A. 1992. *Holy Siege: The Year That Shook Catholic America.* HarperSan Francisco.

Brinkley, Alan, Frank Freidel, Richard N. Current, and T. Harry Williams. 1991. *American History: A Survey.* New York: McGraw-Hill.

Brown, Jerry. 2016. "A Stark Nuclear Warning," *The New York Review of Books,* July 14.

Brown, Raymond E., S.S. 1997. *An Introduction to the New Testament.* New York: Doubleday.

----------. 1994. *The Death of the Messiah: From Gethsemane to the Grave: A Commentary on the Passion Narratives of the Four Gospels,* 2 vols. New York: Doubleday.

----------. 1993. *The Birth of the Messiah: A Commentary on the Infancy Narratives in the Gospels of Matthew and Luke,* new updated edition. New York: Doubleday.

Bruno, Kenny, and Joshua Karliner. 2002. *Earthsummit.biz: The Corporate Takeover of Sustainable Development.* Oakland, CA: Food First Books.

Burns, James MacGregor. 2013. *Fire and Light: How the Enlightenment Transformed our World.* New York: St. Martin's Press.

Butt, Yousaf. 2015. "How Saudi Wahhabism Is the Fountainhead of Islamic Terrorism," *The World Post,* March 22.

Carroll, James. 2014a. "Who Is Jesus Today?" *Harvard Divinity Bulletin* 42: 3/4 (Summer/Autumn).

----------. 2014b. *Christ Actually: The Son of God for the Secular Age.* New York: Viking.

----------. 2001. *Constantine's Sword: The Church and the Jews: A History.* New York: Houghton Mifflin.

Casanova, Jose. 2007. "The Great Separation," *The Immanent Frame,* SSRC, December 7.

Cavanaugh, William T. 2016. "Religious Violence as Modern Myth. In *Field Hospital: The Church's Engagement with a Wounded World*. Grand Rapids, MI: Eerdmans.

----------. 2015. "Return of the Golden Calf: Economy, Idolatry, and Secularization since *Gaudium et Spes*," *Theological Studies* 76:4 (December).

----------. 2009. *The Myth of Religious Violence: Secular Ideology and the Roots of Modern Conflict*. New York: Oxford University Press.

Choksy, Carol E.B., and Jamsheed K. Choksy. 2015. "The Saudi Connection: Wahhabism and Global Jihad," *World Affairs Journal*, May-June.

Clifford, Sister Mary Dorita, B.V.M. 1969. "Religion and the Public Schools in the Philippines: 1899-1906." In *Studies in Philippine Church History*, ed. by Gerald H. Anderson. Ithaca, NY: Cornell University Press.

Cloutier, David. 2015. "The Theological Heart of Laudato Si'," *Commonweal*, June 18.

Clymer, Kenton J. 1986. *Protestant Missionaries in the Philippines, 1898-1916: An Inquiry into the American Colonial Mentality*. Urbana, IL: University of Illinois Press.

Cobb, John, Jr. 1992. *Sustainability: Economics, Ecology, and Justice*. Maryknoll, NY: Orbis Books.

Cochran, Gregory, and Henry Harpending. 2009. *The 10,000 Year Explosion: How Civilization Accelerated Human Evolution*. New York: Basic Books.

Commonweal. 2016. The Editors: "Lights, Camera, Contraception? The USCCB's Dubious Take on Religious Liberty," May 17.

Conley, John J. 2015. "An Elusive Integral Ecology," *America*, August 3-10.

Constantino, Renato. 1978. *Neocolonial Identity and Counter-Consciousness: Essays on Cultural Decolonization*. White Plains, NY: M.E. Sharpe.

----------. 1975. *The Philippines: A Past Revisited*. Quezon City, Philippines: Tala Publishing.

Cox Harvey. 2016. *The Market as God*. Cambridge, MA: Harvard University Press.

----------. 1999. "The Market as God: Living in the New Dispensation," *The Atlantic*, March.

----------. 1988. *The Silencing of Leonardo Boff: The Vatican and the Future of World Christianity*. Oak Park, IL: Meyer-Stone Books.

Crooke, Alastair. 2016. "You Can't Understand ISIS If You Don't Know the History of Wahhabism in Saudi Arabia," *The World Post*, June 3.

----------. 2014. "Middle East Time Bomb: The Real Aim of Isis Is to Replace the Saud Family as the New Emirs of Arabia," *The World Post*, November 3.
Crosby, Michael H. 2014. "Evolutionary consciousness points to a Trinitarian cosmic order," *National Catholic Reporter*, June 6-19.
Crossan, John Dominic. 2010. *The Greatest Prayer: Rediscovering the Revolutionary Message of the Lord's Prayer*.
----------. 2007. *God's Empire: Jesus against Rome, Then and Now*. HarperSan Francisco.
Cullinane, Michael. 2003. *Ilustrado Politics: Filipino Elite Responses to American Rule, 1898-1908*. Loyola Heights, Quezon City: Ateneo de Manila University Press.
De la Costa, H., S.J. 1965. *Readings in Philippines History: Selected Historical Texts Presented with a Commentary*. Manila: Bookmark.
De la Vaissiere, Jean-Louis. 2015. "Two years and counting: Pope's opponents play waiting game," *Yahoo News*, March 12.
Desmond, Joan Frawley. 2013. "Bishop Tomas Tobin: Why I Switched to the Republican Party," *National Catholic Register*, October 24.
Dionne, E.J. 1996. *They Only Look Dead: Why Progressives Will Dominate the Next Political Era*. New York: Simon and Schuster.
Domning, Daryl P. 2001. "Evolution, Evil and Original Sin," *America*, November 12.
Duffy, Eamon. 2015. "Who Is the Pope?" *The New York Review of Books*, February 19.
----------. 2011. *Ten Popes Who Shook the World*. New Haven, CT: Yale University Press.
Economy, Elizabeth C. 2014. "China's Imperial President: Xi Jinping Tightens His Grip," *Foreign Affairs*, November/December.
Ehrman, Bart D. 2014. *How Jesus Became God: The Exaltation of a Jewish Preacher from Galilee*. HarperOne.
----------. 2003a. *Lost Christianities: The Battles for Scripture and the Faiths We Never Knew*. New York: Oxford University Press.
----------. 2003b. *Lost Scriptures: Books That Did not Make It into the New Testament*. New York: Oxford University Press.
Eichengreen, Barry, and Peter B. Kenen. 1994. "Managing the World Economy after the Bretton Woods System: An Overview." In *Managing the World Economy: Fifty Years after Bretton Woods*, ed. by Peter B. Kenen. Washington, DC: Institute for International Economics.
Eitzen, D. Stanley, and Maxine Baca Zinn. 1989. "The Forces Reshaping America." In *The Reshaping of America: Social Consequences of the*

Changing Economy, ed. by D. Stanley Eitzen and Maxine Baca Zinn. Englewood Cliffs, NJ: Prentice-Hall.
Elsbernd, Mary. 1995. "Whatever Happened to *Octogesima Adveniens?*" *Theological Studies* 56:1 (March).
Erickson, Jacob J. 2015. "Falling in Love with the Earth: Francis' Faithful Ecology," *Religion Dispatches*, June 19.
Etzioni, Amitai. 2015. "The Moral Effects of Economic Teaching," *Sociological Forum* 30:1 (March).
Faggioli, Massimo, 2016. "The Pope's Secretaries, from Capovilla to Ganswein," *Commonweal*, June 2.
----------. 2015. *Pope Francis: Tradition in Transition*. Mahwah, NJ: Paulist Press.
----------. 2014. *John XXIII: The Medicine of Mercy*. Collegeville, MN: Liturgical Press.
----------. 2012. *Vatican II: The Battle for Meaning*. Mahwah, NJ: Paulist Press.
Fallows, James. 2015. "The (Planet-Saving, Capitalism-Subverting, Surprisingly Lucrative) Investment Secrets of Al Gore," *The Atlantic*, November.
----------. 1987. "A Damaged Culture: A New Philippines?" *The Atlantic*, November.
Faroohar, Rana. 2016. "Saving Capitalism," *Time*, May 23.
Ferguson, Niall. 2004. *Colossus: The Price of America's Empire*. New York: Penguin.
Fidora, Alexander. 2012. "Augustine to Aquinas (Latin-Christian Authors)." In *The Oxford Handbook of Aquinas*, ed. by Brian Davies and Eleonore Stump. New York: Oxford University Press.
Finkelstein, Israel, and Neil Asher Silberman. 2001. *The Bible Unearthed: Archaeology's New Vision of Ancient Israel and the Origin of its Sacred Texts*. New York: Free Press.
Fiorenza, Francis Schussler. 2000. "The New Theology and Transcendental Thomism." In *Modern Christian Thought*, Volume II: The Twentieth Century, 2nd ed., ed. by James C. Livingston, Francis Schussler Fiorenza, with Sarah Coakley and James H. Evans, Jr. Upper Saddle River, NJ: Prentice Hall.
Fitzmyer, Joseph A., S.J. 2008. *The Interpretation of Scripture: In Defense of the Historical-Critical Method*. Mahwah, N.J.: Paulist Press.
Foreign Affairs. 2016. "The Power of Populism." November/December.
----------. 2014. "See America: Land of Decay and Dysfunction," September/October.
----------. 2012. "Is Europe Kaput?" September/October.

Fox, Matthew. 1991. *Creation Spirituality: Liberating Gifts for the People of the Earth*. San Francisco, CA: HarperSanFrancisco.

Francia, Luis H. 2010. *A History of the Philippines: From Indios Bravos to Filipinos*. New York: Overlook.

Fredriksen, Paula. 2012. *Sin: The Early History of an Idea*. Princeton, NJ: Princeton University Press.

----------. 2002. "The Birth of Christianity and the Origins of Christian Anti-Judaism." In *Jesus, Judaism, and Christian Anti-Judaism*, ed. by Paula Fredriksen and Adele Reinhartz. Louisville, KY: Westminster John Knox Press.

----------. 1988. *From Jesus to Christ: The Origins of the New Testament Images of Jesus*. New Haven, CT: Yale University Press.

Fredriksen, Paul, and Adele Reinhartz, ed. 2002. *Jesus, Judaism, and Christian Anti-Jusaism*. Louisville, KY: Westminster John Knox Press.

Freeman, Charles. 2008. *A.D. 381: Heretics, Pagans, and the Dawn of the Monotheistic State*. New York: Overlook Press.

Freire, Paulo. 1973. *Education for Critical Consciousness*. London: Sheed and Ward.

----------. 1971. *Pedagogy of the Oppressed*. New York: Herder and Herder.

Fukuyama, Francis. 1992. *The End of History and the Last Man*. New York: Farrar, Straus and Giroux.

----------. 1989. "The End of History?" *The National Interest* 16 (Summer).

Galbraith, James K. 2014. *The End of Normal: The Great Crisis and the Future of Growth*. New York: Simon and Schuster.

Gall, Carlotta. 2016. "How Kosovo Was Turned into Fertile Ground for ISIS," *The New York Times*, May 21.

Gallagher, John, and Ronald Robinson. 1953. "The Imperialism of Free Trade," *Economic History Review* 6:1.

Gardiner, Stephen M. 2013. *A Perfect Moral Storm: The Ethical Tragedy of Climate Change*, with a new afterword. New York: Oxford University Press.

----------. 2011. "Climate Justice." In *The Oxford Handbook of Climate Change and Society*, ed. by John S. Dryzek, Richard B. Norgaard, and David Schlosberg. New York: Oxford University Press.

Geertz, Clifford. 1973. "Religion as a Cultural System." In *The Interpretation of Cultures*. New York: Basic Books.

Gehring, John. 2016. "False Choices and Religious Liberty," *Commonweal*, June 21.

Gibson, David. 2015. "Reform, and the Reform," *dotCommonweal*, March 17.

Go, Julian. 2008. *American Empire and the Politics of Meaning: Elite Political Cultures in the Philippines and Puerto Rico during U.S. Colonialism.* Durham, NC: Duke University Press.

----------. 2003. "Introduction: Global Perspectives on the U.S. Colonial State in the Philippines." In *The American Colonial State in the Philippines: Global Perspectives*, ed. by Julian Go and Anne L. Foster. Durham, NC: Duke University Press.

Golay, Frank Hindman. 1997. *Face of Empire: United States-Philippine Relations, 1898-1946.*
Quezon City, Philippines: Ateneo de Manila University Press.

Gonzalez, Antonio. 2012. *God's Reign and the End of Empires.* Miami, FL: Convivium Press.

Goodheart, Adam. 2015. "How Satan Came to Salem: The True Story of the Witch Trials," *The Atlantic*, November.

Goodell, Jeff. 2014. "China, the Climate and the Fate of the Planet," *Rolling Stone*, September 15.

Gordon, Robert J. 2016. *The Rise and Fall of American Growth: The U.S. Standard of Living since the Civil War.* Princeton, NJ: Princeton University Press.

Gore, Al. 1992. *Earth in the Balance: Ecology and the Human Spirit.* New York: Houghton Mifflin.

Gottlieb, Roger S. 2006. "Introduction: Religion and Ecology – What Is the Connection and Why Does It Matter?" In *The Oxford Handbook of Religion and Ecology*, ed. by Roger S. Gottlieb. New York: Oxford University Press.

Gottlieb, Roger S., *et al.* 2006. "Part III: Religious Environmental Activism." In *The Oxford Handbook of Religion and Ecology*, ed. by Roger S. Gottlieb. New York: Oxford University Press.

Gould, Stephen Jay. 2001. "Introduction." In *Evolution: The Triumph of an Idea*, by Carl Zimmer. New York: HarperCollins.

Gowing, Peter G. 1969. "The Disentanglement of Church and State Early in the American Regime in the Philippines." In *Studies in Philippine Church History*, ed. by Gerald H. Anderson. Ithaca, NY: Cornell University Press.

Greider, William. 1997. *One World, Ready or Not: The Manic Logic of Global Capitalism.* New York: Simon and Schuster.

Gremillion, Joseph, ed. 1976. *The Gospel of Peace and Justice: Catholic Social Teaching since Pope John.* Maryknoll, NY: Orbis Books.

Griffth-Jones, Robin. 2000. *The Four Witnesses: The Rebel, the Rabbi, the Chronicler, and the Mystic.* HarperSan Franciso.

Guerrero, Leon Ma. 1963. *The First Filipino: A Biography of Jose Rizal.* Quezon City, Philippines: Journal Press.

Guillermoprieto, Alma. 2010. "Father Maciel, John Paul II, and the Vatican Sex Crisis," *The New York Review of Books,* May 17.

Gutierrez, Gustavo. 1973. *A Theology of Liberation: History, Politics and Salvation.* Maryknoll, NY: Orbis Books.

Gutting, Gary, ed. 1980. *Paradigms and Revolutions: Appraisals and Applications of Thomas Kuhn's Philosophy of Science.* Notre Dame, IN: University of Notre Dame Press.

Habermas, Jurgen. 2008. *Notes on a Post-Secular Society.* www.signsandsight.com (June 18).

----------. 1975. "Toward a Reconstruction of Historical Materialism," *Theory and Society* 2:3 (Autumn), 287-300.

Hacker, Jacob S., and Paul Pierson. 2010. *Winner-Take-All Politics: How Washington Made the Rich Richer – And Turned Its Back on the Middle Class.* New York: Simon and Schuster.

Halper, Stefan. 2010. *The Beijing Consensus: How China's Authoritarian Model Will Dominate the Twenty-first Century.* New York: Basic Books.

Hamid, Shadi. 2016. *Islamic Exceptionalism.* New York: St. Martin's Press.

Haring, Bernard. 1981. *Free and Faithful in Christ,* Vol. 3: Light to the World. New York: Crossroad.

Harris, Susan K. 2011. *God's Arbiters: Americans and the Philippines, 1898-1902.* New York: Oxford University Press.

Hart, John. 2004. *What Are They Saying about Environmental Theology?* Mahwah, NJ: Paulist Press.

Hartcourt, Alexander H. 2015. *Humankind: How Biology and Geography Shape Human Diversity.* New York: Pegasus Books.

Hasler, August Bernhard. 1981. *How the Pope Became Infallible: Pius IX and the Politics of Persuasion.* New York: Doubleday.

Haught, John F. 2010. *Making Sense of Evolution: Darwin, God, and the Drama of Life.* Louisville, KY: Westminster John Knox Press.

----------. 2003. *Deeper than Darwin: The Prospect for Religion in the Age of Evolution.* Boulder, CO: Westview Press.

Healy, David. 1970. *US Expansionism: The Imperialist Urge in 1890s.* Madison, WI: University of Wisconsin.

Heather, Peter. 2013: *The Restoration of Rome: Barbarian Popes and Imperial Pretenders.* New York: Oxford University Press.

----------. 2005. *The Fall of the Roman Empire: A New History of Rome and the Barbarians.* New York: Oxford University Press.

Henninger, Daniel. 2016. "Obama's Greatest Triumph," *The Wall Street Journal*, March 30.

Heyman, George. 2007. *The Power of Sacrifice: Roman and Christian Discourses in Conflict*. Washington, DC: Catholic University of America.

Himes, Michael J., and Kenneth R. Himes. 1990. "The Sacrament of Creation: Toward an Environmental Theology," *Commonweal*, January 26.

Hobsbawm, Eric. 1987. *The Age of Empire, 1875-1914*. New York: Pantheon.

----------. 1975. *The Age of Capital, 1848-1875*. New York: Barnes and Noble.

----------. 1962. *The Age of Revolution: Europe 1789-1848*. New York: Barnes and Noble.

Hochschild, Arlie Russell. 2016. *Strangers in Their Own Land: Anger and Mourning on the American Right*. New York: New Press.

Horn, Heather. 2011. "Where Does Religion Come from? A conversation with Robert Bellah, author of a new book about faith's place in evolution," *The Atlantic*, August.

Horsley, Richard A. 2003. *Jesus and Empire: The Kingdom of God and the New World Disorder*. Minneapolis, MN: Fortress Press.

----------, ed. 1997. *Paul and Empire: Religion and Power in Roman Imperial Society*. Harrisburg, PA: Trinity Press.

----------. 1989. *The Liberation of Christmas: The Infancy Narratives in Social Context*. New York: Crossroad.

Horwitz, Morton J. 1994. *The Transformation of American Law, 1870-1960*. Cambridge, MA: Harvard University Press.

----------. 1977. *The Transformation of American Law, 1780-1860*. Cambridge, MA: Harvard University Press.

Howell, Patrick J., S.J. 2016. "Book Review," *Theological Studies* 77:2 (June).

Huntington Samuel P. 1968. *Political Order in Changing Societies*. New Haven, CT: Yale University Press.

----------. 1965. "Political Development and Political Decay," *World Politics* 17:3 (December).

Ikenberry, John G. 2014. "The Illusion of Geopolitics," *Foreign Affairs*, May/June.

----------. 2011. *Liberal Leviathan: The Origins, Crisis, and Transformation of the American World Order*. Princeton, NJ: Princeton University Press.

----------. 2008. "The Rise of China and the Future of the West: Can the Liberal System Survive?" *Foreign Affairs*, January/February.

Inwood, M. J. 1995. "Enlightenment." In *The Oxford Companion to Philosophy*, ed. by Ted Honderich. New York: Oxford University Press.
Jenkins, Philip. 2015. *The Many Faces of Christ: The Thousand-Year Story of the Survival and Influence of the Lost Gospels*. New York: Basic Books.
----------. 2011. *Laying Down the Sword: Why We Can't Ignore the Bible's Violent Verses*. New York: HarperCollins.
----------. 2010. *Jesus Wars: How Four Patriarchs, Three Queens, and Two Emperors Decided What Christians Would Believe for the Next 1,500 Years*. New York: HarperOne.
----------. 2008. *The Lost History of Christianity: The Thousand-Year Golden Age of the Church in the Middle East, Africa, and Asia – and How It Died*. New York: HarperOne.
Johnson, Chalmers. 2004. *The Sorrows of Empire: Militarism, Secrecy, and the End of the Republic*. New York: Metropolitan Books.
Johnson, Elizabeth A. 2014. *Ask the Beasts: Darwin and the God of Love*. London: Bloomsbury.
----------. 1990. *Consider Jesus: Waves of Renewal in Christology*. New York: Crossroad.
Jones, Gregg. 2012. *Honor in the Dust: Theodore Roosevelt, War in the Philippines, and the Rise and Fall of America's Imperial Dream*. New York: New American Library.
Judis, John B. 2016. *The Populist Explosion: How the Great Recession Transformed American and European Politics*. New York: Columbia Global Reports.
----------. 2004. *The Folly of Empire: What George W. Bush Could Learn from Theodore Roosevelt and Woodrow Wilson*. New York: Scribner.
Karnow, Stanley. 1989. *In Our Image: America's Empire in the Philippines*. New York: Random House.
Kleinbard, Edward D. 2015. *We Are Better Than This: How Government Should Spend Our Money*. New York: Oxford University Press.
Kearns, Laurel. 2011. "The Role of Religions in Activism." In *The Oxford Handbook of Climate Change and Society*, ed. by John S. Dryzek, Richard B. Norgaard, and David Schlosberg. New York: Oxford University Press.
Keenan, James F., S.J. 2015. "Notes on Moral Theology: Redeeming Conscience," *Theological Studies* 76:1 (March).
Kesselman, Mark. 1973. "Order or Movement? The Literature of Political Development as Ideology," *World Politics* 26:1 (October).

Komonchak, Joseph A. 1994. "Vatican II and the Encounter between Catholicism and Liberalism." In *Catholicism and Liberalism: Contributions to American Public Philosophy*, ed. by R. Bruce Douglass and David Hollenbach. New York: Cambridge University.

Konstam, Angus. 2002. *Historical Atlas of the Crusades*. New York: Facts on File.

Kramer, Paul A. 2006. *The Blood of Government: Race, Empire, the United States, and the Philippines*. Chapel Hill, NC: University of North Carolina Press.

Kristof, Nicholas. 2016. "The Terrorists the Saudis Cultivate in Peaceful Countries," *The New York Times*, July 2.

Krugman, Paul. 2009. "How Did Economists Get It So Wrong?" *The New York Times Magazine*, September 6.

Kuhn, Thomas S. 1970. *The Structure of Scientific Revolutions*, 2nd ed. enlarged. Chicago, IL: University of Chicago Press. First published in 1962.

Kung, Hans. 2010. *What I Believe*. New York: Continuum.

----------. 2007a. *The Beginning of All Things: Science and Religion*. Grand Rapids, MI: Eerdmans.

----------. 2007b. *Islam: Past, Present, and Future*. Oxford: OneWorld.

----------. 1998. *A Global Ethic for Global Politics and Economics*. New York: Oxford University Press.

----------. 1995. *Christianity: Essence, History, and Future*. New York: Crossroad.

----------. 1994. *Infallible? An Unresolved Inquiry*, new expanded edition with a preface by Herbert Haag. New York: Continuum.

----------. 1992. *Judaism: Between Yesterday and Tomorrow*. New York: Crossroad.

----------. 1991. *Global Responsibility: In Search of a New World Ethic*. New York: Crossroad.

----------. 1990. *Reforming the Church: Keeping Hope Alive*. New York: Crossroad.

----------. 1988. *Theology for the Third Millennium: An Ecumenical Perspective*. New York: Doubleday.

----------. 1984. *Eternal Life? Life after Death as a Medical, Philosophical, and Theological Problem*. New York: Doubleday.

----------. 1980. *Does God Exist? An Answer for Today*. New York: Doubleday.

----------. 1976. *On Being a Christian*. New York: Doubleday.

----------. 1971. *Infallible? An Inquiry*. New York: Sheed and Ward.

----------. 1969. "Portrait of a Pope," *The Tablet*, August 23.

----------. 1967. *The Church*. New York: Sheed and Ward.
----------. 1964. *Justification: The Doctrine of Karl Barth and a Catholic Reflection*. New York: Sheed and Ward.
----------. 1961. *The Council: Reform and Reunion*. London: Sheed and Ward.
Kung, Hans, and David Tracy, ed. 1989. *Paradigm Change in Theology*. New York: Crossroad.
Kung, Hans, Josef van Ess, Heinrich von Stietencron, and Heinz Bechert. 1986. *Christianity and the World Religions: Paths to Dialogue with Islam, Hinduism, and Buddhism*. New York: Doubleday.
Kung, Hans, and Julia Ching. 1989. *Christianity and Chinese Religions*. New York: Doubleday.
Kung, Hans, and Walter Jens. 1996. *Dying with Dignity: A Plea for Personal Responsibility*. New York: Continuum.
Kuschel, Karl-Josef, and Hermann Haring, ed. 1993. *Hans Kung: New Horizons for Faith and Thought*. New York: Continuum.
Kuttner, Robert. 2016. "Hidden Injuries: The decline of the white working class and the rise of the Tea Party and Donald Trump," *The American Prospect*, Fall.
Lagasse, Paul, ed. 2000. *The Columbia Encyclopedia*, 6th ed. New York: Columbia University Press.
Lande, Carl H. 1965. *Leaders, Factions, and Parties: The Structure of Philippine Politics*. New Haven, CT: Yale University Press.
Landler, Mark. 2014. "U.S. and China Reach Climate Accord after Months of Talk," *The New York Times*, November 11.
Lawler, Michael G., Todd A. Salzman, and Eileen Burke-Sullivan. 2014. *The Church in the Modern World:* Gaudium et Spes *Then and Now*. Collegeville, MN: Liturgical Press.
Lawrence, Bruce B. 1990. *Defenders of God: The Fundamentalist Revolt against the Modern Age*. London: I.B. Tauris.
Law Stephen. 2014. "Open Letter to Karen Armstrong on 'The Myth of Religious Violence,'" *The Outer Limits*. www.centerforinquiry.net
Lengermann, Patricia Madoo, and Jill Niebrugge-Brantley. 1988. "Contemporary Feminist Theory." In George Ritzer, *Sociological Theory*, 2nd ed. New York: Knopf.
Lilla, Mark. 2007. *The Stillborn God: Religion, Politics, and the Modern West*. New York: Knopf.
Linn, Brian McAllister. 2000. *The Philippine American War, 1899-1902*. Lawrence, KS: University of Kansas Press.

Litonjua, M.D. 2015a. Review of *Fields of Blood: Religion and the History of Violence*, by Karen Armstrong, *International Review of Modern Sociology* 41:2 (Autumn).

----------. 2015b. "Christian Theology after Darwin: Notes for an Evolutionary Theology." In *Border Crossings: Sociological and Theological*. Denver, CO: Outskirts Press.

----------. 2013. "The Pathology of Religious Institutions," *International Review of Modern Sociology* 39:2 (Autumn).

----------. 2012. "A World of Grace and Sin: Karl Rahner and Graham Greene." In *Joint Ventures: Religious Studies and Social Sciences*. Bloomingdale, IN: AuthorHouse.

----------. 2011. "Understanding and Appreciating Hans Kung's Trilogy." In *Creative Fractures: Sociology and Theology*. Bloomington, IN: AuthorHouse.

----------. 2010. "International Free Trade, the WTO, and the Third World/Global South," *Journal of Third World Studies* 27:2 (Fall).

----------. 2008. "The Socio-Political Construction of Globalization," *International Review of Modern Sociology* 34:2 (Autumn).

----------. 2007. "From Political Theology to Political Philosophy, and Back," Review of *The Stillborn God: Religion, Politics, and the Modern West*, by Mark Lilla. www.msj.academia.edu/MDLitonjua

----------. 2001. "The State in Development Theory: The Philippines under Marcos," *Philippine Studies* 49:3 (July).

----------. 1999. "Global Capitalism: The New Context of Christian Social Ethics," *Theology Today* (56:2) (July).

----------. 1998. *Liberation Theology: The Paradigm Shift*. Lanham, MD: University Press of America.

----------. 1994. "Outside the Den of Dragons: The Philippines and the NICs of Asia," *Studies in Comparative International Development* 28:4 (Winter).

Lonergan, Bernard J.F. 1972. *Method in Theology*. New York: Herder and Herder.

Love, Eric T.L. 2004. *Race Over Empire: Racism and U.S. Imperialism, 1865-1900*. Chapel Hill, NC: University of North Carolina Press.

Lovelock, James E. 1979. *Gaia: A New Look at Life on Earth*. New York: Oxford University Press.

Luxmoore, Jonathan. 2016. "Papal letters raise issues around clerical friendships with women," *National Catholic Reporter*, March 11-24.

MacCulloch, Diarmaid. 2009. *Christianity: The First Three Thousand Years*. New York: Viking.

Mann, Thomas E., and Norman J. Ornstein. 2016a. *It's Even Worse Than It was: How the American Constitutional System Collided with the New Politics of Extremism*, new and expanded edition. New York: Basic Books.

----------. 2016b. "Republicans created dysfunction. Now they're paying for it," *The Washington Post*, March 8.

----------. 2013. *It's Even Worse Than It Looks: How the American Constitutional System Collided with the New Politics of Extremism*, paperback edition with a new preface and afterword. New York: Basic Books.

Marcos, Ferdinand E. 1974. *The Democratic Revolution in the Philippines.* Englewood Cliffs, NJ: Prentice-Hall International.

Martens, Jens, and Klaus Schilder. 2001. "Sustainable Development." In *The Oxford Companion to Politics of the World*, 2nd ed., ed. by Joel Krieger. New York: Oxford University Press.

Martina, Giacomo, S.J. 1988. "The Historical Context in Which the Idea of New Ecumenical Council Was Born." In *Vatican II: Assessment and Perspectives: Twenty-Five Years After (1962-1987)*, Vol. I, ed. by Rene Latourelle. Mahwah, NJ: Paulist Press.

Masterman, Margaret. 1970. "The Nature of a Paradigm." In *Criticism and the Growth of Knowledge*, ed. by Imre Lakatos and Alan Musgrave. Cambridge: Cambridge University Press.

May, Glenn Anthony. 1980. *Social Engineering in the Philippines: The Aims, Execution, and Impact of American Colonial Policies, 1900-1913.* Westport, CT: Greenwood Press.

Mayer, Jane. 2016. *Dark Money: The Hidden History of the Billionaires Behind the Rise of the Radical Right.* New York: Doubleday.

McBrien, Richard P. 1994. *Catholicism,* completely revised and updated edition. HarperSan Francisco.

McCarraher, Eugene. 2015. "We Have Never Been Disenchanted," *The Hedgehog Review*: Re-Enchantment 17:3 (Fall).

McCoy, Alfred W. 2009. *Policing America's Empire: The United States, the Philippines, and the Rise of the Surveillance State.* Madison, WI: University of Wisconsin Press.

----------, ed. 1993. *An Anarchy of Families: State and Family in the Philippines.* Madison, WI: University of Wisconsin Press.

McCoy, Alfred W., Francisco A. Scarano, and Courtney Johnson. 2009. "On the Tropic of Cancer: Transitions and Transformations in the U.S. Imperial State." In *Colonial Crucible: Empire in the Making of the American Modern State*, ed. by Alfred W. McCoy and Francisco A. Scarano. Madison, WI: University of Wisconsin Press.

McDonagh, Sean. 1990. *The Greening of the Church.* Maryknoll, NY: Orbis Books.

McElroy, Robert. 2017. "Transcript of speech by San Diego Catholic Bishop Robert McElroy to community organizers," *San Diego Union-Tribune,* February 22.

McElwee, Joshua J. 2016. "In letter to CDF, theologians and bishops call for reform of Vatican doctrinal investigations," *National Catholic Reporter,* April 19.

McKibben, Bill. 1989. *The End of Nature.* New York: Random House.

Meacham, Jon. 2012. "Heaven Can't Wait: Why rethinking the hereafter could make the world a better place," *Time,* April 16.

Meier, John P. 2001. *A Marginal Jew: Rethinking the Historical Jesus,* Vol. 3: Companions and Competitors. New York: Doubleday.

----------. 1991. *A Marginal Jew: Rethinking the Historical Jesus,* Vol. 1: The Roots of the Problem and the Person. New York: Doubleday.

Merton, Robert K. 1985. *On the Shoulders of Giants: A Shandean Postcript.* New York: Harcourt Brace Jovanovich. First published in 1965.

----------. 1973. *The Sociology of Science: Theoretical and Empirical Investigations.* Chicago: University of Chicago Press.

Miller, Kenneth R. 1999. *Finding Darwin's God: A Scientist's Search for Common Ground between God and Evolution.* New York: HarperPerennial.

Miller, Patricia. 2016. "Who Will Catholic Bishops Turn to in Trump Age?" *Religion Dispatches,* May 11.

----------. 2014. "Douthat, Dionne Push Wrong Lesson on Religious Exemptions," *Religion Dispatches,* July 9. www.religiondispatches.org/douthat-dionne-push-wrong-lesson-on-religiousexemptions/?

Miller, Scott. 2011. *The President and the Assassin: McKinley, Terror, and Empire at the Dawn of the American Century.* New York: Random House.

Miller, Stuart Creighton. 1982. *"Benevolent Assimilation:" The American Conquest of the Philippines, 1899-1902.* New Haven, CT: Yale University Press.

Moran, Gabriel. 2016. *Missed Opportunities: Rethinking Catholic Tradition.* Bloomington, IN: iUniverse.

Murphy, Cullen. 2012. *God's Jury: The Inquisition and the Making of the Modern World.* Boston: Houghton Mifflin Harcourt.

----------. 2007. *Are We Rome? The Fall of an Empire and the Fate of America.* Boston: Houghton Mifflin Harcourt.

Murray, John Courtney. 1966. "Religious Freedom." In *The Documents of Vatican II*, ed. by Walter M. Abbott, S.J. Piscataway, NJ: New Century Publishers.

Musicant, Ivan. 1998. *Empire by Default: The Spanish-American War and the Dawn of the American Century*. New York: Henry Holt.

Neusner, Jacob. 1987. *Judaism and Christianity in the Age of Constantine: History, Messiah, Israel, and the Initial Confrontation*. Louisville, KY: Westminster/John Knox Press.

Niebuhr, Reinhold. 1932. *Moral Man and Immoral Society*. New York: Scribner.

Nissenbaum, Stephen. 1996. *The Battle for Christmas: A Social and Cultural History of Christmas That Shows How It Was Transformed from an Unruly Carnival Season into the Quintessential Family Holiday*. New York: Alfred A. Knopf.

Nolan, Patrick, and Gerhard Lenski. 2004. *Human Societies: An Introduction to Macrosociology*, 9th ed., revised and updated. Boulder, CO: Paradigm Publishers.

Nugent, Walter. 2008. *Habits of Empire: A History of American Expansion*. New York: Knopf.

O'Brien, Donal Cruise. 1979. "Modernization, Order, and the Erosion of the Democratic Ideal: American Political Science 1960-70." In *Development Theory: Four Critical Studies*, ed. by David Lehman. London: Frank Cass.

O'Connor, James. 1998. "Is Sustainable Capitalism Possible?" In *Is Capitalism Sustainable? Political Economy and the Politics of Ecology*, ed. by Martin O'Connor. New York: Guilford Press.

O'Connor, Martin, ed. 1998. *Is Capitalism Sustainable? Political Economy and the Politics of Ecology*. New York: Guilford Press.

O'Malley, John W. 2015. "Family Gathering: Rediscovering the Role of the Synod of Bishops," *America*, July 20-27.

----------. 2015a. "Vatican II Revisited as Reconciliation: The Francis Factor." In *The Legacy of Vatican II*, ed. by Massimo Faggioli and Andrea Vicini, S.J. Mahwah, NJ: Paulist Press.

----------. 2015b. "Two Popes: Benedict and Francis." In *Catholic History for Today's Church: How Our Past Illuminates Our Present*. Lanham, MD: Rowman and Littlefield.

----------. 2015c. "Ten Surefire Ways to Mix up the Teaching of Vatican II." In *Catholic History for Today's Church: How Our Past Illuminates Our Present*. Lanham, MD: Rowman and Littlefield.

----------. 2015d. "What Happened and Did Not Happen at Vatican II." In *Catholic History for Today's Church: How Our Past Illuminates Our Present.* Lanham, MD: Rowman and Littlefield.

----------. 2008. *What Happened at Vatican II.* Cambridge, MA: Harvard University Press.

O'Meara, Thomas F., O.P. 2012. Review of *Ist Die Kirche Noch Retten?* By Hans Kung. *Theological Studies* 73:2 (June).

Orfalea, Gregory. 2015. "Hungry for Souls: Was Junipero Serra a Saint?" *Commonweal,* September 11.

O'Shea, Stephen. 2000. *The Perfect Heresy: The Revolutionary Life and Death of the Medieval Cathars.* New York: Walker.

Owen, Norman G., ed. 1971. *Compadre Colonialism: Studies on the Philippines under American Rule.* Ann Arbor, MI: University of Michigan Press.

Pagden, Anthony. 2013. *The Enlightenment: And Why It Still Matters.* New York: Random House.

Paredes, Ruth R. 1989. "The Origins of National Politics: Taft and the Partido Federal." In *Philippine Colonial Democracy,* ed. by Ruth R. Paredes. Quezon City, Philippines: Ateneo de Manila University Press.

Parratt, John. 2004. "Introduction." In *An Introduction to Third World Theologies,* ed. by John Parratt. Cambridge: Cambridge University Press.

Perkins, Pheme. 1984. *Resurrection: New Testament Witness and Contemporary Reflection.* Garden City, NY: Doubleday.

Piketty, Thomas. 2014. *Capital in the Twentieth-First Century.* Cambridge, MA: Harvard University Press.

Pomeranz, Kenneth. 2000. *The Great Divergence: China, Europe, and the Making of the Modern World Economy.* Princeton, NJ: Princeton University Press.

Pooley, Eric. 2010. *The Climate War: True Believers, Power Brokers, and the Fight to Save the Earth.* New York: Hyperion.

Pope Francis. 2016a. *Misericordia Vultus,* Bull of Indiction of the Extraordinary Jubilee of Mercy. Appendix in *The Name of God Is Mercy, A Conversation with Andrea Torniella.* New York: Random House.

----------. 2016b. *Amoris Laetitia,* The Happiness of Married Love, Post-Synodal Apostolic Exhortation, March 19.

----------. 2015a. *Laudato Si',* Encyclical Letter on Care for Our Common Home. www.vatican.va

----------. 2015b. *Visit to the Joint Session of the United States Congress, Address of the Holy Father,* September 24.

----------. 2014. "Address to the Roman Curia," December 23. www.zenit.org/en/articles/pope-s-address-to-theroman-curia

----------. 2013a. *Evangelii Gaudium,* Apostolic Exhortation on the Proclamation of the Gospel in Today's World. www.vatican.va

----------. 2013b. "A Big Heart Open to God," interview with Antonio Spadaro, S.J., *America,* September 30.

Portier, William L. 2015. "Just a Gang of Sinners? *Commonweal,* March 20.

Posner, Gerald. 2015. *God's Bankers: A History of Money and Power at the Vatican.* New York: Simon and Schuster.

Powell, Mark Allan. 2009. *Introducing the New Testament: A Historical, Literary, and Theological Survey.* Grand Rapids, MI: Baker Academic.

Preston, Andrew. 2016. "America's World Mission in the Age of Obama." In *Faith in the New Millennium: The Future of Religion and American Politics,* ed. by Matthew Avery Sutton and Darren Dochuk. New York: Oxford University Press.

Prothero, Stephen. 2016. *Why Liberals Win the Culture Wars (Even When They Lose Elections).* HarperOne.

Putz, Oliver. 2002. "Evolutionary Biology in the Theology of Karl Rahner," *Philosophy and Theology* 17: 1&2 (85-105).

Rabasa, Angel M. 2004. "Overview." In *The Muslim World after 9/11,* by Angel M. Rabasa *et al.* Santa Monica, CA: Rand Corporation.

Rahner, Karl. 1978. "Christology within an Evolutionary View of the World." In *Foundations of Christian Faith: An Introduction to the Idea of Christianity.* New York: Seabury Press.

Ralston III, Holmes. 2010. *Three Big Bangs.* New York: Columbia University Press.

Ratzinger, Joseph/Benedict XVI. 2012. *The Infancy Narratives,* Vol. III: *Jesus of Nazareth.* New York: Random House

Ratzinger, Joseph. 1964. "The Pastoral Implications of Episcopal Collegiality." In *The Church and Mankind,* Concilium Vol. 1. New York: Paulist Press.

Reese, Thomas. 2014. "Theologians critique Dolan's defense of capitalism," *National Catholic Reporter,* July 4-17.

Rieger, Joerg. 2007. *Christ and Empire: From Paul to Postcolonial Times.* Minneapolis, MN: Fortress Press.

Ritzer, George. 1988. *Sociological Theory,* 2nd ed. New York: Knopf.

----------. 1983. *Sociological Theory.* New York: Knopf.

----------. 1975. *Sociology: A Multiple Paradigm Science.* Boston: Allyn and Bacon.
Rizal, Jose P. 1886/1996. *Noli Me Tangere,* English translation by Ma. Soledad Lacson-Locsin. Makati, Philippines: Bookmark.
Roberts, Paul. 2014. *The Impulse Society: America in the Age of Instant Gratification.* New York: Bloomsbury.
Robinson, William I. 2014. *Global Capitalism and the Crisis of Humanity.* New York: Cambridge University Press.
Robinson, Marilynne. 2015. "Awakening: Whom God Loveth He Also Chastiseth," *Commonweal,* October 23.
Rose, Michael R. 1998. *Darwin's Spectre: Evolutionary Biology in the Modern World.* Princeton, NJ: Princeton University Press.
Ross, Robert J.S., and Kent S. Trachte. 1990. *Global Capitalism: The New Leviathan.* Albany: State University of New York Press.
Roth, Dennis Morrow. 1977. *The Friar Estates of the Philippines.* Albuquerque, NM: University of New Mexico Press.
Roth, Russell. 1981. *Muddy Glory: America's "Indian Wars" in the Philippines, 1899-1935.* Hanover, MA: Christopher Publishing House.
Rothrock, Brad. 2015. "Relational Ecology: Thomas Aquinas and the Metaphysical Connection," *America,* August 17-24.
Rougeau, Vincent D. 2008. *Christians in the American Empire: Faith and Citizenship in the New World Order.* New York: Oxford University Press.
Rowland, Ingrid D. 2014. "The Fall of the Vice-Pope," *The New York Review of Books,* June16.
Rubenstein, Richard E. 1999. *When Jesus Became God: The Epic Fight over Christ's Divinity in the Last Days of Rome.* New York: Hartcourt Brace.
Ruhl, Jack, and Diane Ruhl. 2015. "*NCR* research: Costs of sex abuse crisis to US church underestimated," *National Catholic Reporter,* November 6-19.
Russell, Gerard. 2016. "What Chance for Democracy in the Middle East?" *The New York Review,* October 27.
Ryan, Alan. 2012. *On Politics: A History of Political Thought from Herodotus to the Present,* 2 vols. New York. Liveright Publishing.
Ryan, Thomas, S.M. 1994. "Ecology." In *The New Dictionary of Christian Social Thought,* ed. by Judith Dwyer. Collegeville, MN: Liturgical Press.
Salai, Sean, S.J. 2015. "How Synods Work: 21 Questions for John W. O'Malley, S.J.," *America* October 21.

Salamanca, Bonifacio. 1984. *The Filipino Reaction to American Rule, 1901-1913.* Quezon City, Philippines: New Day Publishers.
Salzman, Todd A., and Michael G. Lawler. 2012. *Sexual Ethics: A Theological Introduction.* Washington, DC; Georgetown University Press.
Sandel, Michael J. 2012. *What Money Can't Buy: The Moral Limits of Markets.* New York: Farrar, Straus and Giroux.
Satz, Debra. 2010. *Why Some Things Should Not Be for Sale: The Moral Limits of Markets.* New York: Oxford University Press.
Scherer, Michael. 2016. "Learning to Love Ted," *Time,* April 18.
Schillebeeckx, Edward. 1979. *Jesus: An Experiment in Christology.* New York: Seabury Press.
Schirmer, Daniel B. 1972. *Republic or Empire: American Resistance to the Philippine War.* Cambridge, MA: Schenkman Publishing.
Schloesser, Stephen, S.J. 2015. "Reproach vs. *Rapprochement:* Historical Preconditions of a Paradigm Shift in the Reform of Vatican II." In *50 Years on: Probing the Riches of Vatican II,* ed. by David G. Schultenover. Collegeville, MN: Liturgical Press.
Schultenover, David G., S.J., ed. 2015. *50 Years on: Probing the Riches of Vatican II.* Collegeville, MN: Liturgical Press.
Scott, Margaret. 2016. "Indonesia: The Saudis Are Coming," *The New York Review,* October 27.
Shalom, Stephen Rosskamm. 1981. *The United States and the Philippines: A Study of Neocolonialism.* Philadelphia, PA: Institute for the Study of Human Issues.
Shaw, Angel Velasco, and Luis H. Francia. 2002. *Vestiges of War: The Philippine-American War and the Aftermath of an Imperial Dream, 1899-1999.* New York: New York University Press.
Sibley, Angus. 2011. *The "Poisoned Spring" of Economic Libertarianism: Menger, Mises, Hayek, Rothbard: A Critique from Catholic Social Teaching of the "Austrian School" of Economics.* Washington, DC: Pax Romana, USA.
Sideris, Lisa H. 2006. "Religion, Environmentalism, and the Meaning of Ecology." In *The Oxford Handbook of Religion and Ecology,* ed. by Roger S. Gottlieb. New York: Oxford University Press.
Silbey, David J. 2007. *A War of Frontier and Empire: The Philippine-American War, 1899-1902.* New York: Hill and Wang.
Skidelsky, Robert. 2009. *Keynes: The Return of the Master.* New York: Public Affairs.
Smith, Pamela. 1997. *What Are They Saying about Environmental Ethics?* Mahwah, NJ: Paulist Press.

Smith, Tony. 1994. *America's Mission: The United States and the Worldwide Struggle for Democracy in the Twentieth Century*. Princeton, NJ: Princeton University Press.

Spadaro, Antonio, S.J. 2013. "A Big Heart Open to God: The Exclusive Interview with Pope Francis," *America*, September 30.

Stanley, Peter W. 1984. "Introduction." In *Reappraising an Empire: New Perspectives on Philippine-American History*, ed. by Peter W. Stanley. Cambridge, MA: Harvard University Press.

----------. 1974. *A Nation in the Making: The Philippines and the United States: 1899-1921*. Cambridge, MA: Harvard University Press.

Stavrianos, L.S. 1989. *Lifelines from Our Past: A New World History*. New York: Pantheon.

Steinberg, David Joel. 1990. *The Philippines: A Singular and a Plural Place*, 2nd ed., revised and enlarged. Boulder, CO: Westview Press.

Sugirtharajah, R.S. 2005a. *The Bible and Empire: Postcolonial Explorations*. New York: Cambridge University Press.

----------. 2005b. "Postcolonial Biblical Interpretation." In *The Modern Theologians: An Introduction to Christian Theology since 1918*, 3rd ed., ed. by David F. Ford with Rachel Muers. Malden, MA: Blackwell Publishing.

Sullivan, Andrew. 2013. *Untier of Knots: What is the Meaning of Pope Francis?* dish.andrewsullivan.com

Sullivan, Francis A. 2014. "The Definitive Exercise of Teaching Authority," *Theological Studies* 75:3 (September).

Tagle, Luis Antonio G. 2003. "The 'Black Week' of Vatican II (November 14-21, 1964)." In *History of Vatican II*, Vol. IV: Church as Communion, Third Period, and Intersession, September 1964 – September 1965, ed. by Giuseppe Alberigo and Joseph A. Komonchak. Maryknoll, NY: Orbis Books.

Taylor, Charles. 2011. "Western Secularity." In *Rethinking Secularism*, ed. by Craig Calhoun, Mark Juergensmeyer, and Jonathan VanAntwerpen. New York: Oxford University Press.

----------. 2007. *A Secular Age*. Cambridge, MA: Harvard University Press.

Taylor, George E. 1964. *The Philippines and the United States: Problems of Partnership*. New York: Praeger.

The Tablet. 2015. "Key Influences," June 18.

Thomas, Evan. 2010. *The War Lovers: Roosevelt, Lodge, Hearst, and the Rush to Empire*. New York: Little, Brown and Company.

Thomas, Hugh. 2014. *World without End: Spain, Philip II, and the First Global Empire*. New York: Random House. The first two volumes are: *Rivers of Gold: The Rise of the Spanish Empire, from Columbus* to Magellan (2003), and *The Golden Empire: Spain, Charles V, and the Creation of America* (2011).

Thornhill, John. 2000. *Modernity: Christianity's Estranged Child Reconstructed.* Grand Rapids, MI: Eerdmans.

Thurow, Lester. 1996. *The Future of Capitalism: How Today's Economic Forces Shape Tomorrow's World.* New York: Penguin.

Tolson, Jay. 2015. "From the Editor," *The Hedgehog Review*: Re-Enchantment 17:3 (Fall).

Tracy, David. 1981. *The Analogical Imagination: Christian Theology and the Culture of Pluralism.* New York: Crossroad.

----------. 1970. *The Achievement of Bernard Lonergan.* New York: Herder and Herder.

Traxel, David. 1998. *1898: The Birth of the American Century.* New York: Knopf.

Tyrrell, Ian. 2009. "Empire in American History." In *Colonial Crucible: Empire in the Making of the American Modern State,* ed. by Alfred W. McCoy and Francisco A. Scarano. Madison, WI: University of Wisconsin Press.

Vallely, Paul. 2015. *Pope Francis: The Struggle for the Soul of Catholicism.* New York: Bloomsbury.

Vatican II. 1965. *Gaudium et Spes,* The Pastoral Constitution on the Church in the Modern World. www.vatican.va

Vermes, Geza. 2006. *The Nativity: History and Legend.* London, England: Penguin Books.

Walsh, Michael. 2014. "From Rome's fall to the rise of the powerbroker popes," *National Catholic Reporter,* September 12-25.

Weart, Spencer. 2011. "The Development of the Concept of Dangerous Anthropogenic Climate Change." In *The Oxford Handbook of Climate Change and Society,* ed. by John S. Dryzek, Richard B. Norgaard, and David Schlosberg. New York: Oxford University Press.

Weber, Max. 1958. *The Protestant Ethic and the Spirit of Capitalism.* New York: Charles Scribner's Sons. Originally published in 1905.

Weisberger, Bernard A., and Marshall I. Steinbaum. 2016. "Economists of the World, Unite!" *Democracy Journal,* Spring (No. 40).

Welch, Robert E., Jr. 1979. *Response to Imperialism: The United States and the Philippine-American War, 1899-1902.* Chapel Hill, NC: University of North Carolina Press.

White, Lynn, Jr. 1967. "The Historical Roots of Our Ecological Crisis," *Science* 155 (March 10: 1203-7).

Wilkins, Jeremy D. 2005. "Human Being as Primary Analogate of Being," *St. Anselm Journal* 2:2 (Spring).

Wilkins, John. 2014. "Great Expectations: Pope Francis and the Synod on the Family," *Commonweal*, September 26.

----------. 2014. "Ripples spread out from theologian's work," *National Catholic Reporter*, April 25-May 8.

Wills, Garry. 2015. *The Future of the Catholic Church with Pope Francis*. New York: Viking.

----------. 2014. *Bare Ruined Choirs: Doubt, Prophecy, and Radical Religion*. Mahwah, NJ: Paulist Press. (Originally published in 1972.)

Wolff, Leon. 2006. *Little Brown Brother: How the United States Purchased and Pacified the Philippines Islands at the Century's Turn*. New York: History Book Club. Originally published in 1960.

Woolf, Greg. 2012. *Rome: An Empire's Story*. New York: Oxford University Press.

Wright, N.T. 2008. *Surprised by Hope: Rethinking Heaven, the Resurrection, and the Mission of the Church*. New York: HarperOne.

Young, Robin Darling. 2016. "A Fence in the Water: Southern Segregationism and Today's Republicans," *Commonweal*, October 17.

Zakaria, Fareed. 2016. "Obama pursued transformation as Republicans chose self-destruction," *The Washington Post*, April 7.

Zimmer, Carl. 2001. *Evolution: The Triumph of an Idea*. New York: HarperCollins.

ABOUT THE AUTHOR

M. D. Litonjua (a.k.a. **Meneleo/Bing D. Litonjua**) is emeritus professor of sociology at the Mount St. Joseph University in Cincinnati, OH. He holds a Ph.D. in Sociology from Brown University, an M.B.A. from the University of Missouri-St. Louis, an M.S. in Sociology from the Asian Social Institute (Manila), and Licentiates in Theology and Philosophy from the University of Santo Tomas (Manila).

He has written a monograph on liberation theology, *Liberation Theology: The Paradigm Shift*, a text in the sociology and cultural anthropology of religion, *Structures of Sin, Cultures of Meaning: Social Science and Theology*, 2nd ed., and now five collections of articles, published and unpublished, *Critical Intersections, Creative Fractures, Joint Ventures, Border Crossings,* and *Converting Horizons,* all available at www.amazon.com and www.bn.com

He has published in *Studies in Comparative International Development, Theology Today, Journal of Hispanic/Latino Theology, Chicago Studies, Philippines Studies, Philippine News, International Review of Modern Sociology,* and *Journal of Third World Studies.*

He was also a book reviewer for the *St. Louis Post-Dispatch* from 1984 to 1993.

Some of his writings are accessible at www.msj.academia.edu/MDLitonjua

He can be contacted at md.litonjua@yahoo.com

www.ingramcontent.com/pod-product-compliance
Lightning Source LLC
Chambersburg PA
CBHW030301080526
44584CB00012B/394